Writing Off
The Rural West

Writing Off
The Rural West

GLOBALIZATION, GOVERNMENTS
AND THE TRANSFORMATION
OF RURAL COMMUNITIES

Edited by

ROGER EPP AND
DAVE WHITSON

PARKLAND
INSTITUTE

The University of Alberta Press

Published by

The University of Alberta Press   and   **Parkland Institute**
Ring House 2   11045 Saskatchewan Drive
Edmonton, Alberta T6G 2E1   Edmonton, Alberta T6G 2E1

This volume copyright © 2001 The University of Alberta Press

National Library of Canada Cataloguing in Publication Data
Main entry under title:
Writing off the rural West

   Copublished by: Parkland Institute.
   Includes bibliographical references.
   ISBN 0-88864-378-0

   1. Canada—Rural conditions. 2. Rural industries—Canada. 3. Globalization.
I. Whitson, David, 1945– II. Epp, Roger Ivan, 1958– III. Parkland Institute.
HN103.5.W74 2001   307.72'0971   C2001–910943–1

Printed and bound in Canada by Houghton Boston, Saskatoon, Saskatchewan.
∞ Printed on acid-free paper.
Copyediting by Christina Barabash.
Book design by Carol Dragich.
Image on page 1 by Michael J. Broadway; used by permission. Image on page 107 by Pam
Doyle; used by permission. Image on page 203 by George Webber; used by permission.

The University of Alberta Press acknowledges the financial support of the Government of
Canada through the Book Publishing Industry Development Program for its publishing
activities. The Press also gratefully acknowledges the support received for its program from
the Canada Council for the Arts.

Contents

CONTRIBUTORS

Michael J. Broadway is Professor and Head the Geography Department at Northern Michigan University. He is the author of numerous articles dealing with the meat industry and is co-editor of *Any Way You Cut It: Meat Processing and Small Town America* (University Press of Kansas, 1995). He began his research on Alberta's beef industry in 1996 and has been a frequent visitor to the province over the past five years.

Ken Coates is Professor of History and Dean, College of Arts and Science, at the University of Saskatchewan. He has written widely on northern Canadian issues, including works on the history of the Alaska Highway, the provincial Norths, Aboriginal land rights in Canada, and comparative indigenous rights. His recent book, *The Marshall Decision and Native Rights*, was shortlisted for the 2001 Donner Prize. He is now, with co-author Bill Morrison, working on a study of murder in the Yukon Territory.

Bonnie Dobbs received her PhD in gerontology and is an Assistant Professor in the Faculty of Rehabilitation Medicine and Associate Director of the Rehabilitation Research Centre, University of Alberta. Her research interests focus on the psychosocial consequences of having to stop driving when driving becomes unsafe as a result of medical conditions; and the role that transportation plays in maintaining the health and well-being of individuals, particularly those in rural areas.

Roger Epp is Associate Professor of Political Studies at Augustana University College in Camrose, Alberta. A native of Hanley, Saskatchewan, he has published extensively on international politics but increasingly has shifted his attention to the world from which he and many of his students come. He is a frequent speaker, media commentator, and newspaper columnist on rural issues.

John Everitt has a PhD in Human Geography and is currently Professor and Chairman of the Department of Geography at Brandon University. He has conducted research in both rural and urban contexts since coming to Brandon University in 1973. He specializes in the development and implementation of social science research projects.

Ian Gray is Associate Professor of Sociology and Associate Director of the Centre for Rural Social Research at Charles Sturt University. He has conducted many research projects on rural social and environmental issues in Australia and has published in *Sociologia Ruralis, Journal of the Community*

Development Society, Rural Society, and *The Australian Journal of Social Issues.* His first book was *Politics in Place: Social Power Relations in an Australian Country Town* (Cambridge University Press, 1991) and his latest is *A Future for Regional Australia: Escaping Global Misfortune* (Cambridge, 2001).

Lorelei L. Hanson recently completed a PhD dissertation in Canadian Studies at the University of Alberta, exploring the social construction of nature through an examination of place and space. She has taught at the University of Alberta and Augustana University College. Next she plans to tackle learning French and the fiddle.

Cameron R. Harder is Assistant Professor of Systematic Theology at the Lutheran Theological Seminary in Saskatoon, Saskatchewan. He is the author of *The Shame of Farm Bankruptcy: A Sociological and Theological Investigation of Its Effects on Rural Communities* (unpublished dissertation). Working out of interdisciplinary PhD research with rural people and twelve years in town and country ministry, he has offered workshops and seminars in a variety of contexts aimed at helping rural communities to regain some control of their future.

Norah Keating is a family gerontologist who is interested in the contextual issues faced by seniors as they grow older. Recent work in determining the content and consequences of eldercare in Canada, and the economic impact of public policies on informal caregivers, has led her to explore how differences among types of rural communities affect the informal care-giving networks of frail seniors. She has published many journal articles and several books in the field.

Janice Keefe is an Associate Professor in the Department of Family Studies and Gerontology at Mount Saint Vincent University. Her research interests are in the areas of informal and formal caregiving, rural issues for the elderly, and continuing care policy. She has recently published a report for Health Canada on the nature of caregiving in Canada's rural and urban areas.

Arn Keeling is a doctoral candidate in the Department of Geography, University of British Columbia where he also completed his MA in history. His research interests include the history of conflict between energy development and environmental protection in Canada.

Mustafa Koc is Associate Professor of Sociology at Ryerson Polytechnic University, Toronto. He is co-ordinator (with Jennifer Welsh) of Ryerson's Centre for Studies in Food Security, is a founder of the Toronto Food Research Network, and serves as secretary-treasurer of the International

Sociological Association's Research Committee on the Sociology of Agriculture and Food.

Murray Knuttila is a Professor of Sociology and Dean of Arts at the University of Regina. He is the author of several books including a biography of Prairie farm leader E.A. Partridge and (with Wendee Kubik) *State Theories: Classical, Global and Feminist Perspectives*. He has devoted significant attention to the transformation of prairie agriculture and is involved in ongoing research on globalization and agricultural policy.

Geoffrey Lawrence is recognized as Australia's leading writer in rural and regional social issues. He is Foundation Professor of Sociology and Director of Central Queensland University's flagship research centre, the Institute for Sustainable Regional Development. His most recent co-authored/co-edited works include *Environment, Society and Natural Resource Management* (Edward Elgar, 2001), *Altered Genes* (Scribe, 2001), and *A Future for Regional Australia* (Cambridge, 2001).

Susan Machum is an Assistant Professor of Sociology at St. Thomas University in Fredericton, New Brunswick. Raised in rural New Brunswick, she had her BA from St. Thomas, her MA from Dalhousie University and her PhD from the University of Edinburgh. Her major interests are the sociology of work, women and agriculture, inequality and the environment.

Murray Mandryk has been a journalist for 21 years. He has written a column on Saskatchewan politics for the *Regina Leader-Post, Saskatoon Star Phoenix* and other daily and weekly newspapers in the province for the past eleven years. A national newspaper award-winner for business feature writing in 1988, Mandryk grew up on a farm in Grandview, Manitoba and has also worked for the *Winnipeg Free Press, Fort MacMurray Today* and *Portage la Prairie Daily*.

Bruce Milne attended the University of Victoria, completing a BA and MA in political science, and earned his PhD at the University of Toronto. He was a professor at the University of Victoria, teaching Public Administration, Policy Analysis and Political Theory. Currently serving his second term as Mayor of the District of Sechelt, he is also the Chair of both the Sunshine Coast Treaty Advisory Committee and the Coastal Communities Network.

Darrin Qualman has lived and farmed most of his life in Dundurn, Saskatchewan, just south of Saskatoon. He studied political studies at the University of Saskatchewan. While he discontinued large-scale farming in 1994, he and his wife Donna are currently making and selling hay for dairy cattle and horses. Darrin worked on energy and environmental issues in the early 1990s and became the executive secretary of the National Farmers Union in 1996, a position he still holds.

William Ramp is an Assistant Professor of Sociology at the University of Lethbridge. His research interests are in the areas of agrarian history and social thought, social movements, and collective identity.

Doug Ramsey has a PhD in Geography, specializing in rural resource evaluation, and is currently an Assistant Professor in the Department of Rural Development at Brandon University. His teaching areas are rural tourism, resource development, and research methodology. His research interests relate to analyzing the impacts of external political and economic forces on rural communities and in better understanding how communities respond to such forces.

Bob Stirling teaches sociology at the University of Regina. He comes from a family farm in the Eston-Kindersley area of west-central Saskatchewan. The farm is now part of the Genesis Land Conservancy, a Saskatchewan agency devoted to settling new farm families on the land.

Ian Urquhart is an Associate Professor in the Department of Political Science at the University of Alberta. He is the co-author of *The Last Great Forest: Japanese Multinationals and Alberta's Northern Forests* and the editor of *Assault on the Rockies: Environmental Controversies in Alberta*. When he is not chasing trout in Alberta's Foothills, he studies the politics of natural resource use in the Rocky Mountain West.

Dave Whitson is Professor of Political Science and Canadian Studies at the University of Alberta. His research interests for much of his career focussed on sports and leisure, and he is co-author (with Rick Gruneau of Simon Fraser University) of *Hockey Night in Canada: Sports, Identities, and Cultural Politics* (Garamond, 1993). His more recent research has focussed on the transformation of rural communities across Canada by golf, skiing, and recreational property developments.

Nettie Wiebe is Professor of Church and Society at St. Andrew's College, University of Saskatchewan. She took her PhD at the University of Calgary. She is past president of the National Farmers Union and works actively in social justice and positive human rights, particularly the right to food.

ACKNOWLEDGEMENTS

This book originated in a panel of papers on globalization and rural communities presented to a Parkland Institute conference in November 1997. It was sustained during a long gestation by the support of several people associated with the Institute: Trevor Harrison, who, if memory serves, was first to suggest the idea of a book and who paid the price for it by reading at least two drafts of the manuscript; Bill Moore-Kilgannon; Gord Laxer; Gurston Dacks; Cheri Harris; and Josee Johnston. We know of no other policy-research institute or think-tank in Canada that has taken such a strong and ongoing interest in rural issues, and in bringing them to a wider audience. We hope, in turn, that *Writing Off the Rural West* enlarges Parkland's public profile.

While this book is rooted in a rich tradition of resource-based political-economy analysis, its particular interest lies in the communities of people who live in those rural regions from which that resource wealth is extracted. For those communities, this is a crucial time filled with stress and socio-economic transition. This book bears the imprint of its editors' understanding of what is happening and what is at stake in the rural West. One of us, Roger Epp, was raised in a small Saskatchewan town, part of a four-generation prairie family, and teaches at a university that enrolls a large number of rural students. He is indebted to them, especially those in his Rural Community and Political Theory seminar, for many conversations about the places from which they come. He is also indebted to a number of thoughtful, principled people he counts as friends and active collaborators in making sense of rural change: Dennis Sherbanuk; the revolving coffee-shop membership of a group known as the Kingman Renaissance Research Institute; Ken and Sharon Eshpeter; George Calvin; Adam Campbell; Ed and Fay Davidson; Norman and Marg Dyck; Dale Fankhanel; Dick Haydu; Ken Larsen; Earl Rasmuson; Dennis and Marion Read; Jan Richardson; and David Samm. This book, he trusts, will ring true to their situations and reflect the insights they have willingly shared.

Dave Whitson's research interests in change in rural areas grew out of his observations of tourist developments that were transforming communities like Canmore, Kimberley, and other places in the Rocky Mountain West. This has led to a number of trips over a ten-year period during which he has sampled the skiing, hiking, and cycling that the region has to offer and enjoyed the hospitality of friends who are fortunate enough to live in these communities and to have watched them changing. For three years, this observation was augmented by more systematic research, which was partially supported through funding from the Social Sciences and Humanities Research Council. In the course of several visits, he met many people in Canmore and in several communities in the BC interior who kindly made time to share their views. He is particularly grateful to Elaine Spencer and Tim Lang in Canmore; to Sandy and Daryl Abraham in Kamloops; and to Sue Jackel in Sechelt for repeatedly putting him up in their homes, for sharing with him their own thoughts on the growth of tourism in the region, and for putting him in contact with other thoughtful people in their communities. He has also benefitted from many talks with research colleagues Jean Harvey, Alan Law, and Hart Cantelon about the effects of tourism in other communities across Canada, and from conversations over the years with Rick Gruneau, Jay Coakley, and Ian Urquhart.

A book this size is a managerial as well as an intellectual undertaking. First, its many authors not only contributed their knowledge of particular communities and dimensions of the rural West; they also met our periodic deadlines and requests for revisions. We had been warned that editors should be prepared to make enemies, but, if anything, the reverse has been true: our circle of friends has grown. Second, we are grateful to those people who read some or all of the manuscript, who offered constructive comments, and who confirmed our sense that this book could make a valuable contribution to the difficult debates about the situations it describes. That list includes Janine Brodie, Laureen Gatin, Brian Harris, J. Paul Johnston, Tim Lang, Bernadette Logozar, Elaine Spencer, and Gillian Steward, as well as members of Parkland's research committee. Third, we appreciate the institutional support provided by our home universities and departments. Finally, we count it a great pleasure to have brought this book to production with the expertise and congenial support of Leslie Vermeer, Cathie Crooks, and Linda Cameron at University of Alberta Press. All of those named have made this a better book. At the same time, we take final responsibility as editors for both its content and its omissions. We know there is more to be said about the complexity of the rural West than could fit into one volume.

Our most important acknowledgments are to members of our families: to Cathie McDougall and Jake Evans, and to Rhonda Harder Epp, Stefan and Elise. More than anyone, they know about the time and attention devoted to this project. Cathie, who enjoys being out in the mountains every bit as much as Dave does, too often had to stay home while this manuscript came to fruition. Rhonda has experienced much the same. For our part, we thank them for the kind of companionship and support without which this book, and all worthy human endeavours, would not be possible.

Writing Off
Rural Communities?

**Roger Epp and
Dave Whitson**

...Ottawa could help if it thought
about Canada correctly—as a country of cities
strung together by countryside.
—*Jeffrey Simpson, columnist,* The Globe and Mail

It's not a transcendent purpose of Canadian life
to preserve these dinky little towns
in the middle of nowhere.
—*Barry Cooper, political scientist, University of Calgary*

THE VIEW FROM BELL'S HILL
Forget Seattle. Forget street demonstrations in Davos, Quebec City, or wherever trade negotiators, protesters, and TV cameras now periodically converge. Some of globalization's most intense and most revealing conflicts can be found much

closer to home, in rural districts like Bell's Hill, south of Lougheed in east-central Alberta. In the summer of 2000, the County of Flagstaff granted a development permit, in the face of considerable local opposition, to Taiwan Sugar Corporation for an 80,000-hog barn complex in the district. If completed, the complex will make Bell's Hill, in raw-sewage terms, the third-largest city in the province.

It is germane to understanding the wider significance of this very local conflict, though, to know that Taiwan Sugar did not come to Flagstaff by accident, when two other Alberta counties had already sent it packing. On the contrary, Taiwan Sugar, and the considerable investment it is prepared to make, has been actively courted by provincial and federal governments. Alberta Agriculture shared the cost of a location study in the County of Flagstaff and provided advice on setting up an intensive livestock operation there (including advice on topics like minimizing local opposition). The provincial government has also continued to resist demands for tougher environmental regulation of large-scale livestock operations, despite the Walkerton tragedy in Ontario and serious *E. coli* warnings in southern Alberta's feedlot alley. Thus, in Bell's Hill, and in other deeply divided rural districts, municipal authorities have been left on their own to assess these kinds of development applications, while lacking the technical expertise to evaluate the risks and the financial resources to enforce whatever environmental conditions they might impose. Moreover, in places like the County of Flagstaff, with a declining population and limited economic prospects, even a few jobs at modest wages is a powerful consideration.

At Bell's Hill, opposition to the Taiwan Sugar project came mainly from farm families worried about environmental and community impacts and, at a deeper level, about their own future in a vertically integrated world of corporate livestock producers and processors. Their self-chosen name said as much: the Flagstaff Family Farm Promotional Society. They launched an appeal, circulated petitions, flooded newspapers with letters, and packed the local hall for the hearings. They sold sandwiches and pies to offset the expenses of legal counsel. They risked irreparable rifts with some of their neighbours. They sat uncomfortably while their "emotionalism" was disparaged and their personal knowledge of local aquifers and streambeds discounted, and while a city lawyer acting for the company urged the appeal board to "face the fact" that the family farm was dead. Late in November 2000, in a split decision, the appeal board upheld Taiwan Sugar's permit. The opposition continues to pursue legal and political appeals, even though people know that the province wants to have the project proceed, for the sake of Alberta's reputation as a province "open for business." Still, many remain confused and angry that the Conservative government—a government that most locals have supported for years—has become more enemy than defender.

This story about Bell's Hill, one small agricultural community in eastern Alberta, serves to introduce two aspects of globalization that will recur throughout the essays in this book. First, it illustrates the prospect of a harsher rural–urban division of labour in the global economy, as governments retreat both from regulatory roles and from redistribution on behalf of disadvantaged regions. Bluntly put, following Calgary political scientist Roger Gibbins, the clean, high-tech prosperity of the "knowledge economy" is concentrated in larger urban centres. Thus, on the Canadian Prairies, cities like Calgary, Edmonton, and Saskatoon thrive, even as the farm crisis decimates rural communities around them.[1] The countryside, meanwhile, is coming to serve two new and very different purposes—playground and dumping ground—as the traditional rural economy declines. In some fortunate regions, those accessible to urban vacationers and retirees, and having the right kinds of opportunities for mountain or marine recreation, "nature" is coming to mean clean and scenic environments for upscale ski and golf resorts, for various forms of back-country recreation, and for holiday homes. In more remote or less obviously scenic locations, meanwhile, where land is cheap and city people seldom come, rural communities are becoming dumping grounds: sites for the messes created by city garbage, by massive resource developments, by low-wage industry, and by intensive livestock production. Urban people are largely unaware of the sights, smells, and health risks associated with such projects—out of sight, out of mind—but even in the wealthiest province in Western Canada, rural people know all too well that the "Alberta Advantage" is not distributed evenly. Beyond the Rocky Mountain Parks and the Highway 2 corridor, economic desperation has led a succession of communities to grasp at environmentally dubious schemes like hazardous waste treatment, strawboard manufacture, tire incineration, and mega-hog barns. Some advantage.

Second, the events at Bell's Hill focus attention on the changing roles of government alluded to above: specifically, on the new relationships that globalization encourages among regional governments seeking to attract investment, transnational corporations, and local communities that may get little say in developments that will transform their lives. This book offers a series of examples, more fully developed than the one outlined here, of how globalization is transforming our countryside and of the roles our governments are playing. With contributions by farm activists, journalists, politicians, and pastors, as well as from scholars interested in rural issues, it also illustrates how rural people are trying to cope with the effects of globalization. Those effects can be as different as the loss of farms or jobs, the loss of community leaders and collective political capacity, cuts to public services like hospitals and schools, environmental threats, and influxes of retirees and tourists who bring with them new sets of cultural expectations. Taken together, these essays are intended to serve as building blocks for a more critical analysis than is common in Canada today of the abandonment of traditional rural industries and communities.

Many Canadians, it must be acknowledged at the outset, are better off as a result of trade agreements like NAFTA and GATT that have opened up our economy to transnational trade and investment. The booming economies of the major cities clearly attest to this. Canadian technology companies have developed new markets for sophisticated products, creating wealth for investors and jobs for suitably qualified workers. Canadian consumers have also benefitted, albeit unevenly, from cheaper goods, including food products, as a result of global competition. In many rural communities, however, and for most of those working in the natural-resource industries that were once the foundation of the rural Canadian economy, there have been few such benefits. Instead, as many of the essays that follow demonstrate, rural Canadians have often paid a heavy price.

Whether we look at agriculture, forestry, mining, or the fishery, prices for primary commodities threaten the viability of small Canadian producers. In industries like mining, this reflects competition from low-cost producers abroad; the result has been either a shift towards capital-intensive mining, with new technologies and fewer jobs, or the shutting down of Canadian operations in favour of overseas production. In other industries, notably agriculture and fishing, independents struggle on in an environment shaped by corporate concentration in the food industry; but often they have few options beyond low-profit roles as suppliers of raw materials, or even contract workers, for companies like Cargill or McCain Foods. As several of our contributors show, government policies are increasingly focussed on securing cost-efficient "inputs" for the Canadian food-processing industry, as opposed to protecting farmers' livelihoods. What matters, evidently, in strategies for "value-added" food production, is aggregate profitability, rather than the fate of small producers. In this environment, independent farmers and fishers find their incomes, their communities, and their futures all vulnerable to decisions made elsewhere: in provincial capitals, in Ottawa, and in corporate head offices that may be located in Toronto or Calgary but are as likely to be in St. Louis or Taipei.

Of course, Canadians working in export-oriented, primary-resource sectors of the economy have always been exposed to world-market fluctuations. By now, moreover, we are not surprised when foreign—or, indeed, domestic—companies put the corporate "bottom line" ahead of the well-being of small communities a long way from head office. However, most Canadians, rural and urban alike, have historically expected their governments to defend their well-being. What has been altered dramatically, as a by-product of contemporary trade agreements, are the roles of governments. Indeed, at every level, the focus of government activity has shifted away from the kinds of policies that once brought better infrastructure and services (roads, schools, and hospitals) to rural Canada—and towards policies designed to attract business. What geographer David Harvey has called the policy agenda of the "entrepreneurial city,"[2] in which urban governments (or arm's length agencies, like Economic Development Edmonton) compete to attract outside investors, is now replicated at the provincial and national levels and sold to the public under mantras like "jobs, jobs, jobs." Public expenditures have been redirected accordingly.

For more than a quarter century, between 1945 and the early 1980s, Canadian federal governments, as well as provincial governments as different as those of Tommy Douglas in Saskatchewan and Peter Lougheed in Alberta, put considerable resources into evening out the disparities between urban and rural standards of living. Likewise, one objective of federal equalization payments and income support programs was precisely to make seasonal work in the resource industries a sustainable way of life, thereby keeping population in rural areas and keeping resource-based rural communities alive. In more recent years, however, all these programs have been radically curtailed, and successive federal governments have pursued a trade agenda that has hit hardest at rural commodity producers. Most notably, they have played "boy scout" with Western grain, implementing WTO rules against subsidies ahead of schedule, while our major competitors in the US and Europe drag their feet. Indeed, Canada's readiness to impose trade sanctions on Brazil in the winter of 2001 and to provide export loan guarantees to support our aerospace industry stands in stark contrast to our refusal to match the subsidies that the US and EEC continue to give to their farmers.[3] When Western premiers went to Ottawa in 1999, requesting aid for Prairie farmers, the Liberal government's response was belated and grudging, with suggestions made that the only long-term solution was fewer small farmers. More recently, in fact, a national newspaper headline summarized bluntly the advice of a senior federal cabinet minister: "get out of grain farming."[4] It is little wonder, in these circumstances, that farm people have become disillusioned with mainstream political parties.

At the provincial level, governments of all political stripes have resorted to some combination of the following to attract companies looking for low-cost production sites or raw materials: favourable tax regimes, long-term access to natural resources, cheap labour, and relaxed environmental standards. Moreover, when provinces compete for these investments, against each other and against regional governments abroad, the result is not unlike the proverbial "race to the bottom"—a race that is repeated at the local level by competing municipalities. In addition, provincial governments seeking to create a positive investment climate have redefined their relationship to municipal authorities. The story of Bell's Hill and Taiwan Sugar is again instructive here. For years, provinces left ill-equipped rural municipalities to make decisions about hog barns and other contentious developments. This had the appearance, at least, of respecting local democracy, though its effect often was to limit what should have been broad debates about environmental threats or alternative economic futures to the much narrower issues of zoning and the municipal tax base. Another downside, as we will see, has been intensely personal conflict among neighbours. Nonetheless, municipalities could—and sometimes did—turn down big developments. As this book went to press, though, the provincial government had announced its intention to introduce legislation that, as the industry and a committee of government MLAs had recommended, would strip municipalities of virtually all decision-making powers over large feedlot and hog-barn projects. Instead, authority for siting, approval, and monitoring would be vested in a "conservation board" staffed by professionals making technical, or, in the jargon of George W. Bush's presidency, "science-based" decisions on the basis of province-wide standards.[5] ILOs would be treated like the oil and gas industry, whose activity is governed by a pro-development regulatory agency that is itself the object of considerable rural frustration. In this way, rural municipalities' requests for provincial environmental legislation would be met by removing them from the picture almost entirely. The agenda here is clear: local objectors should not be allowed to disrupt "development" regardless of its implications for their community and their livelihoods. In a world of mobile investment, they should be grateful for what they get.

GLOBALIZATION, GOVERNMENT, AND AGRICULTURE

Globalization is often treated as a creature of market forces, but it is no less a creature of governments. Since the late 1970s, indeed, Canadian governments at all levels have helped facilitate the processes of globalization that now bind their policy options. They have signed multilateral free trade deals. They have removed controls on currency flows and foreign direct investment, privatized state-owned enterprises, and progressively deregulated utilities that were once considered public infrastructure: in transportation, communications, and electrical power. They have made debt reduction a top priority, and to that end, they have cut public services. They have shifted the tax burden from corporations to individuals to attract investment and retain "business confidence." In effect, our governments have abandoned the defence of the "national economy," let alone particular regions or economic sectors. The single most notable signal of this shift, in Western Canada, was the phasing out of the Crow benefit, after pressure from rail companies, livestock producers, and the Alberta government. Materials distributed to farm households in 1995 offered much optimism, couched in the shiny new rhetoric of globalization. The change was "necessary" to meet new international trade rules; but it would also serve to encourage "value-added" processing of grain, livestock, and other primary commodities, and increase the efficiency of our rail system. The net result, it was confidently predicted, would secure "new potential for farm families and rural communities" and strengthen the Prairie economy.

Yet drive a secondary highway five years later, almost anywhere in the grain belt, and the picture that emerges is not one of prosperity. The horizon is bereft of the familiar elevators that once announced towns and villages. The pavement is likely patched or broken. The road is virtually empty save for tandem trucks that spin a rock at your windshield or crowd you onto a shoulder. At strategic points along the remaining rail routes, near towns that survive as service centres in a contracting economy, you can see their destinations: high-volume terminals bearing the names of grain barons like Cargill and Louis Dreyfus, and what were Prairie wheat pools before their corporate makeovers. Commercial test plots likewise advertise the brand names of seed and chemical conglomerates. There *is* money being made here. However, even a cursory look at Main Street in most rural towns confirms that this money doesn't stay in local circulation for long. In addition, the effects of the withdrawal of government services are also easy to see. Not only are rail lines closed, but post offices and schools, too. If medical facilities survive, the services they offer have been radically scaled back.

Cutbacks in public services have also meant a loss of professional jobs in the community, reinforcing the trend towards rural depopulation. Small businesses are failing and houses sit empty, even with property prices that are astoundingly low by urban standards.

In some places, of course, it is possible to see (and smell) the kinds of developments that characterize industrial food production. In the post-Crow era, as several of the chapters in the first section of the book illustrate, the landscape of prairie agriculture is less about wheat than it is about intensive livestock operations—a shift promoted and facilitated by provincial governments, New Democrat as well as Conservative. In their chapter on Manitoba, a province in which the loss of the Crow has at least quadrupled grain transport costs by rail, Doug Ramsey and John Everitt describe both a dramatic diversification of agricultural activity and a new emphasis on hog production especially following Maple Leaf's relocation of its hog-processing operations from Edmonton to a massive new plant in Brandon in 1999. Indeed, Manitoba has been praised as a model of value-added adaptation to the new economic realities.[6] That transformation, however, has not come without a political price. As Ramsey and Everitt show, the NDP government reneged on an election commitment to return to a single-desk system of selling hogs—a way of giving equal market access to small producers—while its willingness to accommodate ILOs and the demands of corporate hog processing has opened up rural/urban and farm/labour divisions within the party. The general pattern is that family-farm producers are squeezed by corporations that don't need to make money on hogs if they also own or have preferred market access to the processing plants, with the result that wealth is drained from the local community. Mega-barns are also problematic for their low wages and unhealthy working conditions, and for the environmental hazards that follow from inadequate treatment of huge volumes of liquid manure. Yet provincial governments are typically loath to act, especially when they have promised exemptions from environmental and labour standards in order to attract the plants. Qualman questions what purposes, and whose interests, are served by policies that systematically encourage corporate hog production. His observations challenge any automatic assumption that vertical integration of livestock production is "better" and invite us to ask "better for whom?".

In the article that follows, Michael Broadway raises many of the same environmental and labour issues, and poses many of the same questions, this time in the context of beef packing. Broadway, a geographer who has studied corporate concentration in the US beef-packing industry and its move from urban slaughterhouses to lower-cost rural locations in Kansas and Nebraska, here describes the coming of major US packers to Alberta, specifically to Brooks and High River. The picture he paints is not a pretty one. In Brooks, the promise of jobs from the expansion of a small packing plant was initially welcomed as a boost to local employment. However, as things turned out, the plant required more low-paid labour than the local area could possibly supply. This has meant an influx of transient, unskilled workers, often very recent immigrants, leading in turn to housing shortages, racial tensions in the town, and dramatically higher demands on local social agencies, food banks, medical and school services, and police. "At issue," Broadway suggests, "is the degree to which a local community can be responsible for dealing with the social consequences of a provincial economic development strategy and an industry over which it has no control."

Yet if the economic choices available to low-wage boomtowns like Brooks are not very attractive, Bill Ramp and Mustafa Koc suggest that they may be not much better even in cities the size of Lethbridge. They examine the politics that followed from a proposal to build a major plant to process pork for Asian markets in Lethbridge—in a city (and surrounding county) already polarized over feedlot expansion along the Oldman River. Ramp and Koc take us through the divisions that opened up between those supporting a development agenda and those more concerned about air and water pollution and quality-of-life issues. Municipal officials are portrayed as resigned to the realism of imperfect choices in their ongoing search for jobs and tax revenues, while the community is left with a legacy of bitterness that continues to poison the political atmosphere around issues of privatization or cuts to services. This, the authors suggest, was Lethbridge's baptism of fire into the politics of the global economy, a politics which involves more than competition for investment *between* jurisdictions; it also exposes and sharpens divisions *within* communities between those who see opportunities (or, failing that, no other choices) and those who see threats or displacements.

From Lethbridge, we move to New Brunswick, and Susan Machum's account of agricultural restructuring in that province since the Second World War. Although our primary focus in this book has quite deliberately been the rural West, where both of us and most of our contributors live and work, we believe that the story Machum tells should be of interest to Western readers for at least two reasons. First, and most important, she traces the steady shift in the focus of provincial government policies for agriculture, under both Liberal and Conservative administrations, away from policies intended to support family farms and rural communities, and towards policies designed to serve the growth aspirations of corporate food processors. Under the recently elected government of Bernard Lord, indeed, the Departments of Agriculture and Fisheries have been merged into a single, and aptly named, Department of Food Production. The government's aim here is to build up New Brunswick's food-processing industries, even if the "inputs" to those industries (potatoes or fish) can be sourced more cheaply outside the province. What matters most is a cheap and reliable supply for the food processors, rather than the viability of New Brunswick's independent farmers or fishers. We can see in outline, therefore, in one of Canada's most rural provinces, one possible future for parts of the Prairie provinces, if policies that favour corporate food production are not publicly debated. Second, Machum highlights the growing significance of McCain Foods in the New Brunswick economy, a phenomenon that is relevant to Western farmers not only because McCain and its subsidiaries are also active on the Prairies, but more generally because it highlights the growing power of agri-food corporations to influence provincial agricultural policies.

Similar themes crop up again in the final essay in this section, a comparison of the effects of agricultural restructuring in rural Australia and Canada, by Geoffrey Lawrence, Murray Knuttila, and Ian Gray. Lawrence and his colleagues begin with an analysis of the "farm problem," and why governments in both countries have, since soon after 1945, tried to encourage small farmers to leave the land for more "productive" occupations. They then proceed to associate more recent rural restructuring, in both Canada and Australia, with the emergence in the 1980s of an increasingly global system of corporate food production and distribution. Also important, in both countries, has been the election of neo-liberal governments committed to free-trade agendas that promised benefits, on balance, to their increasingly urban populations. The results of this agenda in Australia, where state governments have cut back on rural services in the same ways we have described Canadian provinces doing, include environmental degradation, the departure of many professional people from rural communities, and economic decline in most inland areas (while the coasts become tourist and retirement havens). This inland decline has produced a rural backlash (called "the revolt of the bush" by some Australian commentators) against governments perceived to have abandoned them, but also against groups in Australian society who are seen as beneficiaries of government largesse: in particular, Aboriginal Australians and immigrants from Asia. What is noteworthy here is the uncanny resemblance this bears to the politics of "Western alienation" that has gained purchase in Western Canada, especially outside our major cities. In both countries, populism speaks to people in the rural hinterlands who are anxious about their futures, and often feel that their way of life has been betrayed by governments more concerned to placate other interests.

THE BUSH: RESOURCE TOWNS AND RECREATION

In Canada, of course, "the bush" refers not to the agricultural regions that are the West of popular imagination but rather to that even larger area of rocks and trees that stretches across the provincial Norths. In Western Canada, this encompasses the Shield country of northern Manitoba and Saskatchewan, the boreal forest that occupies much of northern Alberta, the Rocky Mountains, and the mountain and forest country of the British Columbia interior. What is important, here, for our purposes, is just how much of the analysis developed in the previous section is also applicable to hinterland communities across this other "West."[7] These are communities that, just like agricultural communities to the south, have historically made their living from natural resources: from forestry, from mining, and on the west coast from the fishery. However, globalization in these industries, too, along with government policies that favour the interests of integrated corporate producers, has produced demographic and social effects similar to those occurring in the agricultural West, described above. Small independent operators have been swallowed up by larger competitors, and the livelihood of mining and pulp and paper communities has become even more dependent than in the past on developments in foreign markets and on investment decisions made in Japan or in the United States.

You can see the downside of globalization, therefore, in many remote mining and forestry towns across northern Canada, where if a mine shuts down or a proposed pulp mill is vetoed on environmental grounds, the "last best hope" for community survival may lie in attracting blue-collar retirees with cut-rate house prices. This has led to bitter community divisions, not unlike those described by Ramp and Koc, with local political and business leaders begging multinational companies to establish pulp mills or mines, even when the environmental impacts of these operations might be damaging. Local boosters are supported, moreover, by provincial governments anxious to preserve rural jobs. However, new resource developments have been regularly challenged by environmental advocacy groups, often based outside the local community, who have fought the massive environmental "footprint" of forestry or mining megaprojects. Environmental concerns typically are shared by some locals; but when the expert testimony—and the legal advice—comes from outside, the effect can be to fan local resentment of "outside interference" and to make *any* environmentalists (including locals) the perceived enemies of resource workers, their families, and all the businesses that depend on the resource economy.

The development of Northern resources has been further complicated, over the last two decades, by the increasingly forceful assertion of the interests of First Nations communities. Prior to the 1980s, if First Nations peoples were consulted at all (and before the Berger Commission hearings into proposals for a Mackenzie Valley Pipeline in the late 1970s, they routinely were not), their leaders spoke of the damaging impacts that resource megaprojects would have on their traditional way of life.[8] Twenty years later, though, after a series of court decisions that have affirmed aboriginal rights, new generations of First Nations leaders are less likely to oppose resource development outright than to position themselves as stakeholders and seek economic benefits for their own communities. First Nations' interests are being asserted all across the provincial Norths, but nowhere more vigorously than in British Columbia, where the issue of outstanding land claims affects almost any proposed development. Many argue that this has served to deter development, because corporations are understandably reluctant to invest large sums in resource projects on lands that future court decisions may award to First Nations. Against this background, treaty negotiations have become a highly divisive issue in BC provincial politics, with the newly elected Liberal government promising a province-wide referendum on aboriginal self-government.[9]

This is the geographic and social territory of the chapters that comprise the second section of the book. The lead chapter here, by historian Ken Coates, explores the future of Northern BC in the context of globalization in the mining and forest industries that have been the engines of the economy in this region since the 1950s. In an analysis that offers many parallels with Lawrence's account of the rural hinterland in Australia, Coates suggests that as mines like Tumbler Ridge close down and proposed new resource projects are held up by objections from environmental groups and First Nations, Northern BC is "becoming an angry, isolated, and disenfranchised region." In this context, economic distress is readily transformed into populist anger at government, at urban environmentalists, at immigrants, and at aboriginal people. For Coates, the region's best hope lies in local communities and the province reaching mutually acceptable agreements with First Nations. This would create a climate of investor confidence and encourage new resource developments to proceed, to the benefit of everyone. In the current political climate, however, Coates is not confident that such agreements will be reached any time soon.

The next chapter, by political scientist Ian Urquhart, analyzes the conflicts that surrounded one particular development near Hinton, Alberta: the proposed Cheviot Mine, just outside Jasper National Park. The mine was eventually approved after a protracted and bitter hearing process, involving much expert testimony and arguments by environmental groups that the review panel hadn't fully complied with the requirements of environmental impact assessments. Not long after receiving final approval, in late 2000, the company announced that development of the mine was on indefinite hold, because of falling international demand for metallurgical coal. Environmentalists and those concerned with the recreational values of Jasper celebrated this decision, and in the aftermath there was hopeful talk on all sides about the potential for developing tourism and other "environmentally friendly" kinds of employment. However, as Urquhart makes clear, skilled miners will never be satisfied with the part-time work that is typically available in the tourist industry, let alone with being invited to "create their own jobs," as the rhetoric of small-business assistance programs cheerily advises. It may be that the living standards and expectations of rural blue-collar workers *are* incompatible, in some ecologically important places, with environmental protection. However, Urquhart invites us to look beyond the standard arguments of the "jobs vs. the environment" debate, and to think instead about the meaning of "livelihood" in ways that will not be unfamiliar to people who honour the work of farming. He also urges that where resource work *is* shut down in the name of a larger national interest in environmental protection, the nation has obligations to give the workers who are displaced every possible assistance in making new lives.

The remaining three chapters in the section deal with communities where survival is not the issue, but where the recreation-leisure-tourism economy is already a commercial success. You can observe other aspects of globalization, indeed, in these pockets of new prosperity in the rural West: in the Okanagan Valley, where the old economy of agriculture and forestry is now less visible than tourism, retirement homes, and vineyards; in former mining towns like Canmore and Kimberley, which have been successfully refashioned around ski hills, golf courses, and "recreational property"; and in retirement communities like Sechelt on BC's Sunshine Coast, where the local economy has been rejuvenated by newcomers with disposable incomes and cosmopolitan consumer tastes. All of these communities are prospering, to differing degrees, and their good fortune in being convenient to popular recreational environments distinguishes them from the more isolated Northern communities that are the focus of Coates' paper. Yet the advent of a new economy based on recreation and tourism is not entirely unproblematic. It usually means a loss of blue-collar jobs and, despite job growth in the service sector, miners and loggers rarely become restaurateurs or ski instructors. The net result, typically, is turnover in the population and displacement of what used to be the rural working class.

In the first of these essays, Dave Whitson invites us to consider that these communities are now prime examples of the globalization of the recreational property market, and that parts of BC and Alberta have become very attractive to transnational corporations whose business is the production of "world-class" destinations for skiing, golf, and holiday homes. The paper depicts the growth of this industry and examines the ways that it is changing Western Canadian communities that have the right kind of recreational resources. Whitson's research confirms that communities like Canmore, Vernon, and Kimberley are thriving in this new economy, and that most people prefer the problems of rapid growth to those associated with decline. However, the gentrification of the countryside typically leads to shortages of affordable housing, to changes in the retail mix and the local culture of what used to be blue-collar towns, and to changes in the kinds of livelihood that are available there. Whitson asks who loses out in such changes and, like Urquhart, he urges that the burdens of adjustment not be left to rural working people to bear by themselves.

Lorelei Hanson picks up the theme of "old" vs. "new" economies in the context of the foothills of southwestern Alberta, where spacious acreage homes are now proliferating along the eastern slopes of the Rockies. Here, the threat to the traditional ranching economy comes less from resource extraction (though there are some conflicts over oil and gas development) than from the loss of ranchland to acreages and holiday home developments, and more generally from urbanites' capacity to buy up "working" land for its recreational and scenic values. Hanson's focus, however, is less the details of specific conflicts than the continuity of ranchers' opposition, expressed over generations now, to the "disappearance of the open West." She proposes that the idea of the open West is itself a mythical—and ideological—construct that, while honouring a way of life that is passing, also glosses over ranching's history of conflict with other land uses and inhabitants (in particular, the aboriginal inhabitants of the region). More to the point, she argues that the very traditions of individualism and antipathy to government which are so much a part of "Western" mythology make it harder for ranchers to work together politically for the kind of zoning restrictions that might help to contain acreage development.

The spread of holiday and retirement homes, and the transition to an economy based on recreational and "lifestyle" attractions, is much more advanced on the Sunshine Coast, an increasingly popular destination for Vancouver weekenders and for retirees from Vancouver and the Prairie provinces. Here, the mayor of Sechelt, Bruce Milne, invites us to consider the increasing urbanization of this region, not so much in terms of population growth (which, in fact, has been modest) as in the spread of urban tastes and interests into formerly rural places and economies. Land values have risen while local political debates are now marked by proposals for the sorts of recreational amenities that holiday-makers and urban retirees are known to look for: well-equipped recreation centres and, especially, golf courses. The irony, for Milne, is that these phenomena are seldom explicitly acknowledged as markers of urbanization, with the result that residents seldom openly debate whether this is the future they want. But the tensions he describes—over golf courses, over new indoor recreation facilities, and over the taxes that will pay for them—will be familiar even on the Prairies, where the growth of rural acreage subdivisions sustains the populations (and the tax base) of some municipalities, while introducing new expectations and demands—even demands to be protected against farm odours—into local politics.[10]

DEFENDING RURAL COMMUNITIES

Rural communities are, ultimately, the subject of this book. To do them justice it is necessary, at the outset, to dispel the inevitable and patronizing description of them in big-city news stories as "tight-knit," as if social relations in them were relatively uncomplicated. More than a decade ago, in his well-known study of the "crisis in Canada's countryside," Alex Sim wrote:

> I see the rural community, not as a quiet haven to escape a turbulent
> world, but as a battered raft drifting downstream on a river of change.
> It hits a rock and part of it breaks off carrying away some of its
> occupants, while those that remain grapple with other bits of debris in
> a frantic effort to reconstruct the raft. As others try to scramble aboard
> this rural raft, those already on board are undecided whether to
> welcome them or cast them adrift.[11]

Sim's picture may seem unduly pessimistic in some cases, all too familiar in others. More than ever, though, the metaphor "tight-knit" misses the frays, tears, and stresses in the fabric of rural communities. Not only are they often sites of intense conflict over economic futures of the kind already described. Rural people must also cope with the effects of health-care cuts on an aging population. They may live with the psychological pressures of maintaining a third- or fourth-generation farm; with the continual loss of neighbours; with what can be an overwhelming sense of shame, defeat, and hopelessness—personal and communal. Some find themselves overwhelmed by demands on the volunteer agencies to which they have given their time. Often, the necessity of off-farm work, sometimes far from home, means that men and especially women are less available for community activities, while those faced with financial difficulty can withdraw into isolation. Community leaders are worn out, or else gone; co-operative practices are hard to sustain. As a former Saskatchewan farm leader once put it:

> The people I associate with are confused, depressed, and apprehensive.
> They feel betrayed, used, and abused. They find it difficult to trust
> anyone, even themselves. These attitudes and beliefs permeate every
> level of the community. The truth of the matter is that there is no
> longer in the agrarian fabric, trust, spirit, or the practice of
> cooperation—cooperation for the purposes of economic, social, and
> intellectual development for individuals or collective purposes. We now
> find only competition which is negative in nature.[12]

Across the new rural West, indeed, social capital—trust, mutual aid, shared knowledge—is in short supply at the very point when it is needed most, as communities are impoverished by the gradual loss of communally held knowledge and political skills. Drawing on Raymond Williams' discussion of 1970s changes in the Welsh mining valleys and other parts of rural Britain, we want to propose that any adequate analysis of the "great disrupters ... of people's settlements"—that is, of global economic forces—must also try to grasp what has happened "in the minds of those to whom, in effect, all this has been done."[13] The final chapters in the book, thus, focus more directly on how rural communities are coping with the challenges posed by globalization and rural restructuring. More precisely, in many of them, what is most apparent, and what therefore demands analysis, is an inability to respond effectively and cohesively in their own defence. As these chapters show, the challenges facing rural communities have internal as well as external dimensions.

We begin the section with an account by *Regina Leader-Post* columnist Murray Mandryk of what can happen when the two solitudes of rural white and aboriginal communities in Saskatchewan are pressed by economic forces towards closer coexistence. As earlier chapters have suggested, racial tensions are a prominent part of contemporary rural life in Australia and in Northern British Columbia, as well as on the Canadian Prairies. Rural white resentment of aboriginal peoples feeds off issues such as land claims, tax exemptions, hunting rights, and what some see as federal government "handouts." It can be sharpened when farmers' own claims for financial support are turned down by Ottawa. But white prejudice may also be rooted in the kind of rural culture that Cameron Harder describes, in which respect is tied to work; and if that culture is hard on its own members, it can be even more unforgiving of aboriginal people. The unpolished prejudices reflected in some of Mandryk's encounters in the town of Punnichy will likely make some readers uncomfortable, but they are hardly uncommon. At the same time, Mandryk's ultimate point, not unlike the argument made by Coates above, is that, given demographic trends that show aboriginal populations rising while white populations are in decline, some rural communities in the West will survive only if their members can learn to live— and work together—with aboriginal people.

In the chapters that follow, Cameron Harder and Bob Stirling each dispute the idea that the farm crisis is narrowly about declining income. Harder describes with great sensitivity the deterioration of community spirit caused by bankruptcies and family departures, by the sense that a life committed to the good work of land husbandry and food production is now a sentimental anachronism, by the awareness that critical decisions are made far away, and by the loss of community cohesion that follows from conflicts over development. In place of what was once community spirit, there is now "cannibalistic competition" among neighbours, and silence around personal financial stress. What must be understood and overcome in these circumstances, Harder writes, are the debilitating parts of a deeply entrenched male culture of farm pride that dispenses shame as well as honour. Drawing on his previous experience as a pastor, Harder proposes a role for rural churches in taking the shame and loneliness out of financial difficulty and farm failure. He identifies modest reason for hope if "honest conversation" can occur, and rural people "can find the grace and courage to work together."

Stirling develops a different argument that, not unlike Urquhart in the previous section, puts livelihood at the centre of the analysis. In particular, he describes a de-skilling of farm work and a loss of the kinds of knowledge that were once embedded in communities rather than corporate patents. He traces the history of Prairie farmers' efforts to maintain control of their work, in both the horse-powered era and the transition to machines: through their formation of implement co-operatives, their own inventiveness, and their successful demands for public-access university and government research. While this history may have an inspirational quality, Stirling concludes that farmers may now have a hard time regaining control of their work, when the logic of agribusiness and biotechnology promotes proprietary knowledge. Today, Canada has surrendered agricultural research almost entirely to corporate interests, protecting "plant breeder's rights" in law even when the research is conducted at public universities; and it is not uncommon to hear farmers use terms like "corporate serfdom" to describe their relationship to Monsanto and its competitors. In the new era of contract farming, Stirling proposes, "Skill at the work of actually growing something becomes secondary." The result is the loss of traditional forms of collective social capital and political vitality.

The assumption that rural communities are "tight-knit" plays out in a different way in the chapter on seniors by Norah Keating, Janice Keefe, and Bonnie Dobbs. Partly, their point is to challenge the notion—popular in some circles—that government cuts to health care services have hurt rural communities less, because rural people are likely to have informal care networks of family and friends. They remind us that there are considerable differences among rural communities, as well as considerable differences in the circumstances of seniors in these communities. In the first place, there are predictable differences in the availability of informal support networks, depending on whether the community is one where younger family members still work and live. In some communities where older people move to spend their retirement years, for example, seniors can be quite distant from the relatives or old friends who might provide informal support. As far as personal circumstances are concerned, seniors' health and mobility are the largest factors affecting the kinds of support they need. However, their ability to pay for part-time, home-based care, or even home maintenance services can also be very important. What could help many rural seniors avoid institutionalization, Keating and her colleagues conclude, is the development of a comprehensive national Home Care Program, which could provide support and relief to informal caregivers, so that *they* don't burn out.

Arn Keeling's chapter, based on a historical account of one woman's persistent struggle against sour gas pollution, raises the somewhat different issue of what individuals can do when the regulatory agencies that are supposed to protect the environment appear not to be doing that job. As the author points out, the legal framework governing energy and the environment in Alberta has always meant that farmers have had a hard time "proving" that health problems, whether human or animal, were attributable to the activities of the energy industry. However, Keeling's history of the struggle to strengthen Alberta's regulatory framework through the 1970s and 1980s, and the subsequent diminishing of public accountability in the 1990s, makes it clear that renewed and well-publicized tensions in recent years are at least partly the result of the government's weakening of the public bodies through which rural people had learned to defend their interests. Policy shifts in the 1990s towards industry self-regulation and government cuts to staff—both hallmarks of neo-liberalism—reinforce the perception that the energy industry is a much higher priority for the Alberta government. However, they have also given renewed life to what Keeling aptly terms Alberta's tradition of "cantankerous rural advocacy."

The book's concluding chapter, by Roger Epp, circles back to the effects of globalization and rural restructuring in east-central Alberta and to anxieties about the survival of communities in a region that, demographically, resembles much of rural Saskatchewan. To this the chapter grafts a concern for the survival of democratic life, against the grain of what the author frames as a long process of political de-skilling. Here, its argument runs parallel to Stirling's. It recalls a pioneer history filled with radical democratic experiments in order to ask why rural people are now so easily enlisted in an angry anti-politics of resentment. Why have people acquiesced in a patron–client relationship with a provincial government that seems to have abandoned them? And what happens when the requisite skills of democratic participation and collective action are buried two generations deep in local memory? The long-term effect of this de-skilling, Epp argues, is to make rural people more vulnerable to the difficult choices posed by globalization, as their communities shrink and livelihoods are threatened. For all that, he proposes, rural Albertans should not be written off as a political lost cause. Their individual and communal insecurities have yet to find political expression. However, their regard for land, place, and work cannot be reduced to exchange-value; and, for now, many of them cannot imagine living anywhere else. Especially in a farm economy that increasingly resembles that of the early 1920s, the possibility that a democratic politics of community self-defence might again emerge is not entirely far-fetched. Indeed, spirited local protests against corporate hog barns and proposed school closures offer examples of it. Such "unskilled" protests may be the first step—and the last hope—for rural communities.

NOMADS AND NEIGHBOURS?

A fundamental question that is implied throughout this book is whether rural people have any right to remain "in place"—that is, to continue living and working in communities and occupations that have often sustained their families for generations. This question is a valid one for public policy, at a time of scarce public resources and the continuing concentration of people in cities. However, even to ask it in that way obscures the extent to which government policy—far from being neutral—has already encouraged rural depopulation. Indeed, similar questions have been asked for decades with respect to Atlantic Canada and especially its fishing communities. If seasonally employed Maritimers ought to "move to where the jobs are," rather than live off government support, as a Canadian Alliance official scolded in a famous moment of political candour, surely the same is being whispered in political and financial circles about rural people in the West.

Conventional economic wisdom has not hesitated to condemn "obsolete" towns to a "natural death."[14] In this spirit, a vice-president of the Royal Bank, writing in the relative obscurity of an industry journal, has argued that the crisis of North American agriculture is really a consequence of the "fact" that 20 percent of farm operations—the big, technology-savvy, credit-worthy ones—are responsible for 80 percent of production. It is the relatively unproductive majority of farmers who, in his view, cannot compete in a climate of agribusiness consolidation and are continually clamouring for government assistance. Therefore, the policy challenge is to ease these people off the land. Fortunately, in his view, many of those aged 60 and over "will elect (wisely) to exit the industry and cash in."[15] Statistics Canada figures in the fall of 2000 give some substance to this projection.[16]

The people who leave farming, however, are not simply commodity producers; they are members of communities that will bleed with their departure. And to clinically dismiss such communities, and the ways of life associated with them, as obsolete is to diminish the humanity of people who have sustained them over the years. During the time of the last major coal strike in Britain, in the 1980s, Raymond Williams wrote that it was important for miners to protect their communities—not abstractions, but real "places where they have lived and want to go on living, where generations ... of social effort and human care have been invested, and which new generations will inherit." Against that kind of personal and collective investment in communities, Williams described the "logic of a new nomad capitalism, which exploits actual places and people, and then (as it suits it) moves on."[17] This is a description that rings all too true today in many parts of the rural Canadian West, from emptied-out coal towns like Tumbler Ridge and Cassiar, to farming districts like Bell's Hill. If we can accept that "nomad capitalism" is all too apt a synonym for what we now call economic globalization, Williams' analysis of how it operates—absentee corporate owners extracting wealth for absentee shareholders, as if communities didn't matter—should help us to recognize the consequences of globalization for many rural Canadian communities and the people who inhabit them. In the name of globalization, and its companion, competitiveness, the growth of an abstract economy has been placed ahead of the real desires of many Canadians to remain in the places that have been their homes for generations. An alternative approach, and one that before the "free trade" election of 1988 still had some currency in Canadian political debate, would require our elected governments to weigh the demands of "the economy"—which essentially are demands for greater profits—against other definitions of the public good.

An underlying argument of this book is that rural communities should not be "written off" in the language of bankers and economists. To be sure, there is plenty of reason to be pessimistic. In much of the rural West, the issue is already whether there will be enough of a successor generation to sustain communities. Global economic forces and the neo-liberal attitudes and values they have increasingly made "normal" together present serious challenges to the possibility of community resiliency. Public sympathy, shaped by national media, has worn thin for primary producers who, not long ago, were romanticized as the backbone of the country. At the same time, rural people retain stubborn attachments to places they don't abandon lightly, despite the overwhelming bias toward mobility in the surrounding culture. Those attachments suggest other human values to be balanced out in a fuller understanding of livelihood: the importance of neighbours and friends, of satisfying work, of familiar landscapes, and of intergenerational ties. In this light, rural communities might still be considered as promising places: first, for bringing into focus what is at stake for everyone in the prevailing political-economic order; and, second—wherever people *can* still summon the resources to defend themselves—for renewed popular insistence on policies that, in Williams' words, would "begin from real people in real places, and would be designed to sustain their continuing life."[18] At that point, rural people will speak not only for themselves, but for all of us whose lives are increasingly subordinated to the relentless demands associated with productivity and competitiveness and who have come to accept such demands as normal. Accordingly, the defence of rural communities is a matter of much greater significance than their dwindling share of national and provincial populations would suggest.

Notes

1 Roberta Rampton, "Urban west growing," *The Western Producer*, 7 December 2000. A rural–urban division of labour has also been attributed to the Western United States by Robert Kaplan, *An Empire Wilderness: Travels into America's Future* (New York: Random House, 1998).

2 David Harvey, *The Urban Experience* (Baltimore: Johns Hopkins University Press, 1989).

3 Madelaine Drohan, "Brazilian beef ban smells a bit fishy," *Globe and Mail*, 3 February 2001, B9.

4 Robert Fife, "Get out of grain farming: Goodale," *National Post*, 22 May 2001, A1.

5 Alberta Agriculture, "Province to ensure responsible intensive livestock operations," news release and backgrounder, July 4, 2001; also, Ian Gray, "ILOs require provincial rules, report suggests," *Western Producer*, 17 May 2001, 4.

6 See, for example, Fife, "Get out of grain farming."

7 Rural sociologist William Heffernan of the University of Missouri writes: "Increasingly, our agriculturally based communities ... are looking like mining communities" in terms of both ownership concentration and extraction of wealth by absentee owners. "Consolidation in the Food and Agriculture System," *Report to the National Farmers Union (US)*, 1999, 14. See also Ken Coates and Wm. Morrison, *The Forgotten North: A History of Canada's Provincial Norths* (Toronto: Lorimer, 1992).

8 Thomas Berger, *Northern Frontier, Northern Homeland: The Report of the Mackenzie Valley Pipeline Inquiry* (Ottawa: Minister of Supply and Services Canada, 1977). See also Hugh Brody, *Maps and Dreams* (Vancouver: Douglas & McIntyre, 1981).

9 For historical treatments of these debates, see, e.g., Paul Tennant, *Aboriginal Peoples and Politics: The Indian Land Question in British Columbia* (Vancouver: University of British Columbia Press, 1990); and the diverse collection of essays that followed the Supreme Court's important 1997 land-claims ruling, *The Delgamuukw Case: Aboriginal Land Claims and Canada's Regions* (Vancouver: Fraser Institute, 1999).

10 Janet Fitchen, *Endangered Space, Enduring Places: Change, Identity, and Survival in Rural America* (Boulder: Westview Press, 1991), ch. 7.

11 Alex Sim, *Land and Community: The Crisis in Canada's Countryside* (Guelph: University of Guelph, 1988), 16.

12 Roy Atkinson, "The State of Agriculture in Western Canada: The Conflict," in G.S. Basran and David Hay, eds., *The Political Economy of Agriculture in Western Canada* (Toronto: Garamond, 1988), 35.

13 Raymond Williams, "The Analysis Extended," in *Towards 2000* (London: Penguin, 1983), 186-87.

14 Richard Haigh and Daryll Murri, "Survival Strategies in Rural Canada: The Need for New Paradigms," Staff Paper, University of Alberta Department of Rural Economy, 1990, 4-5. See also Lawrence, Knuttila, and Gray (this volume) on similar "orthodoxies" in Australia.

15 John J. Murphy, "From North of the Border," *Journal of Lending and Credit Management*, December 1999/January 2000, 36.

16 Barry Wilson, "Falling farm numbers due to work shift: Stats Can," *Western Producer*, 1 February 2001.

17 Raymond Williams, "Mining the Meaning: Key Words in the Miners' Strike," in *Resources of Hope* (London: Verso, 1989), 124.

18 Ibid., 125.

PART I

Globalization, Government and Agriculture

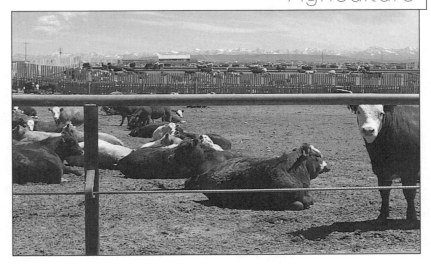

Post-Crow Farming in Manitoba

AN ANALYSIS OF THE WHEAT AND HOG SECTORS

Doug Ramsey and John C. Everitt

The character of rural life in Western Canada has changed considerably over time and so, too, have notions of rurality.[1] In Manitoba, as elsewhere, these changes have been precipitated by three major processes of evolutionary development. First, according to the agricultural census, since 1941 Manitoba has been affected by social changes related to both agriculture and community life, resulting, in turn, in transformations in people's desires, expectations, and possibilities.[2] The net result is that farming, and even the "family farm," is now commonly described as a business rather than a way of life. Second, social and economic developments are inseparable from technological changes that have made rural people more mobile and less isolated than the pioneers in the region, and enabled them to adopt quasi-urban lifestyles.[3] Third, global economic integration, including the implementation of international agreements like NAFTA[4] and the loss of the Crow Rate,[5] which for almost a century had underwritten the shipping costs of export grain production, has had widespread and deeply felt impacts that significantly affect the economic landscapes of the prairies. While this paper makes reference to various points in the agricultural history of Manitoba, its focus is the period between 1991 and 2001, and particularly the immediate pre- and post-Crow (1996) changes. This paper will discuss some of the changes that have resulted from this economic evolution, changes that are transforming rural Manitoba today. Two aspects are presented as pivotal: structural changes brought about by the industrialization of agriculture, and the role of federal and provincial governments in facilitating those changes. The paper further concentrates on two agricultural commodities: one crop, one livestock. First, wheat, the dominant crop in Manitoba, is examined as the agricultural commodity most immediately and directly affected by the loss of the Crow Rate. Changes are discussed within the context of other factors characterizing the post-Crow period, particularly low commodity prices, rising input costs, and extreme weather events in 1997 and 1999. Second, the hog sector is investigated as a post-Crow commodity anticipated and promoted by provincial governments, whether Progressive Conservative or New Democratic (NDP), since the late 1950s. The province's role has included the removal of "single-desk selling" (SDS)[6] in 1996, to the advantage of the packing industry and the disadvantage of small producers; support for the meat-processing sector (construction of the Maple Leaf plant in Brandon from 1997 to 1999); and the promotion of hogs as an alternative to crops for farmers.

AGRICULTURAL DEVELOPMENT AND CHANGE
IN MANITOBA

Crop Production: The Emergence of "King Wheat"

Historically, the prairie west of the late nineteenth century was intended to be a settlement frontier for Canada leading to "the development of one of the world's great agricultural regions."[7] The nature of this transformation did not immediately become apparent, but by 1901, 82 percent of the cultivated land in Manitoba was in grains, and two-thirds of this (1.9 million acres) was in wheat. By 1928, the production of wheat for export had come to characterize the region. At this time, according to historian Gerald Friesen,

> Canadian wheat sales constituted nearly half the world export market.
> An entire society was organized to facilitate this activity. It was built

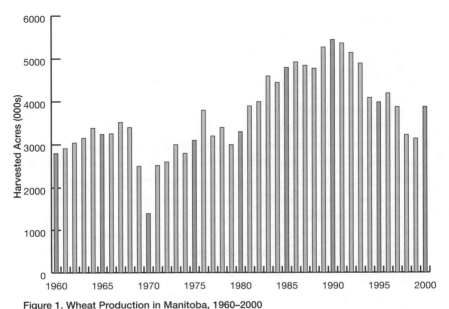

Figure 1. Wheat Production in Manitoba, 1960–2000

Source: Manitoba Agriculture and Food, Program and Policy Analysis Branch (2001)

upon rural village and transportation networks, a grain marketing system, and a family economy attuned to the rhythms of the seasons and the demands of the work itself.[8]

Despite some fluctuations, wheat acreage continued to grow. In 1931, by which time "King Wheat" was unquestionably dominant, the grain economy rested upon sure foundations—although it could be argued that "the fatal prairie habit of dependence on a single export commodity" had also been established.[9]

Although, as indicated earlier, "fundamental changes have taken place in the structure of Manitoba agriculture,"[10] these had not, until recently, affected wheat cultivation in any negative fashion. The amount of cropland has grown over the past fifty years, and wheat acreage increased in step with this general trend. In 1941, 2.4 million acres of wheat were produced; this had grown to 2.9 million acres by 1961; was up to 3.9 million acres by 1981; and reached a high of 5.4 million acres in 1990 (Figure 1). Since that date, however, changes have occurred. In 1992, there were only 5.1 million acres of wheat, and this number fell to 4.9 million in 1993 and dropped to under 4 million by 1995, representing a 27-percent decrease over a 4-year period. Although high world wheat prices led to an increase in the 1996 acreage to 4.2 million (a 5-percent increase over the previous year), this total dropped again in 1997, 1998, and 1999 as prices slumped—and, as we shall see, as the impact of the loss of grain transportation subsidies began to show. As noted in Figure 1, in 2000, the area of harvested wheat returned to 1997 levels.

The Keystone Agriculture Producers (KAP) estimate that grain transport costs have quadrupled since the mid 1990s, rising from approximately $10 to $40 per tonne, or even more, depending on proximity to a mainline.[11] Unfortunately, the true costs of this change were not immediately felt as the Crow was eliminated at a time of higher grain prices. With lower grain prices and rising input costs—in particular, fuel costs—grain farmers in Manitoba are at a competitive disadvantage. For example, KAP notes that wheat prices are approximately $1.77 per bushel lower than in 1995 and fuel costs have increased approximately 40 percent, which translates into an increase of $4.50 per acre.[12]

Livestock Production

Since 1960, three periods of increased hog production in Manitoba can be noted: 1968–73, 1983–88, and 1995–2000. Price appears to be a motivating factor in only one of these growth periods. While the value per hog fluctuated between $36 and $55 in the years 1960 to 1972, in 1973 the price rose to $82 per hog. Yet in the following year, hog production declined from 1.3 million to 1.1 million. Price influenced an increase in hog production in 1983, as the price per hog rose from $112 in 1981 to $136 in 1982. Following a price peak in 1987 at $138 per hog, the following two years were met with a decline in both price and production. Hog production has increased in Manitoba in each year since 1990.

By far, the greatest increases in production occurred between 1990 and 2000 (Figure 2). Between 1990 and 1995, the price per hog fluctuated between $102 and $125 per hog. In 1996 and 1997, record prices were paid, $147 and $146 per hog respectively. Prices plummeted in 1998 ($104) and 1999 ($100); however, this appears not to have deterred hog producers. It is interesting to note that while production rose drastically between 1990 and 1999, the total number of hog farms declined from 3,150 to 1,450 over the same period.

A number of reasons can be cited for the recent continued rise in hog production and decline in number of hog producers in Manitoba. First, it is important to understand that the industrial nature of large-scale hog production facilities does not allow farmers to simply "get in" or "get out"—the investment is of a more long-term nature. With declining prices, it is much easier for smaller producers to exit than larger ones. Second, the loss of SDS in 1996 has

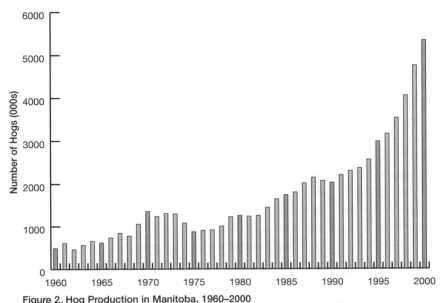

Figure 2. Hog Production in Manitoba, 1960–2000

Source: Manitoba Agriculture and Food, Program and Policy Analysis Branch (2001)

meant that farmers sell directly to processors who require certain numbers in order to receive delivery, which has the effect of squeezing out smaller operations. Third, with the current crises facing crop farming, there are few alternatives for farmers in southern Manitoba. A fourth reason relates to the Maple Leaf plant in Brandon and the perceived stability it brings to the market place in offering a destination for hogs raised by Manitoba producers. Thus, hog production will most likely continue the trends of the last decade. In fact, Manitoba presently accounts for slightly more than 20 percent of Canadian hog production. However, as the Brandon plant moves to a second shift, as proposed for 2003, it will be interesting to observe whether Manitoba producers will still be providing most of the hogs.

Diversification on Manitoba Farms

Diversification in an agricultural context has come to encompass a number of changes, including engaging in off-farm employment, performing non-agricultural activities on the farm, specializing in a different commodity, and adding a new commodity to the existing farm operation (this latter is the traditional definition of diversification). Changes in both crop and livestock sectors on Manitoba farms, particularly those which relate to diversification attempts, can be described by reviewing the reasons cited by the province for such changes. The provincial agricultural ministry states that changes in the livestock sector alone have been brought about by farmers diversifying risk, loss of the Crow Rate, technological advancements, investment, production integration, development of alliances, and growth in the processing sector.[13] The Livestock Stewardship Panel, to be discussed later, identified eight factors in the rise in hog production: crisis in the grain sector, risk diversification, loss of the Crow Rate, rising global demand for meat products, programs supporting rural diversification, technological and genetic developments, trends toward an integrated supply chain, and provincial support of the hog-processing sector.[14]

On the land, there has been an increase in the planting of other (i.e., non-wheat) crops, as well as of higher yielding (but lower quality) varieties of wheat. Other crops include canola, flax, potatoes, and sunflowers. In addition, there has been an increase in other "specialty" farm products, some of them quite exotic: honey, emus, ostriches, llamas, alpacas, elk, hemp, maple syrup, lentils, buckwheat, and mustard seed are only examples. A further development has been an increase in pluriactivity on the farm. Pluriactivity has led to an increase in the number of people involved in farm-related "industrial" opportunities, such as the production and export of leaf-cutter bees to pollinate alfalfa, flax bread production, grass-seed production, and equipment manufacturing. Coupled with this, there has been an increase in non-farm-related work, mostly off-farm. Sometimes both "partners" have full-time, off-farm jobs. In addition, other forms of supplemental economic activity have been tried, such as farm vacations, bed-and-breakfast operations, agri-tours, and other tourism-related enterprises (see also Lawrence et al., this volume). Here, rural and farming "know-how" have been combined with an interest in rural life by (usually) urban dwellers, arguably leading to a further urbanization of rural life, as "hosts" learn to supply the kinds of home amenities and meals that visitors typically expect.

FEDERAL CHANGES IN GOVERNANCE AND SUPPORT: WHEAT

Many reasons for changes in the wheat sector can be identified, but the loss of the Crow Rate seems to have been pivotal. Before concentrating upon changes that result from the loss of this rate, however, it is necessary to discuss the origins and the nature of this agreement known by many farmers as the "Holy Crow." The Crow Rate was a concession made by the Canadian Pacific Railway (CPR) in 1897 (and implemented in 1898–99) to reduce freight rates on specific products—particularly cereal crops such as wheat—in order to get a subsidy to build an expensive spur line from its mainline at Lethbridge, Alberta to Nelson, BC through the Crow's Nest Pass (to reach minerals in the Kootenays ahead of the Americans). In later years, charges were applied to the Lakehead, Churchill, and the West Coast. These rates were given statutory status on grain and flour in 1925. They remained in place (with a few variations, particularly during the First World War) until 1983. From the point of view of Manitoba farmers, the Crow Rate made the shipping of wheat relatively cheap and thus the net price relatively high. In a sense, the Crow Rate had the effect of shortening the distance between Manitoba's wheat farmers and their markets, which, of course, made the farmers more competitive in the world market.

In recent years at least (and arguably for much longer in the minds of railway company executives), the revenues raised from the shipping of grain were less than the costs of transportation.[15] Therefore, they were seen as a subsidy to the farmer, although their immediate financial benefit was offset by a deterioration in rail service that was induced by the low freight rates. Many branch lines, in particular, were given little or no repair for many years, and services became poorer, slower, and in some instances almost non-existent. But branch lines could only be abandoned with permission from the Board of Transport Commissioners—which meant struggles with local farmers that were expensive and time-consuming in themselves. Various agreements between the railways and the government took place over the years. In 1977, the Hall Commission report was produced. It recommended abandoning 2,615 miles (ca. 4,200 kilometres) of rail-line, keeping 1,813 miles (ca. 2,900 kilometres), and referring 2,344 miles (ca. 3,800 kilometres) to a new Western transportation authority for further review.[16] However, relatively few changes resulted from this document, and those that did take place were not seen, by farmers, at least, as getting at the heart of the problem.

In 1983, the federal Liberal government introduced the Western Grain Transportation Act (WGTA). Its passage proved to be definitive, although it was preceded and followed by much discussion and disagreement.[17] To say the least, it was a controversial policy change, about which much bitterness still lingers across the Prairies.[18] The WGTA made provision for the railways to be paid a subsidy, with shippers paying a share of future rail cost increases. Over the next decade the subsidy was gradually reduced, leading to further problems with branch-line upkeep and related matters. In 1996, the subsidy was removed, but the farmers received a "one-off" payment based on acreage and land quality.

The effects of "the Holy Crow" were far reaching. Apart from wheat farming, it also influenced the "industrialization" of the Prairies (or rather, the lack of it),[19] the upkeep of railways, and (to the point of the present discussion) the production system of farms. Thus, the Crow Rate affected the whole structure of agriculture, rail transportation, and agro-industry in the West, and its termination inevitably produced profound dislocations.

Beyond the loss of the Crow Rate, grain farmers have been affected by a range of other forces in recent years including excessive moisture and precipitation in 1997 and 1999, low commodity prices, and rising production costs. Further, because of the totality of factors negatively impacting Prairie farmers, rural communities are witnessing an exodus of young people who do not want to engage in a farming career. Repeated calls have been made by individuals, municipalities, agricultural organizations, and the Manitoba government about the need to assist Manitoba farmers, but to little avail.[20] Even the $92-million farm aid package (Manitoba's portion) fails to meet the needs. As one Manitoba farmer stated, "that won't even pay for a quarter of my spray bill."[21]

PROVINCIAL CHANGES IN GOVERNANCE: HOG PROCESSING AND RAISING

In order to understand structural changes taking place in the hog sector, it is necessary to examine recent trends in the hog-processing industrial sector in Manitoba. As noted by others,[22] concentration of hog-raising operations is influenced by the location of large-scale meat processing plants. Prior to mid 1999, hog processing took place in Schneider's plants in Winnipeg (45,000 hogs per week) and the Springhill plant in Neepawa (20,000 hogs per week). In July 1999, the first shift at the newly constructed Maple Leaf plant in Brandon began. Soon after, an average of 45,000 hogs were, and are, being processed each week. While both the Winnipeg and Brandon plants have suggested proposals to double production, Maple Leaf Foods' purchase of the Schneider's operation in January 2001[23] casts doubt on these projections. Maple Leaf, at least, is planning to introduce a second shift at the Brandon plant in 2003, with a view to doubling output to an average of 90,000 hogs per week. Workplace issues raised by others[24] have been evident at the Brandon plant, notably absenteeism (particularly the day after pay day), alcoholism, and high employee turnover.[25] Evidence of company concern about employee turnover can be found in recent contests that award employees with gifts for good attendance records in January 2001[26] and July 2001[27] as well as Maple Leaf personnel touring Atlantic Canada to recruit new employees.[28] Further, the city of Brandon already faces housing shortages, an issue that will be amplified with the expansions currently taking place at the Shilo military base just west of Brandon.[29]

Environmental issues have been raised repeatedly with respect to effluent from the plant. Of particular concern were two points in the summer of 2000, when breakdowns in the ultraviolet system for disinfecting waste water occurred—a breach of Maple Leaf's agreement with the City of Brandon. On the subject of water, the city and province provided $12-million for the plant which is exclusively used by Maple Leaf (thus all results aim directly at the operation) but operated by city engineers. Further, the City plans to convert its chlorine system to the ultraviolet system in question at an additional cost to taxpayers.[30] The Maple Leaf plant, however, was built without following the requirement for Clean Environment Commission hearings—a provincial legislative requirement. It was on this point that a coalition of concerned citizens developed an organization called Hogwatch Manitoba. This group monitors the hog sector in Manitoba and disseminates its information at public events (e.g., the Rural Forum Convention in Brandon in April 2001) and through a website.

The divisions developing in Brandon are best illustrated in the fact that a Hogwatch organizer ran, unsuccessfully, for Mayor of Brandon in the 1999 municipal election—opposed only by the incumbent, a key proponent of the Maple Leaf plant. Garnering only ten percent of the vote, the Hogwatch candidate ran on two main platforms related to the Maple Leaf plant: the environmental impacts and issues related to housing shortages.[31] Given the margin of victory by the incumbent, it appears that Brandon voters were comfortable that such impacts would either be mitigated or at least offset by the benefits to employment and the economy.

Two other organizations, the Manitoba chapter of the Sierra Club and the Westman Coalition, secured the Canadian Centre for Policy Alternatives to conduct a review of both hog production and processing in Manitoba. A symposium was held in Brandon in October 1999 and featured twenty-three invited presentations (including Michael Broadway, an author in this volume) and six unscheduled presentations. An open-microphone question-and-answer session followed each presentation. The symposium was facilitated by an independent chair and six commissioners. The panel's final report was released to the public in May 2000 and raised public health, social, economic, and environmental issues.[32]

This initiative appears to have embarrassed the NDP government, newly elected in September 1999, into studying issues of "sustainability" in the hog-farming sector. In March 2000, the government appointed a Livestock Stewardship Panel to solicit views on the expansion of the hog industry. One of the first actions of the Panel was a discussion paper released in June 2000.[33] In order to obtain public input, ten public meetings were held in six communities throughout Manitoba between 29 June and 1 August 2000. In total, 225 presentations were made and 150 written submissions were collected. In addition, the Panel sought information from other sources, including a tour across Canada to investigate the experiences of other jurisdictions.[34] It is important to note that the Panel was not investigating whether or not to allow future construction of Intensive Livestock Operations (ILOs); rather, its mandate was to strike a balance between the environment and development, with ILOs assumed as the primary mode of hog production. The Panel termed this mandate "finding common ground." The final report was released in December 2000 and included thirty-five recommendations in four key areas: role of the provincial government, publicly available information, role of ILOs, and decision processes for siting ILOs.[35] These recommendations acknowledge both ILO and less-intensive hog-production systems. While as of June 2001 the government has made no formal response to the report, it is pursuing implementation of the recommendation to decrease the minimum size of operations that require Manure Management Plans from 400 to 300 animal units.

This report and the NDP government's continued support for both the hog-processing and industrial hog-production sectors warrants a discussion of "party" versus "government" policy. The provincial party has longstanding policies that support the notion of the family farm, single-desk selling, and labour rights. However, the implementation of such policies is in question following the provincial convention held in Winnipeg in February 2001. Of the nine hog-related resolutions submitted to convention, three were debated.[36]

First, a motion calling on the federal government to recognize the farm crisis was given unanimous consent by delegates.[37] The provincial government followed this up with a motion in the legislature that also received unanimous consent by all parties. The motion called upon Ottawa to recognize the scale of the agricultural crisis in Manitoba and to provide $500 million in emergency assistance. The all-party standing committee on agriculture then conducted public meetings across the province to hear the voices of concerned citizens. The results of these meetings and the unanimous resolution have been presented to the federal government. As of June 2001, neither the recognition nor assistance has been forthcoming.

Second, a motion calling for a return to single-desk selling was also supported by a large majority, although no vote count was called.[38] This resolution sparked the longest debate of the convention and resulted in one delegate being called to apologize to another.[39] When Glen Hallick, a rural delegate from Morris, made an amendment to include support to those displaced by the loss of single-desk selling, Susan Hart-Kulbaba, former Manitoba Federation of Labour President, responded that such an amendment was the equivalent of including former union members in a vote on a new contract. Hallick shouted across the delegate floor: "Don't suck up to the corporations."[40] Amid the confusion and emotion, the amended motion passed. However, it appears moot for two reasons. First, Rosann Wowchuk, Minister of Agriculture, supports the motion only if the farmers want it. How many displaced hog farmers will engage in such a discussion remains to be seen. Second, Premier Gary Doer is on record as promising Maple Leaf that there will be no return to single-desk selling.[41] In a media interview following the debated motion, Doer went further stating that "the majority of producers don't want to return to [single-desk selling]."[42] One official suggested that these comments were based on two factors: 1) calls made by individuals to Provincial Government and Agricultural offices; and 2) the Premier's and Agricultural Minister's rural tours to farms and communities in southern Manitoba.[43]

Third, a motion asked for a moratorium on further construction of ILOs until the issue could be assessed. The debate included long "speeches" by two cabinet ministers expressing concerns that such a moratorium would have negative impacts on farmers and industry. The convention chair called for a vote while speakers were still lined up at both the "pro" and "con" microphones. After the first vote defeating the motion, a point of order from one delegate asked for a counted vote. The results of the second vote were 142 against, 64 for. Those voting for the motion were mainly the two Brandon riding associations (unarguably the region most affected by the Maple Leaf plant) and southern agro-Manitoba riding associations (unarguably the most affected by ILOs). Thus the influence of Winnipeg and northern Manitoba is felt not only in practice but also in political debate within the NDP. While this may not reflect a formal "split" in the party, it appears that there is a lack of understanding of the impacts ILOs could have on the rural landscape and in rural communities. The issues of ILOs in rural Manitoba are diverse and complex within communities.

In the summer of 2001, for example, the fire chief of the volunteer fire department in Lowe Farm, Manitoba resigned his position of seven years because of concerns related to ILOs, which are not required to follow the same building code requirements (e.g., sprinkler systems) as other commercial operations. Because of this, there are insurance issues and concerns about animal and firefighter safety.[44]

Although the issues that have arisen in hog-producing and meat-processing communities across North America have been raised, the largely urban media, such as the *Winnipeg Sun* and *Winnipeg Free Press*, have reported little on these issues. To their credit, the NDP included two public meetings in Winnipeg as part of the consultation process of the Livestock Stewardship Panel as well as the Task Force on Agriculture in April 2001.

FUTURE PROJECTIONS: THE POST-CROW HOG PHASE OF AGRICULTURE IN MANITOBA

There is no certain future in agriculture, and the post-Crow era of farming in Manitoba is no different in this regard. Having said this, some comments can be made about trends that could take place on the agricultural landscape of Manitoba, which, because of its central location, is the province hit hardest by the loss of the Crow Rate. First, it is likely that we will see the production of more specialty crops, ranging from oilseeds to horseradish. Due to increased livestock numbers, moreover, there will likely be more barley acreage for feed—and even more so if new hull-less varieties are developed that are better for human as well as animal consumption.

Second, the search will continue for "value-added" opportunities, although there is some doubt how far this can go. It seems counter-intuitive that everybody can go into value-added processing. And, as one observer has commented, "Where will all of the capital for this come from?" It is worth noting that with the industrialization of hog production and the concentration of hog processing, the trend toward ILOs provides few opportunities to individual (as opposed to corporate) farmers for value-added production. Indeed, remaining farmers will be pressed towards greater efficiencies, in both production technologies and marketing.[45] Related to this, a stream-lined grain-handling system is evolving that will involve fewer rail lines, more independent (non-unionized) short lines, and fewer but larger elevators.[46] This trend, however, will most likely increase farmers' costs of production, particularly with rising fuel prices. It will also require greater provincial spending on highway maintenance.

Third, as has become evident, more livestock is being produced—in particular, cattle and pigs. Some observers have suggested that in time Manitoba will change into a facsimile of Alberta of the 1980s, whereas Alberta, presented with a post-Crow market advantage as a result of its location nearer to West Coast ports, will become more like the Manitoba of old. Although such change seems likely, at least on the Manitoba side of the proposition, the degree of transformation is still unclear. One additional element in the livestock sector is that more horses will be "produced." Although it is extremely unlikely that the 1941 figure of 300,000 horses will ever again be reached, the number is currently on the rise, from under 41,000 in 1991 to more than 44,000 in 1996. Horses are already an important commodity, producing pregnant mares' urine (PMU) for estrogen. The "surplus" foals are sold for recreational purposes, exported, or sold to feedlots, although at this point very few horses—only five in 1999[47]—are slaughtered for meat in Manitoba.

CONCLUSIONS

It is possible that the rural Manitoba landscape will soon be almost unrecognizable compared, say, to 1983 or even 1996. The first five years since the loss of the Crow Rate have been a period of great change, though it is difficult to project that change into the future. Nor is all change Crow-related. Surely the other forces affecting cereal producers in particular (excessive moisture, low commodity prices, rising input costs) have impacted decision-making. For all that, two puzzles remain. First, why do farmers continue to grow wheat, albeit on reduced acreage, if their own governments discourage it and if it can be produced (or at least transported) more cheaply elsewhere on the prairies and in the world? And, second, will a livestock-dominant pattern emerge in Manitoba that is similar to that of Alberta? A number of points emerge from these two questions that ought to be recognized.

1. New wheat varieties that are higher-yielding (Prairie) than traditional (Red) are now being grown by some farmers—even though their quality may be lower. This trend has resulted from a major philosophical change for many farmers who have prided themselves on growing the highest-quality wheat possible.

2. There is still a worldwide demand for wheat and demand is projected to increase—particularly in countries of the South. As farmers in Manitoba tend be optimistic, they still feel they will be able to fill this demand at a profit. In the short term, they may

simply need to cover cash and labour costs and thus can sell at a lower price. In the long run, they also have to cover fixed costs, but contemporary farmers are much more computer-oriented and up-to-date with world affairs than was once the case. If climatic conditions worsen, for example, in the United States or Argentina, they can plant more wheat and take advantage of higher prices. However, having said this, it is unlikely that a farm will make it by just producing wheat; rather, if prices stay up, wheat can continue to supplement higher-value forms of production.

3. Inertia is a factor in farming as in other industries. Many people still grow some wheat, even with low returns, because they always have done so. In addition, their machinery is geared to grain production and not to other crops, and change might be expensive in the short term—and uneconomic, especially for aging farmers close to retirement.

4. Although canola and other crops can be more profitable (in some years), farmers need to plan a rotation of four or five crops because of fertility, disease, insect, and weed problems. Wheat is a relatively easy crop to rotate. Coupled with this reality is the fact that canola recently has "lost its glass slipper" as prices have slumped, yield and disease problems have surfaced, and high tariffs in Japan (Canada's biggest canola market) have discouraged local crushing. This decline has raised questions around what was once touted as a promising "value-added" industry for Prairie communities. Farmers have then often returned to wheat and barley.

5. Some lands and microclimates in the Prairies are better suited to grains than other crops. Some observers have argued that other lands, particularly in the extreme southwestern corner of Manitoba and in parts of Saskatchewan (e.g., Palliser's Triangle), should never have been cultivated at all but rather left to pasture and rangeland.[48]

6. The location of ILOs has become a particularly contentious issue in many rural municipalities.[49] Municipal support, or non-support, will have an impact on the emerging pattern and density of ILOs in southern Manitoba. This could lead to issues similar to those faced in the hog sector of North Carolina in the 1990s, which saw both an explosion in total hog production and an implosion or concentration into a few counties.[50] Certainly, divisions within communities are

increasing, as illustrated in the almost daily coverage recently in *The Brandon Sun.*

7. The opportunities for farmers to develop ILOs is tied to the Maple Leaf plant in Brandon. While the immediate future of the plant is one of increased production, there is no guarantee that Maple Leaf, with its virtual monopoly on hog processing in Manitoba, will remain in Brandon in the long term.[51] What becomes of the producers if production is moved out of Manitoba? This is a real concern, particularly given the contentiousness of ILO location and the high turnover and other issues currently faced by the Brandon facility.

Although farming in Manitoba is undergoing severe restructuring, the best bets are that the "agro areas" of the province will continue to constitute a farming region into the foreseeable future. What kind of farming sector will survive, and who will work in it, is a more open question. Farmers continue to sell their farms and move out of farming, with consequent impacts on adjacent communities. In many cases their children have decided that farming offers little for them. A survey of the graduates of 8 rural Manitoba high schools in 1996 found that only 6.6 percent planned to choose farming as a career.[52] At the same time, agriculture is still the basis of the provincial economy, as well as rural life; and political decisions, as this paper has shown, are important in shaping the nature of both. Agriculture may not be the economic saviour of rural communities, but it is a critical piece of the puzzle and deserves to be treated as such by all levels of government.

Notes

1 John Everitt, with Kenneth Beesley and Gerald Walker, "Towards an Understanding of the Perception of Rurality: Canadian Perspectives," in Bryon D. Middlekauff (ed.), *Proceedings, New England-St. Lawrence Valley Geographical Society.* Volume XXV (Plymouth, New Hampshire: Plymouth State College, 1996), 28–52.

2 William J. Carlyle, "Agriculture in Manitoba" in John Welsted, John Everitt, and Christoph Stadel (eds.), *The Geography of Manitoba* (Winnipeg: University of Manitoba Press, 1996), Chapter 15; Everitt et al., 1996.

3 Carlyle, 1996.

4 John Ryan, "The Effect of the North American Free Trade Agreement on the Manitoba Economy" in John Welsted, John Everitt and Christoph Stadel (eds.), *The Geography of Manitoba* (Winnipeg: The University of Manitoba Press, 1996), 264–65.

5   The Crow Rate was implemented in 1897 as a concession by the Canadian Pacific Railway to reduce freight rates, particularly for cereal crops.

6   Single-desk selling (SDS) is a system for selling agricultural commodities where all producers sell their product to one agency which then negotiates with, and sells to, the customer. For example, marketing boards such as pork, tobacco, dairy, and egg are considered SDS systems.

7   Gerald Friesen, *The Canadian Prairies: A History* (Toronto: University of Toronto Press, 1984), 301.

8   Friesen, 1984, 301.

9   Friesen, 1984, 328–29.

10 Carlyle, 1996, 220.

11 Keystone Agricultural Producers, "Keystone Agricultural Producers Presentation to Senate Committee on Agriculture and Agri-food" (March 2000).

12 Keystone Agricultural Producers, 2000.

13 Manitoba Agriculture and Food Web Site. http://www.gov.mb.ca/agriculture/news/lsteward/stewardship3.html. Site visited 25 June 2001.

14 Ed Tyrchniewicz, Nick Carter, and John Whitaker, "Finding Common Ground: A Report Prepared for the Government of Manitoba by the Livestock Stewardship Panel" (Winnipeg: Government of Manitoba, December 2000).

15 This point of view has always been argued by people on the prairies, who feel that the railways' arguments are, at best, simplistic. See, for instance "An Historical Analysis of the Crow's Nest Pass Agreement and Grain Rates: A Study in National Transportation Policy," in *A submission of the Province of Saskatchewan to the Royal Commission on Transportation, 1960* (Regina: Queen's Printer, 1961).

16 Garry Fairbairn, *From Prairie Roots: The Remarkable Story of the Saskatchewan Wheat Pool* (Saskatoon: Prairie Producer Books, 1984), 222.

17 Report of the Grain Handling and Transportation Commission. *Grain and Rail in Western Canada*, Volume 1 (Ottawa: Government of Canada, 1977).

18 John Dietz, "Post Crow Farming: Are You Ready," *Farm Forum Spring* 1996: 12. Page Newton, "What Will You Do Without the Crow?" *Grainews* March 1995: 41.

19 Friesen, 1984, 193.

20 For example, Ron Friesen, "Farm Crisis Collapsing Rural Economy, Municipalities Warn," *The Manitoba Co-operator* 58,36 (12 April 2001): 15; Ron Friesen, "Chretien Avoids Farmers While in Winnipeg," *The Manitoba Cooperator* 58,44 (7 June 2001): 3; Ron Friesen, "Ag Forum Long on Concepts, Short on Details," *The Manitoba Cooperator* 58,46 (21 June 2001): 1,3.

21 Ron Friesen, "Payments Start to Flow," *The Manitoba Co-operator* 58,44 (7 June 2001): 1,2.

22 Michael J. Broadway. "Planning for Change in Small Towns or Trying to Avoid the Slaughterhouse Blues," *Journal of Rural Studies* 16 (2000), 37–46.

23 Rod Nichol, "Maple Leaf Buys Schneider Plants," *The Brandon Sun*, Tuesday, 6 January 2001, A1, A2.

24 Michael Broadway, 2000.

25 Discussion has also taken place regarding changes in intake at the Brandon Correctional Institute. The position of management is that, while stating that Brandon Corrections is collecting data on trends with intake and the Maple Leaf plant, no differences had been observed between the Maple Leaf plant starting production in July 1999 and June 2001. However, discussions with two corrections officers tell a different story, one which includes an increase in intoxicated persons who are either are, or were, employed at the plant. This intake tends to increase on pay days. The individuals wished to remain anonymous.

26 Rod Nickel, "Union, Maple Leaf Drive Home the Need for Perfect Attendance," *The Brandon Sun*, Tuesday, 16 January 2001: A1.

27 Rod Nickel, "Second Shift Will Strain Housing," *The Brandon Sun*, Thursday, 15 July 2001: A1, A2

28 Tali Folkins, "Maple Leaf Pleased With Atlantic Recruiting Results," *The New Brunswick Telegraph-Journal*, Tuesday, 1 May 2001: C2.

29 Rod Nickel, "Pats May Accelerate Shilo Move," *The Brandon Sun*, Monday, 25 June 2001; Rod Nickel, Thursday, 5 July 2001: A1, A2.

30 Rod Nickel, "Hog Plant Commits 'Major Breach'," *The Brandon Sun*, Wednesday, 13 September 2000: A1, A2.

31 Steve Burgess, "High on the Hog," *Saturday Night*, March 2000, 64–66.

32 Christine Common-Singh, Celia Guilford, Roderick Macdonald, W.J. Turnock, and John Welsted (Commissioners), *Large-Scale Hog Production and Processing: Concerns for Manitobans*. Commissioners' Report on the Citizens' Hearing on Hog Production and the Environment, Brandon, Manitoba, October 1999 (Winnipeg: Canadian Centre for Policy Alternatives, May 2000).

33 http://www.gov.mb.ca/agriculture/news/lsteward/stewardship0.html

34 http://www.gov.mb.ca/agriculture/news/stewardship/stewardship.html

35 Information Services, "Livestock Stewardship Panel Submits Report to Government" Manitoba Government News Release, 22 January 2001.

36 *Subject to Debate: Resolutions, Manitoba New Democratic Party, Convention 2001.* Winnipeg, February 2001.

37 Emergency Resolution #1 (Agriculture). Distributed to the Convention Floor by Interlake NDP Riding Association (10 February 2001).

38 Emergency Resolution #2 (Agriculture). Distributed to the Convention Floor by Turtle Mountain NDP Riding Association (10 February 2001).

39 Helen Fallding, "Hog Debate Breaks Out at NDP Provincial Convention," *The Brandon Sun*, Sunday, 11 February 2001: A1, A2.

40 Fallding, 2001: A1.

41 Fallding, 2001: A1.

42 Fallding, 2001: A1.

43 Key Informant Interview conducted 9 July 2001. The individual wished to remain anonymous.

44 Ron Friesen, "Fire Chief Quits Over Hog Barns," *The Manitoba Co-operator* 5 July 2001.

45 Andy Sirski, "Loss of Crow Will Not be the End of Prairie Farmers," *Grainews* March 1993: 5.

46 Alec H. Paul, "Short Lines, Main Lines, Branch Lines, Dead Lines: Rural Railways in Southwestern Saskatchewan in the 1990s" in John Welsted and John Everitt (eds.) *The Yorkton Papers: Research by Prairie Geographers*. Brandon Geographical Series No. 2 (Brandon: Brandon University, Department of Geography, 1997) 122–35.

47 Manitoba Agriculture and Food, *Manitoba Agriculture Yearbook: 1999*, 2000.

48 Doug Ramsey, *Issues Affecting the Sustainability of Agriculture in Manitoba: A Summary of Four Focus Groups*, A report prepared for Ducks Unlimited Canada, Killarney, Manitoba, 2000. These comments came from the focus-group meeting in Deloraine in April 2000.

49 Interview with Lyndenn Behm, rural reporter with *The Brandon Sun*, June 2001. Examples of coverage of ILOs in southwestern Manitoba include Lyndenn Behm, "Batten Down Hatches for Hog-Barn Storm," *The Brandon Sun*, Sunday, 29 October 2000: A1 and Lyndenn Behm, "Reeve Won't Hold Hog Barn Vote," *The Brandon Sun*, Friday, 25 May 2001: A3.

50 Owen Furuseth, "Restructuring of Hog Farming in North Carolina: Explosion and Implosion," *Professional Geographer* 49,4 (1997): 391–403.

51 Ron Friesen, "Hog Watch Envisions New Role For Springhill," *The Manitoba Co-operator* 58,30 (March 2000): 18.

52 "Farming Shunned by Rural Graduates," *The Brandon Sun*, 26 June 1996: 8.

Corporate Hog Farming

THE VIEW FROM THE FAMILY FARM

Darrin Qualman

WHO WILL OWN THE ECONOMY?

The corporate takeover of agriculture is proceeding, not acre by acre, but sector by sector. In the United States, Tyson Corporation has cornered the chicken market through contract production and ever-larger production units. Small-scale, independent chicken farmers are nearly extinct in that country. Canada's supply-management system has slowed this trend, but the US government, working through trade agreements, increasingly threatens our system.

In Canada and the US, feeding cattle for slaughter is increasingly the business of large feedlots. Many of these feedlots are owned by large packers such as Cargill and IBP.[1] In addition, these packers control, through contracts, a significant portion of the cattle they do not own. While corporations have left the cow/calf business to family farms, they are taking control of cattle feeding to ensure supply for their slaughter plants.

Over the past century, some of the best farmers in Canada and the US turned to seed production as a way to increase their revenues and profits. These farmers bought seed varieties, propagated them, and sold the resulting seed to other farmers. Genetically modified seeds, patenting, the privatization of research, and the takeover of the seed industry by a few huge corporations have made it increasingly difficult for independent seed producers to survive and reduced the profitability of those who persevere. As seed development moves from publicly funded research stations to corporations such as Monsanto, it becomes nearly impossible for independent seed growers to gain access to the newest and best-selling varieties unless they enter into vassal-like contracting arrangements with the seed/chemical/gene giants.

Corporate agribusiness is also making inroads into North American dairy production. J.G. Boswell plans to open a four-dairy complex in King's County, California. The complex will be the world's largest with over 47,700 cows on 7000 acres.[2] George and James Borba plan a 28,572-cow dairy on 4700 acres elsewhere in California.[3] Again, Canada's supply-management system helps keep dairy production in the hands of farm families, but that system is under attack from corporate interests and the American government at World Trade Organization (WTO) talks and elsewhere. If our system falls, the resulting restructuring will transfer Canadian dairy production to a few corporate producers.

This brings us to hogs. The corporate takeover of hog production that began in the US in the 1980s came to Western Canada in the mid 1990s and was accelerated by the price collapse of 1998 and 1999 (more on this below). It is now mostly accomplished. This takeover is remarkable for its swiftness and its seeming irrevocability.

The corporate takeover of agriculture is one of the last battles in a long war over who will own the economy—local families or distant investors. Fifty years ago, local families owned the shoe stores and clothing stores. Corner confectioneries were independent—each owned by a local family; the Mac's and 7–11 signs had yet to go up. Local families owned the restaurants and were not compelled to remit annual franchise fees to Los Angeles head offices in return for advertising campaigns and computer-designed decors. Even many grocery stores were locally owned. Over the past fifty years, nearly every sector of our economy has passed out of the hands of local families and into the control of a decreasing number of increasingly large and powerful corporations. The farm sector is the single exception. But as the last holdout, it is besieged.

This transfer of ownership has political as well as economic consequences. Thomas Jefferson believed that political democracy rests upon economic democracy. He supported widely distributed ownership of land and businesses. He saw the independent farmer, craftsperson, and shopkeeper as the basis of democracy. He understood, from English history, that if a tiny elite wrest control of the economy from the multitudes, that elite will also covet and purloin political control. It is only natural for those who *own* the country to want to *run* the country. The successes that corporate hog producers and pork packers have had in convincing legislators to weaken environmental protections and labour standards, and to remove the price protection that small producers once had in the form of single-desk selling agencies, offer concrete examples of these economic interests exercising political power—to the point where the wishes of citizens are ignored in a democracy.

This chapter analyzes the recent history and the impact of corporate concentration in the hog industry, on both family-farm producers and rural communities. It challenges the job-creation claims made on behalf of corporate mega-barns and argues instead that they are part of a larger global economy that continues to drain wealth from rural areas—with the complicity of governments.

THE CORPORATE TAKEOVER OF HOGS

Traditionally, farm families raised hogs in thousands of small and medium-sized barns spread across rural Canada. Their barns held anywhere from a few dozen to a few hundred sows. Often, these were diversified farms and the families used the hogs to "add value" to low-quality feed grain; to diversify their operations and, thus, reduce risk; to provide winter work and work for younger family members; and to provide manure to fertilize crops. Because hog numbers were small, production was dispersed, and manure was kept dry, these farms avoided problems such as manure leakage into groundwater.

In the mid 1990s, non-farmer investors and corporations began building huge hog barns in Western Canada. These corporations and individuals sought to replicate the corporate mega-barn model developed in North Carolina, Missouri, and other US states over the previous decade. In 1996, Saskatchewan produced over one million hogs on 2201 farms.[4] One mega-barn owner, Heartland Livestock (a division of Saskatchewan Wheat Pool, a $3.3-billion-per-year corporation), plans to produce (or control the production of) 1.5 million hogs annually by 2004.[5] Heartland is producing 330,000 per year currently.[6] In Alberta, one corporation, Taiwan Sugar, will build a single barn complex that will produce up to 150,000 hogs annually.[7]

The model of choice for Western Canadian mega-barn promoters is to produce a million or more hogs annually in several barn complexes. Each barn complex consists of 4 to 8 large barns clustered over a few square miles, containing approximately 2400 sows in total and producing about 50,000 slaughter hogs per year. Mega-barns are not family farms; they are corporate in form and in effect, if not always in technical definition. Some Western Canadian barns are owned by corporations such as SWP/Heartland Livestock. The balance are built by investors who are paid from profits and seldom do the actual work of feeding or caring for the hogs.

Big Sky Pork Inc. is one of Western Canada's leading mega-barn promoters, builders, and managers. Big Sky's goal is "to combine strategic investors with established hog producers to develop a world class pork production company. [Big Sky] will develop, build, and operate facilities to produce premium quality pork."[8] Big Sky currently manages 14 sites and 9000 sows with an annual production of approximately 203,000 hogs for slaughter.[9] Quadra Group is another mega-barn management service that assembles capital, oversees construction, and manages barns. Quadra manages 17 farrow-to-finish hog operations in Saskatchewan and Manitoba which together produce about 250,000 hogs annually. Six years ago Quadra produced just 12,000 hogs.[10] Other major producers in Western Canada include Sunterra of Alberta, Peace Pork, Elite Swine, and Puratone.

VERTICAL INTEGRATION

Mega-barn owners and managers, already powerful players in the hog industry, are adding to their power through vertical integration. They are signing production agreements that tie them to large packers or they are selling ownership shares in their companies to the packers. From the other direction, packers are expanding into production or seeking linkages with large producers. Corporations that own hog barns and packing plants—and often feed mills and other related businesses—are called "vertically integrated." Saskatchewan Wheat Pool (SWP) is currently the clearest Western Canadian example of vertical integration. It buys feed grains through Canada's largest elevator network; it owns CanGro processing, one of the largest producers of animal feed in the West; it owns barns through its Heartland subsidiary; it owns livestock sales facilities; and, until a recent sale to Quebec-based Oylmel, it had a 44-percent ownership share of—and retains a supply arrangement with—packer Premium Brands Inc. (formerly Fletcher's) with its main plant in Red Deer, Alberta. Explaining its

"Barley to Bacon" strategy, SWP states: "the [hog production] industry has witnessed...the consolidation of the industry into a smaller number of more vertically-integrated players... Our aim is to secure a consistent supply of quality pigs for the higher margin aspects of our operation while utilizing the Pool's expertise in grain procurement, livestock management, and food processing."[11] What SWP means is that producing feed for hogs and killing and packing hogs are both very profitable (these are the "higher margin aspects" of the pork production chain). SWP, like other vertically integrated companies, raises hogs to secure supplies for its packing plant and markets for its feed products.

Almost every mega-barn producer is vertically integrating. All of Quadra Group's pigs are contracted to Premium Brands Inc. until 2004. The deal gives Quadra a $4-million advance to expand its barns.[12] Premium Brands has also purchased a 40-percent ownership stake in Peace Pork—a northern Alberta producer which produces approximately 110,000 hogs annually. And it has formed an alliance with Rocky Mountain Pork of Alberta.

Big Sky has signed a deal with Mitchell's Gourmet Foods (owned by giant packer/producer Smithfield Foods) which gives it $5-million to build barns; Smithfield gets security of supply. Maple Leaf Foods, a spin-off of the McCain Foods empire and one of Canada's largest pork packers, bought Manitoba-based Landmark Group in 1999.[13] Landmark Group included Landmark Feeds, the largest livestock feed company in Western Canada (Maple Leaf already owned feed producer Shur-Gain and the addition of Landmark Feeds gives it 30 percent of the Canadian feed market), and Elite Swine, a hog genetics and production management and co-ordination company. According to the *Western Producer*, Elite Swine manages the production of one million hogs per year.[14] United Grain Growers (42 percent owned by US food-processing giant Archer Daniel's Midland) has purchased 32 percent of Puratone which is involved in 30 feed, hog, and poultry companies in Manitoba and Alberta, and produces about 400,000 hogs per year.[15]

Perhaps the best illustration of the vertical-integration trends outlined above can be found in the world's largest pork producer/packer, Smithfield Foods Inc. Smithfield's annual sales (to April 30, 2000) totalled $7.8 billion [CDN$]; its profits were $113-million.[16] In November 1998, Smithfield bought Schneider Corporation of Kitchener, Ontario. Schneider was one of Canada's largest packers and food processors with 1997 sales of $813-million. Through its operating companies, Schneider manufactures and sells a wide variety of processed meat, fresh pork, poultry, and grocery products from plants in Ontario, Quebec,

Saskatchewan, Manitoba, and BC. In May 1999, Smithfield purchased North Carolina-based Carroll's Foods for $231-million of assumed debt and $107-million in stock. With the purchase, Smithfield became the largest hog producer in the US with over 6.7 million in annual hog production. In November 1999, it tried unsuccessfully to buy Tyson Food's pork group. Tyson is the fifth-largest US hog producer at 2.5 million annually. It is the number-one producer of broiler chickens: over 155 million pounds weekly. In January 2000, Smithfield bought Murphy Family Farms, the second-largest hog producer in the US. With the Murphy purchase, Smithfield's total hog production rises to over 12 million hogs per year: approximately 60 percent of its packing plants' capacity. It is likely that Smithfield will soon build mega-barns in Canada to feed its packing plants.

THE EFFECTS OF VERTICAL INTEGRATION

Vertical integration changes the economics of hog production. Independent farmers need to make a profit on their hogs. The unprecedented crash of hog prices in late 1998 left family-farm hog producers reeling and forced many out of the business. Vertically integrated corporations are less dependent on making money on the hogs they produce. If the price of hogs dropped very low, a corporation which owned both mega-barns and packing plants would see large losses at the barns, but equally large increases in profits at its packing plants. If the output of its barns closely matched the capacity of its packing plants, for every dollar the corporation lost on pig production, it would make an extra dollar at its plants. Low hog prices are far less damaging to a vertically integrated corporation than to an independent, family-farm hog producer.

It is interesting to note that few, if any, of the prime movers behind hog production expansion in Western Canada rely on making a profit in their barns. Companies like Quadra and Big Sky are paid management fees whether the barns make money or not. SWP/Heartland will make up at its packing plants and feed mills any money it loses at its hog barns. The small number of vertically integrated firms who come to dominate the industry often prefer lower hog prices even though they own barns. Low prices allow them to take their profits in their packing plants and to secure additional hog supplies from independent producers at low cost.

Vertical integration has other negative effects. When packers own hogs, they take their own hogs first. The result is that independent farmers lose market access. In addition to owning hogs, packers also often sign supply contracts with mega-barn producers, further restricting market access for smaller producers.

Mega-barns are driving family farms out of the business, not because family farms cannot produce hogs as cheaply, but because, in an industry dominated by large sellers and buyers, small producers have trouble gaining market access. Those who wish a demonstration of this situation should attempt to supply their local supermarket with vegetables.

In addition to reducing market access, packer ownership and contracting hinders price discovery. When a significant portion of the hogs move from a corporation's barns into its packing plants, many more move under long-term supply contracts, and only a minority sell at public auction, it is difficult to discover the "fair market price" for a hog. US cattle producers report that large beef packers use the cattle herds they own to depress prices. These producers claim that when cattle prices rise above levels that packers feel are desirable, the packers withdraw from the market and draw from the cattle herds they own— their "captive supply." Since fat cattle need to be sold within a short time frame to capture a profit, this packer withdrawal quickly depresses prices. Once prices fall, it is alleged, packers resume buying from farmers and the packers restock their captive supplies. It is not unreasonable to suspect that some corporate pork-packing-plant owners choose to own what seemingly are low-profit hog mega-barns for much the same reasons: to ensure supply and to exert downward pressure during times of price increases.

In 1992, the University of Nebraska issued a report which predicted that a 10-percent level of vertical integration results in a 13.3-percent decline in hog purchases from independent producers and a 6-percent price decrease to independents. A 50-percent level of vertical integration results in a 26-percent price decrease.[17] Confirming these projections, *Hogs Today* magazine indicated that North Carolina had already reached the 50-percent level of integration and that prices to independent producers were 24 percent below those on direct purchases from large producers.

The solution to these three problems—lack of access, lack of price transparency, and packers pushing down prices—is single-desk selling. This is a system where a single agency markets all the hogs in a province on behalf of all producers and pays them equally for comparable hogs. Single-desk selling ensures that all sellers have equitable access to the market and that they receive fair and equitable prices. It also gives small- and medium-sized family-farm producers market power when dealing with huge, vertically integrated packers.

Until recently, Manitoba, Saskatchewan, and Alberta hog farmers had single-desk selling agencies. All were terminated as a result of pressure from large hog producers and packers. Thus the entry of large, vertically integrated hog producers/packers not only restricts farmers' access to markets, obscures price signals, and pushes down prices; these same corporations invariably push for and win an end to the single-desk selling agencies that formerly protected farmers from such market abuses.

COMMUNITY DEVELOPMENT AND JOBS?

Corporate mega-barn promoters promise jobs and investment to potential host communities. Before examining the realities of those promises, let us ask why rural communities lack investment capital and jobs. The globalized, free-trade economy increasingly works to extract wealth from the areas where it is produced—often rural areas—and to propel that wealth to major urban financial centres. Rural Western Canada is a vast wealth-creation machine. If you throw a stone in a rural area, you hit an oil field or a grain field; a potash, uranium, diamond, coal, or gold mine; a herd of cattle; or a stand of timber. This great wealth, however, is not captured in rural areas. Instead, rural areas are struggling: farmers are facing bankruptcy, stores are closing, schools are increasingly empty, young people are leaving, roads are disintegrating, and the economy is contracting. In contrast, urban centres such as Vancouver, Calgary, or Toronto, where shareholders are clustered, are doing well.

Faced with this huge outflow of wealth from rural areas, and often unable to understand the global economic system which drives the outflow, rural citizens and communities begin to see themselves as poor. They begin to see growing food, producing wood, or mining minerals as unimportant—"yesterday's industries"—and to see Internet merchandising and mutual-fund management as the valuable activities in the new economy. Misinterpreting their situation, and unable to understand why they have no local money for investment, they go looking for *outside* investment as a salvation. The mantra in rural Canada is that towns and villages need to attract outside investment in order to create jobs and save the community. To this end, well-meaning mayors, rural councillors, county officials, and citizens work to attract barley-malting plants, pasta plants, and hog mega-barns. This view and strategy is reinforced by every level of Canadian government.

Not only is the search for outside investment misguided, it rarely produces the promised results. Let's look at mega-barns as an example. Mega-barn proponents promise three benefits: jobs, community investment, and local markets for feed grains. These claims are deceiving because they compare the jobs, investment, and feed grains markets created by mega-barns to a false alternative: no hog production at all. It is true that producing a million hogs per year in 20 mega-barn complexes will create more jobs, investment, and feed grain demand than producing no hogs at all, but it will produce substantially fewer of these benefits than the real and existing alternative: producing a million hogs on hundreds of family farms. Family farms employ more people per pig, retain profits in the community, and buy more supplies locally.

Family-farm hog production slows the extraction of wealth outlined above. Unlike corporate producers, when local families produce hogs their farms, they receive the profits and spend a significant portion of them in their communities. When corporations produce hogs, the profits are quickly extracted from the area. Family-farm production supports the local economy in other ways too. Raising hogs requires feed, building materials, veterinary drugs, machinery, and other supplies. Small producers buy most of their supplies locally while large producers tend to stock many barns in many communities with supplies purchased in one location—usually a large city.

A Minnesota study found that smaller producers (<$400,000 [US] in annual sales) made 79 percent of their business expenditures within 20 miles of their farms versus just 47.5 percent for large producers (>$400,000).[18] A 1997 study found that 49.1 percent and 46.6 percent of small- and medium-sized producers respectively bought their building supplies within 10 miles of their farms, as opposed to only 27.6 percent of large producers. Two to three times as many small- and medium-sized producers buy their hog equipment within 10 miles of their farms as do large producers.[19]

Mega-barn proponents claim they create local markets for feed grains. This claim is suspect for two reasons. First, it fails to acknowledge that the family-farm hog producers that the mega-barn will displace already use feed grains. Second, it is unlikely that mega-barn operator will pay a cent over "market price" for grain. Market price is determined by world price—it is simply world price less freight costs to port. It is unlikely that mega-barns will significantly increase the quantity of feed grains consumed or the price paid.

We should be as suspicious of claims that hog mega-barns will create jobs. A typical 2400-sow complex employs about 15 people. However, each of these mega-barns will drive as many as 50 traditional small farmers out of the hog business or push those that remain to take off-farm jobs to make ends meet. A University of Missouri study by John Ikerd showed that smaller, independent producers employ three times as many people as mega-barns producing an equal number of hogs: "If new contract hog units were to replace independent operations producing the same number of hogs, approximately two hog farmers would be left without jobs for each new job created."[20]

Mega-barn proponents admit that their profits come largely from lower labour costs per pig. They accomplish this by substituting technology and capital for labour. This is not the same, however, as saying that large producers are more "efficient" or have a lower cost of production. It simply means that they choose to invest in computers and machinery rather than people. Mega-barn operators also use fewer workers in decision-making and management, and employ them far from the community. Corporate mega-producers use mass-production technologies—large production units, standardized genetics, automated feeding, and central marketing and accounting—to transfer most management functions to managers at corporate headquarters. If managers do not live or work in the community, their salaries will not be spent there. Thus, the main benefit claimed by mega-barn proponents—job creation—is questionable. Instead, quality employment opportunities for farmers and other rural citizens continue to disappear. Replacing family farms with corporate mega-barns will accelerate, not reverse, that trend.

Further, the jobs that the mega-barns create will be relatively low quality. High levels of animal dander, fecal dust, and ammonia can combine to cause unsafe working conditions. The American Lung Association has found that nearly 70 percent of swine confinement workers experience one or more symptoms of respiratory illness. Another 58 percent suffer chronic bronchitis.[21] On a family farm, by contrast, hog production is usually one part of a mixed operation. The farmer works in the barn for part of the day, but he or she also works in the field growing crops and in the home office managing the business. In contrast, mega-barn employees work for long hours inside the barn. This prolonged exposure increases the potential for health damage. Traditionally governments have granted family farms an exemption from labour standards legislation in recognition of the need to work long hours during certain seasons and the increased control that family members have over their working conditions. In order to pave the way for hog expansion, many governments have exempted mega-barns from labour standards and health and safety regulations by allowing them to be classified as family farms, not as the industrial facilities they are.

While hog mega-barns offer few economic benefits, they bring the potential for serious environmental costs. Hogs produce large quantities of manure that must be moved out of the barns. Most mega-barns liquefy manure to move it. Feces and urine are washed through the floor slots with water and pumped into earthen pits. A common size of these pits is seven million gallons, but they can range much higher. A 50,000-hog-per-year barn complex creates as much manure as a 45,000-person city. Although hogs and people share much the same physiology and many of the same diseases, liquid hog manure is not treated. Highly concentrated and in huge qualities, this manure becomes a potential toxin. As it is handled in most mega-barn complexes—put in earthen pits with neither liners nor covers—the manure gives off terrible odours, multiplies fly numbers, lowers property values, and threatens to poison surface and ground-water. Liquefying the manure increases its tendency to move, both horizontally and vertically.

Those who claim that mega-barns do not leak or dump manure should look at the evidence. A recent study listed dozens of spills that occurred in 1999 at large, corporate livestock production facilities in ten US states:[22]

- In April 1999, a Murphy Family Farms (now Smithfield) facility in North Carolina spilled more than 1.5 million gallons of manure into a swamp adjoining a tributary of the Northeast Cape Fear River. Investigators believe tree roots punctured the lagoon wall.
- In October 1999, employees at a Seaboard Farms facility in Oklahoma over-applied manure to farmland until it ran off. Some 102,000 gallons of manure were recovered.
- In December, a Carroll's Foods (now Smithfield) hog lagoon in North Carolina spilled 200,000 gallons of manure into the Turkey Creek and a nearby wetland. The spill occurred when employees left a pump running overnight.
- During 1999, facilities operated by Premium Standard Farms in Missouri had a series of 25 spills and discharges. The spills totalled over 224,000 gallons.
- In February 1999, employees at a Tyson-owned hog factory farm in Arkansas dumped between 30,000 and 120,000 gallons of manure into a ravine.

- Overall, in 1999, large-scale livestock producers spilled or dumped manure over 100 times in the 10 states surveyed, for a total of more than 4.5 million gallons.

The report concluded: "Lagoons and other 'technologies' used at factory farms are not working and threaten public health, wildlife, and the quality of our rivers, lakes, and coastal waters."

Smithfield Foods, which may soon be Canada's largest producer/packer, is also a chronic polluter. In 1997, a US court fined Smithfield $18.5-million [Cdn], the largest fine ever imposed under the Clean Water Act. Smithfield's Virginia slaughterhouse had been dumping pollutants into the Pagan River for five years.[23] Despite these clear dangers and despite overwhelming evidence from the US, Western provincial governments have refused to take the environmental threat posed by mega-barns seriously. In many jurisdictions, these barns are exempted from environmental assessment laws that apply to other industrial developments. Governments have changed environmental laws specifically to accommodate the hog industry, so that it can use exactly the same manure-handling techniques that have proven so inadequate in the US.

GOVERNMENT MONEY

In addition to corporate and packer linkages, exemptions from labour-standards laws, and preferential treatment regarding environmental assessment, mega-barn operations also benefit from direct public investments. The Saskatchewan government has been perhaps the most aggressive in this respect. Through its Crown Investments Corporation, it recently invested $15-million in Big Sky mega-barn complexes at Rama and Ogema.[24] The Saskatchewan Opportunities Corporation (SOCO) gave Big Sky a $500,000 equity investment and a $1.5-million loan to fund construction of 2400-sow mega-barn complexes at Humboldt, Kelvington, and Preeceville.[25] SOCO loans have also been granted to Birsay Livestock Ltd. for $700,000; Carrot River Valley Pork Producers (Heartland Livestock) for $1-million; Horizon Pork Producers Ltd. (Heartland Livestock) for $1-million; and Red Coat Pig Investors Group Ltd. (Quadra) for $250,000. Sinnet Pork Farms Ltd. received a $250,000 equity investment from SOCO.

The Manitoba government, meanwhile, gave subsidies and tax incentives totalling $7-million to Maple Leaf to induce it to build a $120-million pork-packing plant in Brandon.[26] Governments representing all parties—failing to acknowledge the extractive nature of the free-trade, globalized economy and its

FIGURE 1: ALBERTA PER-FARM REALIZED NET INCOME:
1926–2001 (2001 DOLLARS)
Sources: *Agricultural Economic Statistics*, Statistics Canada, Catalogue # 21-603E; *Consumer Prices and Price Indexes*, Statistics Canada Catalogue # 62-010-XPB; and *Historical Overview of Canadian Agriculture*, Statistics Canada Catalogue # 93-358-XPB.

corrosive effects on rural areas, and desperate to stem the outflow of economic blood from these areas and slow the evacuation of rural regions—have resorted to lowering standards, deferring taxes, and turning over citizens' tax dollars to attract outside capital and create jobs. Worst of all, governments often do all these things in disregard of citizens' clearly articulated wishes.[27] The globalized economy is characterized by increasingly powerful and mobile corporate capital, increasingly docile governments, and increasingly insecure workers and local residents.

THE ECONOMIC IMPACT OF HOG MEGA-BARNS

The farm income crisis began in the late 1980s, continued nearly unabated, and intensified over the past three years. Alberta provides a good example of the effects the crisis is having on farmers' net incomes. Figure 1 illustrates that for 40 years, between 1942 and 1982, Alberta's per-farm realized net income, adjusted for inflation, remained more-or-less stable: oscillating between $10,000 and $27,000. Since 1982, incomes have found a new equilibrium, oscillating between $0 and $17,000 per farm. An average Alberta farm in 1999

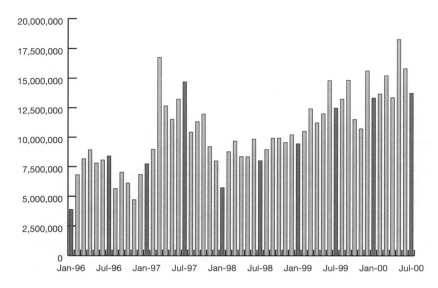

FIGURE 2: CANADIAN HOG/PORK EXPORTS TO ASIA: 1996-99

Source: Data provided on request from Agriculture and Agri-Food Canada: Trade Evaluation and Analysis Division.

enjoyed a realized net farm income of just $3,090.[28] Realized net farm income is not the same as profit. It is calculated before any allowance is made for wages for farm family labour, management, or return on investment.

Alberta realized-net-farm income levels in the late 1980s and throughout the 1990s fell to levels not seen since the Depression. The same thing happened in Saskatchewan and many other provinces. Figure 1 shows clearly that something disastrous happened to farming in the mid 1980s, coinciding with a worldwide move toward deregulation, export expansion, privatization, and government spending cuts that left farmers vulnerable in an agribusiness production chain increasingly dominated by large corporations. In Western Canada, the federal government terminated the Crow Rate and then the Crow benefit; focussed on expanding agri-food exports; dismantled or weakened farmers' single-desk marketing agencies; and made sharp cuts to safety net and stabilization programs.

In the midst of this prolonged farm income crisis came the hog price collapse of 1998–99. The collapse began in October 1998 and continued for almost a year. At its worst—November and December 1998—prices fell to $25/hundred pounds or cwt (dressed weight). These prices were down markedly from the $70–$90/cwt range for the same months in previous years.[29] The hog

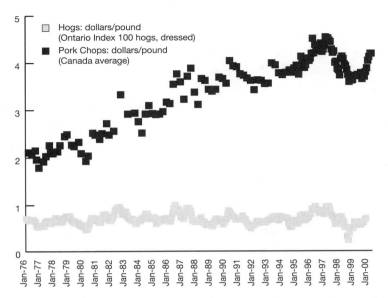

FIGURE 3: HOG AND PORK CHOP PRICES: 1976-2000
Sources: *Consumer Prices and Price Indexes*, Statistics Canada Cat. # 62-010 and *Livestock Statistics*, Statistics Canada Cat. # 23-603.

The current industrial pork production, processing, and distribution

price collapse pushed an estimated one-third to one-half of Western Canada's family-farm hog producers out of the business. The takeover of the sector by vertically integrated, corporate-owned mega-barns makes it unlikely that these families will resume hog production.

Politicians, economists, and the media blamed the hog price collapse on oversupply and the collapse of the Asian market. Figure 2 paints a more ambiguous picture. Canadian pork exports to Asia did decline, but they did so almost a year before the 1998–99 price collapse. By October 1998, exports had already recovered significantly—to a level surpassed only by seven months of record exports in 1997. Exports in 1999 were far above 1996 levels, yet prices were far lower. For all that, Asia consumes just seven percent of Canadian exports. It is hard to believe that a relatively small decrease in exports to this relatively small market could cause prices to fall far below levels seen in the previous 23 years.

Nor is the hog price downturn easily explained by looking at the retail price of pork. As Figure 3 shows, while hog prices have remained roughly the same over the past 25 years, packers and retailers have used their market power to increase the consumer price of pork chops by over 200 percent.

The current industrial pork production, processing, and distribution system is treating neither farmers nor consumers fairly. Farmers are forced to accept hog prices unchanged since the 1970s and consumers are asked to pay ever-increasing prices for pork. Like the grain-price downturn, analysts often point to an oversupply of pork and hogs as the cause of the price collapse. If we grant, for the moment, that oversupply was the cause, it is instructive to look at how the other links of the pork production and distribution chain fared during this alleged glut of pork.

Maple Leaf and Premium Brands Inc. were two of Canada's largest pork packers at the time. Over the twelve-month period from October 1998 through September 1999, those companies recorded *record* profits of $72.9-million and $6.3-million respectively.[30] In its first-quarter report in 1999, Maple Leaf cited low pork prices as a significant contributor to its profitability, stating: "Maple Leaf Pork benefited from favourable commodity markets." In its second-quarter report, the company noted that "Maple Leaf Foods International recorded excellent results due to strong demand from global markets, particularly in Asia." In its third-quarter report, Maple Leaf credited its profitability partly to "strong pork sales into Japan." The pork glut and collapse of Asian market seems not to have affected packers in the same way as farmers. Despite record profits, Premium Brands' managers were not completely satisfied. CEO Fred Knoedler cited "a shortage of hogs in Western Canada" as one factor holding back his company's revenues and profits.[31] The hog price crisis becomes curiouser and curiouser when one learns that farmers were suffering due to hog surpluses and packers due to hog shortages.

The hog price collapse cannot be explained by supply and demand data. Moreover, at the same time that farmers were facing low prices, allegedly caused by a glut of pork, packers were turning that glut of pork into bacon and pork chops. The most likely explanation is that increasingly large and powerful vertically integrated pork producers used their market power to drive down wages to workers, drive down prices to farmers, maintain high prices to consumers, and reap record profits. There are sound reasons as a result to expect that increased corporate control and vertical integration of the hog production and packing sectors will decrease prices and profits for independent farmers.

To attract large corporate hog producers and pork packers to their provinces, governments have exempted these corporations from environmental protection laws and worker health and safety standards, and have stripped farmers of their single-desk selling agencies. When these actions proved insufficient, governments stepped in with direct taxpayer investment in barns and tax breaks for barns and packers. All of this was done despite compelling evidence that family-farm hog production creates more employment and community economic development, and is better suited to environmental protection. A study published by the Nebraska-based Centre for Rural Affairs has concluded that "an agricultural structure that was increasingly corporate and non-family owned tended to lead to population decline, lower incomes, fewer community services, less participation in democratic processes, less retail trade, environmental pollution, more unemployment, and an emerging rigid class structure."[32]

Governments do have a choice. They can support family farms and rural communities through measures which protect farmers' market access, the environment, and workers' rights. Or they can continue to weaken such protections and clear the way for the transfer of control of (and economic benefits from) hog production to a handful of corporations. We must be clear, however, that this is the opposite of rural economic development.

The global economy—structured by the World Trade Organization, the International Monetary Fund, and the North American Free Trade Agreement—works to extract wealth from rural areas and to transfer it to absentee shareholders. Drained of wealth and capital, rural communities go looking for outside investment such as corporate mega-barns. The irony is that transferring hog production from local families to corporations such as Smithfield and Maple Leaf *facilitates and accelerates* the extraction of wealth and capital. The proposed solution only exacerbates the problem. Unless governments and citizens face the realities of the extractive nature of the global economy, they will be able to do little more than fashion palliative[33] strategies, such as luring outside investment that will provide transitional jobs that help "manage" the economic destruction of rural areas and the long-term decline of rural Western Canada.

Notes

1   Cargill and IBP control 74 percent of Canadian beef slaughter capacity.

2   "J.G. Boswell to operate four farm, 47,700 cow nation's largest dairy complex," *The Agribusiness Examiner*, 16 April 2000.

3   "Borbas advance dairy plan," *The Bakersfield Californian*, 16 May 2000.

4   SPI Marketing Group, *1996 Annual Report* (Regina: Saskatchewan Wheat Pool, 1996), 12.

5   Saskatchewan Wheat Pool, *1999 Annual Report* (Regina: Saskatchewan Wheat Pool, 1999), 5.

6   Ibid.

7   Mary MacArthur and Roberta Rampton, "Taiwan pork firm slims down to three loca-
     tions," *Western Producer*, 20 January 2000.

8   Big Sky Pork Inc., *Proposal for the development of Limited Partnership II*.

9   Conversation with Big Sky manager.

10   "Fletcher's in Alliance With the Quadra Group," *Meat Industry Insights*, 22 April 2000.

11   Saskatchewan Wheat Pool, *1999 Annual Report*, 24.

12   Premium Brands Inc. News Release, April 19, 2000.

13   Maple Leaf News Release, September 10, 1999.

14   Roberta Rampton, "Stability likely for hog sector," *Western Producer*, 9 March 2000.

15   Roberta Rampton, "UGG buys one-third share of Puratone," *Western Producer*,
     27 May 1999; Roberta Rampton, "Stability likely for hog sector," *Western Producer*,
     9 March 2000.

16   Information on Smithfield's Foods is based on company news releases and annual reports.

17   Azzeddine Azzam and Allen Wellman, *Packer Integration into Hog Production: Current
     Status and Likely Impacts of Increased Vertical Control on Hog Prices and Quantities*,
     University of Nebraska, 1992.

18   John Chism, "Local Spending Patterns for Farm Business in Southwest Minnesota."
     Unpublished thesis, University of Minnesota, 1993.

19   John Lawrence, Daniel Otto, and Seth Meyer, "Purchasing Patterns of Hog Producers:
     Implications for Rural Agribusinesses," *Journal of Agribusiness*, Spring 1997.

20   John Ikerd, "The Economic Impacts of Increased Contract Swine Production in
     Missouri: Another Viewpoint." Sustainable Agriculture Systems Program, University of
     Missouri, 9.

21   Iowa State University: University Extension, *Livestock Confinement Dust and Gases*,
     http://www.cdc.gov/niosh/nasd/docs6/mn98016.html

22   Clean Water Network and the Izaak Walton League of America, *Spilling Swill: A Survey
     of Factory Farm Water Pollution in 1999*, December 1999, 1–18.

23   United States Department of Justice, "Appeals Court Upholds Ruling Against Smithfield
     Foods for Polluting Virginia River," News Release, Wednesday, September 15, 1999.

24   Ed White, "Hog industry catches Saskatchewan's eye," *Western Producer*, 27 July 2000.

25   Saskatchewan Opportunities Corporation, *SOCO Report*, various issues.

26   Ian Bell, "Poaching practice causes ruckus," *Western Producer*, 1 June 2000.

27   Almost no one, e.g., disputes that the vast majority of citizens in Flagstaff County are
     opposed to the mega-barn complex proposed by Taiwan Sugar Corporation.

28   Latest income figures for Alberta and other provinces are available at
     www.agr.ca/policy/epad/english/fi4cast/july2000/frmincm/frmincm.htm

29   Hog prices from *Livestock Statistics*, Statistics Canada Cat. # 23–603.

30   Maple Leaf and Premium Brands/Fletcher's Quarterly Reports.

31   Premium Brands/Fletcher's News Release, November 10, 1999.

32   *Corporate Hog Farming Update! Spotlight on Pork* (Walthill, NE: Center for Rural Affairs,
     1994).

33   "palliative: *n.* 1: to reduce the violence of (a disease) 2: *to cover by excuses and apologies*
     3: to moderate the intensity of" (*Webster's Dictionary*, Ninth Edition).

Bad to the Bone

THE SOCIAL COSTS OF BEEF PACKING'S MOVE TO RURAL ALBERTA

Michael J. Broadway

Over the past 30 years, successive Alberta governments have sought to diversify the province's economy. Instead of exporting raw materials, a concerted effort has been made to increase the amount of value-added processing in the province. This strategy consists of offering investors access to the province's abundant natural resources and providing a low-tax, pro-business environment. In agriculture this has led to major investments by foreign-owned agribusiness corporations, particularly in beef processing, to the point where the Canadian industry is now consolidated in Alberta. In 1989, Cargill opened a state-of-the-art packing plant in High River. Five years later, IBP (formerly Iowa Beef Packers) purchased Lakeside Packers of Brooks and immediately announced an expansion of the plant. Prior to this injection of US-based capital, beef processing was largely Canadian-owned and consisted of small plants scattered across the country in major cities. By the beginning of the twenty-first century, most of those old urban plants had been closed and production shifted to smaller, rural centres like High River and Brooks, following a trend established in the US. These new plants have created thousands of jobs and provided a market for locally raised fed cattle and feedstuffs. But, in Alberta and elsewhere across North America, the beef industry has also managed to pass on the social costs of its production system to local communities in the form of increases in crime, homelessness, and the demand for indigent care. Industry expansion in Alberta has coincided with provincial government cuts to social services in the name of debt reduction and a balanced budget. As a result, responsibility for meeting the social costs of the industry's operation has threatened to overwhelm social service agencies and local, volunteer-run charities. This article identifies the factors behind the expansion of beef processing in Alberta and documents the social costs that have accompanied its rural industrialization strategy. It asks how much of the burden of a provincial export-oriented economic strategy should be borne in a concentrated way by people in the small communities where plants happen to be located.

GLOBALIZATION AND THE RESTRUCTURING OF ALBERTA'S BEEF-PROCESSING INDUSTRY

At the onset of the 1960s, North American beef packing began a process that would result in its transformation from an urban to a rural-based industry and in the creation of a series of low-wage boomtowns on the US High Plains. In 1961, a new company, Iowa Beef Packers, opened a plant in the western Iowa town of Denison. IBP's cost-cutting practices here signalled the start of a new era for the industry characterized by wage rollbacks and by the construction of plants close to a supply of fed cattle. While beef processing in Canada lagged behind in terms of adopting the cost-cutting practices pioneered by IBP, the recent consolidation in Alberta represents an extension of an industrialized agricultural system that aims to lower production costs by achieving economies of scale and by substituting capital for labour. Both the Cargill and IBP plants have much larger slaughter capacities than the multi-species plants that historically dominated the industry. Cargill's plant, when it opened, had the capacity to kill 6000 cattle per week with 410 production workers, while Canada Packers' older Winnipeg plant slaughtered just 3000 cattle with 475 workers.[1] In the aftermath of the Cargill plant opening, less efficient plants in urban areas closed.

Beef processors have used capital to reduce labour costs by developing the "disassembly line" and boxed beef. IBP introduced the former in the early 1960s. It requires workers to be stationed along a line and be responsible for a single step in the preparation of a carcass. The company argued at the time that this system required less skill than the multiple tasks performed by butchers in older plants; on that basis, it refused to abide by the terms of the industry-wide union master contract and lowered wages. Boxed beef, meanwhile, means that instead of shipping a carcass, fat and bone are removed at the plant and meat is cut to retail specifications before being vacuum packaged for shipment. This innovation appealed to supermarkets and the hospitality industry, as it allowed them to reduce their costs by employing fewer butchers. It also allowed the packers to ship more meat and keep valuable byproducts for additional sale.[2] An October 1993 study estimated that the average cost of transporting fed cattle from Alberta to southwestern Ontario was $112.50 per head, while the equivalent figures for carcasses and boxed beef were $49.50 and $28.91 respectively.[3]

The globalization of agricultural production has been facilitated by technological innovations in transport and data transmission and by the removal of trade barriers.[4] Improvements in refrigerated transport and packaging allow for the shipment of perishable products over vast distances, while the electronic transmission of information via the Internet links potential buyers with sellers and allows for more informed purchasing decisions. The Canadian–US Free Trade Agreement, the North American Free Trade Agreement, and the Uruguay Round of the General Agreement on Trade and Tariffs are all based on the premise that increasing trade stimulates economic growth. As part of these agreements, countries reduce tariffs, lower export subsidies, and withdraw domestic price supports. In 1995, Canada's federal government announced that the Western Grain Transportation Program, which provided Prairie farmers with an annual half-billion dollar subsidy to the cost of shipping their grain to export terminals, would be cancelled. The immediate effect was to push Prairie farmers to grow feed grains for local markets and, in turn, to encourage an expansion of intensive livestock operations.

THE ALBERTA ADVANTAGES

US-based beef processors have been attracted to Alberta because of the availability of large numbers of fed cattle. Between 1984 and 1999 the number of fed cattle in the province increased from 1.1 million to 2.4 million. During the same period, Alberta's share of Canada's fed cattle production rose from 47 to 70 percent.[5] The reasons for this increase include ample supplies of barley and irrigated crops for silage, good sources of fresh water, low precipitation (which results in less mud, cleaner cattle, and efficient feeding conditions), and relatively moderate winter temperatures (which allow for good feed conversion).[6]

The provincial government has facilitated the industry's consolidation by promoting meat-packing as a means of value-added processing and job creation. To assist Cargill's construction of its High River plant the government provided the company with $4-million for the construction of a wastewater treatment plant.[7] It also provided grants and loans totalling $16 million to help Lakeside become "the largest slaughter and beef processing plant in Canada."[8]

To attract foreign capital the provincial government promotes Alberta as "having the lowest overall taxes in Canada " and "wage costs much lower than in the United States."[9] Since the mid 1980s, meat-packing wages have fallen while organized labour's position has weakened. Prior to 1984, wages were determined by means of an industry-wide national contract that had existed since 1947. But Calgary-based Burns challenged this bargaining system, claiming that high costs had made it unprofitable and demanded that the union representing its work-force bargain on a plant-by-plant basis. The United Food and Commercial Workers (UFCW) union refused. Burns charged the union with bargaining in bad faith; labour relations boards in Ontario, Alberta, and Manitoba subsequently upheld the company's position. The UFCW called a national strike but in its aftermath wages fell with the establishment of a two-tiered wage system. At Lakeside Packers in Brooks, replacement workers were hired at $3.00 below the national hourly rate and worked throughout the strike.[10]

Labour's position was further undermined after the bitter 1986 strike at Gainers' Edmonton plant. In 1988, the provincial government approved a new labour code that gave the cabinet the power to decertify unions that conduct illegal strikes and allowed the Labour Relations Board to limit picketing. New barriers to union certification were erected with the requirement of a vote even when all members of a company's workforce sign union cards, while the Board's right to certify a union when management has interfered with an organizing drive was removed.[11] When Cargill opened its plant it employed a non-union labour force (that has subsequently been organized) with starting wages $4.00 an hour less than at plants in Calgary and Lethbridge.[12] Lakeside's labour force remains non-union despite recent efforts to organize the plant. Starting wages at both facilities in 2000 remain below 1984 levels.

The construction of large slaughter capacity beef-processing plants on the US High Plains has produced thousands of jobs. In southwestern Kansas there are 5 plants that employ over 10,000 workers. Finney County is home to two facilities. Between 1980 and 1985 it saw the addition of over 3500 beef processing jobs and 800 spin-off positions, mostly retail clerks, fast-food workers, and motel employees—typically low-paid and part-time. Indeed, despite the creation of over 4000 jobs during this period the county's per capita income fell relative to the state figure.[13]

On the High Plains, beef processing has created significant social costs for rural communities with increases in crime, school enrollment, and demands for social services. Soon after IBP's Finney County plant opened, the company had exhausted local labour supplies and began recruiting workers from outside the region. The newcomers, many of whom were Southeast Asian refugees and Latinos, helped boost the population of the county's major centre, Garden City, from 18,000 in 1980 to 24,000 in 1985. This sudden growth created a housing shortage that was alleviated by the construction of a 500-unit trailer court. Some newcomers arrived penniless, resulting in large increases in the number of indigents in need of food and shelter.[14]

The packers recruited young, single adult males and recent immigrants due to their high mobility. Yet both groups added to the social costs of economic development. Males between the ages of 18 and 24 have the highest incidence of committing crimes and are highly susceptible to alcohol abuse. Reported crimes in Finney County rose by 40 percent between 1980 and 1986, while significant increases in child abuse and the need for psychiatric and alcohol-related care were also reported.[15]

The recruitment of young immigrant families assured an increase in the demand for social services. Between 1980 and 1988, the number of children enrolled in Garden City public schools rose by nearly 2000. To meet this demand, three new elementary schools were built. Minority enrollment during this period doubled to 34 percent. The school district's ability to meet the educational needs of Latino and Southeast Asian students was constrained by a shortage of bilingual instructors and high pupil turnover.[16] A longitudinal study of newcomer students in the mid 1980s found that two years after their arrival in Garden City over two-thirds of them had left the school district.[17] Still, despite the high turnover rate, the influx of young migrants meant that by 1987 Finney County had the second highest birth rate in Kansas.

Similar social changes have been documented in other small towns with packing plants and have been attributed to the nature of the industry.[18] Low wages mean that the plants have a limited multiplier effect and that many other newly created jobs are also low-paying. Most of the tasks along the packer's disassembly line can be performed with a limited knowledge of English, which makes these jobs attractive to non-English speaking immigrants and refugees. The nature of line work ensures workers will experience a high level of repetitive motion injuries, the most common being carpal tunnel syndrome.[19] Low wages, injuries, and the nature of the work contribute to monthly turnover of six to eight percent among line workers.[20] These general patterns established in the US suggested that High River and Brooks, too, would experience an influx of immigrants, housing shortages, and increased social disorders and demand for social services.

HIGH RIVER

Cargill's Excel plant is located about three kilometres outside of High River, south of Calgary. The plant's labour force consists mostly of new immigrants, primarily Southeast Asians, East Indians, Iraqis, Iranians, and Latinos. Monthly turnover among line workers in 1996 averaged 8 percent, which meant that approximately 100 workers left and were replaced.[21] A 1997 strike against the company listed unsafe working conditions and line speed as among the workers' major grievances.[22]

Although the Excel plant shares many similarities with its US counterparts in terms of its labour-force characteristics and working conditions, High River has so far avoided many of the social problems experienced by small communities with packing plants. The local school district has yet to experience a significant increase in enrollment or in the demand for special services, nor has there been a jump in the local crime rate. The absence of any significant social impacts is explained by High River's shortage of affordable housing and the preference among line workers to live in Calgary and commute to the plant. In 1995, 852 of the plant's 1208 employees lived in Calgary, while 201 employees—mostly clerical and managerial workers—lived in High River.[23] High River markets itself as a retirement and bedroom community for commuters who work in Calgary. These two functions have effectively kept the cost of housing beyond the means of most low-paid workers at the plant. The experience in Brooks has been much different.

Population and housing issues

Brooks is situated 186 kilometres southeast of Calgary and 111 kilometres west of Medicine Hat. IBP's Lakeside plant is located along the Trans-Canada Highway five kilometres northwest of the town centre. Prior to the plant's expansion in December 1996, the town's civic census reported a population of 10,110; four years later the corresponding figure was 11,584. By early 1997, after hiring 700 mostly local workers at a weekly turnover rate of approximately 40 to 60, Lakeside's Human Resources Manager acknowledged that the company had "pretty much exhausted the local labour supply." As a result the company began to recruit workers from Newfoundland and Nova Scotia, where the collapse of the cod fishery had produced unemployment in excess of 30 percent in many East Coast communities. It also recruited immigrants, especially through Calgary's Catholic Immigration Society, which seeks to place newcomers in entry-level positions. The plant's increasing number of immigrant workers led to the establishment of an on-site immigration service for workers in fall 1998. The service's leading users are from Iraq, Cambodia, Somalia, Ethiopia, Bosnia, Pakistan, Sudan, and Nigeria; most clients are seeking advice on how to proceed with family reunification.

In mid 1997, the town announced a zero-vacancy rate for rental accommodations. A 1995 consultant's report had advocated that the town promote the construction of new single-family homes in hopes that this would create a vacancy chain, with local people "moving up" to newer homes and leaving cheaper properties vacant for newcomers.[24] The report proposed constructing 900 to 1400 units between 1995 and 1997, but only 284 were completed. Moreover, when Lakeside doubled its production workforce in 1998 with the addition of a second shift, just 78 units were added to the housing stock and 48 the following year.[25] The inevitable housing shortage means that newcomers have the options of living in the surrounding rural area, or in Medicine Hat, or doubling or tripling up in town units that should accommodate just one household. Direct field observations indicate that some newcomers elect to live in new trailer courts that have been built in the surrounding rural area. Sagebrush Estates, situated east of Brooks, had just four trailers in fall 1996; two years later it had over forty occupied units. The option of living in Medicine Hat and commuting to the plant has been facilitated by Lakeside's provision of a chartered bus service.

The shortage of rental housing also led Lakeside in 1997 to provide 168 dormitory-style units for single employees at the plant. A chain link fence topped with barbed wire surrounds the compound. Entry is through a guardhouse. Meal vouchers for use in the plant's cafeteria are provided for occupants awaiting their first cheque. The housing is designed to be transitional; to make that clear, rent increases the longer a person stays. The company deducts rent, meal vouchers, and other costs that workers incur from their cheques. Lakeside's Human Resources Manager acknowledged that one unfortunate consequence of the scheme was that many workers were essentially broke even after receiving their first cheque. At one point, the company sought a permanent solution to the town's housing shortage by seeking planning permission for a trailer court on the north side of Brooks, but the town denied the request.

Social services

Many newcomers arrive penniless in Brooks. Under Alberta's welfare system, they may be eligible for a one-time transitional assistance payment. But between the time they arrive, make an appointment with a Social Services intake worker, and receive that transitional payment, they need shelter and food. For persons without friends or relatives in the community, the Brooks Salvation Army provides lodging and food assistance. The amount spent providing these services has increased dramatically since 1996, as has the amount for clothing, furniture, medicine, and other forms of assistance. In 1997 the total cost of providing all forms of assistance was $9990, but in the first 6 months of 2000 the equivalent figure was $23,084. Most of the funding for these services is received in the form of donations from local residents.[26]

The Brooks food bank was established in October 1998 for the specific purpose of "providing temporary emergency access to food." During its first year of operation it distributed 4514 food hampers that are designed to sustain an adult for 7 days.[27] A survey of food bank clients in the year 2000 found that 70 percent of them work at Lakeside and that a further 12 percent started work at the plant and then quit. The average client is assisted 2.4 times. Like the Salvation Army, the food bank is largely dependent upon local donations of money and food. Demand has increased steadily, though the service was interrupted for several months when the food bank was forced to vacate the premises it was occupying. It reopened in July 2000 in the Brooks Community Centre after paying for renovations to satisfy building code requirements. It now pays rent of $600 a month to the city. Further evidence of the impoverished nature of newcomer families is provided by the establishment of a school breakfast program in one elementary school in fall 1999 and plans to expand the program to other schools.

At the same time that increasing demands have been placed upon the voluntary sector, applications for one-time transitional payments from Alberta Family and Social Services (AFSS) increased by 820 percent between 1996 and 1999, while the number of transients receiving assistance increased by 300 percent. The amount a person receives under the transitional assistance program varies. If they live at Lakeside, they receive $229 for food, clothing and personal items; if they live elsewhere, an additional $168 is provided for shelter. Neither amount covers the typical one-month's rent damage deposit required by rental properties, so Lakeside now provides recruited workers with funds to cover such costs. The amount provided by AFSS in supporting the initial settlement costs is considerable. Assuming very conservatively that half of the 1999 aid recipients did not live at Lakeside, the amount the provincial government provided to support the labour force amounted to over $185,000.[28]

The increase in the demand for transitional assistance reflects Lakeside's recruiting practices as they extend increasingly to Maritimers, immigrants, and, most recently, laid-off workers from British Columbia's resource-based industries. While the AFSS data precludes the identification of gender and marital status, it is clear that the overwhelming majority of persons receiving payments are single. Over time it would be expected that the proportion of single persons moving to the area would decline as incentives are provided to existing Lakeside workers to attract family and friends to work at the plant.

There is little evidence of an increase in school enrollment.[29] But the number of annual births recorded at the Brooks Health Centre rose by 28 between 1997 and 2000, indicating that enrollments are likely to increase in the near future. More significantly, the local school district has experienced an increase in demand for English as a Second Language (ESL) instruction and for special services for children with severe physical, emotional, and social disabilities. The school district obtained funding to hire a half-time person to provide ESL instruction beginning in fall 2000. The number of students receiving special services has nearly doubled between 1998–99 and 2000–2001 school years. A local school official attributes this increase to an influx of persons of low socio-economic status. Funding for these programs is provided by provincial government grants.

The emergency centre at the local hospital has also experienced a significant increase in usage. Average monthly emergency room visits rose 38 percent between 1996 and 1999, reflecting the difficulty that many newcomers have in obtaining access to a primary-care physician. The clinic is open 10:00 AM to 5:00 PM, Monday through Friday, so for those persons who cannot obtain time off work to see a physician, the emergency room is a practical alternative. Emergency workers also note that some patients cannot afford to pay for prescriptions and so return a few days later with a worsened condition.

Social disorders

Lakeside's recruitment of young, single adult males has been the primary factor in a 70-percent increase in reported crimes between 1996 and 1999.[30] The local 12-member RCMP detachment now has the highest criminal-code load per officer of any detachment in the province, though its staffing levels have remained unchanged. A detailed analysis of local crime statistics indicates that a large proportion of the increase in criminal activity is associated with alcohol consumption. Between 1996 and 1999, the number of persons reported for disturbing the peace increased from 66 to 377, while the number of intoxicated persons went from 128 to 309 and violations of the provincial liquor act went from 172 to 261. Accompanying these increases have been several highly publicized fights between newcomers and established residents outside local bars. In 1998, the owner of one bar installed security cameras to act as a deterrent against future problems, while a letter was written under the auspices of the Provincial Liquor Commission to all bar owners warning them that existing regulations regarding the serving of intoxicated persons would be strictly enforced. These measures helped reduce the number of intoxicated persons from a 1997 peak of 401 to 309 in 1999, but the sustained increase in reports of disturbing the peace suggests that this problem has not been eliminated.

Property crimes have also increased. Motor vehicle thefts went from 41 in 1996 to 101 in 1999, while the corresponding figures for thefts of property less than $5000 are 333 and 468. These increases reflect the high turnover and mobility among newcomers and the accompanying loss of a sense of community. High employee turnover is endemic to beef processing and as more people become "unknown" in a community it becomes difficult for persons to identify strangers around another person's property and thus prevent theft.

Concurrent with the rise in violent crimes, the number of women and children seeking shelter from abusive relationships has also risen.[31] The Brooks and District Women's Safe Shelter Society was formed in 1997 after a formal needs assessment that predated Lakeside's expansion. Since the shelter's establishment, 254 women and children had been served as of May 2000; 70 percent of them were from outside the region. The Society has now purchased a four-bedroom house in Brooks with the help of federal funding. It competes with a comparable facility in Medicine Hat for the same limited funding sources.

The evidence from Brooks and its counterparts south of the 49th parallel indicates that beef processing's cost-cutting strategies produce similar social consequences for communities on either side of the border. In moving to Alberta, IBP and Cargill have utilized the same business practices that have enabled their successful domination of the industry in the US. The nature of the work and high employee turnover ensure a continuous demand for labour, which is met by recruiting transient young adult males. High River has avoided the social consequences associated with this strategy only because most of Cargill's labour force is able to commute from Calgary.

The elimination of trade barriers and the provincial government's pursuit of outside investors have helped bring lots of beef-processing jobs to Brooks; they have provided a market for locally raised cattle and feed grains. But the industry's expansion has also generated high social costs. Provincial government cost-cutting has meant that Brooks residents have been left to fill in the gaps in the social safety net. Local volunteers now donate considerable time and money to meet the needs of indigent newcomers. Before the plant expanded few such needs existed. In an era marked by government preferences for tax cuts rather than social spending, and by an ideology of self-reliance, there is little likelihood that these circumstances will change. Indeed, the evidence from this study suggests that local volunteer agencies will have to increase their fund-raising abilities to meet future newcomer needs for food, shelter, and other basic life supports, given the plant's insatiable appetite for workers. Lakeside has tried to address the town's housing shortage with the erection of temporary accommodation and an effort at rezoning land for a trailer court. The province, meanwhile, has met its statutory responsibilities of providing school grants and transitional assistance payments (which amount to a labour-force recruitment subsidy). But, by default, funding for indigent care has become a responsibility of the local citizenry. The long-term sustainability of this approach is questionable. What is fundamentally at issue in places like Brooks is the degree to which a local community should be responsible for dealing with the social consequences of a provincial economic development strategy and an industry over which it has no control.

Notes

The author thanks the following individuals for providing information for this study: Marijana Agicic, Kevin Bridges, Connie Dulle, Chris Ernst, Norma Galloway, Bonita Levie, Greg Lynch, Bill Peterson, Jody Rutherford, and, in particular, Roberta Rogers who provided insightful comments in the preparation of the manuscript. Any mistakes or omissions are the sole responsibility of the author.

1   Joel Novek, "Peripheralizing Core Labour Markets? The Case of the Canadian Meatpacking Industry," *Work, Employment & Society* 3 (1989): 162.

2   Michael J. Broadway, "From City to Countryside: Recent Changes in the Structure and Location of the Meat and Fish Processing Industries," in *In Any Way You Cut It: Meat Processing and Small Town America*, eds. D. Stull, M.J. Broadway and D. Griffith (Lawrence, KS: University Press of Kansas, 1995), 18–19.

3   Canadian International Trade Tribunal, *An Inquiry into the Competitiveness of the Canadian and Cattle and Beef Industries* (Ottawa: Ministry of Supply and Services, 1993), 21.

4   K.K. Klein and W.A. Kerr, "The Globalization of Agriculture: A View From the Farm Gate," *Canadian Journal of Agricultural Economics* 43 (1995): 551–2.

5   *Fed Cattle Production* (Calgary: Canfax ResearchServices., n.d.)

6   Canadian International Trade Tribunal, *Competitiveness*, op. cit. p. 17.

7   Mark Stevenson, "Playing Rough in a Tough Business," *Alberta Report*, 13 December 1991, 21.

8   Johanna Powell, "More Upheaval for Beef Plants," *The Financial Post*, 4–6 May 1991.

9   Alberta Economic Development, *Highlights of the Alberta Economy*, 1998, 1, 24.

10 Anne Forrest, "The Rise and Fall of National Bargaining in the Canadian Meat-Packing Industry," *Relations Industrielles* 44 (1989): 396.

11 Alain Noel and Keith Gardner, "The Gainers Strike: Capitalist Offensive, Militancy, and the Politics of Industrial Relations in Canada," *Studies in Political Economy* 31 (1990): 56.

12 Stevenson, "Playing Rough," 21.

13 Michael J. Broadway and Donald D. Stull, "Rural Industrialization: the Example of Garden City, Kansas," *Kansas Business Review* 14 (1991): 4.

14 Ibid., 8.

15 Michael J. Broadway, "Meatpacking and its Social and Economic Consequences for Garden City, Kansas, in the 1980s," *Urban Anthropology* 19 (1990): 339–40.

16 Ibid., 332.

17 Michael J. Broadway, "Settlement and Mobility Among Newcomers to a High Plains Boomtown in the 1980s," *Journal of Cultural Geography* 10 (1990): 56.

18 Michael J. Broadway, "Hogtowns and Rural Economic Development," *Rural Development Perspectives* 9 (1994): 44–50. See also Mark Grey, "Pork, Poultry and Newcomers in Storm Lake, Iowa"; and, Lourdes Gouveia and Donald D. Stull, "Dances With Cows: Beefpacking's Impact on Garden City, Kansas and Lexington, Nebraska," both in Stull et al., eds., *Any Way You Cut It*.

19 Martin E. Personick and Katherine Taylor-Shirley, "Profiles in Safety and Health: Occupational Hazards of Meatpacking," *Monthly Labor Review* 112 (1989): 5.

20 Anita Wood, *The Beef Packing Industry: A Study of Three Kansas Communities in Southwestern Kansas: Dodge City, Liberal and Garden City, Kansas*. Final Report to the Department of Migrant Education (Flagstaff, AZ: Wood and Wood Associates, 1998).

21 Michael J. Broadway, "Where's the Beef? The Integration of the Canadian and U.S. Beefpacking Industries," *Prairie Forum* 23 (1998): 26.

22 David Heyman, "Lost Time due to Injury a Cargill Issue," *Calgary Herald*, July 21, 1997.

23 Broadway, "Where's the Beef?", 26.

24 Sturgess Architecture, "Affordable Housing for Brooks: A Preliminary Study with Recommendations" (Calgary, 1995).

25 http://www.albertafirst.com/geographic_Profiles/community_Profiles 26 These figures were obtained from the Salvation Army's Family Care Centre in Brooks. The Centre's expenditures on food dropped sharply in 1999 once a food bank was established in town.

27 These figures were obtained from the Brooks Food Bank Foundation.

28 These figures were obtained from Alberta Family and Social Services, South Region, Calgary. My calculation of the total is as follows: 50 percent of recipients in 1999 = 298. 298 @ $229 = $68,242; 298 @ $397 = $118,306. Thus the total amount is $68,242 + $118,306 = $186,548.

29 Bruce Parker, "Student Numbers Don't Reflect Population Growth," *Brooks Bulletin*, 9 September 1998.

30 These figures were obtained from the Royal Canadian Mounted Police, Brooks Detachment, Operational Statistics, 1996–1999.

31 These figures were obtained from the Brooks and District Women's Safe Shelter Society.

Global Investment and Local Politics

THE CASE OF LETHBRIDGE

William Ramp
and Mustafa Koc

In a globalizing economy, regions, cities, and communities are struggling to survive as viable settings for the enactment of human identity and purpose. The borderless nature of economic, social, and cultural interaction has made ever more problematic the meaning of a sense of place and its relation to community. At the same time, new definitions and configurations of the local continue to make their appearance.[1] Local adaptations to, *and* resistance to, the pervasive forces of globalism play an important role in this process. Local conflicts reflect different perceptions *and* realities of global linkages, and their implications for economic development, political autonomy, and social justice. This chapter addresses some of the dilemmas faced by communities in relation to two features of the globalization process: neo-liberal schemes for governmental restructuring and the new economic climate in which investment projects are proposed and debated. It focusses specifically on a recent set of events in Lethbridge, Alberta, which brought into play competing notions of globalism, government, and local development. These events also provide insights into patterns of local conflict, resistance, and adaptation.

Lethbridge is a regional retail and service centre of approximately 69,000 people. It is located south of Calgary in a dryland belt which was transformed in the early twentieth century by irrigation agriculture. The area now produces large amounts of grain, oilseeds, potatoes, sugar beets, hay, and other crops; it is also home to dairying, an intensive cattle-feeding industry, and a number of hog producers. While the city was long a centre for coal mining, the railways' conversion to diesel combined with a long-term general decline in the coal industry has led to a concentration on industrial and retail services to the surrounding agricultural community. A flour mill, pasta plant, and other processing industries cater to the agricultural sector, as do several farm and industrial machinery dealerships. There is also a long-established federal agricultural research station. In the past 35 years, provincial government investment in post-secondary education has given the town a university and a community college. In addition, government money fostered a small aero engine and communications technology sector in the 1970s. In the past few decades, Lethbridge has attracted a significant population of retired people from the surrounding region, and increasingly from across and beyond the province. The city's First Nations population has also undergone rapid growth since the 1970s, but this growth has yet to be reflected in political or economic influence, contributing to an undercurrent of political unease.

In 1996, following initial contacts made with city officials at a Taipei trade show, Taiwanese investors showed an interest in establishing a major hog-processing facility in Western Canada to produce pork products for what was then a burgeoning Asian market. Partly driven by disease, which had cut into Taiwanese production for Japan, the location would also allow investors to tap into and expand the existing intensive-livestock industry in southern Alberta. Lethbridge's municipal government eagerly courted the Taiwanese investors as part of a long-term strategy of developing agricultural-products industries in Lethbridge and area, in order to build on what were seen as existing strengths in the local and regional economy.

This effort, however, quickly ran into controversy. An active group of local citizens began to raise questions both about the project itself and the manner in which the city was promoting it. Concerns were raised about the environmental impact of the plant, the types of jobs it would create, possible social disruption in the community, and the appropriateness of foreign investment. Over the next year, this debate would turn increasingly bitter and specific, with charges and counter-charges levelled about an alleged cover-up of environmental, legal, and procedural problems. Eventually, the investors withdrew, and coincidentally, the Asian boom collapsed, taking with it not only dreams of the hog plant but also the livelihoods of a number of Alberta pork producers, who had been encouraged to expand in the hopes of growing export demand. This episode, which left both "sides" bruised, and proponents of the plant rueful, served as a signal baptism of fire into the politics of the global economy. While the battle over the proposed plant has died down, our interviews with former proponents and opponents made it clear that it remains a touchstone for continuing debate over the manner in which Lethbridge should articulate itself to the global economy.

GLOBALIZATION AS A PROCESS

The term globalization has only recently become part of popular jargon in many parts of the world, as people in different localities come to realize that the social and economic conditions affecting them have something to do with events taking place elsewhere. But as a process of expansion and intensification of commodity relations on a world scale, an integration of domestic markets, and the emergence of an international division of labour, globalization has been with us for half a millennium. In that time, it has repeatedly destroyed or transformed previous social, economic, and political regimes and institutions. Even under the best circumstances, these transformations have been fragmented and uneven. Some regions and localities have been integrated into this process; others have been bypassed. Development and underdevelopment, integration and marginalization persist as contradictory features of today's global economic order.

Perhaps the most significant transformation in the final two decades of the past century has had to do with the nation-state. Although it is still an important actor in the international arena, its sovereignty increasingly is limited by trade rules and by the pressures of the global economy; it is less able to pursue strategies of national autonomy without risking major economic sacrifices and political turmoil. At the same time, local, regional, and (especially in Canada) provincial governments have become more important. Increasingly, competition for investment, including regulatory and tax concessions, occurs at subnational levels. In this political and economic environment, local and regional differences are important factors in investment decisions. Far from being a universally integrative force, the global movement of capital has been very selective, often ignoring large territories, ethnic communities, nations, cities, or neighbourhoods. The new global networks tend to create islands of integrated communities, but also vast "peripheries" (spatial as well as social), all around the globe.[2] As a result, unevenness of development has become more pronounced, and implications for national-level policies have become even more complex. At the same time, as we shall see in the case of Lethbridge, what a given region has to offer to specific *types* of industry is important. So is the differential flow of costs and benefits of participation in the global economy to those local groups with a voice in municipal and regional affairs.

Canadian municipalities have had less flexibility than their American counterparts in pursuing such positioning strategies, given their limited powers under provincial government jurisdiction. As James Lightbody has noted, "the essential theme which has guided the Canadian provincial-local relationship is one of 'control and guidance.'"[3] In recent years, the particular course of government restructuring in Canada has strengthened a patron-client relationship between provinces and municipalities, as the former have gained political influence at the expense of the federal government. Comparative studies show that local and regional governments in the United States typically are able to employ a wider range of financial incentives such as tax abatements, loans, or loan guarantees, in pursuing investment. Yet even within Canada there can be variations from province to province, so that many cities can "compete for development fairly autonomously."[4] Alberta, for example, offers more discretion to local governments in certain financial matters, especially under the new *Municipal Government Act*, while Ontario has a more paternalistic policy. The issue of how Alberta municipalities make use of their discretionary powers is raised below.

RESTRUCTURING THE LOCAL STATE

The contradictory nature of municipal government as both an agent of central control and an obstacle to it has made it an important arena of political conflict over recent development strategies. Since the 1970s, old questions about the relative merits of centralization and decentralization have re-emerged in the context of government restructuring. In their attempts to confront problems of economic competitiveness, industrial decline, and deficits, provincial and federal governments have transferred part of the fiscal burden to local governments. Politically, decentralization also created an appearance of power-sharing while tending both to conserve the economic resources of the centre and to shift blame for deteriorating economic conditions (and infrastructure) from the central to the local state. Changes to federal unemployment insurance legislation in 1990, for example, pushed the unemployed toward welfare programs jointly funded by municipalities.[5] Cuts in transfer payments handed municipalities part of the responsibility for local and regional employment development, infrastructure investment, and service delivery. These cuts, combined with loss of tax revenue as a result of economic recession, led in turn to various municipal restructuring schemes, influenced by neo-liberalism, that often included cuts in labour expenditure (lay-offs, pay cuts, early retirement, etc.); organizational remodelling (closing or combining departments); reductions in services; and revisions of tax policy. These strategies were often accompanied by the introduction of various economic development programs, such as "shop locally" campaigns, and by attempts to retain existing businesses and to attract global corporate ventures to the area.[6] These attempts were presented as opportunities to bring "revenues" to the local government and "jobs" to the community, against the threat of tax hikes and reduced services. While public reaction generally has been positive, it has not been free of controversy. What may appear in the abstract to business and governments as a locational decision for investment often conflicts with local people's more grounded and emotive conceptualizations of "social space," as a place to live, as a community.[7] The types of concessions offered to new ventures, as well as the possible impacts of new developments on local property values, employment, local traffic, quality of life, and the environment, lead to conflicts. On one side are the dominant interests of the local elite, or what has been called the "growth machine"[8]; on the other are citizens who reflect the diverse interests of class, gender, ethnic, and neighbourhood groups. Those interests may be represented through local coalitions or social movements formed around such concerns as the environment, housing, and poverty. In this way, the struggle for a better position in the global economy is likely to take place not only between various localities but also within them.

NEO-LIBERAL DISCOURSE ON LOCAL GOVERNMENT RESTRUCTURING

Neo-liberal discourse on local state restructuring has been derived from a populist critique of the state, bureaucracy, and taxes, combined with a business-oriented vision of reorganization as essential to efficiency. In many parts of the world, neo-liberalism has effectively used examples of public concern and disappointment in its defence of the need to "reinvent" governments and public agencies at all levels. The new vision for the state is analogous to that of private business driven by the profit motive. It is focussed, first, on responding effectively to consumers (or "clients") of its services, and, second, on complementing but not interfering with the market economy. According to neo-liberal ideology, global economic challenges require a flexible, down-sized municipal government, responsible for the integration of a locality into the world economy. John Bulloch's observations as president of the Canadian Federation of Independent Business summarize this perception quite clearly:

> Canadians have to look to micro solutions: individuals taking control of their own lives through upgrading and self-employment; businesses creating their own futures by becoming more technological, international and entrepreneurial; and communities working together to solve problems. To deal with the issues that concern everyday Canadians, it's thumbs down to big corporations, big unions, big bureaucracies, big medicine, big law, big constitutions, and it's thumbs up to individual empowerment, small scale enterprise, specialization, flexibility, sub-contracting, self-employment, part-time employment, networking, and all types of informal co-operation and problem-solving at the local level. It's a new world of transnational corporations interacting with separate economies at the local and regional level, a world where national governments are reduced in terms of their real power and influence.[9]

But this populism of micro solutions is far from a "small is beautiful" approach. What is envisioned here is a decentralized and deregulated economy, where municipal governments will create the services and infrastructure for the private sector, community groups will supply voluntary services to replace or reduce welfare costs, and the locality will be attached to global networks through connections offered by transnational corporations.

THE LETHBRIDGE STORY

On June 4, 1997, Mayor David Carpenter of Lethbridge announced that a Taiwanese pork-processing company, Yuan Yi, intended to take up land in Lethbridge to build a plant, at an estimated cost of $50 million, which would eventually process up to 8000 hogs per day. The Yuan Yi project was promoted heavily by the city and much of the business community. The city estimated that the plant could introduce up to 400 new jobs to Lethbridge and $900-million in annual spin-off benefits to the local economy. Subsidy costs to municipal taxpayers, including utilities hookups, rezoning, financing assistance, and technical support for an application to Alberta Environment, were projected to be in the region of $1-million. An information meeting concerning the proposal was held July 15, 1997 and attended by 350 people; however, no members of city council or representatives of Yuan Yi attended. As controversy surrounding the project, and the city's promotion of it, grew, a public hearing was scheduled for July 28. It was attended by some 750 people, and concerns were expressed about the environmental impact of the plant and the possible implications of a rezoning bylaw. On August 16, the City Treasurer noted that a mistake in calculations meant that the estimated municipal cost of the project would be closer to $8.1-million. On August 27, a group of Lethbridge citizens filed legal action to overturn the decision to rezone and sell land to Yuan Yi on the grounds that the city had not acted in the best interests of citizens, that citizens were denied the right to petition for a plebiscite, and that information regarding economic and environmental impacts was not made available.[10]

Throughout the remainder of 1997, and the first two months of 1998, controversy continued to rage over the project, as reflected in daily coverage in the local newspaper, several public meetings, a court decision and an appeal, and submissions to Alberta Environment and Environment Canada. On November 7, Alberta Environment's Regional Director, Peter Watson, ruled that 2200 letters asking for an environmental assessment of the hog plant by his department represented people who were not personally and directly affected by the proposed plant, and that therefore their request could not be granted. Three days later, Alberta Environment issued an approval of the project. On February 13, however, the Alberta Environmental Appeal Board heard further concerns from local citizens. The controversy was still in full swing when, in March, Yuan Yi announced cancellation of the project, due, it said, to delays. It was noted at the time that the cancellation also coincided with the downturn in Asian economies.

TAKING AND MAKING SIDES

Public supporters of the Yuan Yi project, including city council and key figures in the city administration, claimed that it would have been a good fit with the existing economic emphasis on agricultural processing and primary production. They argued that the jobs were needed, that the spin-off benefits to the local economy would be significant, and that the local agricultural sector needed access to international markets. (Yuan Yi had intended to export much of its product to Asia.) The Yuan Yi project would also have coincided with the provincial government's economic strategy, which saw intensified agricultural production for international markets as key to Alberta's prosperity.

Opponents raised concerns about power supply for a plant that would need large amounts of refrigeration, about wastewater holding and treatment, about odours, and also about the quality of the jobs that would be created. They raised the example of Brooks, a smaller community that had been negatively affected by a large packing plant and the influx of transitory and unskilled workers (see Broadway, this volume). In addition, the citizens who had launched the court challenge raised concerns about legal and democratic procedures relating to the land transfer and rezoning, and to the lack of opportunities offered to the public to be part of the decision-making process.

Cancellation of the project in March 1998 resolved none of these arguments and left the city with a bitter ideological hangover that was expressed in mutual recriminations. It was in this context that the authors of this chapter, and their researchers, commenced interviews with local government figures, business and community leaders, and selected members of the public in Lethbridge on the subject of globalization and government restructuring. The Yuan Yi incident provided an obvious focus for such discussions.

Opponents of the Yuan Yi initiative generally saw it as something imposed on them by a city government too eager to adopt a sort of "megaproject" mentality and too willing to neglect or sell out the public interest in favour of a business agenda. City hall was accused of taking for granted the necessity of keeping up with the global economy, whatever its consequences, and even of being an "outright agent and legal extension of a global corporation."[11]

City politicians and officials in favour of the project, on the other hand, tended to see the opposition as too stuck in the past, unwilling to see Lethbridge "grow." The need for growth (to supply jobs to local young people, to keep up the tax base, etc.) was generally taken for granted. At the same time, the mayor, some members of council, and senior city administrators agreed readily that mistakes had been made and that they would handle things differently the next time, if a next time came. The Yuan Yi debacle was, in fact, the subject of a series of reflective sessions engaged in by senior city staff.

One mistake identified by city officials was about public relations. They proposed that the project had not been promoted effectively enough and that the city, having misjudged the ferocity of opposition to the plant, had not got positive information out quickly to enough people. A second problem discussed was that the city government had allowed itself to get too far out ahead of the public on the issue, thus leaving itself exposed. Administrators and some members of council proposed in hindsight that a series of public forums to test the waters and set development agendas would have been a good idea, both to gauge public opinion and to educate the public. Third, it was argued, Yuan Yi was not used to launching projects in a North American context, did not expect the public opposition, and, given its market commitments, could not afford the delays consequent on the opposition and regulatory procedures. Yuan Yi itself did little in the way of public relations.[12]

Some city politicians and administrators reported that their approach to new investment had been affected by the Yuan Yi experience. A senior administrator commented that smaller municipalities could not "sell" themselves to international business in general any more: multinational corporations had their own reasons for locating where they did and were unlikely to be swayed either by a bidding war among municipalities or by propaganda campaigns. The city would continue to advertise itself and its advantages, especially for particular types of industry suited to existing local economic strengths, but would see its role as one of facilitating rather than soliciting or subsidizing international investment decisions. Instead, the city would emphasize a strategy of cutting red tape and "getting out of the way" of those business investors who did express interest. In addition, city officials seemed increasingly interested in helping to provide opportunities for established local businesses to grow in accordance with a "slow and steady" rather than "boom and bust" development model.[13]

This approach to development was tied to a new philosophy of municipal government that had been developing through the 1990s. Under Alberta's *Municipal Government Act* (1995), municipalities had gained a significant increase in latitude in local and regional decision-making. This increased latitude was somewhat selective, in that it involved a centralization of fiscal and taxation power at the provincial level while downloading responsibility for regulatory and development decisions on municipalities, which in some cases lacked a strong provincial legislative framework, or sufficient fiscal, organizational or technical capacities, to make or enforce decisions effectively. In addition, the regionalization of provincial government services (as in the creation of regional health authorities), while intended to bring service delivery closer to the people and to increase efficiency by eliminating unnecessary bureaucracy and organizational duplication, was slow to deliver on its promise, leaving municipalities with the burden of "symptoms of a larger problem" in the form of social issues like homelessness, poverty, and gaps in health and social service delivery.

But while it could be argued that the *Municipal Government Act* was part of a provincial governmental restructuring plan meant to offload responsibilities (e.g., for certain environmental and zoning approval issues) without increasing revenues, a number of city politicians and administrators in Lethbridge, as elsewhere in the province, emphatically did not see it that way. They welcomed their new freedom from province-wide restrictions.[14] Those same politicians and administrators, however, expressed no desire to use this new freedom to expand their reach; rather, they adopted a philosophy of "minimal government." In Lethbridge, this was taken to entail the privatization of certain city services (swimming pools and water being two contentious examples), the streamlining and standardization of business regulations, and the adoption of a less interventionist approach to investment recruitment. City officials saw their mandate as getting out of the way of private business and doing their part to provide opportunities for it to flourish. The job of municipal government was to set and enforce a fair regulatory climate, to set standards for the operation of services provided in-house or contracted out, to operate those local services that could not be contracted out, to keep taxes low, and to promote business as the basis for the economic well-being of the citizenry. Two senior administrators suggested that municipal residents needed to be weaned from a psychology of dependence and to get used to a model of government that no longer told citizens what was best for them.[15]

In the course of our interviews, it became apparent that senior city officials in Lethbridge had come up with a relatively coherent vision of municipal government and its role, a vision that they believed in sincerely. Practically, though, they agreed that they operated on a bit of a tightrope, balancing the different interests of the citizenry (in lower taxes, but also in well-run services and in regulatory enforcement to preserve the local quality of life), and of business (in less regulation and restriction).[16] City leaders also expressed an increased interest in regional partnerships for economic development and in overcoming a history of residual suspicion or rivalry between the city and its surrounding municipalities. In both Lethbridge and Red Deer, mayors, council members, and others spoke of the need to develop regional partnerships in economic development—implicitly seeing competition as an inter-regional or inter-provincial matter rather than a municipal one. The emphasis at the level of the municipality or region was on inter-municipal consultation (rather than formalized institutional structures) and on developing specific economic strengths or niche opportunities.

It is important to note here that one effect of the Yuan Yi episode was to reinforce one of the *philosophical* tenets of neo-liberalism as a *practical* approach to investment issues. As an economic philosophy, neo-liberalism decries any attempts by government to skew the market, including attempts to "lure" investment through various kinds of fiscal and infrastructural incentives. Lethbridge's city government has become increasingly cautious about trying to compete with other municipalities in an incentives or concessions game, but not simply because of philosophical scruples. Rather, the perception is that municipalities, with limited resources and fiscal flexibility, simply cannot win at such a game. Such strategies now tend to be seen as questionable: whether they would result in significant increases in investment at all; whether they would attract investment with little commitment to the city; and whether they would even have much of an interim effect. However, that does not mean that munic-ipalities will not feel continuing pressure from both citizens *and* some sectors of local business to offer lures.

One important fallout of the Yuan Yi debacle in Lethbridge was its effect on the political climate of the city: namely, to sharpen an already existing polariza-tion. Those who actively supported the Yuan Yi proposal expressed a genuinely wounded surprise over the level and (perceived) stridency of the public opposi-tion; in response they have tended to personalize their reaction to it. Thus, for example, a local reporter on agricultural affairs referred privately to the opposi-tion as driven by "environmentalist" scare stories, and expressed dismay over what he saw as a new enthusiasm for the use of the courts as a "blocking" tactic.[17] Some officials and politicians—the mayor included—offered a demographic explanation for the opposition, referring to a highly articulate and educated group of retired people who, in the interest of a nostalgic vision of small-town quality of life, tended to develop a blanket opposition to "change" and "growth." Generally, proponents of the hog plant tended to characterize their opposition as nay-sayers who had seized on and manipulated a highly symbolic issue. They noted, with irony, that an established local packer had since converted to hog production without controversy. In turn, a number of those in the opposition tended to characterize city politicians and administrators as an "old boy network": overly secretive, cliquish, blinded by class background, unwilling to acknowledge the public interest over business preferences, blindly adhering to a "business is best" philosophy, or neglecting the diverse strengths of the local economy to focus narrowly on agricultural processing.[18] Both "sides" in the dispute represented themselves as speaking for a silent majority. This polarization has carried over into more recent municipal issues, such as the privatization of city pools, a controversial building permit, location of a new retail centre, cutbacks in city bus services, housing and social policy, downtown revitalization, and the city's response to provincial electrical deregulation.

More recently, city officials have begun to explore ways of developing a wider debate over future economic development in Lethbridge, one which, according to Darrel McKenzie, the city's Economic Development Officer, would include the question of whether or not economic growth is good, or whether it should be limited. In addition, McKenzie has suggested a revision to the historical emphasis on agricultural processing as an economic mainstay of the city, suggesting that "research commercialization" in agricultural biotechnology and food processing might give Lethbridge an edge in the "new economy."[19] While these suggestions may well generate further controversy, they may also signal a growing openness to new economic development options, and to an enhanced public process for debate and decision-making.

While the Yuan Yi incident threw issues of globalization into a harsh new light for the citizens of Lethbridge, it may also have diverted attention from some equally important issues. Although McCain Foods has established a large new french-fry-processing plant near Taber, to the east, it is unlikely that any Lethbridge city government will as aggressively promote a major development on the scale of Yuan Yi in the future. Globalization will affect the citizens of Lethbridge in more subtle ways; for example, through the commitment of their present municipal leaders to a model of minimalist government, regulatory streamlining, and privatization. This model is put forward in highly convincing ways: "no one wants" government inefficiency, paternalism, or obstructionism. Yet this commitment to minimalism, and the continuing division of responsibility between municipalities and the provincial government (especially in the areas of health and social welfare), means that small-city government will find it more difficult to address quality of life issues in the future. Until relatively recently, these issues appeared to be relatively low on the municipal government horizon in Lethbridge.[20] Perhaps because of their middle-class professional or business backgrounds, the (doubtlessly genuine) concern of city politicians and senior administrators for those about to fall off the edge of the global economy has tended to be voiced in the language of "opportunity, initiative, and skills," and the need therefore for education and training. But these are not fields that city governments are equipped for, or feel they can take major responsibility for. While front-line workers in social services voice the opinion that the city could and should do more in the way of housing, sponsorship of community projects, services, or fee reductions, council also faces vocal opposition to tax increases; and, in any case, the money and authority to address social and health issues directly still lies with federal and provincial governments. (The city's response to this dilemma is, of course, variously interpreted, with questions being raised about which taxpayers tend to be listened to, and what interests and philosophies drive the city's spending and policy priorities.)[21]

In an interview for this project, David Carpenter, the city's mayor, spoke of the problem municipalities faced in dealing with "symptoms" of underlying social and economic problems: the symptoms were often visible and occasionally costly for municipal governments, but their causes (and solutions) lie elsewhere—for example, in provincial or federal policies on social service funding and delivery, fiscal restraint, or regulatory policies. One example has proved his words prophetic: the deregulation of Alberta's electricity supply left city consumers facing major rate hikes. Although the city was not responsible in any direct way for deregulation or the price increases, it was directly affected by them and felt compelled to respond politically to the issue, both in representations to the provincial government and in bruiting the possibility of generating power locally. In turn, public anger was turned against the city to such an extent that a petition was started for an early council election.[22] In the controversy, electrical deregulation, price hikes, and city-imposed electrical rate riders were linked to other issues such as recent cuts to bus service and privatization of city pools—and the blame laid at the municipal doorstep. At the same time, the city's finances have been severely affected by the sudden rise in electricity prices.

The example of Lethbridge, then, teaches us to be wary of oversimplifying the impact of globalization on local communities. As often as not, such "communities" are riven by internal political differences, which may reflect many things: among them class and demographic division; the existence of different or opposed political or cultural elites; the isolation of such elites from each other or from more disadvantaged or silent groups; the existence of constituencies with different stakes in both local and global economies; and the political structure of the municipality in question. Since the Yuan Yi incident, a number of subsequent developments, both in and outside Lethbridge, would appear to confirm this. For example, the routing of an export highway bypass around Milk River led to polarization in that community between local proponents of the bypass and landowners subject to expropriation. A proposal by the Taiwan Sugar Corporation to locate a giant hog-raising facility in the nearby County of Forty Mile led to a massive public outcry and the withdrawal of the proposal, prompting the company to look elsewhere in Alberta, with the same divisive effect between, on one hand, municipal officials and business owners and, on the other, large numbers of residents (see introduction, this volume).

The danger in such developments is that political divisions can weaken the ability of local communities to deal effectively with the economic and political challenges they face. Yuan Yi and similar events have heightened political awareness in Lethbridge and have led to increased scrutiny both of local municipal issues and of environmental issues in the surrounding county, especially with regard to intensive livestock operations. This is all to the good. But a tendency to personalize the issues (as mainly the fault of a "cliquish" city council, a group of stubborn "senior citizens," alarmist "environmentalists," or an arrogant "business elite") takes attention away from a set of issues that must be addressed if effective and human-oriented responses to globalization and government restructuring are to develop effectively at the local level.[23] That set of issues has to do with the *systemic* organization of inequality in local communities. Who has access to the public forum or the local media? Who has the ability to articulate a point of view effectively? Who has the material resources to do so? What potential constituencies remain marginalized and silent? Who has close connections to local and provincial politicians and business leaders, or to global business, and who does not? The point of such "who" questions should *not* simply be to demonize those so identified, but to ask *why* such inequalities exist and *how* they are reproduced locally.[24] And, as importantly, how are the selective blindnesses that accompany particular positions and particular interests in the community *reproduced*, sometimes despite the best intentions of those occupying the positions and holding the interests? How are the pressures to adopt, and adapt to, a model of minimalist government and of market dominance felt and understood differently by different groups, and why?

In short, the impact of globalization and government restructuring on a city like Lethbridge is likely to be felt in other ways than competition for, or the parachuting in of, a new global-scale megaproject. Citizens will feel the sting of globalization and restructuring through decisions like that of the provincial government to deregulate and privatize electrical power generation and supply. They may also feel it through the potential employment and service effects of decisions by the municipality to outsource local services to private agencies—often corporations with headquarters out of province or at least outside the city. They will feel it in municipal service cuts as local governments decide on fiscal priorities. In short, they will feel it through changes in the cost, billing, and quality of services and utilities. Some might experience a benefit from globalization, as established local companies find and supply niches in the global or continental economy, as is already happening in Lethbridge, with Ellison Milling, a division of Parrish and Heimbecker. They will also eventually reap the consequences, good or bad, of what has become a broad *de facto* consensus between local government and business: that the future of Lethbridge and the surrounding area rests on a backbone of agricultural production and processing. In the long run, this means that the local economy, instead of competing against many other regions for investment-in-general, will become focussed on a specialized role, one that is said to suit its strengths. But these particular strengths have a number of potential downsides: the historical tendency of primary commodity prices to fall; the general reduction in labour requirements of both modern agriculture and agricultural processing; the long-term environmental vulnerability of irrigation agriculture; growing controversy over intensive livestock production; and, possibly, future disputes with adjacent First Nations over land and water rights. These issues, among others, will engage the different political and ideological coalitions and fractions generated by the Yuan Yi episode. Whether they will be engaged shortsightedly or not will depend a great deal on the strategies and interactions of local interests and local groups.

Neo-liberal interpretations of local development assume that regions and localities will play an increasingly significant role in a global economy, as competitive spaces in which communities are continuously improving conditions for investment. There is an understanding that offering the best possible conditions in this new competitive economy will help to attract new ventures or keep jobs and maintain the economic livelihood of communities. These conditions are not just limited to incentives, as in earlier economic development programs, but now involve restructuring of the local state and state-society relations; indeed, such restructuring has appeared to eclipse the attractiveness of an incentive-based strategy for Lethbridge. Global pressures turn into excuses to demonstrate the inevitability of change and to justify the necessity of restructuring schemes. But history has demonstrated, time and again, that the "inevitability" of any process is contingent—that is, defined by the social relations and political struggles of the time. While different constituencies may share a perception that "change" is necessary, the direction and outcome of that change will be decided partly at the local and community level by *political* means. Whether in the form of nostalgia for the past, conservative resistance to modernization, populist defences of locality and community, or co-operative movements for democratic self-determination, resistance to corporate visions of globalism and their consequences will continue to shape the course of the restructuring we have experienced in the last couple of decades. But it will not do so in a vacuum. These local movements have the potential to bring communities together and to offer a locally defined sense of global space, *if* they can manage to link effectively with other communities and localities and *if* they can generate strong local support with a coherent, practical, and defensible vision. They also have the capacity to split and weaken communities depending on how they address the local as well as global interests arrayed against them, and how they respond to the political rationales and strategies adopted by those interests. A key issue will be the nature of opportunites for public participation in local decision-making. The new global citizen may very well come out of these battles over globalism: the future character of that citizen is in our hands.

Notes

The authors wish to acknowledge the invaluable research and editorial assistance of Sheila Collar, and the research assistance of Dana Dawson, Viola Cassis, Allison Roest, and Brandy Monilaws. Our thanks also to the editors, Parkland Institute readers, and Peter Ibbott for helpful critiques, comments, suggestions, and forbearance. Work on the project out of which this chapter was written was supported by grants from the Social Sciences and Humanities Research Council of Canada and the Province of Alberta Research Excellence Envelope.

1   D.J.A. Douglas, "The New Rural Region: Consciousness, Collaboration and New Challenges and Opportunities for Innovative Practice," in W. Ramp, J. Kulig, I. Townshend, and V. McGowan, eds. *Health in Rural Settings: Contexts for Action* (Lethbridge: University of Lethbridge, 1999).

2   See, for example, E. Soja, *Postmodern Geographies: The Reassertion of Space in Critical Social Theory* (London: Verson, 1989); Robert D. Kaplan, *An Empire Wilderness: Travels*

into America's Future (New York: Random House, 1999); Saskia Sassen, *Cities in A World Economy* (Thousand Oaks, CA: Pine Forge Press, 1994).

3 James Lightbody, "The Strategic Planning Component in the Policy making Process for Municipalities in Canada," *Policy Studies Journal* 21 (1993): 97.

4 A.L. Reese, "Local Economic Development Policies in Ontario," *Canadian Public Administration* 35 (1992): 239.

5 Lightbody, "The Strategic Planning Component," 95.

6 See Sassen, *Cities in a World Economy*; Mustafa Koc, "Global Restructuring and Communities," in B. Wolensky and E. Miller, eds., *Social Science and the Community, Proceedings of the Conference on the Small City and Regional Community*, XI (University of Wisconsin-Stevens Point Foundation Press, 1995).

7 H. Lefebvre, *The Production of Space* (Oxford: Blackwell, 1991).

8 J.R. Logan and H.L. Molotch, *Urban Fortunes: The Political Economy of Place* (Berkeley: University of California Press, 1988).

9 John Bulloch, "Tips for the tough job of economic restructuring," *Canadian Speeches*, March 1993, 10.

10 Rhonda Ruston, "Rights and Freedoms," *Lethbridge Herald*, 2 April 1998.

11 See, for example, Tony Hall, "Hogocracy," *Canadian Forum*, October 1997; and "Hogocracy and Municipal Law in Alberta," *Encompass Magazine*, October 1997.

12 Interview, D. McKenzie, Economic Development Department, City of Lethbridge, June 13, 1999; interview, G. Weadick, member of Lethbridge city council, August 10, 1999.

13 Interviews, McKenzie, B. Horrocks, City Manager, City of Lethbridge, 1999.

14 Lethbridge's mayor, David Carpenter, was among those who took this position in our interview, July 13, 1999.

15 Interviews, McKenzie, Horrocks.

16 It should also be noted that the interests of different sectors of the business community can conflict, with some calling for more government intervention in specific areas (especially public investment in projects seen as investment lures), and others for less.

17 Interview, R. Swihart, *Lethbridge Herald*, 1 November 1999.

18 Interviews, J. Huffman, editor, *Alberta Free Press*, October 21, 1999; R. Barsh, Professor of Native American Studies, University of Lethbridge, July 3, 1999.

19 D. Mabell, "City may look toward biotechnology business," *Lethbridge Herald*, 1 January 2001.

20 An administrator in human services with the City voiced some frustration over the fact that no social impact study of the Yuan Yi project had been done. When she raised the idea with a senior staff member, it was received positively and she was told to go ahead and do one, but she was not given additional time or resources to do so (Interview, R. Annis, Leisure Services Department, August 3, 1999).

21 In Lethbridge, proposed cuts to city transit services became a major public issue, while in Red Deer, an interviewee in the social services field complained that that city's focus on a new civic centre had eclipsed arguments for increased transit funding, which would have allowed the unemployed and working poor better access to jobs and services. See, for example, J. Ecklund, "Poverty in the spotlight," *Lethbridge Herald*, 5 January 2001; G. Gauthier, "Housing committee just 'spinning wheels' say participants at SACPA meeting," *Lethbridge Herald*, 19 January 2001.

22 J. Helmer, "City comes up $4 million short," *Lethbridge Herald*, 20 March 2001; and J. Helmer, "Petition calls for investigation of city council," *Lethbridge Herald*, 26 October 2000.

23 Another danger lies in the personalization of "global" investment as "foreign" investment. Yuan Yi and Taiwan Sugar have been high-profile news in Alberta. But it must be pointed out that any major corporation, Canadian or not, is of necessity a "global" player today.

24 C.P. Marlor, "Oldtimers, Newcomers and Social Class: Group Affiliation and Social Influence in Lethbridge, Alberta." Unpublished MA thesis, Department of Anthropology and Sociology, University of British Columbia, 2000.

De-prioritizing Agriculture

LESSONS FROM
NEW BRUNSWICK

Susan Machum

Our supermarket shelves are filled with row after row after row of foodstuffs for sale. As we walk the aisles selecting one product over another the choices seem endless. But as food consumers we often have no idea about where our food is actually coming from; who grew the fruits and vegetables we fill our carts with; what kind of conditions they worked under; or what parent company was responsible for researching, developing, and marketing the array of processed food items from which we make our grocery selections. Amongst these "ready-made" products it is sometimes hard to see the raw materials that went into their creation. Brand names stand out far more than the farmers. In such a context it is hardly surprising that most food consumers are unaware of what is happening to Canadian farmers.

More than a decade ago Brewster Kneen proposed that Canadians "are becoming increasingly separated from their basic food supply."[1] In this process, which he calls *distancing,* the physical and social connections between what we eat and where it comes from are increasingly obscured. Distancing effectively insulates food consumers from the changes in how food is produced, and from the trials and tribulations of the people who are actually growing our food. It encourages us to see companies like McCain Foods, Quaker Oats, and Campbell Soup as the food producers rather than the potato farmers, wheat farmers, and livestock producers who lie at the base of the food chain.

Occasionally we do become aware of the plight of our farmers, their families, and the rural communities they live in. But it is usually at moments of crisis. When the food we take for granted might not find its way to our supermarket shelves, we take notice. So we paid some attention when, as the twentieth century drew to a close, farmers and their families—across Canada but especially in the Prairie provinces—urged politicians and the public to recognize the major financial crises they were facing as a result of crop failures, inadequate crop insurance, foreign subsidies, and low commodity prices. Their farms and their communities were in crisis. They would be forced out of business if the federal and provincial governments did not provide assistance, and a way of life that is part of Canada's history would be gone. Demonstrations, phone-ins, and public meetings did produce some assistance for financially troubled farmers. However, it is not yet clear whether it was enough to make a real difference.

This crisis in agriculture is not new. Nor is it restricted to the wheat-exporting economy of the Prairies. It is one bout in a long and continuing drive by multinational corporations and governments to metamorphose agri*culture* into agri*business*. The role of governments in this process is seldom made explicit. Instead, shifting agricultural practices and the subsequent transformation of agriculture from small, family-owned operations to larger enterprises is portrayed as a "natural" outcome of modernization, competitive markets, and, these days, globalization. This outcome might well have been predictable, given the shifting priorities and changing opportunities that emerged in the economic environment that followed the Second World War; but, of course, nothing happens automatically. This article argues it was the combined actions of farm families, governments, and the growing food-processing industries that together transformed our rural communities.

Using New Brunswick as a case study, the article examines how this province's farm community has been steadily eroded in the postwar era. Specifically it considers the extent and degree to which rural communities in New Brunswick have been affected and altered by ongoing changes in the agricultural industry that not so long ago defined them. It pays particular attention to the role successive provincial governments have played in the structural transformation of agriculture in this province, and it argues that transformations in food—and the conditions under which food is grown—have repercussions that reach far beyond the farm gate. Moreover, although New Brunswick is perhaps more widely associated with forestry and fishing, in the minds of other Canadians, family farming had a long and successful history in parts of rural New Brunswick. Thus, this case study in the industrialization of New Brunswick agriculture—and in particular, the ways that successive New Brunswick governments since the 1960s have promoted corporate, export-oriented agriculture— may be of interest to farmers in other provinces, where the switch to industrial food production might yet be contested.

NEW BRUNSWICK'S CHANGING AGRICULTURAL SCENE

Compared to other Canadian provinces, New Brunswick is unusual in that it has not lost its rural population base even though farming has steadily declined.[2] While there have been ups and downs in the rural population, throughout the postwar years approximately half the province's population has continued to live in rural areas. However, the actual farm population has declined dramatically: 149,916 people lived on farms in 1951 while only 10,975 did so in 1991. Put another way, 29.1 percent of the New Brunswick population farmed in 1951 while four decades later only 1.5 percent of the population continued to farm. What this has meant for rural communities is less of a dependence on farming as the basis of livelihood: 43 percent of the rural population farmed in 1951, while less than 2 percent did so two generations later.[3] As people stopped making their living from farming, the number of farm operations fell from 26,431 census farms in 1951 to 3252 in 1991.[4]

As a consequence, most of the barns and outbuildings which once dotted rural New Brunswick are dilapidated or gone today. The cream cans that used to sit at the end of farm lanes waiting for the rattling truck to take them to the creamery are now hand-painted decorations sitting on doorsteps or waiting in craft stores for nostalgic consumers to take them home. The public buses that used to pass through these communities three times a day gave up these rural roads two decades ago, in favour of a new highway system that cuts through provincial forests to connect New Brunswick's urban centres. Meanwhile, new houses have been built on what used to be farmland. Two hands are now all that's needed to count the remaining farms along the thirty-mile stretch of old provincial highway I call home, a road the New Brunswick tourism department has recently coined the "Scenic River Route" along the Saint John River.

Indeed, "scenic routes" now abound in rural New Brunswick, as formerly working landscapes are promoted as places of leisure—or nostalgia. Country roads are no longer overflowing with farmhouses, barns, and outbuildings, as working farms are supplanted by commuter and weekend homes. Gone are the days when farm families exchanged produce and livestock, and supplied their local store with eggs in exchange for staples they could not produce for themselves. For that matter, most of the local corner stores, like the three that used to be within a mile of the house I grew up in, are gone, replaced by supermarket chains and "super" stores located in larger centres. Rural families and farm wives often travel twenty to fifty miles to do their grocery shopping—an event which is now a regular household activity for farm wives in a way it wouldn't have been before the transformations described here. Before New Brunswick's economic expansion in the postwar years, most family farms were self-sufficient operations growing, harvesting, and preserving the family's food requirements. Excess production was bartered with the local store or sold for cash earnings.[5] While commercial agriculture did exist, this kind of subsistence farming predominated in New Brunswick into the mid 1950s.[6]

However, from roughly this point on, farms grew bigger and mixed farming moved towards specialization. Relatively unmechanized farms where people did the work became highly mechanized farms, and the farm community shrank in size and population. Ecologically sustainable integrated farming practices gave way to more productive but unsustainable modes of farming; and farms once dependent on their own inputs of seed, fertilizer, and pest control became dependent on chemicals, seeds, and biocides purchased from multinational agrochemical companies. Self-financed, formerly debt-free farms became bank-financed operations, often heavily in debt. Indeed, the majority of smaller New Brunswick farms that followed advice to expand were at some point unable to withstand the debts they procured in order to buy machinery and expand production. High interest rates and continuing low prices for agricultural commodities created severe financial problems for farms built on credit.[7] Most farms that attempted to engage in the capital accumulation cycle went bust. A relative few were more successful and continue to sustain the elusive promise of success. But even for the "successful" farms and farm families there is no security. Stress, off-farm employment, debt, and fear of foreclosure are as much a part of the contemporary farm enterprise as the soil and the seeds.

Yet, even though the structures of the rural economy and the agricultural sector have certainly changed, New Brunswick's rural communities have not disappeared or emptied out. Moreover, despite broad shifts in agricultural practices, smaller subsistence farm operations still continue to exist alongside larger commercial operations. For example, in 1996, 46.5 percent of New Brunswick's farms grossed less than $10,000 in farm cash receipts while almost a quarter of the province's farms earned over $100,000 in gross farm receipts.[8] Yet, while these figures suggest that subsistence farms remain, many of these depend on family members' off-farm income to survive. Others could best be characterized as hobby farms, that is, where the owners raise crops or keep livestock for pleasure, and farming is not intended to be a major source of family livelihood. Whichever—and statistics don't distinguish between these sometimes blurred types of part-time farms—it is likely that there are even fewer families earning their living from farming than population and census data would suggest.[9]

New Brunswick agriculture has always featured a wide variety of farming operations. In fact, Darrell McLaughlin identifies four kinds of contemporary farm enterprises with varying forms of production operating in the province: the hobby or subsistence farm, the family farm, the corporate family farm, and the corporate farm.[10] The first two types involve petit-bourgeois production while the last two are forms of capitalist production. According to McLaughlin, hobby or subsistence farms are not engaged in commodity production for commercial sale. These farm units have no interest in or impact on the market. Most have at least one person or more engaged in off-farm work, and the farm does not provide them with their living. On the other hand, family farms are commercial petit-bourgeois operations. They are trying to stay in farming to maintain a way of life, not accumulate capital. They rely largely on family labour. Meanwhile, corporate family farms are small capitalist operations that are family owned and operated but dependent on wage labour. They represent small capitalist enterprise in farming and think of themselves as businesses in farming. They are engaged in the effort to expand their operations to create a self-sustaining cycle of capital accumulation. This group is the most important group for policy-makers and tends to be the most influential in "mainstream" farm organizations (like Federations of Agriculture) and in state policy formation. Corporate farms are corporate owned and operated, with farmers hired as managers and workers who execute company plans, as in any other business.

Because corporate farms employ only wage labour, they are not part of the "family farm" sector. They are factories-in-the-field, but they have not proved to be the wave of the future that was predicted in the 1960s and 1970s.

The resilience of subsistence agriculture and petit-bourgeois production has sometimes been portrayed as the persistence of backward thinking and traditional ways. I want to argue, though, that it is better understood as a marker of the determination of farmers and farm families to keep land in the family, to keep working in what they believe is an honourable occupation, and to feed themselves and their communities (the relative strength of these motivations, of course, varies with individuals). On a broader scale, it also reflects resistance on the part of growing numbers of food consumers to corporate/government efforts to reorganize food production, delocalizing it and forcing farmers into the position of simply growing "inputs" for processing factories, whose corporate owners then sell brand-name food products into continental and global markets.

THE NEW BRUNSWICK GOVERNMENT'S AGRICULTURAL POLICY: PROMOTING CHANGE

The predominant pattern of agriculture in New Brunswick until well after the Second World War was rural "occupational pluralism." Farm families combined subsistence and semi-commercial agriculture with waged work in tree-harvesting and lumber mills, various trades and crafts like blacksmithing, and a variety of waged work in nearby towns.[11] Though there certainly was commercial agriculture in New Brunswick, particularly commercial potato and dairy production, farming in New Brunswick was, for most farm families, part of a round of seasonal occupations. As the 1951 Annual Report from the New Brunswick Department of Agriculture notes:

> General conditions for dairying were not improved over the 1949–1950 period. Beef prices were high in comparison with dairy products, the cost of mill feeds was heavy, and many dairy farmers were engaged in the temporarily more lucrative lumber industry at the expense of dairy production.[12]

Off-farm opportunities became more abundant and lucrative in the wake of World War II, which quickly led to many people abandoning farming as the primary source of their income in the fifteen years immediately following the War. The biggest exodus occurred between 1956 and 1961, when over half the rural population who had been farming ceased to do so, and the number of census farms decreased from 22,116 to 11,786.[13] It is reasonable to argue that this exodus from farming represents people voluntarily leaving farming for urban and industrial opportunities inside and outside the Maritimes.[14] The shrinkage in the number of New Brunswick farms from the late 1960s represents something different, with people being involuntarily driven out of farming by the changing political-economic conditions of agriculture. It is clear, moreover, from the province's own records that it has not been an idle bystander in the exodus from farming; on the contrary, it actively sought to encourage the "modernization" of agriculture and to create the economic conditions that led inexorably to concentrated ownership.

In 1967 when the New Brunswick Department of Agriculture was renamed the Department of Agriculture and Rural Development, it stated its mandate was "to encourage the establishment of economic farm units and efficient food production" while increasing "income and employment opportunities for rural people."[15] These goals were to be achieved by "enlarging and consolidating farm units" while at the same time increasing the number of employment opportunities in rural communities.[16] The latter meant, in practice, the promotion of food-processing factories in small towns. "Enlarging and consolidating farm units" can only be accomplished by either increasing the land base or having some families leave farming while their neighbours incorporate these farm operations into their own units, making themselves thereby into "bigger and more efficient" business enterprises. This approach was clearly also the goal of the Federal Government Task Force Report on Agriculture in 1969, which "recommended the elimination of smaller, unprofitable farms in favour of large, efficient units and even corporate farming in Canada to provide the massive capital needed for modern, cost efficient, mechanized agriculture."[17]

An examination of dairy and potato farming in New Brunswick shows that this goal was attained. The number of dairy and potato farms has steadily declined while the average production capacity of these farms has risen steadily. Specifically, dairy farms in the province declined from 19,751 in 1951 to 2800 in 1971, and again to 637 in 1991 and 496 in 1996. Meanwhile, the average number of cows per dairy farm increased from four to thirteen to thirty-seven to forty-three over the same time period.[18] Likewise, the number of potato farms in the province declined sharply from 20,004 in 1951 to 1212 in 1971, and again to 442 in 1991 and 439 in 1996; meanwhile the average acreage per potato farm increased from 2 to 59 to 115 to 123 acres.[19] With fewer farms producing more, milk production remained stable between 1971 and 1991.[20] Similarly, fewer potato farms are planting comparable acreages. For example, in 1961, 8190 farms in New Brunswick grew 54,165 acres of potatoes; while in 1996, 439 farms grew 54,064 acres of potatoes.[21]

One can only imagine that the government's true agricultural policy agenda of fewer but bigger farms would not have been well received. This is because their strategy has been to ambiguously manipulate the notion of the "family farm," presumably to avoid criticism of this policy. By changing the meaning of "family farming" while still continuing to use a term that remained a rallying cry for many rural people, the state could enlarge and consolidate farm units without a political backlash. These tactics were occasionally revealed explicitly, as in this 1974 statement from the New Brunswick Department of Agriculture:

> Alarmist stories about the impending disappearance of the family farm, vertical integration, and the take-over of the farming business by large corporations have little foundation in New Brunswick. It appears the family farm is likely to remain the basic form of production unit. The concept and philosophy of the family farm is to be preserved, *but its connotation must be altered* [my emphasis added]. To preface a program by the title "family farm" does not define the issue at hand.[22]

The "issue at hand" for the state and for agribusiness capital appears to have been how to strengthen family-owned farming enterprises that were large enough and business-like enough to meet the needs of the agri-food system, at the expense of smaller and more traditional family farms whose modes of farming emphasized feeding the family and serving local markets.

From its own perspective, the Hatfield government was trying to modernize agriculture through the promotion of more efficient family farms capable of making reasonable profits. At the same time, they were also trying to meet the increasing needs of New Brunswick's food-processing industry. The two goals seemed compatible since the elimination of small, "inefficient" family farms would pave the way for larger, more efficient operations that were capable of being reliable suppliers to the expanding processing industry. But this agenda would—and did—result in a shrinking farm community, which led to a political outcry. The government agreed to conduct an "Agricultural Resources Study" (ARS) that would investigate the state of agriculture in New Brunswick and propose an agricultural development plan for the province. However, the mandate of the ARS study itself shows the "dual character" of the provincial government's agribusiness strategy:

...to initiate a major study of all aspects of the management and utilization of the Province's agricultural resources. The overall objective of the Study is to find ways to promote the fullest use of agricultural resources in such a way as to maximize farm income, to strengthen the vitality of the family farm, to encourage new job creation in food processing industries and to increase food production.[23]

The study lasted from October 1974 to November 1977 and documents the state's interest in sustaining "family" farms while also promoting the growth of the food-processing industry—an industry which was and is dependent on ever-increasing amounts of raw material at ever-lower prices for its own sustained growth and profits. Therefore, in order to meet the processors' needs, the province encouraged farms to expand, mechanize, and modernize into "cost-effective commercial operations." A civil servant writing to the Agricultural Minister acknowledged that government policy was designed to push small farmers out of the industry:

Provincial and federal government policies have openly emphasized industrial development and the "rationalization" or reduction in the number of farms. The intent, actual and/or perceived, of many farm policies has been to entice farmers to produce food for a particular market (viz. processing industry, export market, urban population, etc.) without adequate long-range safeguards for the farmers' investment and continuing income.[24]

This attitude of triage for farmers was accompanied by policies which supported the growth of food-processing firms, upon whom the government had placed its hopes for economic development connected to agriculture. Food processing, not farming, was to be the future of "agriculture." A draft version of the Overview section of the ARS study makes this point:

In direct contrast to primary agriculture, food processing has enjoyed an uninterrupted steady growth since the early 1950s and the total contribution of agriculture related industries over the next decades could be one of the most significant factors in the development of the provincial economy.[25]

By the 1970s, as far as the government was concerned, farming was the tail of agriculture and food processing the dog. Farmers were to be suppliers to food-processing corporations, and farming simply the production of raw materials for the food factories.

It should not be surprising, in this context, that it was the food-processing industries in which the provincial and federal governments were investing large sums of money. This was especially true in the case of McCain Foods, who were becoming a New Brunswick success story as they expanded into a multinational food-processing company. The best summary of just how much public money was lavished on McCain Foods is found in the Senopi Consultants Ltd. report done in 1980 for the National Farmers Union. This report observes:

> The full extent of government hand-outs has never been revealed. However, it is known that the McCain group of companies for its operations in New Brunswick alone has received over $6.5 million in loans guaranteed by the Province of New Brunswick; over $9 million in bonds guaranteed by the Province; DREE grants of almost $8 million plus a no-interest loan of $1.5 million from the New Brunswick Industrial Finance Board; and a fixed tax agreement for the ten year period, 1965–1974, which amounted to a "tax loss" for the province or a "grant" to the company of $80,960.
>
> What is unknown is assistance the company got under smaller, less well-known government programs. Other hand-outs consist of government assistance of a less-obvious nature and ones to which a price tag cannot easily be attached. For example: the federal Agriculture Canada research station at Fredericton has laboured for years to come up with a good "processing potato" that is better suited to New Brunswick's short growing season than the "Netted Gem." The government-salaried scientists think they have the answer in the "Shepody"... Low provincially-legislated minimum wages for the non-unionized McCain plants; federal training-on-the-job programs to pay part of the seasonal labour costs; and government assistance for the export trade are just a few examples of the less obvious government assistance to the McCain organization.[26]

However, while McCain Foods and the food-processing industry in New Brunswick flourished, farm families increasingly found themselves caught in a cost-price squeeze.

The state and agribusiness corporations did not, however, want to put all farmers out of business. If they did the processing industries and corporations would have to do all the farming themselves and that would be more costly than buying the raw product from the farmer. McCain Foods, for instance, was very explicit about their dependence on potato farms:

> The farmers are not going broke, and we don't want them to go broke. If they go broke, McCain goes broke and vice versa.[27]

The problem is, evidence indicates that many farmers did go broke. In the early 1980s many farms that had expanded and mechanized on credit, at the behest of the food processors and the provincial government, found themselves in trouble as input costs escalated while commodity prices stagnated or fell. Ironically, it was often the smaller, "backward," more traditional farms that were better able to weather these economic conditions, since they tended to be more diversified and less indebted.

Despite this, the agricultural priorities introduced by the Hatfield government in the 1970s did not materially change with the landslide victory of the McKenna Liberals in 1987. Predictably, moreover, the advent of the Free Trade Agreement in 1988 did nothing to alter New Brunswick's agribusiness-oriented strategy. What can be found, indeed, in the Department of Agriculture's Annual Reports from 1988 through until the mid 1990s is language that suggests an attitude of "business as usual" and continuity with the policies of the past. In 1994, for instance, they reaffirm their commitment "to continue to support the family farm concept as the basic unit of production in the industry"[28]—when by this they mean corporate family farming as outlined above (i.e., families who are farming in a business-like way, as suppliers to corporate food processors). And their mission statement repeats the now familiar mantra:

> The goal of the Department of Agriculture is to encourage, facilitate and provide direction for the continual growth and development of a viable, competitive and environmentally sustainable agri-food system in New Brunswick.[29]

In the latter years of McKenna's Liberal government, though, it became increasingly clear they were no longer interested in "family farms"—whether they be traditional family farms or corporate family farms—but simply in businesses. This was manifest in New Brunswick Department of Agriculture and Rural Development publications that no longer referred to "family farms," farmers, or even *farm* businesses in their mission statements, or statements of objectives.[30] For example, in February 1998, the Department described their mandate as follows:

... To increase the level of economic activity in the agri-food industry and promote entrepreneurship and economic growth in New Brunswick.

- Provide clients with the appropriate tools for growth, development and increased self-reliance. Such as information systems, access to capital, risk management, training, technology and technical expertise;
- Maximize returns from the market; and
- Create a healthy "entrepreneurial environment" through the reduction of unnecessary regulations and other barriers to development.[31]

In the use of such language, the government of New Brunswick had decisively put aside any pretence of concern with "family farms," or indeed farms of any kind. Now, the provincial Department historically concerned with agriculture saw its mandate as promoting "the agri-food industry"; rather than serving farmers, they were serving "clients." Apparently there was no longer any need for euphemisms; but it did not bode well for farm families or their farms that the concept of farming had been dropped altogether.

Yet what is even more disturbing is that the new New Brunswick government of Premier Bernard Lord is no longer interested in agriculture at all. The Conservative government elected in the summer of 1999 has repeatedly argued there is a need for aggressive government restructuring, less spending, the elimination of government departments, and the general cutting of "excess" government services—this after eleven years of a Liberal government that followed this precise agenda. In its first budget, unveiled in March 2000, the Conservative government stunned the agricultural community when it proposed to completely eliminate the Department of Fisheries and the Department of Agriculture and amalgamate them into a new, leaner Department of Food Production. Perhaps, though, the farm community shouldn't have been so shocked, since food production has always been a code word for food processors—as opposed to food growers—in this province.

Farmers reacted swiftly and in surprising concert, sensing a dramatic shift in the ground under their feet. The farm community rallied quickly and took to the streets, demonstrating and protesting the proposed changes: both to the restructuring of the Department of Agriculture and Rural Development and to the deep and immediate cuts proposed to many programs that had assisted food growers in the past. After many meetings and confrontations between the province's farmers and government officials, the planned amalgamation was halted—at least for the time being. Nevertheless, many long-standing programs aimed at farming were cut, putting in jeopardy the financial security of farm families who have relied on these programs. Some of these cuts are now being phased in, rather than being swept away in one motion. But in the end this might amount to no more than death by a thousand cuts instead of one chop of the axe. Given the policy direction indicated by the Lord government, what seems likely is that farm families are going to be facing more and more pressures to "restructure" the ways that they farm and sell their produce, as we move into a more global economy.

What New Brunswickers—and other Canadians watching where this province's agricultural industry is heading—really need to be asking is what these proposed policy changes signal about the government's commitment to the existence of farming in the province. Are farmers in this province growing food for local markets? Or are they mostly growing "inputs" for the food-processing industry, at the lowest possible prices? Are they going to be competing with each other or with farmers in Maine, Idaho, or the Caribbean?

These are important questions, not least because in the past McCain Foods has not hesitated to import potatoes from Maine whenever they were cheaper than New Brunswick potatoes.[32] In the global economy, companies are moving their operations to wherever they can maximize profits, and it is no different in the food industry. If it is cheaper to grow food elsewhere and import it for final processing in locations closer to intended markets, it's easy enough to foresee that McCain Foods and their competitors will do this. Already few of us know where our produce comes from, and we have even less knowledge of the production history of the ingredients that go into our ready-made convenience foods.[33]

This agenda of increasing the food-processing industry's profits—growing dollars rather than growing food—affects not just the farm community, therefore; it affects everyone who eats convenience foods. The trends in New Brunswick described here should serve as a warning to all Canadians interested in agriculture, as well as those who care about the nature of the food they eat. Yet, while increasing numbers of consumers (especially in Europe) *are* very concerned about the food additives and genetically modified organisms increasingly present in the food they eat, the majority of us in North America seem to be embracing what Waxman[34] calls "take-it-or-leave-it eating"—i.e., we happily consume new prepared food products that the food processors and fast-food restaurants put in front of us. Our complacency in this respect may cost farmers their livelihoods, and us control over a very central part of our lives:

> All [processed and manufactured foods] are prepared by someone else, who is making the decisions on ingredients, flavor and texture. All three [foods in restaurants, ordering in, prepared and semi-prepared foods] represent food making that is beyond our control. When we adopt these, or a combination of these, as a significant proportion of our diet, we are truly eating in ignorance. When we abdicate in this fashion, we surrender yet another sector of our lives....[35]

If Waxman is right that this constitutes "cooking dumb and eating dumb" and that convenience foods "represent the lowest common denominator of taste,"[36] we are in the process of reaching the lowest common denominator in this province. Yet we seldom make the connections between our eating habits and the willingness of successive governments to "write off" small-scale agriculture in New Brunswick, in other provinces, and indeed in other countries. We need to understand that our readiness to leave what we eat to others—typically, multinational food corporations—has implications for everyone involved in food production, at any stage. By accepting "business as usual," we are endorsing a food system in which the multinationals will continue to offer us brand-name food products that are engineered for profit and little else; and we are *also* encouraging a food system in which independent farmers have little economic place and are inexorably being pushed off the land.

I grew up on what government officials would call a subsistence farm. Both my parents worked. We did not have a lot of money but we had a lot to eat: a lot of good, wholesome food that we either grew ourselves or bought from other local farmers. Not today. I still live in the community I grew up in, and the old farmhouses are occupied; however, the farms themselves are gone. I and my neighbours now depend on "super" markets for most of our food. Our gardens are much smaller, and we don't can or freeze enough to feed us until the next harvest. As our lifestyles change, valuable household skills are being lost, as well as tacit knowledge about gardening, food preservation, and preparation.

The way I see it, agricultural policies that support multinational food corporations over small farmers serving local markets constitute a step backwards, rather than progress. Why? Because as our food travels farther and farther to get to us, it's harder to know what exactly we are eating—both literally and metaphorically. How many pesticides and chemicals are we consuming when we eat? Are the farmers and workers now growing our food in other places (in Canada, the US, and Mexico) able to put enough food on their own tables? When food was grown in local communities for local markets such questions could be easily answered. No longer. As our knowledge of what we are eating and who grew and/or prepared it erodes, so too does our confidence in our food erode, along with the health of our rural communities. As a woman in my mid-thirties with a young child, this scenario scares me.

As I write in mid 2001, the Lord government may have been slowed, at least temporarily, in their agenda of promoting "the industry" rather than farmers. However, there is no evidence that they have abandoned it. In a province where food production has increasingly come to mean the manufacturing of "value-added" food products by processors like McCain Foods, with farming under-stood as little more than ensuring a flow of raw materials to those processors, it is entirely conceivable that a Department of Food Production might not encompass support for local farming at all. Whether we realize it or not it, the logic of the Lord agenda would support New Brunswick-based food processors importing their raw materials—i.e., the potatoes or vegetables traditionally grown by New Brunswick's farm families—from the cheapest international sources. And this is happening in part because citizens and consumers have become increasingly content to simply leave the decision-making to others.

I have argued in this paper that successive provincial governments in New Brunswick have supported food processing over food growing. Yet they have not acted alone. The federal government, the food-processing companies, other agribusiness corporations (seed and fertilizer companies, farm machinery companies), and even some farm families have supported and endorsed these policies. Food consumers have also done so indirectly, by filling their grocery carts with more and more processed food. As a result, we have been slowly dismantling our agricultural sector, and with it our ability to feed ourselves. It is time to re-evaluate what we are doing and what we are eating, and the conse-quences of our actions for rural Canada. When a province like New Brunswick, with a historically strong rural society (and even its own home-grown food-processing corporation!), can contemplate removing "agri-" from the scene altogether, it should be obvious that the business logic of industrial food production is in danger of ploughing under the "art" and practices of cultivating the land. This should give anyone who cares about rural life in Canada—or food in Canada—cause for concern. Food is one of the basic requirements for life. Is it desirable that such a basic part of any society as the food system be organized in such a way as to distance it from the control of the population? Is it acceptable that control of our food be vested in the hands of corporations whose primary interest is in profits, whatever the consequences for the environment or public health? Where does the privilege of profit end, and the public's right to confidence in our food system begin? These are the questions I think we as Canadians need to be asking and answering.

Notes

Part of this article encompasses research and work done for my doctoral thesis at the University of Edinburgh. I would like to thank the Doctoral Fellowships Division of the Social Science and Humanities Research Council of Canada, the Overseas Research Scholarship of the British Council, and the Women's Doctoral Fellowship of the New Brunswick Department of Advanced Education and Labour for financial support during my tenure at the University of Edinburgh.

1   Brewster Kneen, *From Land to Mouth: Understanding the Food System* (Toronto: NC Press Limited, 1989), 31.

2   Another exception here is Prince Edward Island, which continues to support a large rural farm base. See Ray D. Bollman and Brian Biggs, "Rural and Small Town Canada: An Overview" in Ray D. Bollman (ed.), *Rural and Small Town Canada*. (Toronto: Thompson Educational Publishing Inc., 1992), 1–44.

3   These figures are calculated from data obtained in the 1951 Census of Canada, Table 1 and Statistics Canada, Catalogue 95–324, *Agricultural Profile of New Brunswick — Part 2*. Statistics Canada (Ottawa, December 1992).

4   Statistics Canada, Catalogue 93–358–XPB, *Historical Overview of Canadian Agriculture*. Statistics Canada (Ottawa, July 1997), 18–19.

5   Carter describes a similar scenario in Northeast Scotland where farmers sold part of their crop for cash in order to pay taxes. In Carter's case the time period is much earlier— 1840 to 1914—when compared to New Brunswick where this was still occurring in the 1950s. See Ian Carter, *Farmlife in Northeast Scotland 1840–1914: The Poor Man's Country*. (Edinburgh: John Donald Publishers Limited, 1979).

6   See Ray D. Bollman, and Pamela Smith, *Integration of Canadian Farm and Off-farm Markets and the Off-farm Work of Women, Men and Children*. Statistics Canada Analytical Studies Branch, Research Papers Series, No. 16, (Ottawa, 1988); and Michael Trant, "Farm Producers, Past and Present' in *Canadian Journal of Agricultural Economics/ revue canadienne d'economie rurale*, Vol. 33, June 1986, 122–144.

7   According to Pugh, every year in Canada 4,000 families are forced out of farming. See Terry Pugh, "Index on Farming." *Canadian Forum*, Vol. LXX, No. 805, December 1991, 32.

8   Statistics Canada, Catalogue 95–175–XPB, *Agricultural Profile of the Atlantic Provinces*. Statistics Canada (Ottawa, July 1997).

9   It is worth noting that in the postwar years provincial governments often made a distinction between "census" farms and viable, "commercial" farms. For example, in 1971 there are 5,485 census farms in the province but the Department of Agriculture of the day argues there are only "2,603 commercial farms in New Brunswick in 1971," from New

Brunswick. "Family Improvement Program, Evaluation 1974." Planning and Development Branch, New Brunswick Department of Agriculture and Rural Development, (Fredericton, September 1, 1974), 14.

10   Darrell McLaughlin, *A Critical Review of Rural Sociology in Advanced Industrial Societies.* Unpublished BA thesis, St. Thomas University, Department of Sociology (Fredericton, April 1990).

11   This "pluriactivity" continues to be a part of New Brunswick agriculture especially on small farm holdings where farm families would be living far below the poverty line if they only relied on farm income. For example, over a quarter of the province's dairy and potato farms are extremely small operations producing a minute amount of the province's total milk and potato production. In 1991, 29 percent of New Brunswick's dairy farms milked between 1 and 17 cows accounting for a mere 4 percent of the province's total herd. See Statistics Canada, Catalogue 93–348 (Ottawa, 1992), 322–323. Similarly, 28 percent of the province's potato farms grew 1–17 acres of potatoes but only accounted for 1 percent of the province's total acreage. See Statistics Canada, Catalogue 93–348 (Ottawa, 1992), 296–297.

12   New Brunswick. *Department of Agriculture, 1951 Annual Report.* Queen's Printer for New Brunswick (Fredericton, 1951), 26.

13   Statistics Canada. *Agricultural Profile of the Atlantic Provinces.* Statistics Canada, Catalogue 95–175–XPB (Ottawa, July 1997).

14   This analysis is widely shared, and is made explicit in E.B. DeMerchant, *From Humble Beginnings: The Story of New Brunswick Agriculture*, New Brunswick Department of Agriculture and Rural Development and the New Brunswick Federation of Agriculture (Fredericton, 1983), 66.

15   New Brunswick. *Department of Agriculture and Rural Development, Annual Report 1967.* Queen's Printer for New Brunswick, (Fredericton,1967), 10.

16   Ibid., 35.

17   DeMerchant, op. cit., 66

18   Statistics Canada. *Historical Overview of Canadian Agriculture.* Statistics Canada, Catalogue 93–358–XPB op. cit., 18–19, 141.

19   Ibid.

20   Statistics Canada. *Agricultural Profile of New Brunswick — Part 2.* Statistics Canada, Catalogue 95–324 (Ottawa, December 1992), ix.

21   Statistics Canada. *Historical Overview of Canadian Agriculture.* Statistics Canada, Catalogue 93–358–XPB, op. cit., 18–19.

22   New Brunswick. "Family Improvement Program, Evaluation 1974." Planning and Development Branch, New Brunswick Department of Agriculture and Rural Development (Fredericton, September 1, 1974), 14.

23   New Brunswick. Report of the Agricultural Resources Study. Province of New Brunswick, November (Fredericton, 1977), 3.

24   David Malcolm, "New Entrants into Family Farm Enterprises in New Brunswick: A Report to the Minister of Agriculture and Rural Development," (Fredericton, May 1976), 4–5, archived material from the ARS study.

25   Taken from the draft version of the "Overview of Agriculture in the New Brunswick Economy," found in New Brunswick Agricultural Resource Study archive material, 8.

26 Senopi Consultants Ltd. *A Report on the Situation of New Brunswick Potato Farmers for the National Farmers Union.* Mimeo, May 1980, 37–39.

27 Harrison McCain as quoted in Stephen Branch, "McCain Foods Limited: Regional, National and Now Multinational," *The Atlantic Advocate*, January 1983, 11.

28 New Brunswick. *Department of Agriculture, Annual Report 93/94.* Queen's Printer for New Brunswick, (Fredericton, December 1994), 7.

29 Ibid.

30 New Brunswick Department of Agriculture and Rural Development web site, February 1998.

31 Ibid.

32 Karen McLaren, *Farmers, Feds and Fries: Potato Farming in the St. John Valley*, Round One pamphlet, No. 7, March 1977, 1–8.

33 Brewster Kneen, *Invisible Giant: Cargill and Its Transnational Strategies.* (Halifax: Fernwood Publishing, 1995).

34 Nahum Waxman, "Cooking Dumb, Eating Dumb" in Katharine Washburn and John Thornton (eds). *Dumbing Down: Essays on the Stripping of American Culture.* (New York: W.M. Norton and Company, 1996), 297–305.

35 Ibid., 307.

36 Ibid.

Globalization, Neo-liberalism, and Rural Decline

AUSTRALIA AND CANADA

Geoffrey Lawrence, Murray Knuttila, and Ian Gray

The European-style systems of agriculture imported into Australia and Canada were designed to provide cheap staples (wheat, lamb, and wool from Australia; fish, fur, timber, and wheat from Canada) to an industrializing Britain. To a large extent, then, primary production in both countries had a global focus, with most of what has been produced leaving the shores of both nations as raw, unprocessed products. The national policy adopted by successive Canadian governments during the late nineteenth century was an explicit attempt to foster national industrial development via protective tariffs, agricultural expansion, and the export of key staples, primarily cereal grains. This policy remained in effect until after the great depression when structural economic changes associated with the Canadian-American co-operative war effort began the process of continental economic integration. By the 1970s, Canadian governments and the business elites had essentially abandoned the initial objectives of the national policy. That is, until the mid 1970s production and distribution in both nations occurred under a mantle of protection, subsidization, and state regulation—something which has largely disappeared in recent decades. Rural communities were, to a limited extent, "planned" communities, with governments in both nations providing infrastructural support for railways, roads, schools, law courts, police stations, and other facilities and services. Such state involvement was consistent with the desire for spatial and social equity. Commitment to such ideals has now been replaced with a more narrow focus on free markets, "user pays" and "self help"—as part of neo-liberalism.

In many rural towns, government-employed service workers are now being dismissed or relocated, leaving those towns without an appropriate level of services and without a secure "middle-class" base from which to draw leadership and direction. The aged and other disenfranchised groups in inland rural towns are, in particular, disadvantaged by the removal of services. While governments are being targeted for having abandoned the needs of rural people, there is little evidence that, despite protest, political parties intend to alter their policies. In this chapter we argue that neo-liberal policies—which are the handmaiden of globalization—are leading not to a prosperous future for farmers but to economic and social polarization within rural society.

THE "FARM PROBLEM" AND GLOBALIZATION

For neo-liberal economists, the move to a more globalized world in which freer trade prevails is viewed as essential if agriculture is to prosper. Its current failure to prosper is believed to be a result of a combination of factors: the specific nature of traded agricultural commodities, low commodity prices, unfair world competition, and the way assets are "fixed" in farming.[1] The agricultural economists' approach to understanding the problem of farm viability focusses on the inevitable "pressure" that continued economic growth—viewed as essential for Australia's well-being—puts on the farm sector:

> The essence of the "farm problem" … is that economic growth causes
> net incomes in agriculture to increase less than those in the non-
> agricultural sector. The problem arises partly because of the nature of
> the demand farmers face … Demand for agricultural products does not
> respond a great deal to falls in prices, nor to rises in consumers'
> incomes. As an economy grows and national income increases, there is
> a decline in the proportion of extra income spent on food. Inevitably

then, the share of national income going to agriculture declines relative to the share going to the rest of the economy. In addition, the supply of agricultural commodities increases more rapidly than the demand because of technological change. The result of supply outstripping demand is that prices fall and farmers have to increase output to maintain income, which they do by adopting new technology, and the cycle goes on.[2]

Furthermore, many farmers cannot be "enticed" from farming because of a combination of lifestyle considerations and their inability to obtain fulfilling and well-remunerated off-farm employment (one reason for which is declining work options in rural regions—not only for the poorly educated, but increasingly for the better educated). The best they can do is to produce more output per input of labour—largely by utilizing new technology—or by increasing the scale of their operations.

> The ... economic forces that farmers confront add up to the conclusion that, with economic growth in the community in general, there will eventually either have to be fewer farmers ... or poorer farmers. The third option is for farmers to be subsidized by taxpayers and consumers. This option has been widely adopted in the USA and Western Europe.[3]

From the standpoint of neo-liberal economists only the first two scenarios are to be countenanced: the third is unacceptable because it involves state intervention, considered to lead to market distortion. This is despite the fact that the intensification of agriculture as well as persistent low income in agriculture has been implicated in continued environmental degradation;[4] that high stress levels and general social malaise are a feature of contemporary farming;[5] and that there is only faint hope of persuading competing nations to remove subsidies. The views of the neo-liberal economists, such as those quoted above, have salience for the debate in Canada where the abandonment of the producer subsidies embedded in the Crow Rate, the closure of railroad lines across the West, and the centralization of grain-handling facilities were all deemed necessary.

For those advocating a neo-liberal economic strategy, such actions are consistent with the logic of allowing the market to "decide" what is worth retaining and what must pass in the interests of progress. For neo-liberals, social arrangements are seen to flow logically and advantageously from the market. It is inefficient to assist producers who are not economically viable, nor is it desirable to seek to "save" country towns whose economies are in decline. Indeed, according to Gordon Forth of Australia's Deakin University, towns below 4000 people should be encouraged to die: "Many of these towns are going to go into decline, and the population will not only become smaller but poorer and increasingly disadvantaged."[6] Governments ought not to be involved in propping up small communities, and if market forces dictate that towns or regions must shrink, then so be it. This is a "natural" outcome that will move people and resources into more appropriate endeavours.

The argument above is, in modified form, the ideology that currently holds sway in Australia, and is coming to prominence in Canada, too. It is one which overlooks a number of factors: that the "free market" is a myth (and that in most nations economic decisions are greatly tempered by political and social considerations); that the attempts of governments to expose their farming industries to international competition only serve—in a world of continuing protection abroad—to disadvantage their agricultural producers rather than enhancing prospects for growth; that the "level playing field" is a metaphor promulgated to justify industry restructuring, but which results in de-industrialization; and that economic "signals" are only one set of signals which producers will take into consideration when making decisions about location and resource use.[7]

"Agri-food restructuring"—or, more broadly, "rural restructuring"—is the term used by sociologists to depict the forces that are altering the rural areas of the developed capitalist world. Agricultural/rural restructuring is concerned with an understanding of the place of local agriculture within a wider system of food production and distribution and of rural settlement within the wider global economy.[8] Farmers—increasingly under contract—are integrated more directly than in the past with transnational corporations (TNCs), and the TNCs themselves are becoming more prominent in agricultural marketing and supply. Most farmers continue to produce bulk commodities—no longer exclusively for statutory marketing boards, but for the TNCs. However, many farmers are seeking ways to "value-add" and "niche market" their products, and to respond to the demands of the so-called "green consumer."[9] Farmers are also becoming "pluriactive": working off the farm in greater numbers, as well as developing new kinds of income opportunities on their farms.

Thus, alongside dominant tendencies toward efficiency and productivity—the driving forces predicted, and lauded, by neo-liberals—smaller rural producers have found opportunities to stay in agriculture via the niche marketing of exotic fruits or native species, or by tapping into "postmodern" phenomena like ecotourism or farm stays. Indeed, as leisure and recreation begin to figure increasingly as economic options, some rural destinations (and operators) in both Australia and Canada are actively catering to this demand. For example, the provision of retirement homes, wetland tours, heritage festivals, or the staging of local cultural events has allowed some communities to move away from their dependence on agriculture and develop new "service" industries. However, this kind of "restructuring" is not occurring evenly throughout rural space. Some locations, advantaged by climate, proximity to coastal areas, or on the "tourist" path between (or close to) capital cities, appear to have benefitted differentially. The question we must ask is this: will the new income "opportunities" associated with restructuring suffice to counter those forces that are undermining family farm-based agriculture? And are these solutions realistic in all farming areas?

THE STATE AND THE "GLOBAL"

In line with global structural tendencies and neo-liberal doctrine, the state in Australia has sought to withdraw from direct support of industry (the winding back of tariffs, removal of direct subsidies, and other forms of protection). In deregulating the financial markets, in reducing support for industry, and in selling off government assets, Australian governments have actively sought to expose Australian producers to global trade regimes, ones based largely on the needs and interests of TNCs. One result of this is that many Australian rural regions have become "de-industrialised."[10]

In Canada, the shift from national to global economic development strategies appears even more pronounced, because it required the dismantling of a series of deliberate and conscious state measures historically designed to facilitate domestic development. It is important to note that there was an intermediate period during which the orientation of economic policy was continentalist, meaning oriented to the North American continent. The logic of the Allied war effort during World War Two led to joint and co-operative production, and as a result many Canadian companies became integrated into transnational networks of production and distribution, while others were simply bought by American-based multinationals. The ultimate outcome of the war effort was a Canadian economy that was integrated into US industry on an unprecedented scale. By the end of the war it appeared obvious to many business leaders in Canada that their best financial interests lay not in the pursuit of a domestic (that is, Canadian) development strategy, as had been envisioned by the founders and subsequent proponents of the national policy, but rather in the direction of continental integration.

Yet the implications of this shift in corporate and public economic development strategies for prairie agriculture were not immediately apparent, in part because of a series of unique historical developments. The emergence of what sociologist Harriet Friedmann refers to as the postwar international food regime resulted in a period of relatively high demand and prices for many agricultural products, especially cereal grains.[11] Canada was able to benefit from the postwar economic boom because US corporations operating in Canada benefitted from US government spending on Japanese and European reconstruction, the Marshall plan, and the military and space races. In addition, increased immigration, the baby boom, the pent-up wave of consumer spending, plus state spending on the required social infrastructures, all stimulated the economy. Several Prairie provincial governments attempted to use the boom in commodity prices and the development of raw material extraction industries to diversify their economies.[12] However, we now understand that during the 1950s and 1960s several key processes were underway, processes that would ultimately change the face of Prairie agriculture.

During the late 1960s the federal government instigated a major study into the future of Canadian agriculture. The study concluded that there were too many farmers in Canada and recommended that approximately two-thirds of them be eventually eliminated. During the controversy that followed many politicians disavowed themselves of the recommendations. Nevertheless, an important seed had been planted, namely that it was time to begin to look at the restructuring of Canadian, and in particular Western Canadian, agriculture. Throughout the 1970s and the ensuing decades, the financial structures of the Canadian economy also began to change, due to the relentless concentration of capital. This resulted in more and more sectors of the economy being controlled by a diminishing number of larger producers, increasingly organized along transnational lines, with operations and interests in many national jurisdictions. What followed in agriculture was the now-familiar instabilities in different commodity prices, closures in locally owned support industries (e.g., feed suppliers and packers), and the subsumption of "family farm" agriculture by large corporations.

It is apparent, indeed, that cereal grain and mixed Western agriculture will play a new and different role in the "globalization" agenda for Canada. At the start of the new millennium, and in the wake of the Canada–US free trade agreement and the North American Free Trade Agreement, it is clear that small independent landowners, including farm families seeking to maintain traditional modes of agricultural production, cannot count on support from agribusiness interests in their efforts to convince governments to assist them to stay in business. Quite the contrary. In Australia, recent governments have sought to ameliorate some of the worst effects of market forces on trade in agricultural commodities by endorsing the formation of new regional bodies to "exploit" new options. However, such bodies have been provided with only limited funding, and they have no legislative or statutory powers.

It might be asked, here, why should the state foster co-operation between business and government at a level "between" state and local governments? One answer is that rural local governments have been notoriously "backward" in seeking new production options, and the regional bodies are viewed as potential sources of new impetus. Another is that it recognizes that in a globalizing economy where capital is highly mobile, the "region" is increasing in prominence, as firms bypass traditional administrative structures in order to negotiate access to desirable regional spaces. However, while many Australian regions are desirable in terms of natural resources, labour costs remain much higher than in the developing economies to Australia's north. So, rather than locating in regional Australia, many TNCs are taking produce and sending it overseas for second or final stage manufacture. The "regional Australia" solution thus appears to be no solution at all—unless, of course, wage deregulation can provide rural/regional Australia with a comparative advantage over regions abroad. And wage deregulation—which is a euphemism for wage decline—might be expected to lead to increased polarization *within* countries, as those in the cities bargain for higher wages, while those in the countryside, desperate for jobs, accept lower-paid work. The significance of such a scenario for rural regions in Australia and Canada has only just begun to be researched. It would seem almost certain to create more disadvantaged rural spaces, as explained below.

IMPACTS OF, AND REACTIONS TO, NEO-LIBERALISM
Global economic forces—in concert with domestic neo-liberal policies—appear to be, at least in part, responsible for five distinct effects.

1. Economic decline in inland areas and the "fundamentalist back-lash"
In relation to Australian agriculture, in the ten years from 1985–86 to 1994–95, one in every twelve rural properties had disappeared (most were amalgamated

with other properties in an effort to increase viability). In 1994–95 Australia had 115,368 viable rural properties—defined as those producing $20,000 worth of on-farm produce in that year.[13] Among commodity groups, the dairy industry experienced the greatest decline in numbers (3,100 farms lost: an average annual rate of 2.2 percent). This was followed by wheat and other "broad-acre" cropping properties, where the number of farms dropped from 82,430 to 70,883 or by 1.7 percent per annum.[14] Losses in agriculture produced declines in other rural industries, and in rural populations:

> Areas of declining population were mainly in provincial, rural or remote areas. Reasons for decline included unemployment, the rural recession, contraction of government services and a drift of families and young people to capital cities for secondary school or tertiary education …With the loss of young people, many country regions (suffered) … problems associated with an ageing population profile and the need for more services for elderly people.[15]

Yet the rationalization of services is itself another factor in the downward spiral experienced by rural Australia. With governments withdrawing services and with many branch firms closing, people are migrating from country towns. Those moving are those most likely to find work elsewhere, leaving already-disadvantaged groups such as the aged and the undereducated to cope with the declining services.[16] There are exceptions to these patterns, notably in hinterland towns based on thriving mining operations. However, according to one observer, rural life in Australia is generally marked by "poorly performing local economies … declining employment opportunities; low and often inadequate household incomes; out-migration of youth; negative health outcomes associated with stress and low incomes … and reduced access to services …"[17] (for Canada, see Coates and Keating et al., this volume).

In this context of decline and threat, a disturbing feature of social life in rural (and, it is important to note, wider) Australia is the extent to which present economic problems are being attributed to ethnic and racial minorities. The actions of Aboriginal people seeking land rights, together with the increasing presence of Asians in the inner cities of state capitals, are viewed by some as causing a deterioration in the Australian way of life.[18] Former member for the federal seat of Oxley Pauline Hanson founded her One Nation party on the belief that Aboriginal people receive too much welfare and that Asian migration to Australia is too high. She complains that Australian jobs are being taken by

Asians and demands an immediate halt to further migrant intake from Asia. Her speeches in rural Australia have been very well attended—although, at times, with as many people protesting outside the venues as are listening to her reportedly racist speeches inside.[19] However, Hanson's Party—and Hanson's attitudes—should not be viewed in isolation. Other new political parties and groups—such as Australia First and the City Country Alliance—have also derided Australia's multicultural policy, condemned the pro-Aboriginal verdicts from the High Court, and opposed the tightening of gun laws. The Returned Services League, while not a political party as such, lobbies to have Asian migration reduced and is uncompromising in its dedication to the Australian flag and the Queen of England—powerful symbols of white Anglo-Saxon rule in Australia.

Similar attitudes and sentiments are, of course, heard today in parts of Western Canada, and indeed they were represented in the policies and public pronouncements (concerning both aboriginal rights and immigration) of the Western-based Canadian Alliance Party. Canada shares with Australia a history in which aboriginal peoples were dispossessed of their lands in order to make way for agricultural settlement and resource "development." Even though the Canadian government recognized aboriginal nations in the nineteenth century and signed treaties that gave a legal basis to Canada's takeover of the lands where they had historically lived, the legacy of this for aboriginal peoples has been much the same as that for Australia: destruction of their traditional economy and culture, misguided attempts at assimilation (including forcible placement of children in residential schools in the postwar decades), widespread prejudice and exclusion at the hands of the settler society, and generations of individuals and families severely damaged by these experiences.

First Nations peoples in Canada do enjoy some payments and tax exemptions as a result of treaty obligations. In addition, as in Australia, recent decisions of the Supreme Court have recognized the principle of aboriginal rights to historical territories. In this context, the federal government and some provinces—most importantly, British Columbia—have negotiated "modern" treaties that give territory, limited self-government, and financial subsidies (or compensation) to First Nations. However, just as in Australia, these settlements have provoked a backlash in at least some sectors of the Canadian population. And although this backlash is perhaps most acute in rural areas where the traditional economic bases of settler life (agriculture, forestry, and fishing) are threatened in various ways by "restructuring" (see Coates and Mandryk, this volume), it is certainly not confined to rural areas. Indeed, as Coates notes, the opposition Liberals in

BC (who became the government in June 2001) officially oppose the recently signed Nisga'a Agreement and the whole modern treaty process. Meanwhile, opposition to "special rights" for aboriginals (whether tax exemptions or exemptions from fishing restrictions) is a common theme in the rhetoric of Canadian Alliance MPs.

2. The de-traditionalization of rural society

De-traditionalization can be best understood as the disembedding of patterns of communal authority and custom by the intensification of consumer culture— itself a product of globalizing tendencies.[20] What is occurring is that global processes in commerce and popular culture are undermining older patterns of shopping and community interaction which fostered development of social capital.

In Australia in the mid 1980s—and following the impact of another "rural crisis"—it was clear that farming and rural people were greatly confused (and annoyed) at what many perceived to be the inability of the state to restore a stable "regime" of profit for rural/regional Australia.[21] Research has demonstrated that the social structures of farming—the roles and relationships which had been created and maintained within the system of family farming and which provided it with stability—are constantly being threatened by wider social and economic forces, as well as by the responses of farmers to those forces, specifically the taking of off-farm work.[22]

Off-farm work helped to keep the producers on the land; however, it also altered the capacity of people to engage in voluntary associations, increased stress in marital relations, and altered the social status of producers. Further, it placed new and unfamiliar demands on family members (often undermining the "conventional" and familiar roles of farming couples) and, for some, led to a run-down in farm capital and to environmental deterioration. These produced, in turn, anxiety about the future of the farm as a viable economic entity. Research has revealed the extent to which economic pressures produced conflicting requirements in family farm reproduction, undermining the co-operation that had been the foundation for action at the community level.[23] Similar pressures are manifest in rural communities across Canada (see Machum, Stirling, and Harder, this volume).

3. Removal of social capital from rural regions

People's ability to work together to develop community structures is crucial for social and economic progress. Social interaction, developed through trust and often occurring in a spontaneous or voluntary manner, is considered to be a major component in the success of both individual and community. If collective social capital is the basis of a democratic community, its diminution might be viewed as threatening or at least undermining democracy.[24] There has been a strong cultural tradition in both Australian and Canadian rural society based on maintenance of family-farm relations and viable local businesses. The degree to which voluntary community associations have been a fundamental plank of economic and social life in rural communities has been well described for the Australian situation.[25] As farm-family members increase the extent of their off-farm work, as their incomes from agricultural production fall, as rural dwellers lose jobs, and as those with more opportunity for geographical mobility leave, the ability of rural communities to take collective action is lessened (see Stirling, and Epp, this volume, for Canadian examples). Social capital is believed, in such circumstances, to have deteriorated, severely limiting the ability of communities to do the very things expected of them by neo-liberalism: that is, to be resourceful, "self-reliant," and to provide the intellectual wherewithal to regenerate their own future growth.

The point here is this: neo-liberal ideologies and policies in Australia and Canada are leading to the depletion of social capital at the very time that social capital is considered the key to future development. Rural regions that are unable to find within themselves the requisite leadership or entrepreneurial enterprise get labelled as "backward"; yet this is not because of any intrinsic backwardness, but rather because the state has seen fit to encourage the departure of the very kinds of people whose social skills might have contributed to regional economic growth. If rural communities are to be expected to gather sufficient collective resources to deal effectively with global processes, their social capital must be developed to a level sufficient for social action. Yet government stringencies that are imposed on regions regularly create divisions in local communities, often leading to a weakening, rather than a strengthening, of community social resources.[26]

4. Government promotion of "self help" in rural regions

As outlined above, successive state and federal governments in Australia have reduced expenditures by cutting services and curtailing infrastructural expenditure. Just as in Canada, there have been vocal—but not well-co-ordinated—efforts to politicize the impacts of these policies on regional communities. Given that voting patterns still suggest regional Australia is important in helping to decide which party will win an election—and in an effort to minimize regional disaffection—governments have set up various "task forces" to seek to understand the regional problem and its possible solution. The Kelty Report, commissioned by the former Federal Labor government, examined the problems of the regions. Kelty and his co-authors concluded that public and private investment was the key to regional growth, and recommended a 30-year infrastructure investment strategy, targeting almost all of the main areas of economic activity in regional Australia.[27]

However, Kelty also suggested that a necessary part of such a policy would be measures that "empowered" the regions. While this had a certain appeal—it appeared to give local people an opportunity to develop plans for their own destiny—there was very little said about exactly who would be empowered, by whom, in what way, and to what extent. The notion that regions should control their own destinies, particularly where responsibility is devolved but power and funding are not, can often "become an excuse for inaction by central governments." The present Coalition government in Australia has set in motion policies that lead to the withdrawal of state-funded economic activity from the regions. This has its parallels in Canada in the free-market policies of the Canadian Alliance Party, vigorously supported by neo-liberal citizens' groups like the Canadian Taxpayers Federation and the National Citizens Coalition, whose shared agenda is to scale back the redistributive role of the federal government in Canada and return many kinds of policy responsibilities—and revenues—to the provinces.

The point here is not that local "self help" is an unimportant ingredient in regional development, or that local initiatives are not to be praised. As many studies have shown, local initiatives backed up by state or industry support can be a catalyst for change.[28] It is, rather, that the ideology of "self help" has emerged with a new vigour, and at roughly the same speed at which the Keynesian welfare state is being dismantled. It is as if rural people are being encouraged to accept that it is their responsibility alone to develop the conditions for the future success of their farms and communities at the same time that governments are abrogating their former commitments to rural regions.

5. Continued environmental degradation

At present, the annual cost of environmental degradation to Australia is estimated to be some $2-billion, about half the net annual value of farm production, currently $3.9-billion.[29] Dryland salinity, the result of massive tree clearing, affects approximately 2.5 million hectares. Range land degradation caused by a combination of clearing, overgrazing, and the introduction of feral animals and woody weeds, affects some 44 percent of inland Australia, and about 12 percent of rangelands are now deemed "unrecoverable." The federal government currently spends some $500-million per annum on programs to reduce land and water degradation—a figure that both the conservative National Farmers' Federation and the more progressive Australian Conservation Foundation believe should be closer to $6-billion. What is being proposed is that the nation spend some $6-billion each year on a system which—as noted above—only produces $3.9-billion in annual net production. One might legitimately ask whether the continuation of agriculture makes sense, especially from the point of view of the economic logic embedded in neo-liberal theory.

The Australian government currently funds a number of important initiatives such as Landcare and catchment management, through specially designated federal funds. The extent to which Landcare and catchment management are simply ideologies that obscure the unsustainable character of present practices has been raised by a number of authors.[30] Others believe that some government commitment to better environmental practices—and indeed any attempt to bring rural producers closer to the other users of catchments—is more desirable than no commitment at all.[31]

Canada is home to an influential group of environmentalists who have called for the immediate reduction in environmental exploitation by the nation's resource-based industries. However, despite such enlightened advocacy, the erosion of prairie soils, agro-chemical pollution, waterway destruction, and a host of other ecologically damaging processes—many of which have been directly linked to corporate farming systems—continue apace.[32] Fish stocks have been, in some areas, depleted to the point of extinction, while forests continue to be cleared at an unsustainable rate. Such "eco-hostility" is seen to be promoted, rather than reduced, under a regime of globalization.[33]

THE NEO-LIBERAL EXPERIMENT IN AUSTRALIA AND CANADA
In this chapter we have, in a "broad-brush" fashion, attempted to paint a picture of two nations progressing enthusiastically down the globalization path. Policies of both nations have been fashioned by neo-liberal thinking, and this has lead to governments withdrawing from many forms of economic activity (like agricultural marketing boards), placing their faith in the ability of the marketplace to best determine resource allocation. However, given that that marketplace is a global one, this means leaving decision-making with the large TNCs that dominate global trade. The rural social consequences of the "globalization" of

Australian agriculture and rural society have not been hard to describe, and include:

- exacerbation of trends toward long-term population loss in many of Australia's inland rural areas combined, increasingly, with the development of postmodern service economies (recreation, leisure, retirement) in the more climatically favourable and coastal rural regions;
- decline of social capital in rural regions, leading to a situation in which country towns and rural areas do not appear to have the same political or economic "clout" as in earlier times;
- the de-traditionalization of rural society, leading to uncertainties about change and direction, and to the demise of some of the social institutions (clubs, societies, sports) that once brought community members together;
- the growing promotion by the political Right of an ideology of "self help" in regions undergoing restructuring (and, associated with this, an allocation of responsibility to the local community, if or when it is not able to compete economically); and
- the scapegoating of racial and ethnic minorities who are blamed for the economic problems of the nation.

As far as Canada is concerned, it is important to trace current problems in rural society to the move from a national to a continental economic development strategy after the Second World War. While there was no immediate impact on the relationship between Western agriculture and the larger economy, important changes were underway. Rapid postwar mechanization in agriculture and growing divisions between the interests of large and small farmers began to change the nature of both farming and the farm community. On the national scene, postwar tendencies toward continental integration resulted in more and more Canadian companies becoming incorporated into US conglomerates whose markets were continental and global. By the late 1960s it was apparent that the relationship of Canadian capital to the independent Western farmer had fundamentally changed. The further realignments of the 1970s and 1980s ushered in the current phase, in which the governments cite ideological and practical rationales for massive cutbacks, deregulation, and rationalization in agriculture, as in other areas. In the current era, the dominant logic that informs much public and private discourse, as well as public policy, is the logic of capital accumulation on a global scale. In this logic, the presence of thousands of farms—and farm families—on the Western plains is no longer viewed as practical or desirable (see also Machum's account of New Brunswick, this volume).

It should also be acknowledged, however, that there are some positive sides to the tendencies mentioned in this chapter. For example, an important factor in the de-traditionalization of rural society has been the introduction of new satellite and computer technologies which, together, have the potential to bring rural society closer to the metropoles in terms of tastes, values, and social and economic expectations. And as local culture and power structures might wane, new opportunities exist—at least for those who can afford the new technologies—for links with wider culture. Moreover, the ideology of "self help," when combined with the associated realization that the state is unwilling or unable to act to assist rural towns, might provide the impetus for regional/global connections—the very kinds of links which some writers have suggested are crucial for future development within nation states.[34] Finally, a number of postmodern developments have the potential to assist rural-based populations. These developments include the growth of tourism (especially cultural and ecotourism); the capturing of overseas (niche) markets for primary products; evidence that consumers at home and abroad are increasingly demanding fresh and "green" foods; and the re-definition of rural space as a place of consumption and leisure (see, however, Urquhart and Whitson, this volume).

Just what sorts of futures rural regions of Australia and Canada will have will most certainly be determined by the extent to which neo-liberal policies are enacted and to what extent they are either embraced or resisted. At this time, the rhetoric of widespread economic and social benefits for rural people supposedly emanating from a more market-driven system is largely hollow.

Notes

1 B. Malcolm, P. Sale, and A. Egan, *Agriculture in Australia: an Introduction* (Oxford: Melbourne, 1996)

2 Ibid., 57.

3 Ibid., 58.

4 J. Gow, "Farm Structural Adjustment-an Everyday Imperative," *Rural Society* 4(2), 1994, 9–13.

5 I. Gray, G. Lawrence, and T. Dunn, *Coping with Change: Australian Farmers in the 1990s* (Wagga Wagga: Centre for Rural Social Research, Charles Sturt University, 1993); F Vanclay and G. Lawrence, *The Environmental Imperative: Eco-social Concerns for Australian Agriculture* (Rockhampton: CQU Press, 1995); A. Conacher and J. Conacher, *Rural Land Degradation in Australia* (Oxford: Melbourne, 1995).

6 *Courier Mail,* 5 July 2000.

7 S. Rees, G. Rodley, and F. Stilwell (eds) *Beyond the Market: Alternatives to Economic Rationalism* (Sydney: Pluto, 1993); J. Stewart, *The Lie of the Level Playing Field: Industry Policy and Australia's Future* (Melbourne: The Text Publishing Company, 1994).

8   D. Symes and A. Jansen (eds) *Agricultural Restructuring and Rural Change in Europe* (Wageningen: Agricultural University, 1994); T. Marsden, J. Murdoch, P. Lowe, R. Munton, and A. Flynn, *Constructing the Countryside* (London: UCL Press, 1993).

9   A. Ferguson, "A Case Study in Decentralisation and Rural Economic Development: An International Air Freight Export/Import Terminal at Parkes, NSW," Paper Presented at the *Rural Australia: Toward 2000 Conference*, Charles Sturt University, Wagga Wagga, 2–4 July; I. Gray and G. Lawrence, *The Future of Regional Australia: Escaping Global Misfortune?* (Cambridge: Cambridge University Press, Cambridge, 2001); G. Lawrence, *Futures for Rural Australia: from Agricultural Productivism to Community Sustainability*, Inaugural Address (Rockhampton: RSERC, 1995).

10 F. Stilwell, *Reshaping Australia: Urban Problems and Policies* (Sydney: Pluto, 1993); F Stilwell, *Chaning Track: a New Political Economic Direction for Australia* (Sydney: Pluto, 2000).

11 H. Friedmann, "The Political Economy of Food: A Global Crisis," *New Left Review*, 197, Jan-Feb, 1993, 29–57.

12 J. Richards and L. Pratt, *Prairie Capitalism: Power and Influence in the West* (Toronto: McClelland and Stewart, 1979).

13 *Australian*, June 25, 1997, 3.

14 Ibid.

15 B. Kelty, *Developing Australia: a Regional Perspective*, A Report to the Federal Government by the Taskforce on Regional Development, Volumes 1 and 2, (Canberra: National Capital Printing, 1993).

16 B. Cheers, *Welfare Bushed: Social Care in Rural Australia* (Aldershot: Ashgate, 1998).

17 R. Fitzgerald, "Sustainable Development and Rural Structural Adjustment," in Council of Social Service of NSW (ed.) *Rural Communities Looking Ahead: Papers, Abstracts and Notes from the NSW Rural Policy Conference* (Sydney: NCOSS, 1996), 42–48.

18 A. Davidson, *From Subject to Citizen: Australian Citizenship in the Twentieth Century* (Cambridge: Cambridge University Press, 1997).

19 *Australian*, May 17, 1997, 6.

20 P. Heelas, "On Things Not Being Worse, and the Ethic of Humanity," in P. Heelas, S. Lash and P. Morris (eds) *Detraditionalization: Critical Reflections on Authority and Identity* (Massachusetts: Blackwell, 1996), pp. 200–222; P. Morris, "Tradition and the Limits of Difference," in P. Heelas, S. Lash, and P. Morris (eds) *Detraditionalization: Critical Reflections on Authority and Identity* (Massachusetts: Blackwell, 1996), 223–249.

21 G. Lawrence, *Capitalism and the Countryside: the Rural Crisis in Australia* (Sydney: Pluto, 1987).

22 Gray et al. op. cit.

23 I. Gray, E. Phillips, P. Ampt and T. Dunn, "Awareness or Beguilement? Farmers' Perceptions of Change," in P. Share, (ed.) *Communication and Culture in Rural Areas*, Key Papers 4, Centre for Rural Social Research (Wagga Wagga: Charles Sturt University, 1995), 53–70

24 E. Cox, *A Truly Civil Society: the 1995 Boyer Lectures* (Sydney: ABC Books, 1995); L. Gain, "Equity in Social Policy," in Council of Social Service of NSW (ed.) *Rural Communities Looking Ahead: Papers, Abstracts and Notes from the NSW Rural Policy Conference* (Sydney: NCOSS, 1996), 19–23.

25 I. Gray, *Politics in Place: Social Power Relations in an Australian Country Town* (Cambridge: Cambridge University Press, 1991; G. Poiner, *The Good Old Rule: Gender and Other Power Relations in a Rural Community* (Sydney: Sydney University Press, 1990); R. Wild, *Heathcote* (Sydney: George Allen and Unwin, 1983).

26 I. Gray, D. Stehlik, G. Lawrence, and H. Bulis, "Impacts of the Drought on Australian Rural Communities: Is It Socially Binding or Socially Divisive?" Paper presented at *Windows on the World: 28th International Conference of the Community Development Society*, Melbourne, 22–24 July.

27 Kelty, op. cit.

28 Ibid.

29 *Australian*, 18–20 August 2000, 23.

30 M. Bailey, "Landcare: Myth or Reality?" in S. Lockie and F. Vanclay (eds) *Critical Landcare*, Key Papers Series 5 (Wagga Wagga: Centre for Rural Social Research, Charles Sturt University), 129–142; R. Haworth, "Fine Sentiments vs Brute Actions: the Landcare Ethic and Landclearing," in S. Lockie and F. Vanclay (eds) *Critical Landcare*, Key Papers Series 5 (Wagga Wagga: Centre for Rural Social Research, Charles Sturt University), 165–174; S. Lockie, "What Future Landcare? New Directions Under Provisional Funding," in S. Lockie and F. Vanclay (eds) *Critical Landcare* (Wagga Wagga: Centre for Rural Social Research, CSU), 227–38.

31 A. Campbell, *Landcare: Communities Shaping the Land and the Future* (Sydney: Allen and Unwin, 1994); A. Carr, "Innovation and Diffusion: Landcare and Information Exchange," in S. Lockie and F. Vanclay (eds) *Critical Landcare*, Key Papers Series 5 (Wagga Wagga: Centre for Rural Social Research, Charles Sturt University), 201–216.

32 I. Wallace and R. Shields, "Contested Terrains: Social Space and the Canadian Environment," in W. Clement (ed.) *Understanding Canada: Building on the New Canadian Political Economy* (Montreal: McGill-Queen's University Press), 386–408.

33 Ibid.; and J. McMurtry, *Unequal Freedoms: the Global Market as an Ethical System* (Toronto: Garamond Press, 1998).

34 M. Featherstone, S. Lash and R. Robertson (eds) *Global Modernities* (London, Sage, 1995); S. Lash and J. Urry, *Economies of Signs and Space* (London: Sage, 1994).

PART II

Resource Towns
and Recreation

Northland

THE PAST, PRESENT, AND FUTURE OF NORTHERN BRITISH COLUMBIA IN AN AGE OF GLOBALIZATION

Ken Coates

In August 1994, Queen Elizabeth came to Prince George to open the new University of Northern British Columbia. In the speeches that marked that auspicious occasion, politicians and community leaders spoke of the renaissance of Northern British Columbia and of the region's promising future. In previous decades, the North had endured a series of booms and busts, most noticeably a resource-based boom that ran through much of the 1960s to 1980s. The establishment of UNBC represented a great success story for the North, for the university was created over the objections of many southern interest groups and following a sustained and systematic effort at northern co-operation. The university represented the coming of a new age, a sign that the North has matured as a region, and that a new economy, more self-contained, less cyclical, and more technologically based, could emerge in the region.

Since the opening of UNBC in 1994, the Northern British Columbia economy has been battered by crises in the forest industry, divided by debates about First Nations rights and treaties, and the focus for intense discussion about the balance between environmental protection and resource development. The future of Northern BC appears, at the turn of the century, to be yet another promoters' pipe dream, the short-term prosperity of the forestry boom fading quickly from view. The university has succeeded more than all but its most optimistic supporters argued, but research centres and an influx of southern students have not yet offset the economic losses associated with the decline in the logging industry and the general malaise that has settled over the region.

The North's challenges for the twenty-first century are considerable: adjusting to the reality of First Nations self-government and treaty settlements, coping with the continued transitions in the resource economies, addressing long-standing problems such as the mobility of the non-aboriginal population, ethnic tensions, the difficulties faced by one-industry towns, and the unavoidable realities of distance, isolation, and an extreme climate. To this daunting list can be added the growing economic and social gap between Northern and Southern British Columbia, conflict between developers and environmentalists, limited regional influence in provincial politics, inter-community rivalry, and the "separatist" impulses of the Northeast (Peace River district). Northern BC retains many key advantages, including its considerable natural resource base, the attractions of the Northern "wilderness," and the revitalizing and newly empowered First Nations communities, but it continues to face formidable difficulties.

The experience of Northern British Columbia mirrors that of many resource-dependent and rural parts of Canada. The region has a considerable amount in common with the rural areas of the Prairie provinces and the vast Canadian mid-North. Issues that animate debate in Northern BC are common across most of rural Canada. Just as mechanization and corporate concentration have affected Prairie farm communities, so have these processes shaped the destinies of Northern logging towns. For many decades, the agricultural Prairie West has tended to view its problems in isolation, seeing them as part of the turmoil in global agriculture. While there is value in this understanding, it is also vital that agricultural and non-agricultural sections of the country begin to identify common problems, challenges, and opportunities. There is a political angle to this assertion as well. If the rural constituencies in Canada, including agricultural and non-agricultural areas alike, were to identify common interests, they could combine into a formidable national political force. To date, however, this has not happened.

Northern British Columbia, cocky and confident in the 1960s and early 1970s, faces dramatic changes and appears to be losing control of its destiny. Tumbler Ridge, only a decade ago a showpiece for government-private sector and Canada-Japan economic co-operation, is in the process of closing down its coal mines. The "fire sale" of local homes attracted national attention to the plight of single-industry towns, but less attention has been given to the downstream impact of this closure on other communities all the way from Dawson Creek, near the Alberta border, to Prince Rupert, on the Pacific Coast. Prince Rupert has been reeling from a series of successive difficulties, ranging from financial problems at the local pulp and paper mill to struggles between Canadians and Americans over salmon rights. The fishing industry on the Northwest Coast faces numerous challenges, caused by historic overharvesting of resources and harsh disagreements between industry representatives, First Nations leaders, and governments over the allocation of harvests and fishing seasons. The realities of the early twenty-first century appear to be harsh ones, as provincial and federal governments retreat from their former activist approach to regional development and as foreign trading partners find cheaper and more amenable sources of raw materials (which means without strong labour unions or environmental controls). Prospects for a return to prosperity appear dim, at best, and communities throughout the region struggle to identify opportunities for economic growth and job creation.

If there is any doubt about globalization bringing mixed blessings, Northern British Columbia is an excellent laboratory to test the impact of contemporary worldwide economic, political, and ideological influences. It has become a battleground between First Nations concepts of collective rights and Reform Party/Canadian Alliance views of individual freedoms. Aboriginal groups from the region have both fed and fed off the global indigenous-rights movements, finding support and encouragement as far away as New Zealand and Scandinavia and supporting indigenous groups in Russia and Central America. International investors, particularly from Japan, poured millions of dollars into regional development projects and bought up a significant percentage of regional resource production. But declining interest and the insistence that Canadian firms match international prices has added to labour–management strife, forced the closure of several industrial plants, and otherwise caused economic calamities across the North.

The North's current situation illustrates the difficulties of sustaining a resource-based economy in the late twentieth century. The arrival of coastal and overland fur traders in the late eighteenth century brought profound disruptions to the regional order and established the foundation of Western geographic knowledge, European assumptions, and visions of future resource wealth that would govern the region in subsequent generations. The BC gold rush of the 1850s attracted a surge of prospectors and developers into the central part of the region and, in subsequent years, the gold miners dispersed more widely in search of the next major strike. The coming of the railways, particularly the completion of the Grand Trunk Pacific in 1914, opened large portions of the region for resource development, as did the expansion of commercial fishing along the Northwest Coast. Miners and other developers sought to exploit the evident bounty of the Northern rivers, valleys, and mountains. However, none of these as yet small-scale ventures would vault the northern part of the province into prominence.

Northern British Columbia's time came, in economic terms, following World War Two. Until that time, First Nations experienced relatively little competition for access to the land and harvestable resources of the region. There were only small pockets of non-aboriginal settlement, and these communities generally co-existed reasonably well with the First Nations population, largely through separation. However, because of the postwar resource boom, particularly the development of the interior logging industry, the government built new roads to open the region for development and extended the PGE Railway to Dawson Creek. Companies opened sawmills throughout Northern BC. The development of the pulp and paper industry also drew thousands of plant workers, loggers, and contractors into the region. Finally, the global demand for cheap raw materials resulted in the opening of a series of mines. Entire new towns sprang into being at sites like Granisle and Cassiar. The North's population surged, growing faster between 1950 and 1970 than the province, and indeed the country at large.

There seemed, at the time, no end to the resource-induced prosperity. W.A.C. Bennett's grandiose and controversial Wenner-Gren/Rocky Mountain Trench proposal called for extensive hydroelectric and transportation development in the region. Although this plan fell through, BC Hydro proceeded with the W.A.C. Bennett Dam and Alcan constructed a hydroelectric system at Kemano and opened a massive aluminum smelter at Kitimat. The discovery of oil and gas in the northeast also sparked an exploration and development boom in the Fort St. John area, and resulted in the construction of a gas pipeline to the south.

The resource boom slowed and even stalled in the 1970s. What seemed like a temporary delay in the race toward economic prosperity, however, dragged on. Mines that opened with a flourish in the 1950s and 1960s neared the end of their productive lives. Consolidation in the logging, sawmill, and pulp and paper sectors forced closures. The provincial government, hoping that the downturn was temporary, primed the pump by investing in major resource projects, particularly the extensive and controversial northeast coal industry. By the 1990s, the resource boom had long since passed its peak. Communities stabilized and, in some instances, declined and faded, modern-day versions of Barkerville.

Throughout the development period, it is noteworthy that Northern British Columbia lacked a clear presence in provincial affairs. The continued growth and prosperity of the Vancouver-Victoria region and the growing importance of the southern interior largely masked the economic and social difficulties in the northern half of the province. The North had had its promoters—T. "Duff" Pattullo in the 1930s and W.A.C. Bennett (who headed south from the Peace River country to the Okanagan) in the 1950s and 1960s—but no one stepped forward to take their place. The province's power bases lay firmly in the south, in the union halls and investment offices of Vancouver for the most part, and regional politicians rarely figured prominently in provincial affairs.

The North had, of course, generated enormous returns through the postwar boom. Yet little of this money stayed long in the region. Most of the major investments came from large national or international firms, and the profits from northern resources were typically repatriated quickly to southern hands. Some of the firms, particularly Alcan at Kitimat, invested in their host communities and regions, but most of the companies looked southward. Similarly, many of the individuals who profited from the development boom, and who made personal fortunes from road construction, logging, or mining activities, followed the time-honoured Northern tradition and moved south with their fortunes. Meanwhile, First Nations had experienced substantial dislocations as a result of the resource boom and found their communities in considerable social and cultural difficulty.

ECONOMIC DISTRESS AND TRANSFORMATION

The North's current economic and social condition reveals the contemporary manifestation of long-term reliance on the resource sector. Declining prices for commodities have combined with growing international competition, a depleted resource base, and intense debates over environmental protection and First Nations rights to slow regional development. The once-vaunted forest industry that brought prosperity and growth to the area has fallen on difficult times. Plant closures, consolidations, slow-downs, and layoffs have become the norm, as have routine appeals to the provincial government for emergency loans and assistance schemes.

The North currently faces a very uncertain future. At one extreme lies the continued strength, but uncertainty, of northeast oil and gas. At the other lies the Cassiar "syndrome," the once lively company town built around an asbestos mine that was closed and completely dismantled. A similar fate has befallen the coal-mining town of Tumbler Ridge; although like other communities before it, Tumbler Ridge is attempting to re-market itself as a retirement centre and attract new industry. In July 2000, the mining company began selling off homes at cut-rate prices in an attempt to attract interest. Many of the companies that have continued to do well have resorted to major investments in technology, which in turn have resulted in significant reductions in the local workforce. There has been some attempt to promote tourism and to capitalize on the region's natural beauty, but this initiative has enjoyed little success.

To many non-natives in the North, the economic uncertainty is tied to First Nations land claims. Critics of the contemporary treaty process argue that the lengthy delays in treaty negotiations complicate already difficult and complex resource development procedures. Further, the 1997 Delgamuukw decision on aboriginal harvesting (potentially supported by the 1999 Marshall decision by the Supreme Court) and the agreement signed with the Nisga'a of the Nass River valley have established new rules for resource development, based on substantial First Nations participation in the process. To supporters of the First Nations efforts, the treaties will establish a more stable and sustainable foundation for regional economic development. To opponents, the treaty process, as well as the terms of final agreements and court decisions, only serves to frighten off potential investors and thus contribute to the region's economic malaise.

The North is in economic difficulty and, as a consequence, the regional society is experiencing hard times as well. Relations between First Nations and non-native people ebb and flow. Along the coast, concern about race-based fisheries has generated hard feelings and antagonism. In other Northern communities, discussions at regional advisory committees and treaty advisory committees have helped reduce tensions and misunderstandings. On a broader scale, the resource economy has, for several decades, produced high incomes for men with relatively little technical or advanced education, thereby providing a stable and prosperous foundation for communities across the region. That foundation is weakening, as lay-offs and wage rollbacks, cyclical slowdowns, and labour-saving resource-extraction technologies together reduce the future prospects for blue-collar workers and undercut local economies.

The challenges, to put it simply, are formidable. Northern British Columbia was at the front of the wave of postwar prosperity. However, the same dependence on resources that brought high returns from the 1950s to the 1970s now ensures that the region is on the leading edge of the economic dislocation that is affecting much of rural Canada. As many analysts have argued, the sharp devaluation of the Canadian dollar relative to the United States has only served to postpone the reckoning. The North's resources circulate in a volatile and uncertain global economy. Markets that once seemed assured are being lost to cheap competitors from Chile and Russia, or are falling to more sophisticated producers in Sweden and Australia. High wages used to draw workers and their families into the North, and indeed resource developments once spurred the construction of entire company towns, bringing flow-through benefits to the entire region. Now, stagnant or declining incomes, coupled with increasing costs, force many out of the region, while with little fanfare, most companies are shifting to fly-in camps, using workers from southern cities and increasing their own flexibility to expand or contract operations. This means, in turn, that much of the income earned working on these projects is spent around the province, bringing almost as much return to the Vancouver area as to Northern regions.

First Nations land claims are, at once, an opportunity and a threat. They will, when completed, bring millions of dollars into the region and, if other aboriginal settlements are a guide, much of this money will be reinvested locally or provincially. The agreements will bring certainty to the resource sector, answering a long-standing corporate complaint about the process. It is as yet unclear how national and international companies will respond to expanded First Nations ownership, however, and it may take several decades before relations between developers and First Nations permit orderly and systematic development. Furthermore, there are doubts about the long-term viability of many land claims-based economies, and questions about the ability of some First

Nations communities to rise to the challenges of self-government. The first major land claims agreement signed with the Tainui people of the Waikato District of New Zealand, in 1995, has quickly unravelled, amidst internal charges of professional incompetence. As much as $40-million of a $170-million settlement has been lost in the first 5 years.[1]

Thus, the North is becoming an angry, isolated, and disenfranchised place. Ethnically, it is developing along a very different path than the rest of the province, with relatively few Asians moving into the region. As multiculturalism takes firmer hold in the political arena—witness the debates surrounding the NDP leadership process and the selection of Ujjal Dosanjh as the first Indo-Canadian premier in Canadian history—the North may find itself further separated from the rest of the province. Predictably, moreover, economic distress is producing great personal frustration, which is often expressed as anger at politicians, the bureaucracy, First Nations, and national policies (see also Lawrence et al., this volume). Bitterness is a weak foundation for regional co-operation, but it often surfaces in Northern debates. Add to this the absence of a clear and consistent political voice, very limited urban interest in Northern concerns, intense inter-community rivalries in the North, and one sees a region falling into the politics of despair. Demands for subsidies, special programs, immediate government action, and a halt to those influences (environmentalism and First Nations rights) that are seen to interfere with local prosperity sound more like the voices of Canada's poorer regions than the confidence and independence typically associated with BC and Alberta.

SOURCES OF POPULATION GROWTH

Even a quick look at relevant demographic and financial information reveals the extent to which British Columbia is developing along several separate streams.[2] Northern BC is sharply divided from the rest of the province, and the divisions are becoming more pronounced, not less so. Northern BC's population growth originates from very different sources than that of BC as a whole. In the North, First Nations population growth is a major contributing factor, and aboriginal people will form an ever-larger percentage of the total population over the years (as is occurring in Saskatchewan and Manitoba). In addition, most of the other growth in the interior of BC comes from interprovincial migration; very little is attributable to increased international migration. The population growth of the Lower Mainland, in contrast, is driven by both international and interprovincial migration. Vancouver and area, as a consequence, is becoming more international and more connected to the global economy, while northern regions are remaining substantially Canadian, with fewer ethnic and personal financial ties to other parts of the world.

Although First Nations issues are province wide in scope, the issues take on greater demographic importance in the North. Aboriginal people make up a sizeable percentage of the regional population and this percentage is forecast to grow dramatically in the coming years. As of 1996, the province-wide aboriginal population stood at 139,000 out of 3,724,500. In the North, the proportions were much more substantial (Cariboo, 12,254 out of 165,449; Nechako, 6220 out of 43,033; North Coast, 18,330 out of 68,413; North East, 6025 out of 62,333). The Northern percentages will increase in the years to come, while the Lower Mainland's surging population will demographically marginalize that area's relatively small aboriginal population.

Conversely, Northern BC is not attracting Asian immigration—and the investment that has accompanied it—to the same degree as the rest of the province. In the south, Asian connections have been one foundation for the area's expanding economy; but this does not, for the most part, extend into the North. Census data (total ethnic single response) again confirms a pattern of growing cultural differences. In not a single sub-region of the North are Asian cultures represented among the top five groups. For BC as a whole, however, both Chinese (third largest group) and East Indian (fifth largest) are among the top five. In all of the northern areas, in contrast, First Nations figure prominently (topping the list in the North Coast district), while they have a much smaller presence in the province as a whole. This means that, in ethnicity as in other areas, the face of Northern BC will become increasingly different from the rest of the province. It also suggests that the northern region is not as globally connected or culturally diverse as the rest of the province. Over time, if these trends continue, the cultural and ethnic chasm between Northern BC and the rest of the province will grow wider still, and these differences are likely to be reflected in provincial political and economic affairs.

OTHER DEMOGRAPHIC REALITIES

There are other aspects of the region's social profile that are important to note. Northern British Columbia has long been a mobile society, particularly among non-aboriginal people. Young adults have often been attracted to the region by the prospects of high income and easily found employment. Just as pronounced, however, has been the out-migration of older adults and seniors, who plan to spend their time (and the money that they earned in the North) in warmer southern climates. The long-established pattern of Northerners leaving the region for southern BC is revealed in the age profile for the Northland. Each sub-region in the North has less than 7 percent of its population over 65 years old. For Greater Vancouver, the number is over 12 percent, and the figure stands at over 22 percent for the Okanagan.

In addition, regional employment has suffered sharp declines in recent years. Unemployment rates have not risen as dramatically, in part because Northern unemployed workers have tended to leave the region for higher employment areas (principally southern BC and Alberta). Yet where unemployment in 1971 was one percent below the provincial average, not; it is currently running close to two percent above. In terms of total employment, the lower mainland has experienced a 4.5-percent increase, against a provincial average of 3.6 percent. For the North Coast/Nechako districts, total employment has fallen 1.9 percent and the decline in the Northeast has been even greater (3.3 percent). Once touted as the land of opportunity—and it is important to realize that the safety valve of southward migration helps keep unemployment rates relatively low—the Northland no longer holds the lustre that it once did. There are occasional localized booms—a new plant, a new mine, or a major government project—but the region as a whole has had difficulty employing its local residents, let alone attracting migrants. Moreover, the regional economy has done very poorly in terms of incorporating aboriginal workers, and most First Nation communities suffer through chronic high unemployment. According to provincial and federal studies, prospects for an improvement in the Northern economy are relatively slight. Wood/paper manufacturing, for example, is expected to decline by five percent between 1999 and 2005.

In this context, where Northerners used to highlight the high incomes available in the resource and development sectors, now this rarely figures in regional boosterism. Indeed, comparative incomes have fallen considerably in the last twenty years. All Northern areas were lower than the provincial average in 1991, and that decline has continued. Regional income disparity has been declining since the early 1980s, but this is not because of improvements in wages and salaries. Rather, improvement is due to the effects of sustained and expanded government transfer payments to individuals and families. Such transfers remain the economic cornerstone of many aboriginal communities and, increasingly, some of the non-aboriginal centres as well.

Collectively, this information highlights important aspects of current realities in Northern BC. The North finds itself on a different track—less international, less Asian, younger, poorer, more aboriginal—than the rest of the province. The economic prospects appear discouraging, at best, with few signs of a quick return to prosperity. At present, tensions and divisions over First Nation treaties have driven significant wedges between aboriginal and non-aboriginal residents, although the experience in the Yukon suggests that this element can potentially be turned around.

FIRST NATIONS, THE BRITISH COLUMBIA TREATY PROCESS, AND THE FUTURE OF THE NORTH

Northern British Columbians have become familiar with a unique set of acronyms (RAC, or Regional Advisory Committee; TNAC, or Treaty Negotiations Advisory Committee) and political processes. The BC treaty process began in earnest in the early 1990s, and gained in importance with the election of the New Democratic Party in 1991. Although federal and provincial interest waxed and waned in subsequent years, aboriginal treaty negotiations remain a high provincial priority. Northern BC has, in turn, emerged as a primary testing ground for this critical debate, one that holds the key to the province's future.

The signing of the Nisga'a treaty and the ratification of the agreement by the federal parliament in 2000 has arguably misled Canadians about the state of the Northern treaty process. Nisga'a negotiations began in earnest in the mid 1970s, after the 1973 Calder decision by the Supreme Court of Canada. Those negotiations, undertaken by a unique, powerful, and highly professional group of Nisga'a political leaders, took over a quarter of the century, used up an enormous amount of Nisga'a good will, and changed provincial *and* Northern expectations about the modern treaty process. But the Nisga'a discussions have always been separate from the full BC treaty negotiations, which have enjoyed few successes and which stand, in 2001, on the verge of additional difficulties. Most immediately, the continued political problems of the New Democratic Party and the subsequent election of the provincial Liberals, whose opposition to modern treaties is well known, present a serious threat to the future of treaty negotiations.

At the same time, Northern BC has, through two major First Nations court challenges, transformed the debate about aboriginal rights in Canada. The Nisga'a's Calder case (which actually resulted in a loss before the Supreme Court of Canada) convinced the Trudeau government to open treaty negotiations with First Nations in BC. This huge land area was not covered by the nineteenth-century agreements that saw aboriginal people surrender land title in much of the rest of the country. Through the 1980s and 1990s, a second major court challenge, this one launched by the Gitskan and Wet'suwet'en of north-central BC, asked for formal recognition of aboriginal title. The tortuous path of this case through the courts—it has still not been finally decided—has raised the stakes in BC. First Nations have demanded recognition of their sovereignty over their land, and have demanded expanded access to commercial resources. After a critical loss before Justice Alan McEachern (who used his judgement to offer strong and largely negative opinions about the nature of pre-contact aboriginal life in the region), the First Nations took their appeal to the Supreme Court of Canada. There, they won a new trial and crucial recognition of their rights to harvest resources on their territories.[3]

These legal battles—only a few of the literally hundreds of court challenges involving aboriginal rights in Canada—convinced the NDP government of the need to negotiate treaties across the province. While the treaty process has enjoyed considerable support in southern urban centres, where aboriginal rights are largely an abstract concept, the idea has generated much more negative responses in the North. While this opposition has been portrayed as simply a "red-neck" reaction to aboriginal aspirations, closer examination reveals several distinct lines of criticism. The hardest line, embodied in the Reform/Canadian Alliance position on the matter, simply opposes on principle the idea of "racially based" rights and privileges. Other critics point to the record (and the lack of accountability) of some First Nations administrations and to the continuing shortage of educated leaders and professional employees, and challenge the assumption that the majority of First Nations communities are ready for the kinds of self-government being proposed.[4] Finally, and perhaps most fundamentally, resource-dependent communities in the North worry that the signing of aboriginal treaties might signal the death-knell of a regional economy already under threat from global economic pressures. A strong sense prevails across the North that treaties are a southern, urban imposition, out of touch with Northern realities, and with the potential to cause enormous economic and social dislocation.

Despite these reservations and concerns—or perhaps because of them— Northern BC has the potential (and the challenge) to develop fundamentally different patterns of aboriginal–non-aboriginal relations. One part of Canada, the Yukon Territory, has already moved down this path and, on the social and cultural level, has made important strides in overcoming a history of racial antagonism in the region.[5] Non-aboriginal people in Northern BC do bring different interests and perspectives to negotiations and community consultations. While there are a few bigots and racists in the mix, the vast majority of Northern BC commentators are open to the idea of empowering aboriginal communities, providing that the rest of the region does not suffer in the process. And there is a growing realization, likely to be helped by the Nisga'a settlement, that modern treaties can bring considerable benefits to the region as a whole. Improvements in the First Nations communities can be stalled by the opposition of local non-aboriginal people, if their legitimate interests are not recognized and taken seriously. Conversely, the support and participation of non-aboriginal residents of the North can go a long way toward ensuring the future success of the treaty process.

First Nations people represent approximately ten percent of the population of Northern BC, but a significantly higher percentage of the long-term residents in the area. Although there has been a substantial out-migration to the south, primarily to Vancouver, most First Nations people have stayed in the North, if not on their home reserves. Settling the future of aboriginal rights is, as a result, critical to the region's future. If a pattern of antagonism continues over the next decade, treaties will not be signed, additional court challenges will be launched, and potential investors will look for more secure opportunities. Companies have stated that they are delaying investments in the region until indigenous claims are resolved, and concern has grown that continued debate about treaties will continue to hurt Northern prospects. Aboriginal frustration continues to grow and remains near the point of explosion on many reserves, including several in Northern BC. The pattern across Canada has been for aboriginal protests to generate a backlash, not greater support, and the potential for further conflict in the North is very real. Crucially, there is also considerable prospect for conflict between aboriginal groups, and this has long been a little-known feature of Northern political life. The Gitskan, for example, are bitterly opposed to the Nisga'a treaty, which they claim incorporates some of their traditional territories. Overlaps in aboriginal land claims are endemic in the North, and rivalries are intense.

As in so many other areas, Northern BC finds itself at a critical juncture in terms of relations between First Nations and other citizens. There are some positive signs in the region that the long history of neglect and racial antipathy is beginning to be put aside. Some communities, major corporations, and government departments are working very productively with First Nations groups. Treaty negotiations are proceeding well in some quarters and are encountering turbulence in others. A portion of the non-aboriginal population is firmly and bitterly opposed to the very concept of aboriginal rights, and they tend to dominate both the political arena and the public commentary on First Nations issues. Yet, if several more treaties are signed in the coming years—and that is looking increasingly problematic—the prospect exists for Northern BC to emerge at the cutting edge of First Nations–non-aboriginal co-operation. Conversely, several major conflicts could easily tip the regional balance in the opposite direction, with controversy, blockades, and angry words becoming the hallmark of relations in the region.

While regional opinion remains divided and uncertain, there is little question but that the resolution of aboriginal aspirations in the North is critical to the region's success. Without a settlement of First Nations claims, and without the climate of certainty that successful treaties create, resource companies will shy away from the region, weakening an already vulnerable economy. With treaties in place—and particularly with the tens of millions of dollars that will flow from the federal government into regional communities as a result of settlements—economic development will find a much stronger footing. More to the point, the North currently expends an enormous amount of emotional and political energy on treaty and First Nations rights issues. With these matters resolved, the region will have the opportunity to address other issues and respond more creatively to its many economic, social, and political challenges.

THE FUTURE: PROSPECTS AND IMPEDIMENTS

If the postwar history of Northern BC represented the promise of the resource-dependent model of Canadian development, the future seems destined to reveal its shortcomings. Increasing international competition for resource markets, declining reserves of valuable products, and increasing tension between environmental and development priorities have made the North less attractive to many investors. Technological improvements in industry have reduced job opportunities, so that opportunities for young people appear to be declining dramatically. First Nations issues are alternately viewed as a threat and an opportunity, with settlements seen by some as an impediment to economic growth and by others as the necessary foundation for a new level of stability and interracial co-operation.

Northern promoters continue to hold out hope, as they have done since the early part of this century. The belief in the region's resources remains strong, but investors may have taken unwelcome lessons from the resolutions of the

Kemano and Tatshenshini debates (where, in both cases, conflict between conservation and development was resolved by the provincial government in favour of conservation). The resource sector is unlikely to suffer a cataclysmic collapse, but individual communities will continue to experience the highs and (with greater frequency) the lows of the resource-based economy. Tourism is often touted as a viable alternative, although the lower wages and seasonality of this sector combine with comparatively small markets and intense national and international competition to make tourism an uncertain foundation for regional prosperity. Visionaries speak enthusiastically of the prospects for an information-based economy, founded on the idea that workers can be located anywhere and still participate in production and commercial transactions that may be consummated thousands of miles away. This opportunity is real—as Fargo, North Dakota and Moncton, New Brunswick have discovered—but the competition for such work is fierce and the pay often low. The only substantial prospect for gains in this area rest with strong provincial and federal government initiatives; but for a diverse set of financial, political, and social reasons, government programs to build an information technology industry in Northern British Columbia are unlikely.

Nonetheless, there are reasons for optimism imbedded in a story that, in its broad contours, holds many warning signs. Given the First Nations' generations-long commitment to the region, the money circulating from treaty settlements is more likely to stick in Northern BC than funds raised externally. Oil and gas reserves in the Northeast hold considerable promise, and may provide a potential foundation for a regional processing industry, even though the pattern to date has been to export the raw material for processing elsewhere. Barriers remain, however, and they are formidable. The Government of BC has not had a sustained regional development strategy, and the political imperative to create one is minimal. There have been attempts over the last two decades to jump-start the regional economy, but they have had little impact. In the past few years, short-term aid has been offered to ailing companies and sectors, particularly in the Prince Rupert area, as well as one-off subsidies for other proposed investments. The North has often been its own worst enemy, moreover. Internal struggles between sub-regions—the Northeast versus the Prince George/Nechako region, for example, or Terrace-Kitimat versus Prince Rupert and the Queen Charlottes—have made it easy for provincial politicians to direct attention and resources elsewhere. The successful battle for UNBC demonstrates the potential of regional co-operation; elements of the subsequent evolution of the university reveal the often painful internal dynamics generated by sub-regional politics.

Historically, Canada's northern visions, from the late nineteenth century through to the 1970s, have come from southern Canada. Twenty years ago, First Nations people articulated a contrary vision: of the North as homeland rather than the North as hinterland. In the spirit of this, they also managed to establish new constraints on Northern development, and to convince the federal government to address long-neglected issues of aboriginal rights and aspirations. Today, as the country and province inch towards sustainable partnerships with First Nations people—the Nisga'a treaty remaining, however controversially, one of the most promising developments in this regard—the need for a new kind of shared vision becomes more evident. The vision will not come from southern British Columbia or from Ottawa, however. The pattern of neglecting Northern needs is deeply entrenched and is unlikely to change.

In conclusion, the present currents of globalization and international competition, First Nations rights, technological transition, and environmentalism are creating considerable turbulence in Northern BC. In this context, there is an urgent need to generate a new, regionally based vision of the future, one that goes beyond waiting for the next megaproject to bring renewed optimism. Evidence is mounting from across the country that the natural-resource economy that brought Canada opportunity and prosperity in the postwar world will no longer "work." A new vision for Northern BC must, furthermore, overcome the internal rivalries and jealousies that have so long prevented the emergence of a coherent and consistent Northern voice. The challenge is to overcome internal divisions, develop a realistic appraisal of future prospects, and accept treaty settlements as a building block for future development. In particular, any real vision of the North's future absolutely must demonstrate a substantial partnership between First Nations and other Northerners. To do otherwise is only to encourage conflict, and a continuation of the divided dreams that have long stalled development in the region. The opportunity exists, and the challenges are real. Sadly, the lessons of history suggest that reasons for optimism are relatively few and far between.

Notes

Special thanks to Greg Poelzer, Robin Fisher, Bill Morrison, and Carin Holroyd for their comments on an earlier draft of this paper. They are not, of course, responsible for any errors or omissions that remain. This paper would not have been possible without the research assistance provided by Bradley Coates.

1   The Tainui settlement was signed in 1995. In the years since the treaty agreement, the Tainui have run into difficulties with investments and several key leaders have been singled out for personal criticism and political attacks. The agreement, however, provided the Tainui people with significant amounts of land and investment capital.

2   Statistical information relating to British Columbia is taken from the Government of British Columbia statistics web-site (www.bcstats.gov.bc). This on-line data set provides ready access to a wide variety of provincial statistical information, including material relating to labour force, population, and income.

3   Recent court cases relating to Northern British Columbia can be found on the Supreme Court of Canada/LexUM web-site (www.lexum.umontreal.ca/csc-scs/en/). The most relevant cases are Supreme Court of Canada, R. v. Calder, 1973; Supreme Court of Canada, R. v. Delgamuukw, 1997, and Supreme Court of Canada, Regina vs. Gladstone, 1996.

4   Thomas Flanagan, *First Nations? Second Thoughts* (Montreal: McGill-Queen's University Press, 2000).

5   See K. Coates and J. Powell, *The Modern North: People, Politics, and the Rejection of Colonialism* (Toronto: James Lorimer and Company, 1989).

Blind Spots in the Rearview Mirrors

LIVELIHOOD AND THE CHEVIOT DEBATE

Ian Urquhart

I do know men need work but isn't there another way?

—*Kay Farnham, former resident of Mountain Park, Alberta*

Battles between resource industries, their boosters, and environmentalists are now commonplace throughout the Rocky Mountains and their foothills. Visions of resource-led economic growth and environmental preservation smash against each other. People who feel at home in one vision are shut out of the other. In the American Rocky Mountain West, such conflicts have been portrayed as confrontations between an old resource-extractive economy and a new environmental economy.[1] This essay argues that this portrait of political conflict in the Rockies does not really fit the conflict considered here—the proposal to develop

Cheviot, a gigantic open-pit coal mine in the Alberta Rockies. I propose instead that while advocacy of the old resource-extractive economy is easy to identify, the substance of the new environmental economy remains a mystery. An important irony rests here. Clashing visions of the future of the mountain landscapes touched by the Cheviot proposal share a common flaw: impoverished conceptions of livelihood. The positions of both the project's boosters and its opponents are rooted in ideas about livelihood that more appropriately belong in our past, not our future. This difficulty is compounded, moreover, by aspects of the political and environmental assessment processes that examine and pass judgement on the suitability of projects like Cheviot. Frankly, these institutions and processes seem to have neither the capability nor the will to try to realize richer, more sustainable visions of livelihood.

The idea of livelihood is central to this critique. The term is sometimes used quite generally to describe "conduct" or the "kind or manner of life" led by people. In this respect, it may incorporate immaterial subjects such as faith and spiritual connections with land or with specific places. More generally, however, livelihood stresses earning or gaining the means of living. Here, work is privileged. My interest in livelihood and how developers, environmentalists, and governments think about it is taken first from the writings of people like Donald Snow and Richard White. Snow, executive director of the Northern Lights Institute in Missoula, Montana, takes seriously the Wise Use movement—a *bête noire* of environmentalism in the American West. He believes the intellectual significance, as well as the popular attractiveness of Wise Use arguments, lies in their focus on livelihood. "The central problem with environmentalism," he argues, "is that it lacks a cogent, convincing focus on livelihood, and that has made it vulnerable to Wise Use attacks. The grand cause of protecting the environment *from humans* means that lots of humans now feel unwelcome in what they see as the environmentalists' visionary world."[2]

This outlook is similar to Richard White's sympathetic critique of contemporary environmentalism. For White, too many environmentalists see work as the destroyer of nature; they are blind to the idea that work may be a way of knowing nature. This distrust of work often places humans outside of nature and presents a Hobbesian choice: humans or nature.[3] Such environmentalists look backwards, idealizing a view of "pure nature" where men, women, and their work are airbrushed out of the picture.[4] Working men and working women, on the other hand, star in Wise Use productions. Those who push for massive resource projects like Cheviot often do so in the name of working people. But this vision of livelihood looks backwards too. Workers, in Wise Use scripts, can only live comfortably if the resource project proceeds. Maintain the existing industrial base, attract new resource industries, or face the de-population and impoverishment of the countryside.[5] Little or no time is spent thinking about alternative ways of realizing the comfortable lifestyles most people aspire to.

Livelihood is a very personal issue for me too. I grew up in the shadows of the Cominco smelter smokestacks in Trail, BC, a town in the otherwise scenic Kootenays that owed its existence to mining. At Smoke Eater hockey games, steelworkers joined backcountry recreation enthusiasts (who back then usually were just called outdoorsmen) in cheering on the last Canadian hockey team to win the World Amateur Championships. But their camaraderie could degenerate into conflict if post-game conversations turned to consider Cominco's impact on Columbia River fish stocks or the number of jobs that might be lost if the company installed pollution-control equipment. The tension between preserving jobs in the resource sector and loving pure, wild spaces and their creatures was part of everyday life in the Silver City.

In 1994, Snow argued it was high time to pursue diversification and innovation as general strategies to try to bridge the sort of ideological chasms I saw in Trail and further a version of livelihood that all camps could find desirable. Mutual respect and good will would certainly seem to be needed to travel down this path. I also believe, though, that this job requires public institutions and decision-making processes that are devoted to helping rural communities find Kay Farnham's "another way." Today, these structures are absent from Alberta's political terrain; a better future demands their presence.

HISTORICAL BACKGROUND TO THE CHEVIOT DEBATE

It is easy to see why controversy embroils the Cheviot open-pit coal mine project. Even for Albertans, no strangers to welcoming mammoth resource-extraction projects as neighbours, the scale of Cheviot is staggering. If Cheviot proceeds, its pits and rock dumps will sprawl over approximately 180 square kilometres, a site measuring roughly 24 kilometres east to west and 7 kilometres north to south. If Cheviot's size alone is not enough to guarantee controversy, its location is. The western boundary of the mine would be perched no more than two and a half kilometres east of Jasper National Park, a United Nations World Heritage site.

For the Town of Hinton, the Hinton and Alberta chambers of commerce, and trade unionists, Cheviot's future is vital to the prosperity of Hinton, a town of 10,000 located less than an hour's drive east of Jasper. Local support for the mine is overwhelming. Motorists passing through Hinton in the late 1990s couldn't miss the "We Support Cheviot" banners strung up on either side of the Yellowhead Highway. Opposition to the project is spearheaded by the Alberta Wilderness Association (AWA) Coalition.[6] Its central position focusses upon the mine's threat to critical wildlife habitat and the ecological integrity of Jasper National Park.

Coal mining in the vicinity of the proposed Cheviot mine has a long, hard, and turbulent history. The Mountain Park Coal Company opened the first mine on the Cheviot site in 1911. At first, Mountain Park coal fed the westward push of the Grand Trunk Pacific Railway. Early life in Mountain Park and the other towns that sprang up in a part of Alberta known as the Coal Branch was extremely difficult. If you visit the Mountain Park cemetery today you will see too many crosses marking the graves of children who died before they could walk or talk. The Alberta Coal Mining Industry Commission of 1919 is an important source for other testimonials to the harshness of a Coal Branch miner's life in the early days. Many miners appeared before the Commission, complaining of appalling living conditions in the mining camps and company towns. Cramped, poorly ventilated housing, food tainted by coal oil, overflowing outhouses that contaminated drinking water and led to outbreaks of typhoid and cholera— these were the kinds of conditions the Coal Commissioners learned of during their hearings.[7]

The death of Mountain Park and its mine was foreshadowed by the Leduc oil discovery in 1947. Railways converted from coal to diesel. As petroleum production increased, oil and natural gas took larger and larger chunks of the home heating market. Faced with this shrinking market the Mountain Park mine closed in 1950. The town was bulldozed, leaving the cemetery as the only obvious sign that hundreds of people once lived in that subalpine setting.

While changes in Canadian coal use led to the decline of coal mining after 1950, a new international demand for coal rejuvenated the industry in Alberta's Rockies and foothills in the late 1960s. A hungry, growing Japanese steelmaking industry needed the high-quality metallurgical coal an earlier generation of coal miners had dug out of the mountains surrounding Mountain Park, Cadomin, and Luscar. The Luscar mine, closed in 1956 because of the collapsed domestic market, reopened in 1969 to supply coking coal to Asian steelmakers. This Asian hunger for coal holds an important key to the prospects for the Cheviot project. After serving Asian demand for more than thirty years, the Luscar mine has nearly exhausted the amount of coal that can be profitably mined and is slated to close in 2002. If Asia's appetite remains both healthy and unsatisfied by alternative supplies, Cheviot's proposed production—3.2 million tons of coal annually for 20 years—would replace the Luscar mine's share of this export market.

However, international markets change. For metallurgical coal, market changes ushered in during the 1990s threaten the prosperity enjoyed during the last twenty years. Technological changes in steelmaking, particularly Pulverized Coal Injection (PCI), allow steelmakers to substitute softer, less expensive steaming coal for the very hard metallurgical coal the Coal Branch is famous for. This technological change strengthened Australia's already strong position in the Asian coal market and helped trigger a free fall in the price of metallurgical coal in the last half of the 1990s. The depressed market was a death sentence for chronic money-losing operations such as Quintette Coal near Tumbler Ridge, BC and Smoky River Coal in Grande Cache, Alberta.[8] But it also killed consistently profitable mines, such as the Gregg River mine, located just north of Luscar. Besieged by closures and layoffs, industry insiders warned of "a paradigm shift in the industry."[9] By late 2000, the more than $50 (US) per ton that Cardinal River Coal officials once expected to receive for Cheviot coal seems like nothing more than a pipe dream.[10]

Unlike the pioneer generation of coal miners, most of today's miners whose lives are buffeted by stormy international markets do not live where they work. Most commute to the mines from Hinton, a town that owes its birth to coal mining. Belittled by a "clever" Toronto newspaper writer as "probably best known as the site of the last McDonald's before the mountains," Hinton rode the crest of a booming resource economy throughout much of the late 1980s and 1990s.[11] Between 1991 and 1996 the town's population grew nearly twice as fast as Alberta's. Its 10.1-percent growth rate over these years pushed the town's population to just under 10,000.[12] Judged by conventional yardsticks, economic life in Hinton was arguably better than many other places in Alberta in the 1990s. In 1996, the town boasted a lower unemployment rate than the Alberta average, and a workforce that took home higher average incomes. The importance of the resource economy to Hinton's prosperity is further underscored by the fact the average income for men in Hinton is 27 percent higher than for the average Albertan working male. Moreover, this significantly higher average income figure exists despite the fact that the male workforce in Hinton is not as well educated as the Alberta average.[13]

LIVELIHOOD AND THE CHEVIOT ENVIRONMENTAL ASSESSMENT

The Canadian constitution is silent on the question of which level of government, federal or provincial, has jurisdiction over the environment. *De facto* joint responsibility exists. With joint responsibility came a number of federal-provincial agreements designed to minimize duplication and overlap. The Canada-Alberta Agreement on Environmental Assessment Cooperation is such an agreement. Under its terms, the Alberta Energy and Utilities Board (EUB) and the Canadian Environmental Assessment Agency agreed to establish a single, joint environmental assessment of the Cheviot project. In January 1997, the Joint Review Panel began six weeks of public hearings into the project. On June 6, 1997 the Panel declared that the EUB found Cheviot to be in the public interest and recommended federal approval of the project. In October the Department of Fisheries and Oceans (DFO) gave its regulatory blessing to the project. The AWA Coalition was severely disappointed with this outcome and launched a challenge in the Federal Court of Canada to the Joint Review Panel's recommendation. The Federal Court concluded that the Panel had not properly addressed several requirements for assessments, as outlined in the Canadian Environmental Assessment Act (CEAA), and the Court quashed the DFO's regulatory approval of the mine. It ordered the Joint Panel to reconvene to consider the alternative of mining Cheviot's coal through an underground operation, the cumulative effects of forestry and other mining activity in the area, and two documents that the Canadian Nature Federation had submitted to the first set of hearings. The Joint Panel did this in the spring of 2000. In September, the Panel once again recommended approval of Cheviot.

Some people dispute whether the mandates of federal, provincial, and joint federal-provincial environmental assessment processes are broad enough to entertain matters of livelihood. Andrew Nikiforuk, for example, has charged that the CEAA fails to consider the general socio-economic effects of development proposals.[14] This is simply wrong. In part, the CEAA defines "environmental effect" as "any change that the project may cause in the environment, including any effect of any such change on health and socio-economic conditions, on physical and cultural heritage, or the current use of lands and resources for traditional purposes by aboriginal persons, or on any structure, site or thing that is of historical, archaeological, paleontological or architectural significance." However, Nikiforuk's concerns may be on the mark in respect of Alberta's Environmental Protection and Enhancement Act. There, we cannot find any reference to "environmental effect," let alone the sweeping definition of that phenomenon found in the federal legislation. Instead, the legislation offers a narrower definition of what an "adverse effect" would be: "impairment of or damage to the environment, human health or safety or property."[15] Other sections of the provincial legislation seem more hospitable to questions of livelihood, but only as these are posed and answered by the proponents of resource projects. In provincial environmental assessments, for example, proponents should ensure that their environmental impact assessment reports describe "potential positive and negative environmental, social, economic and cultural impacts of the proposed activity, including cumulative, regional, temporal and spatial considerations."[16] As well, provincial law stipulates that environmental impact assessments reports should consider "alternatives to the proposed activity, including the alternative of not proceeding with the proposed activity."[17] The reader will be excused, however, for speculating that self-interested proponents may carry out these obligations in ways that minimize the threats to their view of the project's value.

Perhaps the most relevant focus here is upon the Alberta-Canada agreement to establish a panel to review the Cheviot project, and the panel's specific terms of reference. In respect to defining environmental effects, the Alberta-Canada agreement replicates, with one exception, the definition found in the CEAA. This exception acknowledged that non-aboriginals, as well as aboriginal persons, may currently use the land and resources for traditional purposes. The Panel's terms of reference called for the review to consider the social and economic effects of the project. Among the factors to be considered in the federal-provincial review were "(t)he Environment, including the socio-economic environment, which may reasonably be expected to be affected by the Cheviot Coal Project" and "(t)he Environmental Effects of the Cheviot Coal Project...." Thus, the parameters of the joint federal-provincial review appear to have been broad enough to welcome interventions on the issue of livelihood. It is germane, therefore, to examine what portraits of livelihood the project's opponents and supporters painted.

This essay looks for discussions of livelihood in several places. It examines the submissions made to the Joint Panel, media commentaries on the first round of public hearings that commenced in January 1997, and the testimony offered during those hearings. It pays particular attention to the testimony offered during the fifth panel of these hearings, the panel established to consider socio-economic issues.

NATURE AND PLAY

Modern environmentalism generally has little respect for work in nature. Most people who work in nature, like those blue-collar workers who operate CRC's gigantic coal-mining shovels and haul trucks, are portrayed as either pawns or villains. Their work destroys nature. Indeed, Richard White's provocative examination of contemporary environmentalism charges: "environmentalists have much to say about nature and play and little to say about humans and work."[18] As harsh as this may strike some ears, it nonetheless characterizes quite well the thrust of the commentary offered by the environmentalists who opposed Cheviot. Throughout the Cheviot saga it was not uncommon to hear environmentalists say they cared for the future of the hundreds of miners who would lose their jobs if the project did not proceed. But environmentalists seldom said much more than that on the subject. In particular, they were silent about how they thought most of the laid-off miners could continue to live comfortable lives in their chosen communities if Cheviot did not go ahead.

An examination of the Coalition's written submission to the Joint Panel makes this point emphatically. Only 3 of its 101 pages were devoted to the sustainability of the local economy and employment. Only three lines of the submission dealt with the need to diversify the economy in the Hinton area. There, the Coalition argued that "an increased emphasis on tourism, recreation and white collar jobs (with today's computer communications capabilities) could play a significant and useful role in diversifying the local economy."[19] That this is not a "cogent, convincing focus on livelihood" was confirmed by the Coalition's testimony during the public hearings. Indeed, when the time came to address socio-economic and human-impact issues, the striking characteristic of the AWA Coalition's interventions was the extent to which nature, not socio-economic affairs, became the focus for discussion. For example, the concept of "human-impact issues" was used to explore the impact the mine and its workers would have upon the alpine landscape and the wildlife found there ("nature" concerns); it was also used to probe the mine's impact upon backcountry recreation activities ("play" concerns).

"Nature" concerns were the first issues addressed during the AWA Coalition's cross-examination of the socio-economic/human-impacts panel. The Coalition began by considering the construction camp CRC proposed to erect to house some of the construction workers Cheviot would need. This proposed camp was a concern for Cadomin residents who worried that this transient workforce would bring rowdiness to their hamlet. The AWA Coalition had a different worry: the environmental impact of CRC's camp upon the Cadomin Caves and the various species of bats that swarm and hibernate therein. The AWA's Dianne Pachal opened her cross-examination with the concern that the construction camp would encroach upon territory earmarked for a future Cadomin Caves protected natural area. The Coalition also was worried the camp would increase the number of visitors to the Cadomin Caves during critical bat mating and hibernating periods.[20] A concern with nature also animated the Coalition's interventions on the subject of greenhouse gas emissions/climate change. This concern also might account for the rather tangential set of questions about water quality that the Pembina Institute's Chris Baker later put to this panel. When his turn came to cross-examine witnesses, he began with questions about the company's program for monitoring the amount of Total Suspended Solids (TSS) contained in water leaving the Luscar mine's settling pond—odd questions to pose to a socio-economic panel.

"Play" concerns also figured prominently in the AWA Coalition's cross-examination. In particular, the Coalition wanted to know what impact the mine would have upon backcountry recreational activities. In pursuing this line of questioning, Pachal very effectively critiqued CRC's consultants for their failure to even consider Cheviot's impact upon how the public might use and enjoy the Mountain Park area in the future. Pachal also was concerned about noise from the mine. However, unlike the people of Cadomin, Pachal wanted to know if noise from mining operations would be audible in pristine wilderness areas such as Jasper National Park or the Cardinal River Divide Natural Area. Parks Canada, she said, had "identified that they are hearing sounds in the Fiddle River area of Jasper National Park, which is to the north and across from Luscar mine; and hence, they are concerned about the noise that could be generated by the current proposed Cheviot mine on the section of Jasper Park and the trails further to the south and opposite the Cheviot mine."[21] A long argument ensued between Pachal and CRC's consultants over whether or not noise levels in the Park and the Cardinal River Natural area should have been studied.

Not all of the Coalition's interventions were restricted to nature and play issues. But when Coalition members spoke to the subject of humans and work, they did not do so with the conviction or preparedness they brought to their interests in wilderness, recreation, and biodiversity. Both Pachal and Baker encouraged the Joint Review Panel to doubt the company's position that the Cheviot project was economically viable and would provide a stable source of employment in the region.[22] The Coalition's arguments were tentative on the crucial subjects of economic diversification and job opportunities for today's miners if Cheviot did not go ahead. The principle of sustainable tourism was championed, but few details were offered about the economic value this option might bring to the regional economy. The Coalition hinted at the possibility that the region might pick up additional coal-mining jobs from less environmentally damaging mine projects. Again, details were sparse. Somewhat hypocritically, the Coalition suggested that laid-off miners might find work in northeastern Alberta's booming oil sands industry, an industry whose expansion plans environmentalists have regularly opposed.[23]

Fundamentally, the mandates of environmental organizations such as the AWA contribute to the failure to seriously engage socio-economic issues. The AWA defines its mission as "Defending Wild Alberta Through Awareness and Action"; it describes itself as "Alberta's frontline advocacy organization advancing the establishment of protected areas."[24] But this orientation is only part of the explanation for the lack of attention the AWA Coalition paid to socio-economic questions during the Cheviot hearings. The AWA and other environmental organizations unsuccessfully sought funding from the Canadian Environmental Assessment Agency to hire experts to help them address the socio-economic aspects of the project.[25] More funding might have led the Coalition to explore these aspects more seriously. It is a point we return to below.

THE FOUR HORSEMEN OF THE APOCALYPSE

If the socio-economic dimension played a minor role in the interventions of environmentalists, it was the central theme of the interventions of Cheviot's supporters. The message delivered by the Town of Hinton, the Hinton and Alberta chambers of commerce, and the United Mineworkers Union was blunt and apocalyptic: a future without Cheviot would be bleak and joyless; Hinton would suffer horribly if the mine did not go ahead. The United Mineworkers underlined that a clear majority of their membership at the Luscar mine expected to leave the area if Cheviot did not go ahead; only ten percent of their members expected to remain in the Hinton area if Cheviot was not approved.[26] The Hinton Chamber of Commerce argued that, without Cheviot, the Hinton economy would suffer "an immediate and devastating impact." The Alberta Chamber warned that, without Cheviot, "most importantly—the quality of life Hinton's residents have enjoyed over the years will visibly diminish."[27] Leaving little to the imagination, the Hinton Chamber argued it would be "a matter of lost jobs and lost economic benefits of catastrophic proportions."[28] Spousal abuse, family violence, and substance abuse might increase too. Hinton would become another Grande Cache, a sister resource town north of Hinton that has suffered years of economic hardship after losing a significant number of resource-industry jobs. The Town of Hinton echoed these positions. Approve Cheviot if governments wanted a healthy socio-economic picture. Take away the mine and the community would be devastated. More than 400 households would vanish; real estate prices would plunge by 20 to 30 percent; the community would suffer serious social disruptions.[29]

Not only were the supporters' arguments apocalyptic, they were also xenophobic. However, the foreigners attacked in these arguments were not Americans, Asians, or Europeans. They were fellow Albertans who did not call the Hinton area "home." The Hinton Chamber of Commerce slammed "special interest groups from outside the area" for opposing Cheviot. Hinton's mayor Ross Risvold essentially argued that only the people of Hinton should decide the project's future. After the first round of hearings he complained about "[a] growing sense of frustration that the people most affected by this important decision have so little impact on the outcome. Is there a lack of concern or consideration for social/economic environmental consequences to the people of Hinton and area?"[30] Later, his criticism of the environmental assessment process became even more acerbic. Environmentalists were urban "academic elites" who "don't seem to have any empathy for the working person or the children of the working person."[31] Environmentalists privileged environmental protection over the community development and quality-of-life interests of the people of Hinton.[32]

Social and economic impact studies commissioned by Cheviot's supporters framed their interpretation of livelihood. If environmentalists could be criticized for paying scant attention to livelihood, Cheviot's supporters could be criticized for having a different kind of blind spot, and for thinking about livelihood in narrow and unimaginative ways. Livelihood could only be sustained by adopting a "business as usual" approach that perpetuated past patterns of work and economic development. Consequently, their socio-economic impact studies had a very clear intent: to demonstrate that Hinton would be crippled if Cheviot was stopped. These studies emphasized coal mining's importance to the regional economy and represented Cheviot as Hinton's only economic option. They paid no attention to what Hinton's future might look like if the Town conceptualized and pursued economic diversification strategies. Their predictions of job losses and out-migration assume a Hinton with nothing else to offer, a Hinton unable to do anything to attract people to live there. This failure to treat economic diversification seriously was a very significant blinker on the vision of livelihood championed by Cheviot's supporters.[33]

POLITICAL WILL, POLITICAL INSTITUTIONS, AND MORE SUSTAINABLE VERSIONS OF LIVELIHOOD

Cheviot's boosters and critics, each with their respective sets of blinkers, disregard Snow's advice that it is high time to pursue diversification and innovation as general strategies to conceive and develop more sustainable versions of livelihood. Environmentalists do not take seriously enough the concerns of working men and women; Cheviot's boosters do not take seriously enough the concerns about environmental sustainability. Neither side is willing to think about community sustainability in imaginative ways that respect the other side's concerns. I suspect that, in Alberta, the route to accepting Snow's advice runs in several directions. It requires an environmental assessment process where more sustainable versions of livelihood are demanded of participants; it also requires governments to put in place institutions with the mandates and expertise needed to support more sustainable versions of livelihood.

The first requirement could be met partially if environmental assessment panels realized that their terms of reference may give them the authority to demand more sustainable versions of livelihood from intervening parties. The terms of reference for the Cheviot Environmental Assessment offered this option to the members of the Joint Review Panel. They did not, however, have the political will to take advantage of it. The terms of reference for the Cheviot review stated that, in part, the Panel should consider the following factors: "[t]he purpose of, need for, and alternatives to the Cheviot Coal Project"; [t]he Environment, including the socio-economic environment, which may reasonably be expected to be affected by the Cheviot Coal Project."[34] If Panel members were genuinely interested in moving past the preservationist/Cheviot-at-all-costs arguments they heard, these terms of reference might have been used to good effect. Intervening parties could have been required to consider non-coal-mining alternatives to Cheviot; furthermore, they might have been asked to reflect upon how Cheviot might limit future socio-economic possibilities in the Hinton area. When these possibilities are ignored, as they were in the Cheviot case, assessment panels are essentially asked to respond to the options offered to them by intervening parties. As I have tried to show in this paper, these options are likely to be backward-looking; they are likely to ignore the possibility of thinking about the idea of livelihood in a richer, more sustainable way.

Satisfying this first requirement also would require giving environmental assessment panels the resources needed to help fund the interventions of groups and associations that want to make this type of argument. The Cheviot case suggests that funding for socio-economic analyses was hard to come by for environmental groups. Environmental assessment review panels are going to have to offer financial assistance to environmental groups like the AWA if they want what are essentially volunteer organizations to explore more sustainable versions of livelihood. Environmental assessment panels could also use their control over intervener funding to help private-sector organizations develop the institutional capacity needed to contribute meaningfully to efforts to map out sustainable versions of livelihood.

The impoverished conceptions of livelihood haunting the Cheviot debate also impose an obligation on governments to assess their own institutional structures. In the language of political science, this raises the issue of "institutional capacity." Does the public sector have the wherewithal needed to offer the citizens of rural communities the resources needed to try to realize more sustainable visions of livelihood? To explore together how they might make "good livings in good environments," to paraphrase Wallace Stegner? Can the state insure that public institutions and public consultation processes commit resources and expertise to addressing these types of questions?

When governments attacked budget deficits in the 1990s, this public-institution-building exercise fell very out of fashion. "Plan" was a four-letter word in more ways than one. In 1995, Alberta effectively killed ten regional planning commissions by withdrawing all of their provincial financial support. To be sure, those regional planning commissions were not perfect. They were sites for sometimes sharp conflicts between the development visions of urban and rural municipalities; they were not specifically charged to promote more sustainable versions of livelihood. Yet, in a eulogy for these commissions, the Chairman of the Edmonton Metropolitan Regional Planning Commission described them in language suggesting they had the potential to make a positive contribution to the sustainable livelihood debate:

> Regional planning commissions are designed to collect and consider a broad range of demographic and geographic information in order to assist governments in making those key decisions that affect where and how people live, where business can best be located to capitalize on human and natural resources, and how best to plan economic development in the interest of preserving a sustainable environment.[35]

Ironically, the Minister of Municipal Affairs' decision to kill these commissions came while other provincial and federal institutions were arguing on behalf of a need to create regional, cross-jurisdictional planning mechanisms in order to pursue sustainable development. When Alberta's Natural Resources Conservation Board approved most of the Three Sisters recreation and tourist project in Canmore, it recommended creating a Bow Valley Planning and Advisory Committee. Such a multi-jurisdictional committee of senior officials was needed because established political boundaries and responsibilities were unlikely to serve well the health of the Bow Valley ecosystem.[36] This call for regional management and planning in the Bow River valley was reiterated several years later by the federal government's Banff-Bow Valley Task Force.[37] The future health of the Banff-Bow Valley area depended upon the development of a joint federal-provincial-municipal strategy.

The value of viewing sustainable development issues through a regional lens now has been acknowledged formally by the Alberta government. In the spring of 2000, the province outlined its intent to develop a Northern East Slopes Sustainable Resource and Environmental Management Strategy (NES Strategy). The area targeted in this strategy is considerable, including portions of the upper Athabasca and Smoky River watersheds and the communities of Edson, Hinton, Grande Cache, and Whitecourt. The terms of reference for this strategy outline a number of desirable objectives. They include:

- a regional vision with goals and indicators, that outlines desired sustainable resource use and considers economy, environment, community and aboriginal interests;
- the identification, prioritization and analysis of values, issues and concerns in realizing our regional sustainable resource management vision;
- strategies to achieve the goals and to resolve outstanding issues and concerns;
- a process to monitor, evaluate, report and improve the NES Strategy.[38]

However, anyone familiar with Alberta's history of resource/environment conflicts may doubt whether any of the four provincial departments responsible for this strategy, other than possibly Alberta Environment, are committed to sustainable development.[39] Too often departments such as Alberta Resource

Development simply reiterate their long-held views on what constitutes desirable resource-development policy, views indistinguishable from those of Cheviot's boosters. Again, what may be needed to push this initiative forward is a separate cross-jurisdictional planning agency.

Some readers may be frustrated by the refusal here to identify the "good guys" in the Cheviot debate. Some, perhaps especially the partisans in the debate, may object to the "plague on both your houses" tone of this essay. I don't apologize for either conviction. For years now I have watched debates between developers and environmentalists in Alberta. They are depressingly predictable and have taken us nowhere because neither side is prepared to think creatively about how the other side's key concerns may be incorporated into "another way" of securing good livings for people in rural Alberta.

Building bridges between these two camps, not erecting higher walls, is the approach I prefer. But I doubt this will be possible until environmentalists acknowledge livelihood's importance and developers step beyond their traditional understanding of what must be done in order to secure good livings in rural Alberta. Environmentalists must supplement their primary concerns with nature preservation and their secondary concern with backcountry recreational values with a more genuine concern about local livelihoods, if they are serious about building lasting bridgeheads into rural Alberta. As things stand now, the priority that environmental groups appear to place on backcountry recreation over jobs fosters the impression in communities like Hinton that they don't care about the people who live there. As visitors from the city, who come to rural areas only to play, how can they be seen in any other light? However, the "outsider" label might lose some of its force if environmentalists could link their legitimate interests in backcountry recreation to well-researched plans outlining how the recreational value of wildlands in the Hinton area could offer livelihoods to people living in the region. By seriously engaging the challenges of rethinking livelihood, environmentalists could make a common cause with the people of Hinton.

For their part, developers must lose their slavish attachment to the idea that the traditional model of resource-led development is the only model capable of delivering good livings. In Cheviot's case, the crisis in metallurgical coal markets may be forcing this realization upon some of the project's boosters. It may increase the political support for alternative models of regional development. On October 24, 2000, Luscar announced that the Cheviot project was postponed indefinitely.[40] Officials of the Japanese steel mills who earlier had signed letters of intent to purchase coal from the Cheviot mine did not extend those commitments when the letters expired. Within hours of the company's announcement, Hinton mayor Ross Risvold declared that his town needed "to pursue a long-term economic strategy with senior levels of government."[41] This realization might be the first step towards reformulating livelihood into a richer, more sustainable idea.

But old habits die hard. If both sides in this debate are going to think creatively about how they can address the other's key concerns they are going to need help from government. Environmental assessment review panels must push this envelope and insist on an important place for sustainable versions of livelihood in their work. It's also high time we let the idea of planning out of the doghouse and opened up the public purse to help rural communities imagine what a more sustainable version of livelihood might look like and mean to them. Without these sorts of government commitments, I doubt we will ever produce the sort of answer Kay Farnham hoped to hear.

Notes

I would like to thank David Whitson, Roger Epp, and several anonymous reviewers for their comments on an earlier draft of this essay.

1   Samuel P. Hays, "The New Envrionmental West," *Journal of Policy History*, Vol. 3 (1991).

2   Donald Snow, "The Pristine Silence of Leaving It All Alone," *Northern Lights*, Vol. IX, no. 4 (Winter 1994), 13.

3   Richard White, "'Are You an Environmentalist or Do You Work for a Living?': Work and Nature," in William Cronon (ed.), *Uncommon Ground: Rethinking the Human Place in Nature*, (New York: W.W. Norton and Company Inc, 1996).

4   Ibid., 182.

5   Snow, "The Pristine Silence of Leaving It All Alone," 13.

6   In addition to the AWA, the coalition also included the Canadian Parks and Wilderness Society, the Jasper Environmental Association, the Canadian Nature Federation, and the Pembina Institute for Appropriate Development.

7   An edited version of the Commission's hearings is found in David Jay Bercuson (ed.), *Alberta's Coal Industry 1919*, (Calgary: Historical Society of Alberta, 1978).

8   See "Coal mine's early closure costs 500 jobs," *The Edmonton Journal*, 2 March 2000; "Teck shuts B.C.'s Quintette mine early," *The National Post*, 2 March 2000; "Offer for indebted mine refused," *The Edmonton Journal*, 25 April 2000.

9   "Low coal demand forces Luscar to lay off 95," *The Edmonton Journal*, 22 April 1999.

10 Amicus Reporting Group, *Proceedings taken at a hearing of the Alberta Energy and Utilities Board at the Crestwood Hotel*, 186.

11 "Rocky Mountain showdown: planned coal mine near Jasper pits environmentalists against industry," *The Toronto Star,* 16 November 1996.

12 Hinton's population was 9,961 according to the 1996 census.

13 In 1996 the average income for the male workforce in Hinton was $42,142. The same average for Alberta was $33 129. The percentage of male workers in Hinton who had not finished high school stood at 38.5 percent; the Alberta average was 33.6 percent. While 15.5 percent of male workers in Alberta had completed university only 7.2 percent of the male workforce in Hinton were university graduates.

14 Andrew Nikiforuk, "'The Nasty Game:' The Failure of Environmental Assessment in Canada," (Toronto: Walter and Duncan Gordon Foundation, 1997), 10.

15 Alberta, Environmental Protection and Enhancement Act, section 1 (b).

16 Ibid., section 47 (d).

17 Ibid., section 47 (h).

18 White, "'Are You an Environmentalist or Do You Work for a Living?'," 173.

19 Alberta Wilderness Association, Pembina Institute for Appropriate Development, Canadian Parks and Wilderness Society (Edmonton), Jasper Environmental Association, Ben Gadd, "Submission to the Joint AEUB/CEAA Panel on the Cheviot Mint Project," (mimeo.), January 1997, 98.

20 *Proceedings,* 2453.

21 *Proceedings,* 2506–2507.

22 This theme also was raised by Ben Gadd in his testimony on behalf of the AWA Coalition. See *Proceedings,* 2929–2942.

23 The Coalition raised another general subject—Cheviot's possible impact upon human health—during its interventions. Chris Baker pursued this subject in respect to benzene emissions. See *Proceedings,* 2552.

24 Alberta Wilderness Association, "About Us," http://AlbertaWilderness.ab.ca/AWA/Aboutus.htm; Alberta Wilderness Association, "History," http://AlbertaWilderness.ab.ca/AWA/history.htm

25 See the comments of Jennifer Klimek in *Proceedings,* 43. It is unclear how the AWA Coalition would have used socio-economic expertise. Ben Gadd suggested that the Coalition would have used any funding it received for socio-economic research to question the economic viability of the mine. See his comments at *Proceedings,* 2929.

26 A survey done for the United Mineworkers of American Local 1656 found that 61 percent of the membership expected to move if Cheviot did not replace Luscar.

27 Alberta Chamber of Commerce, "Presentation to Alberta Enery [sic] and Utilities Board and Canadian Environmental Assessment Agency," 13 January 1997.

28 Hinton and District Chamber of Commerce, "Presentation to Alberta Energy and Utilities Board and Canadian Environmental Assessment Agency with respect to Cardinal River Coals Limited Application Nos. 960313 and 960314," 13 January 1997.

29 Town of Hinton, "Presentation to A.E.U.B./C.E.A.A. Re: Cheviot Mine."

30 Ross Risvold, letter, 24 August 1999.

31 "Layoff warning if Cheviot mine not quickly approved," *The Edmonton Journal,* 9 September 1999.

32 For the Alberta Chamber of Commerce, environmentalist arguments about preservation were unsubstantiated. "It's unfortunate," the Chamber added, "but we are victims of the process here today. Victims of a media-induced frenzy that would pit those interested in promoting the economic and community development interests of this region against those that promote environmental preservation—that's the bottom line…." Alberta Chamber of Commerce, "Presentation," 13 January 1997.

33 The Town only seems to have considered diversification as a worthy option when it was forced to recognize that the area would lose coal mining jobs, regardless of Cheviot's future. In May 2000, Luscar surprised the Hinton area with the announcement that the Gregg River mine would close and put approximately 250 workers out of a job. The closure forced the Town to begin to explore economic diversification options. See "Hard times ahead for Hinton," *The Edmonton Journal*, 26 May 2000.

34 Alberta Energy and Utilities Board and Canadian Environmental Assessment Agency, *Report of the EUB-CEAA Joint Review Panel, Cheviot Coal Project*, (June 1997), Appendix B, 8.

35 Ken Allred, "Government wiping out planning commissions," *The Edmonton Journal*, 23 February 1995.

36 Alberta, Natural Resources Conservation Board, *Decision Report—"Application to Construct a Recreational and Tourism Project in the Town of Canmore, Alberta,"* (25 November 1992)

37 Canada, Banff-Bow Valley Task Force, *Banff-Bow Valley: At the Crossroads*, (Ottawa: Minister of Supply and Services Canada, 1996).

38 Alberta Environment, "Final Terms of Reference, Northern East Slopes Sustainable Resource and Environmental Management Strategy, March 30, 2000," 1.

39 The other three departments are Alberta Agriculture, Food and Rural Development, Alberta Resource Development, and Alberta Economic Development. The hostility of a department like Alberta Resource Development to environmental values was illustrated by the province's Special Places 2000 Program. Opposition from Alberta Resource Development (then called Alberta Energy) helped compromise Special Places' wilderness protection objective. See Andrew Nikiforuk, "Oh Wilderness: The Promise of Special Places 2000 Betrayed," *Alberta Views*, Vol. 1, no. 4 (Fall 1998).

40 Luscar, "Cheviot Mine Postponed-Luscar Mine to be Closed by Mid-2002," (press release), 24 October 2000.

41 "Hinton faces exodus as Cheviot shelved," *The Edmonton Journal*, 25 October 2000.

Nature as Playground

RECREATION AND GENTRIFICATION
IN THE MOUNTAIN WEST

Dave Whitson

In *The Culture of Nature,* a wide-ranging meditation on North Americans' changing associations with nature and with the land, Alexander Wilson suggests that over the postwar decades, nature has become, for most Americans and Canadians, primarily a playground.[1] Outdoor recreations like skiing, golf, camping, and water sports have become part of the "lifestyle" of the urban middle classes; and as a result, sites for these activities—ski hills, golf courses, cottages and campgrounds, and marinas—have burgeoned across the North American landscape, wherever suitable terrain and improved accessibility make weekend recreation feasible. In the lake country north of Toronto, Ottawa, and Montreal, demand for recreational real estate quickly drove up property prices, and recreational uses supplanted mixed farming on land that had usually been marginal for agricultural purposes. In other regions, notably the Alberta foothills and the southern BC interior, agriculture and forestry have remained important in local economies. Yet demand for golf, skiing, and second homes has created opportunities to make even *more* money from recreation and recreational property, and this has led to changes in the population and landscape of once-rural regions like the Okanagan and the eastern slopes of the Rockies.

It represents a significant departure from our past as a nation of agriculture and resource extraction if most Canadians now relate to nature primarily as a place of leisure and if many rural regions are now more valuable as "recreation resources" than for the farming and forestry once associated with them. Not all rural areas, of course, have the right kinds of terrain and scenery. However, for those that do, new economic possibilities have opened up. Wilson suggests that this transformation has its roots in the postwar urbanization of North America, and the prosperity and rising living standards that accompanied it. Before this, even though rural people had always enjoyed the recreational possibilities available in their particular environments, rural recreation was relatively casual and uncommercialized. Demand for nature holidays, and for the range of specialized commodities and services now associated with outdoor recreation, followed population shifts from rural areas into cities and into waged or salaried employment. It was a response by burgeoning urban and suburban populations to the circumstances of their new postwar lives. In these conditions, "nature became a place of leisure on weekends and summer holidays; it became attached to the schedules and personal geographies of an urban society."[2]

Along with urbanization, postwar trends that contributed to the boom in outdoor recreation included rising levels of disposable income among both the middle and skilled working classes, and the growth of leisure as a democratic social expectation. It is ironic today to recall the confident futurism of the 1960s, in which the advent of the "leisure society" was widely predicted. Yet reductions in the working week and increases in annual holidays were standard items on collective bargaining agendas in the 1960s, and real if temporary progress was made in this direction. When more leisure time was accompanied by rises in real incomes sufficient to finance recreational equipment and travel, weekends and vacations in the countryside became normal routines in the lives of more and more Canadian families. Indeed the cottage, or a family camping vacation, quickly came to be significant occasions for the practice of "family," as postwar parents sought to respond to a social ideology that idealized family togetherness, while steadily confining to the realm of holidays the actual times and activities that many families could share.[3]

As the expansion of national highway systems in both the US and Canada made national parks in the mountain West more accessible and other provincial highways (Hwy. 400 in Ontario and later the Coquihalla in BC) brought country once considered remote to within a 3–5 hour drive of major cities, travelling to mountain and lakeside vacations and even second homes became an annual ritual for many Canadian families. Recreation became an increasingly familiar rural land use, and the money invested in recreational property began to increase. The cottage lifestyle became accessible to a wide cross-section of postwar Canada, with the result that for many "boomers" and their parents, the cottage remains a site of fondly remembered family events. At the same time, urban money chasing recreational property would steadily push up rural land prices in the more attractive and accessible areas, and this would combine with the costs of new leisure commodities and lifestyle expectations to make cottaging a steadily more expensive proposition.

FROM COTTAGES TO CONDOS: "SPORTIFICATION" AND GENTRIFICATION

In the early postwar years, cottages were typically simple summer dwellings, of basic wooden construction, without insulation, and often without electricity or indoor toilets. Indeed, for most cottagers of the 1950s, it was precisely the contrasts with city amenities and lifestyles that were part of the cottage's special place in their lives. Moreover, the standard fun of cottage days in this era still consisted of activities like swimming, berry-picking, canoeing, and fishing: activities that required little in the way of accessories, user fees, or other expenditures. They exemplified the possibilities of non-commodified fun, of having good times at little or no cost. Over the course of the 1960s and 1970s, the characteristics of recreational homes, and the lifestyles associated with them, began to change. Newly built cottages tended to be bigger and to include electricity, running water and indoor plumbing, and better heating and insulation. Before long, it was not uncommon for families to have at the cottage all of the modern appliances that made life easier at home, as well as telephones, record players, televisions, and later (in the 1990s) computers. As these amenities became more normal, it is not surprising that many cottages came to look (and cost) more like urban homes.[4] Certainly, there were families who resisted these trends; but postwar children were growing up in a world where more home comforts were taken for granted and where "standards of living" now included an unprecedented array of leisure equipment and activities. In these circumstances, parents often felt some pressure to satisfy their children's expectations, and most tried, within their means, to do so.[5] At the cottage, this would gradually normalize the presence of telephones, televisions, motorboats, and new forms of commodified fun.

Water-skiing, golf, and skiing all illustrate these new tendencies in postwar family recreation. These are all activities that require the purchase of (more or less) expensive equipment, and often lessons too. Golf and skiing further require the payment of substantial access fees, whether in the form of member-ships or daily passes. What is noteworthy here, beyond the rise in costs itself, is a blurring of older differences in ethos between outdoor recreations and sports, as the former take on the latter's characteristic emphases on skill development, performance, and competition. This has contributed, over time, to the "sportification" of many outdoor activities—cross-country skiing, mountain biking, and rock climbing—and as Everest climber Sharon Wood notes, to a whole new industry in outdoor adventure instruction that is visible in towns like Canmore.[6] However its most immediate effect was to generate enormous interest in performance-enhancing equipment.

This was achieved, at one level, through advances in technology and design that made equipment lighter, safer, and easier to use. New developments in both downhill and cross-country skis and bindings, for example, enabled chil-dren and older adults (of both sexes) to enjoy sports that were once the preserve of fairly serious athletes. In addition, though, fashion has become important, and design advances have combined with changing fashions in outdoor clothing and equipment to produce annual revisions of product lines that quickly render perfectly sound gear old-fashioned. These interconnections between product innovation, fashion, and marketing were familiar in other consumer goods industries, of course; but since the 1970s, they have been skilfully deployed by brands like Patagonia, Salomon, and The North Face, normalizing levels and styles of consumerism not previously associated with outdoor recreation.

It should be remembered that, in leisure as in other spheres of life, "the urban and the affluent organized their lives around consumption earlier than did the rural or the poor."[7] In addition, the early decades of cottage consumerism brought seasonal prosperity to significant numbers of "locals": marina operators, grocers, property owners with land to sell, and (most of all) contractors. However, affluent lifestyles were quickly transforming into images of popular aspiration in an upwardly mobile society; and as golf and skiing, in particular, became part of the cultural capital of the business and professional classes, interest in these sports would start to change the face of many rural areas. This is because each of these sports requires significant land assembly, extensive transformation and contouring of that land, and increasingly heavy capital expenditure.

Again, it is useful to trace the progression of norms over successive postwar decades. In the 1960s, although architect-designed golf courses began to sprout around the edges of our major cities, rural courses were still relatively unpretentious, often nine-hole layouts. As long as their "tourist" trade was limited to school vacations, golf courses in regions like Muskoka or the Okanagan remained small-scale ventures run by local entrepreneurs. Ski hills were even more marginal investments, virtually everywhere outside of the Rockies and the Laurentians. Substantial capital was required to develop any choice of runs and to install even simple lift technologies, and before the advent of snowmaking (itself expensive, of course), a ski operator in Southern Ontario or the BC Interior could be bankrupted by a single season of poor weather. Ski hills survived, often under successive owners, around Collingwood in Ontario, in several interior valleys in BC, and in the Eastern Townships in Quebec—all regions that offered excellent skiing when conditions were right. However, they were typically undercapitalized and couldn't accommodate high volumes of vacationers. Like the golf courses of these same regions, they remained local operations, awaiting outside investors with bigger plans and more money.

These would begin to materialize in the early 1980s, in direct relationship to booms in the economies of metro Toronto, Vancouver, and Calgary and Edmonton during these years. These booms had created substantial wealth in the business and professional classes of these cities, and unprecedented numbers who could afford winterized holiday homes. Meanwhile, new highways like the Coquihalla and the Okanagan Connector made ski destinations in the BC Interior feasible for weekenders from Vancouver and Seattle. In this context, larger investors developed resorts that competed to serve this demand with better, higher value-added facilities. This meant expanding the skiing to include a greater variety of runs and substantially increasing both the capacity and comfort of the tow systems. It also meant developing on-site restaurant and après-ski facilities, so that skiers could enjoy a stylish holiday and, not incidentally, spend more money. Most importantly, though, it meant real estate development on a scale that would ultimately transform regions like the Okanagan, the Bow Valley, and the Collingwood area of Ontario. Towns like Kelowna, Vernon, Canmore, and Collingwood have all mushroomed well beyond what used to be their boundaries; and many of these developments aptly illustrate the maxim that the property development industry is about the creation and sale not just of new living spaces but of the lifestyles associated with them.

Three aspects of these lifestyle-oriented property developments will concern us here. First, and most importantly, these are developments aimed at "incomers": primarily business and professional people from nearby metropolitan centres who are attracted to an area for its holiday possibilities. Indeed, the influx of outside money and population associated with gentrification (as in the urban context) is precisely what creates economic growth. Yet affluent newcomers, buying with money made in bigger and richer economies, tend to want features like cathedral ceilings, European kitchens, and multiple garages, all of which add significantly to unit costs. The result is that new developments are often priced beyond what people working in the local economy, or at least the old local economy, can afford. This can lead to *de facto* residential segregation and often sharply rising rents as older rental accommodation is upgraded and converted to condominiums. Moreover, people who have paid a quarter million dollars for their homes often want the municipal services they have taken for granted in the cities they have left behind: paved roads, snow removal, and (following Milne, this volume) modern recreation centres. However, as Canmore town planner Steve de Keijzer observes, the improvement and diffusion of town services can raise property taxes beyond what locals are used to, creating political divisions between the two groups.[8]

Another corollary of gentrification can be seen in the kinds of suburban sprawl that now characterize communities like Kelowna and Canmore, and in the kinds of commercial services that spring up to cater to the new residents. Suburban-style malls with franchises of national chains (e.g., Safeway, Subway, Home Depot) create price competition for longtime local merchants. Meanwhile, when downtown premises change hands, shops that traditionally supplied household needs are supplanted by boutiques selling "value-added" goods and services: brew pubs, art and craft galleries, specialty outdoor clothing shops, and now financial services. Gradually, the commercial texture of the rural service centre is transformed by businesses catering to the needs and tastes of urban holiday-makers, retirees, and "telecommuters." These tendencies began to manifest themselves in US mountain communities in the 1980s—in places like Telluride, Park City, Taos, and Moab—and they are visible today in all of the Canadian communities identified above.[9]

Gentrification, it can be proposed, inevitably involves adding value to property and changing the character of communities, whether in urban neighbourhoods or rural towns. However, these same processes also produce personal and cultural dislocations that the upbeat promotional brochures of the holiday and property industries seldom acknowledge. Gentrification leads to competitions for space and for public resources, competitions in which affluent newcomers enjoy significant advantages. This can produce economic and political divisions around issues like zoning, property taxes, and what municipal services will be funded (road improvements and snow removal vs. affordable housing or youth services, for example). Today, in a resort community like Canmore, accommodation costs have risen so steeply that people working in the new service industries often struggle to make ends meet. Young single workers, who have often come to ski themselves, can make do with shared accommodations (often overcrowded and sometimes illegal). For those with families, however, according to town official Dales Judd, the housing market is more difficult. People working in the public services need two professional incomes in order to afford a modest house; while for waged workers, the options are trailer parks or long commutes from nearby communities where housing costs remain lower (from Cochrane to Canmore, for example, or Pemberton to Whistler). Judd here concurs with de Keijzer that planning for affordable housing is one of the most difficult challenges facing such communities.[10]

THE NEW LEISURE INDUSTRIES AND THE "WORLD-CLASS" RESORT

All of these tendencies—the commodification of outdoor recreation, growth fuelled by outside money, suburbanization, and gentrification—are presented in sharpened forms by 1990s developments that favour well-capitalized, corporate-operated resorts. The driving forces here are globalization and the emergence of transnational resort corporations whose business is precisely the production of recreational destinations for tourists, homeowners, and investors—a business that has been facilitated by the removal of obstacles to foreign ownership of property in many places, including Canada.[11] This has made recreational Canadian real estate attractive to buyers (individual buyers, as well as corporations) from Japan, Europe, and America, all societies where land in beautiful places is both less available and more expensive.

At the same time, the scale of capital investment and the specialist expertise now required to build "world-class" ski hills and golf courses have led to corporate consolidation in these industries. Resorts unable to upgrade their facilities to the standards set by well-known destinations lost customers in droves. The result was, just as in other rural industries discussed in this volume, that small operators were driven out of business or taken over by corporate investors with the capital to finance expansion. One example of the latter pattern has seen Intrawest Corp. of Vancouver, developers of Blackcomb Resort near Whistler, take over Panorama in the BC interior, Mont Tremblant in the Laurentians, Whistler itself, and several American mountain resorts. The effect of these acquisitions is to make TSE-listed Intrawest the second-largest ski-resort operator in North America. Indeed, in Intrawest, Canadian expertise and capital have created a global player in the mountain resort business, while one of its Canadian competitors, Resorts of the Canadian Rockies, has also expanded from their original property at Skiing Louise to six other mountain resorts in Alberta, BC, and Quebec.

However, another version of this same dynamic has seen the Japanese giant Nippon Cable, one of Japan's largest ski operators, take over the former Tod Mountain near Kamloops and invest heavily in bringing that formerly local operation up to "world-class" standards. When Nippon took over in 1992, although Tod boasted the longest vertical drop in the BC interior and some of the best snow and ski terrain east of Whistler, the mountain was underdeveloped in terms of runs and tows, and it had only a day-use cafeteria by way of amenities. Now, after 8 years and more than $150 million in investment, the renamed Sun Peaks features vastly expanded skiing, 6 high-speed lifts, and a mid-mountain restaurant. Just as important is the village that has taken shape at the base of the mountain, complete with new hotels, condominium developments, and private homes, as well as a variety of upscale shops and restaurants. Now, "with tourists from Japan and Europe adding a stop here after a week at Whistler/Blackcomb, Sun Peaks is quietly developing into not only a provincial, but an international class skiing mountain."[12] According to Canadian ski legend Nancy Greene, Sun Peaks can now compete on climate, value, and atmosphere for skiers looking for a quality Canadian ski experience.[13] The resort has also added a golf course and other attractions that add to its year-round appeal.

Several dimensions of the new economics of the resort industry are worth highlighting here. The basic requirement is the capital necessary to enhance the skiing: by developing more runs on the mountain and by improving the speed, comfort, and capacity of the lift system. When these are in place, more skiers can get up and down the mountain more often, and a resort can offer a greater variety of interesting runs to skiers at every level of ability. As Intrawest observes,

The customer's demand for a premier ski experience requires capital-intensive technology that is considerably more expensive than previous generations of hardware.[14]

However, today's ski vacationer expects more from a holiday than just good skiing, and Intrawest and other successful resort operators have also recognized the importance of offering an attractive ambience. This starts with better food on the mountain itself, and extends to an attractive "mountain village" where destination skiers can enjoy fine dining, shopping, and other forms of après-ski entertainment. Again, investment in the non-ski facilities that contribute to the total "mountain resort experience" requires considerable capital. However, Intrawest found, at Blackcomb and Whistler and more recently at Mont Tremblant, that "adding value" to both ski and non-ski facilities pays off, both by attracting more visitors *and* by increasing the average amounts that each visitor spends. Maximizing each figure, indeed, becomes the object of corporate strategy:

> In order to maintain profitability, ski resorts must increase per capita spending and, at the same time, increase the use of available capacity during non-peak periods. Consistent with this strategy, successful mountain resorts must also find ways to create a 12-month operating year.[15]

The latter usually involves two mutually reinforcing strategies: developing alternative off-season recreational attractions and developing more home units. The historical difficulty with the economics of skiing has been the seasonal character of its revenues, and today, the scale of investment required virtually dictates that resorts must develop off-season attractions. Thus it is not surprising that, up and down the US mountain West, "Attempts to establish a year round economy have brought about golf courses designed by Arnold Palmer and Jack Nicklaus, racquet and health clubs, and every kind of music, art and balloon festival you can imagine."[16] In Canadian destinations, the development of "soft adventure" products—whitewater canoeing, mountain biking, guided walks, and nature photography—has been an important focus, especially in locations like Sun Peaks and Fernie where the narrow mountain valleys limit the development of golf. However, real estate development remains the most important single thing, not least because, as noted above, it provides a source of capital that helps to finance new ski facilities. It is also important because homeowners (and their families and friends) increase the midweek customer base for the resort, and for other businesses in the community.

According to Intrawest's calculations, "a typical lodging unit at an Intrawest resort generates approximately $16,000 in revenue every year."[17]

Thus, it is hardly surprising that real estate development is central to Intrawest's long-term corporate strategy, with at least 15,000 units scheduled for development at Intrawest resorts around North America over the next 12–15 years. Intrawest has developed a systematic approach to planning, design, construction, and marketing, the key to which lies in the integration of different aspects of resort-building:

> We start with a mountain and enhance the skiing. Then build an animated place so that people stay longer. All this attracts more skiers who come more often, spend more money and bring their friends. More real estate is built and attractions are added, drawing yet more people…[which] leads to the expansion of year-round facilities, maximizing the value of shops, hotels, convention facilities and restaurants… As occupancy and room rates climb, so does demand for resort real estate, creating a surge in real estate sales. All this results in a total resort experience which brings year-round destination visitors, generating the financial critical mass which…leads to more [resorts].[18]

The synergies that Intrawest envisages between the different features of a successful mountain resort (and, indeed, a successful mountain resort corporation) are clearly explicated here, including the linkages between real estate and year-round facilities. This is because purchasers of resort and retirement homes are likely to choose communities where there are recreational opportunities available throughout the year. The biggest warm-weather attraction in this market is golf, with the result that almost every winter ski destination is now also the site of one or more designer golf courses, even places where constructing and maintaining a "world-class" golf course can create significant pressures on fragile mountain and valley environments. This is because golf has become, perhaps even more so than skiing, the lifestyle sport of the business and professional classes. Thus any resort destination that wants to attract these high-spending people—whether for conventions or sales meetings, on vacations, or in retirement—must offer challenging and well-kept golf courses, in scenically beautiful environments (again, see Milne, this volume).

Indeed, the perceived importance of golf to recreational land development and the development of a recreation and tourism economy has been illustrated repeatedly in Alberta, where the provincial government approved "world-class" golf and property developments (by Three Sisters and SilverTip) in the Canmore area, in the face of fierce opposition by environmentalists and others concerned with wildlife habitat in the Bow Corridor. The attitude of at least some provincial Tories was revealed in an e-mail by former political advisor Rod Love, where he referred to opponents of more golf development as "communists" and urged the Economic Development Ministry to "get aggressive" in helping Three Sisters move ahead.[19] More recently, local and provincial environmentalist groups have been joined by Canmore Town Council in opposing a major golf and ski development proposed by Genesis Land Development for the Spray Lakes. This proposal was provisionally approved by the province despite a 1999 policy that had appeared to preclude new resort development in Kananaskis Country.[20]

In British Columbia, too, the provincial (NDP) cabinet overruled the province's Agricultural Land Reserve Commissioners and approved development of a 27-hole golf course, 1000 housing units, and a guest ranch, at Six Mile Ranch on Kamloops Lake.[21] In this case, it is noteworthy that the developer enjoys almost unanimous support in Kamloops, including business and labour organizations as well as local politicians. This is not only because of the immediate prospect of jobs but because the land is widely seen by Kamloops-area people to have more economic potential as a "recreational resource" than it has ever had for agriculture or ranching. However, the development has been controversial because of opposition from Vancouver-based environmental groups, as well as from local First Nations bands who have made claims to the land, as they have also done more recently at Sun Peaks.

It would require another paper to adequately discuss the growth of the golf industry and its social and environmental impacts in places like the Caribbean, the southwestern United States, Hawaii, and Australia.[22] What is germane here is simply to note that golf is now almost essential to the economics of any Canadian ski resort: from Whistler and the Okanagan resorts, through Canmore and Kananaskis in the Alberta Rockies, to Ontario and Quebec. In addition, golf courses (and privileged or exclusive access to them) are also the central selling points in many other property developments, including retirement home developments in parts of the country where skiing is not an option. These are appearing in parts of southern Vancouver Island and southern Ontario, just as they did in many of the southern states, where the private ownership structure of the golf "club" also serves as a legal way of maintaining the exclusivity of gated communities.[23] The concept of the gated community is, fortunately, not nearly so established in Canada as it has become in the southern and western

US. Yet even the beginnings of such "lifestyle communities," as property developments anchored by golf courses or marinas are often called, should alert us to the social segregation that follows almost inevitably from the price structure of these developments.

Finally, it is worth noting that golf, too, is becoming corporatized, as stand-alone courses find it difficult to upgrade their playing and clubhouse facilities to the standards that today's patrons expect. In corporate dynamics not unlike those in the ski industry, publicly traded ClubLink now owns and operates more than ten golf courses in southern Ontario, including several formerly independent resort courses in the cottage country north of Toronto. ClubLink is particularly interested in the potential of golf resorts and in "repositioning" what used to be family golf courses in the Muskoka region. "Golf is becoming the key amenity in marketing upscale resorts, especially for the conference business ... and corporate entertaining."[24] Indeed, in developing upmarket real estate in conjunction with its resort courses, and in building a luxury hotel (to be operated by Delta Hotels) at its championship Glen Abbey course near Oakville,[25] ClubLink is adapting strategies modelled by Intrawest in the ski industry.

What is illustrated in the success of both Intrawest and ClubLink is just how big an industry the production of "world-class" skiing and golf has become, and how the production of upscale sporting destinations is changing both the landscape and the demographic makeup of rural Canadian communities that have the right kinds of space and scenery. With respect to the landscape, what matters is that both of these sports take up large tracts of land and require that the land be reshaped and groomed in ways that can have significant environmental effects. For golf in the urban fringe, this may involve only modest sculpting of terrain already "tamed" for agricultural or other purposes. In the case of skiing, though, as well as golf courses in mountain regions, the development of sporting venues involves the conversion, to groomed and contoured forms, of terrain that was hitherto "undeveloped" and thus available for non-commodified forms of recreation like hiking or cross-country skiing. This creates economic opportunities, as land development always seeks to do. However, it also reduces that stock of relatively "wild" places in which free outdoor pastimes can be enjoyed by Canadians. This presents a particular dilemma in our Rocky Mountain parks, where resort operators (Sunshine and Skiing Louise) have sought permission to develop more accommodation, more skiing, and more golf, all in order to compete with the likes of Whistler, Mont Tremblant, and *their* competitors in the US and Europe.[26] Nancy Greene of

Sun Peaks has proposed that we may need to limit the number of beds that can be developed in popular national parks like Banff if we want to save the park itself. However, she points out that if we do this, the price of staying in Banff may increase beyond the means of most Canadians.

> So perhaps what our governments should be looking at is buying up some of the hotels and beds in Banff National Park and making them available exclusively to Canadians, maybe some for school groups, Elder hostels, places where Canadians can experience the Parks without having to pay the cost of an international bed.[27]

Greene recognizes this as "a very radical position" but considers it worth discussion.

URBAN LIFESTYLES IN RURAL PLACES

As far as demographic change is concerned, the basic issue is that "world-class" developments and the kinds of tourists and residents they are designed to attract inevitably alter the social and commercial makeup of the communities where they are situated. As sophisticated tourists and affluent urban refugees form a critical mass capable of supporting cappuccino bars, good restaurants and bookstores, and shops selling state-of-the-art gear for outdoor sports, resort communities become more urbane and upmarket in their commercial makeup than they were in their days as mining towns or agricultural service centres. One effect of this gentrification of commerce can be to leave some "old-time" residents feeling like strangers in their own communities; and indeed towns like Canmore and Kelowna have now grown and changed so much that they have become, effectively, different communities. At the same time, it is also true that some of the new businesses that cater to urban tastes and interests provide welcome new opportunities for other locals who have long wanted options (commercial choices as well as cultural choices) that traditional resource towns seldom offered. For many women and young people, for example, new ventures like vegetarian restaurants, arts co-ops, good bookstores, and summer festivals come like a breath of fresh air. They offer new kinds of jobs and new ways of being, and for some they make these communities more diverse and interesting places than they were before.

Nonetheless, it is hardly surprising that these changes are not universally popular, either with traditional blue-collar residents or earlier urban émigrés who may have chosen life in fishing or logging communities at least partly because of the character of the local culture. In this spirit, American wilderness essayist Edward Abbey complained thirty years ago about many features of the postwar recreation boom that were identified in earlier sections of this paper. Abbey took particular issue with building highways into parks and other beauty spots, with "improving" US national parks so that they could accommodate car campers and motor homes, and with the transformation of quirky old mining towns like Telluride into fancy ski resorts.[28] Such "developments," for Abbey, prefigured the urbanization of the rural West and the loss of rural culture. Likewise, John Nichols' novel (and film) *The Milagro Beanfield War* depicts a struggle that is at one level ethnic, between rich urban Anglos and poor Hispanic farmers in northern New Mexico. However at another level, Nichols' story also depicts the same dynamics described here: the impacts of a proposed recreational development (in this case, golf and fishing, along with holiday homes), on a rural community, and the dislocations that can be foreseen when outsiders' recreation becomes a more valuable land use than the traditional ways that rural people have made livings from the land.

One needs to distinguish here between the effects of urbanization—where this means not the spread of cities themselves so much as the spread of urban tastes and interests into rural areas—and those of gentrification, where that means (as indeed it does in urban areas too) the transformation of neighbourhoods by outside money and the displacement of former residents. There are, indeed, many urban people retiring to places like Vernon and Sechelt and Kamloops for their recreational and climatic attractions. However, while those who buy their new homes from resort developers are indeed buying at higher prices than most local buyers can afford, there are also other "incomers" who buy their homes (and other goods) from locals and who participate in these communities in other ways, too (see Milne, this volume). Even more important, perhaps, as a harbinger of the future are the increasing numbers of young people—including young business and professional people, but also other young people making lifestyle choices of their own—who are opting to work in rural locations in ways that have nothing to do with the traditional economy.[29] The result, observes Montana writer Donald Snow, is that we now find communities with incongruously urban amenities in some beautiful and out-of-the-way places: around Yellowstone and Glacier national parks in Montana, in the interior valleys of Colorado, and in the canyon country of Utah.[30] In Canada, we might add to this list the Okanagan and the Kootenays in the BC interior, the Sunshine Coast and Gulf Islands, Canmore, and "Harrowsmith country" in southeastern Ontario.

Here, it is worth considering the thoughts of ski developer Matt Mosteller on Colorado, where the transition from a resource-extraction economy to one based on tourism is effectively complete and where tourism is now worth far more to the state, in real dollars, than either mining or forestry.[31] In Colorado, the ski industry is now mature, in the sense that new resorts are unlikely to be developed, both because the best locations are gone and because the costs and environmental restrictions associated with developing new areas would now be prohibitive. In this context, the value of real estate in a small (and relatively isolated) resort like Telluride has doubled in the last five years. Thus, it is not hard to see why, from an industry point of view, the interior of BC now looks like "the last best West," for future recreational developments. Moreover, Mosteller suggests, investment in upgrading existing resorts—such as Kimberley, Fernie, Tod Mountain, and Red Mountain—is more cost-effective than trying to build completely new ones (at Jumbo Pass, for example, or Melvin Creek, where resort proposals remain in limbo as a result of environmental and First Nations opposition). The climate and snow conditions in these locations are ideal, and some infrastructure is already in place, at 1980s costs. This, in turn, makes the prices at which both holidays and real estate can be offered on the global market highly attractive. Indeed, even in locations where prices have already appreciated in recent years (e.g., Fernie or Sun Peaks), they are still cheap in comparison with Colorado resorts, with Jackson Hole, with Europe, or with Whistler. Thus, resort companies are already taking advantage of the opportunities they represent, with new waves of home-buyers and holiday-makers already on the drawing board, if not yet on site. Nonetheless, upgrades to "world-class" standards, and holidays and real estate products aimed at international markets inevitably mean price increases, lots of newcomers, and other changes to "funky" resorts that long-time locals object to.

It is important, though, to be clear about what (if anything) we should find objectionable in this scenario. Although Snow pokes gentle fun at the proliferation of "cappuccino cowboys" in the American West, he is quick to acknowledge that it would be churlish to knock the aspirations of these increasing numbers of urban refugees "who want to borrow the liberties and sensibilities of rural life, and have figured out the daunting question of livelihood in place(s) that have never yielded an easy living to anyone."[32] If relocating from urban areas to communities that offer ready access to nature-based recreation is becoming a common lifestyle choice, one form of that late twentieth-century geographic and social mobility that Raymond Williams has called "mobile privatisation,"[33] it would be as pointless to oppose this as it would have been to oppose suburbanization in the 1960s. Equally, it is hard to see why we should object to the urbanization of rural cultures—if this means good bookstores, coffee, and internet access—except out of nostalgic affection for past ways of life and for the smaller and more homogeneous communities that characterized older kind of rural economy. If the mining, fishing, forest, and agricultural economies that sustained communities in rural Canada in the past are destroyed by globalization, it is hard to imagine that the cultural practices associated with those ways of life can live on, except in museums, "heritage days," and other simulations of local history.

Other lessons can be drawn from communities like Kamloops and Vernon, where recreation and tourism are growing rapidly but where the "old economy" also remains a significant source of employment. In Kamloops, pulp mills were the most prominent feature of the local landscape through the postwar decades, and (along with the railways) they were the region's major employers.[34] Yet, as many professionals who came to the city to pursue their careers discovered, the Thompson Valley offers a wealth of lifestyle attractions—golf, skiing, lakes, and cottage property—all at prices that their metropolitan counterparts could only dream of. Now, Kamloops is being "discovered" by others who might once have dismissed it as a blue-collar town—and not just retirees, but faculty and students at a growing university, young professionals, and a burgeoning core of small high-tech businesses. Following Tom Power's analysis of recent in-migration into Montana and other Rocky Mountain states, it can be suggested that people with choices about where to build their careers or businesses are increasingly choosing to locate in communities that offer lifestyle attractions.[35] And Kamloops is now actively promoting itself, both as a tourist destination and as an attractive and affordable place to live. According to Mayor Mel Rothenberger, the development of Sun Peaks has been important to the city's economy (especially to the construction trades), as has the hosting of events like the Canada Games and Memorial Cup. Kamloops is also emerging as an increasingly popular golf destination.[36] Most important of all is that each of these elements—along with the university and the new restaurants and bookstores downtown—have contributed to diversifying the image that others have of Kamloops—and indeed that Kamloops has of itself. Kamloops is now widely seen as having more to offer, both to visitors and to its own young people, and Rothenberger suggests that, over the long term, this is the best foundation for economic diversification and future prosperity.

Nonetheless, it is important to recognize that the long-term trends discussed in this paper—the commodification of recreational land, the growth of global tourism, and the spending power of newcomers—are not simply changing the character of Canadian resource communities. They are often displacing the rural working class who have historically called these places home. In just this context, it is worth recalling English sociologist Stuart Hall's suggestion that "cultural change" is often a polite euphemism for the processes by which some cultures, and the people who live them, are actively pushed aside so that others can take their place.[37] And when this happens, it *is* legitimate to be concerned about the fate of those who are displaced. As places in the West with the right kinds of recreational resources have become playgrounds for urban (and increasingly global) money, workers have too often found themselves pushed aside, either to the fringes of their own communities or to the margins of cities that ex-urbanites have chosen to leave behind.

Property development, as we have noted, is precisely intended to attract new people and new money into a community, and any major influx of affluent residents creates a range of economic opportunities in real estate, construction, and services. Yet Canada's experience of resource booms should teach us that rapid regional growth can have dis-integrating effects upon and within communities, creating displacement and social fissures that hinterland local governments haven't the resources (or sometimes the will) to repair. This is not a new issue; we noted that even the early transformation of "cottage country" often led to higher accommodation costs and taxes for rural working people and to divisions between newcomers and "locals" over provision of services to property vs. services to people. However, the globalization of the recreational property market through the 1990s has dramatically pushed up property prices in the most attractive "lifestyle" destinations, further widening divisions between those with the means to make money from these developments and those who work for wages. These divisions are clearest around the issue of affordable housing. In resort communities across the US mountain West—e.g., Aspen, Jackson Hole, Telluride, Sun Valley—working people (both in the old economy and the new service economy) can no longer afford to live within the community,[38] and this same phenomenon is appearing around Canadian resort communities, from Banff–Canmore to Whistler. What happens is that incomers push up the price of land and housing, and in the absence of municipal measures aimed at mitigating market forces, the superior capital of the incomers almost inevitably prevails.[39]

At the same time, we need to recognize that places like the Okanagan and Canmore are much more affluent, and easier to make a living in, than they were a generation ago. Moreover, it is not difficult to find older residents in these communities (and in Vernon or Kamloops) who welcome the fact that the new tourism and leisure economy has made it possible for their children and grand-children to remain in (or return to) the community, rather than making their lives in Vancouver, or further afield. Indeed, despite fluctuations in the tourist economy, neither agriculture nor mining nor forestry has ever delivered such sustained prosperity for these regions, and it bears remembering that many mountain communities have actively sought ski and retirement developments, if not as direct alternatives to mine/mill closures (as in the case of Kimberley), at least as strategies for economic diversification (e.g., in Golden). It further bears remembering that some places are more fortunate than others in *having* the kinds of recreational resources that attract tourists and new residents, and that if growth brings with it some of the problems I have outlined in this paper, there are other rural communities where closure of a mine or the decline of the farm economy has simply meant an exodus of those with any options at all and a collapse of property values for those who remain (see Coates and Mandryk, this volume). This points to three final thoughts.

First, as traditional rural industries struggle and community leaders search for ways to diversify their economies, it is important to remember that strategies cannot focus solely on holding onto the landscapes and economies of the past.[40] Other Canadian communities, notably in the suburban areas around our major cities, are also experiencing dramatic demographic and cultural changes today, and it is hard to imagine that rural communities can remain as they were simply by putting up obstacles to the kinds of development outlined here. This means, in turn, that one crucial struggle in mountain communities, just as in other rural locales, must be for creative community planning mechanisms (such as BC's "Community Futures") which assist local people in developing their *own* plans for different futures, rather than having those futures determined by outside interests, as has happened so often in the past across rural Canada. Finally, though, if the "mobility rights" popularly associated with globalization also imply any right to remain "in place,"[41] it is important that rural working people have choices and are not simply pushed to the margins when people who have choices want to turn the places that have been the source of their traditional livelihoods into spaces of leisure and "lifestyle."

Notes

This is a revised version of a paper first presented at Parkland Institute Conference at the University of Alberta.

1   Alexander Wilson, *The Culture of Nature: North American Landscape from Disney to the Exxon Val*dez (Toronto: Between the Lines, 1991).

2   Ibid., 26.

3   Doug Owram, *Born At the Right Time: A History of the Baby Boom Generation* (Toronto: University of Toronto Press, 1996), ch 3, 4. For another perspective on "family" issues, see also M. Cerullo and P. Ewen, "The American Family Goes Camping: Gender, Family, and the Politics of Space," *Antipode*, 10(4): 35–45, 1984.

4   See John Barber, "Out of Reach: The changing face of cottage country," *Globe & Mail*, September 4, 1999, A7; also Greg Halseth, *Cottage Country in Transition: A Social Geography of Change and Contention in the Rural-Recreational Countryside* (Montreal: McGill-Queen's University Press, 1998).

5   Owram, *Born At the Right Time*, 93.

6   Interview with author, February 2000, Canmore, Alberta.

7   Owram, *Born At the Right Time*, 94.

8   Interview with author, February, 2000. See also Don Snow, "As the Mirage Begins to Fade," *Northern Lights*, 10(2), 1994, 3.

9   See R. Ringholz, *Little Town Blues: Voices From the Changing West* (Salt Lake City: Gibbs Smith, 1992), as well as Snow, op. cit., for insightful discussions of the US experience.

10 Interview with author, February, 2000; for a US example, see Mike Medberry, "Sun Valley: Just Another Perfect Place in the Mountains?," *Northern Lights*, 7(1), 1991, 12–13.

11 Samuel Britton, "Tourism, Capital, and Place: Towards a Critical Geography of Tourism," *Environment & Planning (D): Society & Space*, 9, 1991, 451–478.

12 *Edmonton Journal*, 24 January 1998, H4.

13 Interview with author, January 2000.

14 Intrawest Corp., *Annual Report*, 1994, 21.

15 Ibid., 21.

16 Ringholz, *Little Town Blues*, 14

17 Intrawest Corp., *Annual Report*, 1997, 19.

18 Ibid., 12–13.

19 *Canmore Leader*, 29 February 2000, A1, A6, A7.

20 See *Canmore Leader*, 7 March 2000.

21 *Globe and Mail*, 28 February 1998, A10; 4 March 1998, A22.

22 See Brian Stoddart, "Wide World of Golf: A Research Note on the Interdependence of Sport, Culture, and Economy," *Sociology of Sport Journal*, 7(4), 1990, 378–388; also Wilson's comments on the struggle at Oka in 1990, *The Culture of Nature*, op. cit., 1–2.

23 See E.J. Blakely & M.G. Snyder, *Fortress America: Gated Communities in the United States* (Washington: Brookings Institute/Lincoln Institute of Land Policy, 1997). Also, Jim Robbins, "Jackson, Wyoming," *Northern Lights*, 7(1): 19–21, 1991.

24 Bruce Simmonds, Club Link CEO, cited by Leonard Zehr, *Globe and Mail Report on Business*, 31 October 1997, B12.

25 D. King, "Want to pull a Glen Abbey all-nighter?," *Globe and Mail*, 31 October 2000, P1.

26 See Bill Corbett, "The Battle for Banff," in Ian Urquhart (ed.), *Assault on the Rockies: Environmental Controversies in Alberta* (Edmonton: Rowan Books, 1996), 129–136.

27 *Communique*, December 1999.

28 See, "Polemic: Industrial Tourism and the National Parks," *Desert Solitaire* (NY: Ballantine Books, 1968), and "Telluride Blues: A Hatchet Job," *The Journey Home* (NY: Dutton, 1977).

29 T.M. Power, "High Quality Natural Environments and Local Economic Development," in Ian Urquhart (ed.), *Assault on the Rockies,* op. cit., 197–199; see also Milne, this volume.

30 Donald Snow, "Cappucicno Cowboys," *Northern Lights*, 7(4): 3, 1994.

31 Author's interview with Matt Mosteller, VP Marketing and Real Estate Sales, Resorts of the Canadian Rockies, Kimberley, August 2000.

32 Snow, "Cappuccino Cowboys," op. cit., 3.

33 Raymond Williams, *Towards 2000* (Harmondsworth, UK: Penguin, 1985).

34 Colourful Social Credit cabinet minister 'Flying Phil' Gagliardi is reputed to have told visitors who objected to the smell of the mills in the 1960s that it was the "smell of money."

35 See Power, "High Quality Natural Environments and Local Economic Development," op cit.

36 Interviews with author, January 2000, August 2000.

37 Stuart Hall, "Notes on Deconstructing 'the Popular'," in Raphael Samuel (ed.), *People's History and Socialist Theory* (London: Routledge, 1981).

38 Mike Medberry, "Sun Valley: Just Another Perfect Place in the Mountains," op. cit., 12.

39 A.M. Gill & P. Williams, "Managing growth in mountain tourism communities," *Tourism Management*, 15, 1994, 212–220. Some developers (e.g., Intrawest, and Resorts of the Canadian Rockies) recognize affordable housing for workers as an important issue for the kinds of communities they are seeking to build and are trying to develop solutions.

40 Thomas Power, *Lost Landscapes and Failed Economies* (Washington, Island Press, 1996).

41 Nick Blomley, "The Business of Mobility: Geography, Liberalism, and the Charter of Rights," *The Canadian Geographer* 36, 3 (1992): 236–53.

The Disappearance of the Open West

INDIVIDUALISM IN THE MIDST OF AGRICULTURAL RESTRUCTURING

Lorelei L. Hanson

> Our lives are ceaselessly intertwined
> with narrative, with the stories that we tell
> or hear told, those that we dream or imagine
> or would like to tell, all of which are reworked
> in that story of our own lives that we narrate
> to ourselves in an episodic, somewhat
> semiconscious, but virtually uninterrupted
> monologue. We live immersed in narrative....
> —*Peter Brooks,* Reading for the Plot

One of the most enduring and celebrated stories told about settlement on the Canadian prairies is that of "winning the West." This is a story about conquest and promise, progress and risk, and a vast frontier landscape there for the taking by hard-working, tenacious, self-reliant pioneers. It is a story that has been broadly reproduced over the past century in movies, literature, and song, and that in a contemporary setting can be witnessed in its most performative, carnivalesque form at rodeos and cowboy poetry gatherings, and on television and movie screens in the form of the still popular Western.

Such stories are not inconsequential. Stories shape us; in many ways we are the stories we tell about ourselves. Montana writer William Kittredge speaks of stories as maps or paradigms in which we see our purposes defined: "That's what stories are for, to help us see ourselves as we go about the continual business of reimagining ourselves."[1] As mirrors of ourselves, the stories we tell must continually be reinvented. As our lives change, so too must the maps. To not do so, to stick to old stories and fail to incorporate into our narratives the changing conditions of society and the land, is to risk that which we covet, or to become anaesthetized museum pieces in a world that has long ago passed us by. We are in trouble when the stories that we live with don't work anymore and we hold on to them anyway.

The following is a story about a ranching community that settled on—and continues to make a living off—the land that surrounds and is fed by the upper Oldman River in southwestern Alberta. It is drawn from research exploring the social construction of place and nature through an ethnographic community case study. Like parts of the larger work, this chapter discusses a story about myth, transition and displacement, and the many communities that have shared the foothills and grasslands of the Oldman basin over the years.

Specifically, I examine as a myth the story of origins often associated with ranchers in the upper Oldman River basin. The word *myth* is sometimes used to refer to a fabrication, a lie, but in a broader conceptualization myths are facts and fictions woven together into collective narratives that act as settled assumptions about people, places, and events. The origin myth of the Oldman basin, I argue, offers an important context in which contemporary events can be understood. In particular, connections can be drawn between the mythic past and people's current distrust of government to make sense of why local residents seem so resigned to the changes befalling their community, as more outsiders look to the region as an ideal location for a recreational or retirement home, and why ranchers seem unable to act to protect the future for small family ranches in the area.

The upper Oldman River basin is geographically situated in southwestern Alberta, bordered to the south by Waterton Lakes National Park, to the east by the Peigan Reserve, to the north by the Porcupine Hills and Whaleback montane, and to the west by the Continental Divide (the Alberta–British Columbia border) and the Crowsnest Pass (see Figure 1). The land is traversed principally by three rivers—the Oldman, Crowsnest, and Castle—which curve through the mountains and across the foothills before spilling out across the open prairie. The upper Oldman basin covers an area of approximately 4000 km² and can be described broadly as windy territory where the Canadian Prairie abruptly meets the Rocky Mountains. Approaching from the east, one gains a panoramic view of the sharp, striated peaks of the Rockies, bordered by an undulating thin green-and-tan ribbon of gentle ridges and valleys which level out into vast, golden, hummocky till plains stretching back east into Manitoba. In many ways this part of southwestern Alberta is unique both from an ecological and human history perspective, yet the upper Oldman River basin shares with many other regions throughout the Canadian and American West landscape imprints which resulted from similar concessions, ignorances, and dreams.

Historians remind us that to understand the complex realities of today we must be well informed about the linkages between the past and the present and be able to distinguish fact from fiction. In the American and Canadian West, untangling the threads of connection between contemporary conditions and more distant events, and deciphering what is imagined or mythic from events that actually occurred, is not always an easy task. The West as an empty, frontier landscape that was transformed by brave, independent pioneers into an Eden of fields of plenty to feed the nation has a strong hold on the collective imaginations of many Canadians. The idea that these early settlers brought peace, prosperity, and reason to the region feeds countless dreams and visions of the contemporary West. Yet, more than a century after the first Europeans arrived, environmentalists, aboriginal peoples, historians, and many others have begun to question whether these tales are more about myth and romance than historical events.

Western writer Marilynne Robinson describes myths as "complex narratives in which human cultures stabilize and encode their deepest ambivalences."² In her estimation, the popularity of myths is in part due to the way in which they arrest discrepancies by providing an emblematic, momentary form to contradictions which gives the appearance of resolution. Myths allow cultures to maintain

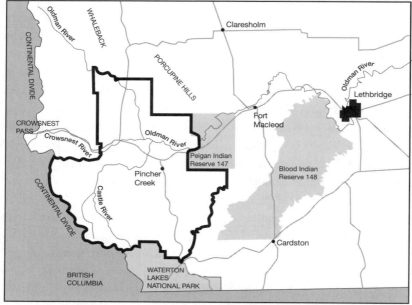

FIGURE 1: THE UPPER OLDMAN RIVER BASIN
Source: Oldman River Regional Planning Commission, *Oldman River Region-Regional Plan,*
Lethbridge, AB, unpublished, September 1984.

stories that contain incompatible ideas in stable relation to each other. It is not
that myths are out-and-out falsehoods. Myths often capture elements of various
realities, but they inevitably fail to capture fully the messiness, complexity,
contradiction, and dynamics of human experience.

Origin tales, which are often central to a community's history, function
particularly well as myths because they provide an abiding and stabilizing narrative. Projecting backward from some present time, origin myths authorize the
current regime as if it is inevitable. For Westerners, these origin myths often are
focussed on a group of people who, against all odds, demonstrated physical and
moral courage.

In the Oldman basin, the origin narrative is a story many of the residents
retell as a characterization of their contemporary community and a story with
which many of them personally identify. This story is about resilient, self-reliant
ranchers who, through sheer determination, triumphed and built a prosperous,
healthy community despite harsh political, economic, and physical circumstances. Environmentalist Robert Stacks describes the origins of the community

this way: "the turn of the century ranching community, their roots [are] the deepest."³ Paul Torrington, who grew up in the area and remains close to many members of his family who still live there, concurs that when people are asked about the history of the area, "they talk about the old-time ranchers...."⁴ Local history volumes tell a story about the beginnings of permanent European settlement in the upper Oldman basin that parallels the story these residents tell.⁵ As one local resident and history buff wrote, "it was from eighteen-eighty when some of the early police had taken their discharge from the force that the real settlement began."⁶

One of the most telling indications of the significance of the ranchers as the first settlers in the areas is captured within local vernacular by the term "Old Stock." Although not familiar to all who reside in the area, Old Stock is an expression frequently heard in the conversations of those who have lived there most of their lives. It is a term specific to the region, rarely heard in neighbouring communities, some of which are only 50 kilometers away. It distinguishes the people who "belong" to this place, those who were the "true settlers," from the rest—the "Imports." The term Old Stock is a clever and telling metaphor. By its allusion to livestock it orients attention exclusively to the role of ranchers in founding the community. And, as Peggy Walsh, an Import, says, it provides a means of identifying a way of life and moment in the history of the upper Oldman River region that is of great significance to many of the current residents:

LH: Old Stock. How does somebody become Old Stock? Like if your son had stayed in this area would he be Old Stock?

PW: I think Old Stock homesteaded here ...

LH: ... Old Stock's only the people, yeah, but ....

PW: ... that first owned the land ...

LH: So that would be the first, so the late 1800s right?

PW: Hmm, hmmm ... I don't know how long that time would be. I haven't a sense of that because I haven't asked these people when they came here. Just a sense of these big families and their ancestors homesteaded the area, and that's the reason there's so many of them, belong to these original families.⁷

Aside from a smattering of Mounties, most of the first European ranchers came from the United States. The Americans' familiarity with the region was largely a result of their use of trade and travel routes, established by native peoples, that cut through the upper Oldman basin following the edge of the Rocky Mountains and stretching from the Liard River of the Yukon down to the Marias River in Montana.[8] In addition to Americans, many people from the British Isles and Western Europe also eventually found their way to the area.

Canada's unique system of grazing leases was one of the principal factors that enticed many of them. With the signing of Treaty 7 in 1877, the entire area became Crown land under the control of the Dominion of Canada, which made most of it available for utilization. A person or company could lease up to 100,000 acres of land for 21 years at a rate of 1 cent per year. The sole requirement was that there had to be one cow for every ten acres leased.

Historian W.L. Morton writes that the first American ranchers on the Canadian prairies were often seen as ideal settlers because they never really openly challenged any of the new country's institutions. However, according to Morton, they were also politically not aligned with those who resided in central Canada, retaining business ties with the US as well as a latent republicanism within their families. This was not a radical form of republicanism but a form of republican simplicity that had at its roots a deep doubt of the utility of politics and the state. Morton argues that this skepticism, when combined with ranchers' quiet refusal to accept the whole spirit of Canadian politics, contributed greatly to the final apolitical outlook of many Prairie people.[9]

Prior to the arrival of the railroad and influx of farmers into the Oldman region, the ranchers held a broad sense of their place in the world and proprietorship over the region. With the establishment of the Indian reserves, the early white residents inhabited a world that was largely unmarked by human presence. Separated from one another and the markets by considerable distances, a rancher's network of relations was limited and dispersed. Many of today's residents tell stories of their grandparents or parents riding a good part of a day to go to a dance, or herding their cattle to market in Calgary, over 200 kilometres away.[10] Further, many of the ranchers had little or no sense of connection to the municipal district in which they resided.[11] Instead it was the land and their way of life to which they felt attachment.

While the Dominion government was anxious for settlement, it considered ranching "merely as an interim measure of reserving western lands for Canada in the absence of significant farm settlement."[12] In the early years, the leasehold laws supported the ranchers. Evidently the government felt obliged to protect the large capital investments made by individuals and corporations in the cattle industry, in spite of increased pressure by existing and prospective farmers. But in 1882, through an order-in-council of John A. Macdonald's government, ranchers were put on notice that any leases that did not provide for voluntary surrender of lands for homestead purposes would be terminated by 1896. The government's one concession to the ranchers was an opportunity to purchase one-tenth of their lease at the price of $2.00 per acre.[13] Although they had previously been the benefactors of government policy, this concession was too small to maintain most ranchers' trust in the government.

The government's intention, however, was to open up new territory for farming. According to William Irvine, this move was a central part of the National Policy of the Conservatives under John A. Macdonald; it was extended and broadened by the Liberals under Wilfrid Laurier. The purpose was to incorporate the Western prairies into the national economy as a producer of agricultural exports to gain for the Dominion government foreign exchange from international markets.[14] In response, the Canadian Northwest Territories Stock Association, initially a local organization created for rounding up cattle, was revived primarily to fight these developments. The Stock Association had limited success. The price of Crown lease land available for purchase was reduced from $2.00 per acre to $1.25 per acre, but ranchers had little luck garnering much support for their ultimate goal, which was to protect the ability of livestock to graze freely in southwestern Alberta. The defeat of the Conservative government in 1896 marked the end of almost all active political support for the ranching community.

The homesteading vision was an immediate success. Within ten years nearly every available section of land had been applied for.[15] By 1890 much of the land surrounding the small hamlet of Pincher Creek—established eight years earlier—was part of ranching or farming homesteads. The land was quickly transformed from open prairie into real estate plots, a change that was not appreciated equally by all. In the words of one of the first ranchers in the area:

> ... 1900 saw the curtain beginning to lower, and the old, wide-open prairie changing into a vast checker-board of rectangular, wire-fenced patches of cultivated land. The cowboy with his horse and lasso and branding iron was supplanted by teams of ploughs and binders and threshing machines. And it seemed not without a touch of pathos, that the old pioneer spirit was also fenced in, as was the land.[16]

Combined, the shift in government policy, the severe winter of 1906–07, and completion of a nearby Canadian Pacific Railway line marked the death of the open range in southern Alberta and changed the role of the cowboy forever. The days of the big cattle companies and the round-up were gone. Ranchers in the upper Oldman River basin would not forget how the government had paved the way for the sodbusters to "crowd them out."[17]

A TALE OF STASIS, A TALE OF TRANSFORMATION

The story of the "original families" in the upper Oldman basin pinpoints the arrival of the North West Mounted Police (NWMP) and American ranchers as the founding of this community. It describes the escape to the frontier of courageous but ornery Western personalities who were descended from self-exiled people and who dealt with their quarrels with society by walking away from them.[18] However persistent and popular, the story is not only incomplete but paints a diorama that has more in common with the trailers of a John Wayne Western than it does the history or current state of the community.

For one thing, ranchers clearly were not the first families or communities to inhabit the upper Oldman basin. The first recorded presence of human habitation in the southern Canadian Rocky Mountains, traces of which have been found in the Crowsnest Pass, just to the west, dates back to about 11,000 years ago. Various cultures have resided in the area since then. The Kootenai, Blackfoot, and Shoshoni peoples' use of the area dates back about 2000 years.[19] Eventually, as a result of either sickness or war, the Shoshoni people were weakened and migrated south, leaving the territory to the Blackfoot. The Blackfoot travelled across the grasslands from the Bow River to the Missouri, their path determined to a great extent by the cycles of the seasons and the path of the bison. The upper Oldman basin provided them a favoured winter haunt with an abundance of game and protection from inclement weather.[20]

Hence, the first European settlers did not just happen upon a garden in need of caretakers, a frontier, or an unsettled wilderness. The aboriginal people saw their homelands not as edges of the world, but rather the centre.[21] In discussing his people's early years in the region, Peigan member Henry Plains Hawk described them living in the whole area from the Red Deer River south into Montana and knowing it as their home territory. Throughout this area they would store food in case of bad weather or need of food: "[It] had land marks and [they] had ways of travelling through the territory. People lived in certain areas for a certain reason."[22]

Neither did the ranchers just happen upon the "ideal" rangeland. On the one hand, explorers Captain John Palliser and naturalist Henry Youle Hind declared the area north of the 49th parallel and east of the Rockies into Manitoba unsuitable for habitation by Europeans.[23] On the other hand, the Dominion government advertised the Oldman basin as the land of Eden. Its depiction of this part of the northwest as an agricultural paradise was a part of the attempts to populate the region quickly with ranchers as a means of protecting it from American interests. The truth about the area lay somewhere in between these two accounts.

Nonetheless, when the NWMP and American cowboys ventured into the Oldman basin they discerned it as a land full of promise and opportunity. In part, the prospective settlers' view was a result of luck. The ranchers had timed their arrival just right climatically, as the winter of 1878 was unusually mild.[24] That year the warm chinook winds blew frequently throughout the season, clearing and melting the snow crust off the grasslands and allowing cattle, which will not use their hooves or noses to paw through snow, to get to food and forage all winter long.[25]

Again, the truth about the ecology of the region was more complex than many of the first ranchers appreciated. The eastern half of the region is semi-arid land that most years does not get enough rainfall to support annual grain production. The massive root systems of the indigenous mixed grasses the ranchers first encountered retained enough moisture to allow for several years of good grazing and ploughed crops of wheat and other grains to flourish. Yet several years after their arrival, the ranchers found they were dependent upon the very unreliable opening up of the skies and calm summers in which the west winds did not dry out everything, including the soil, for the lush grasses to return. The harsh winter of 1886–87 convinced many that the chinook could not be counted on and that summer haying was necessary. That year many ranchers reconsidered their hands-off approach to livestock raising after they took a loss of between 25 and 60 percent of their herds because the cattle were unable to reach beyond the heavy snowpack to the grass below.[26]

Further, while the Oldman basin origin tale makes the farmers sound like they were simply opportunists who destroyed sound ranching enterprises, the arrival of farmers to the region helped to provide an assured food supply and improve conditions for many of the early settlers. The farmers in the Pincher Creek district rapidly became leaders in illustrating the viability of growing wheat, barley, and oats in southern Alberta.[27] By 1907, a harvest of two million bushels of wheat was predicted.[28] As well, those who took up farming strengthened the symbolic and political boundaries of the Municipal District (M.D.) of Pincher Creek by nurturing a communal spirit.[29] The new immigrants were often young families who settled fairly close to one another. Their needs incited the building of schools, churches, and community halls within the hamlet of Pincher Creek and across the region. As a result, the sense of community changed significantly. Several farmers in the region also took up the cause of developing a co-operative, which would become a part of the United Farmers movement, while others formed local recreational clubs and political organizations. The arrival of the railroad in 1897–98 resulted in more efficient and easier contact with the outside world that translated into an increased influx of immigrants to the area. Farmers were the first but would not be the last to challenge the ranchers' proprietorship of the land.

After the turn of the century, development within the upper Oldman basin increased rapidly. In 1902, Alberta's first producing oil well was drilled at Oil City in the southwest corner of the region, close to what is now Waterton Lakes National Park. This discovery initiated a small, short-lived investment boom within the area. Coal mining and the lumber industry really took off in the same time period. The first mines opened along the western edge of the region in Beaver Mines in 1907. Meanwhile, local lumber companies began to feed not only local mills but others situated in Fort Macleod and Lethbridge.

It was not until after the Second World War that the development of oil and gas had any real impact on the community. In 1947 Canadian Gulf Oil discovered a major wet gas field approximately 20 kilometres southeast of the town of Pincher Creek.[30] Later, in 1957 the British American Oil Company (now Gulf) assumed responsibility for this field and constructed a $25-million natural gas-processing plant nearby. It was completed in 1959 and operated until 1982.

Shell Canada drilled its first successful well in the region in 1957 in an area just outside the Castle Forest Reserve in the southwestern corner of the region. A second well was drilled within the forest reserve. Nearby, Shell also initiated construction of a gas-processing plant that was completed in 1959. In 1963, Shell and Gulf jointly built a third gas-cycling plant in the Lookout Butte field. Construction of this third plant meant that, in total, employment was created in the oil and gas sector for 225 families in the region.[31]

The impact of natural gas development within the upper Oldman River region was dramatic. People were not only employed in the construction of the plants but, combined, the two companies employed nearly 400 people at their heyday, with approximately a third of the town's population and wealth directly linked to the gas industry.[32] Increased employment opportunities attracted new residents to the community and new developments within the region and town. New schools were built to accommodate the influx of families, stores were expanded, businesses started, and residential construction boomed. By the early 1980s, the town's population had risen to 3800 residents, roughly what it is today. The effect of oil and gas development on the community, however, was as much social as financial. According to one resident:

> ... it added a new element. There was new comers coming in, there was suddenly a much larger base, things like that. It meant that the economic agenda, or the economic control wasn't in the hands so much of the ranching and farming ... this gas industry added a whole new dimension ... It was a much more diversified economy than it was in the 1920s or it was in 1890. So it added a completely new element which certain portions of the long-term population base certainly found a little different. There was also sorta new versus the old aspect and sorta the ramifications that come around control issues and all of that. There was also disagreements over the environmental issues, especially with the gas industry. Concern about pollution coming from the plants... There were some concerns in certain portions of the agricultural community that their cattle could die if they got, that the fumes, the leftover fumes out of the gas plant were not handled properly sort of thing. Especially if you lived downwind from there, from the gas plants.[33]

THE NEW "SETTLERS"

Two decades after the heyday of oil and gas development, an equally rapid transition of land use has beset the community—one that threatens to further disassociate the ranchers from their central position in the community. Particularly in the last five years, the upper Oldman region has experienced a trend that has been sweeping through many resource-based communities in the West: the arrival of new pilgrims from the city and the consequent displacement of those making a living off the land. An affluent and mobile workforce, retirees, and people in search of a better quality of life are seeking out recreational property or a location for a second or retirement home. The land most desired is along the western edge of the region, beside the trickling waters and lodgepole pine of the rocky foothills—traditional ranch land. In 1996 the Municipal District's planning office received more applications for building permits than in any previous year. By the early fall of the following year, this number had been surpassed by two-thirds.[34]

For ranchers living along the same western edge of the region, however, tourism and acreage interest has meant escalating land prices. As Ruth Melindy describes:

> ... a lot of the [new residents] are acreage owners who are buying quarter sections for recreational purposes or for retirement or whatever. And they are coming from the cities and far away and ... since they aren't making a living off the land they are buying it for recreational prices. So it's really hard for people trying to make a living here to, well you can't expand any more because you can't compete with the retired lawyer from Calgary who is paying $2000 an acre to buy his retirement home or his weekend home. A ranch that hardly makes any money anyways, can't pay $2000 an acre ....[35]

In spite of escalating land prices and increased pressures for ranch land, many in the region contend that this is and will forever be an agricultural community. According to one resident, "... the ranching and the farming sectors have always established the foundation of the community and they always will."[36] Not all agree with this community analysis. Newcomer Alan Timms believes that the changes that have occurred in the Oldman basin over the past half century will continue to radically transform the economic and social base of the community. In Timms' words:

> [They have b]linders. When you look at this community as a whole I would say this community may have a strong basis in agriculture but when you look at it the tourism base has certainly got a big sector. I just look at it from just a health perspective as well. I look at the number of restaurants in Pincher Creek. I mean Pincher Creek has got 2700 people and it has more restaurants than the Crowsnest Pass which has almost 7500 people living in its corporate boundaries. So in my viewpoint a lot of the businesses depend upon tourism dollars, not agriculturally based dollars. And if you look at the way high-use tourism areas have actually started being developed is a result of the fact that people go there to visit. As soon as they start to see the community and start to enjoy the assets it has literally they come here to retire, they come here to live, they come here to work, they live here because they

want to live here. And that's just because there's fresh water, there's good air, there's fewer people, and like you say, it's a friendly community, and there's relatively low levels of crime. With those sort of factors involved and you're raising a family, and the schools are good, the services are good, you have a hospital in your town, you have a golf course, ski area, hiking trails, fishing, boating, what else can you ask for raising a family? So people who tell you that this is going to stay an agricultural place forever, no way. I see Pincher Creek as having the same status as Canmore in the near future.[37]

Statistics Canada data confirms a steady decrease in the economic role of agriculture. According to 1986 census data, 33 percent of those 15 years of age or older in the upper Oldman River basin were employed in agriculture or other resource-based industries, 34 percent in construction and manufacturing, and 33 percent in service industries.[38] In 1996 the number of people who worked in agriculture or primary industries had dropped to 29 percent, and in manufacturing and construction to 12 percent, whereas those employed in the service sector had risen to 59 percent.[39] While more people in the area are employed in agriculture than any other single occupation, over the past several decades the contribution of agriculture to the economy of the region has been steadily shrinking.

Some ranchers in the upper Oldman River region quietly lament this break in continuity in the political economy of the land. They speak with combined disdain and sadness of all that they know disappearing. In the words of one of the local ranchers:

When these people come out with thousands and thousands of dollars and start building great big fancy houses and telling their neighbours what to do and how to do it, some resentment builds up there ... Like they don't sort of realize the value of land or how we need the land to make a living from it. That if we have a cow slip a calf because she's been chased over the hill too hard or something, that this is important to us ... Ahh, there goes ranching I suppose. They certainly tie up a lot of good land. But I'm not quite sure what else you can do.[40]

As these sentiments depict, ranchers generally take an active interest in the land that they tend. In many ways it is the focus of their lives. This centrality of place is exhibited in the poems, songs, sculptures, and paintings they create and in their discussions of their communities. Obviously, the land is not only a place to call home to these folks, but a point of reference from which they view their lives and the rest of the world, that is, it is a "centre of meaning, intentions or felt values."⁴¹ As the following quote reveals, ranchers' ties to the land didn't disappear with the loss of the open range:

> It was the attachment to the place, this particular place, this actual ranch. I don't have a real big attachment to ... [the nearby towns] ... or anything, but just this piece of land, this is where the attachment comes from. And I just kept looking for opportunities to be able to come back here. And there's just no way I'll ever sell it, I'll never let it go because it does belong to me but not in the financial sense at all. I don't know ... it's hard to describe. I can't imagine not being here. I can't imagine this place ... anybody else living here or even the land [not being] ours. It's still a part of this area and part of what I am attached to and I can't imagine anybody else ever moving into it because there's such a history here, and if there was anybody else here they wouldn't know that history, it would be totally lost.⁴²

Most ranchers in the area know their land, be it leased or owned, as well as most folks know their backyards.

Yet mixed with this connection and knowledge of place has been a complicity that has allowed grazing land to be turned into dream homes and chemical lawns. While they venerate the land and have been fairly successful in maintaining public display and celebration of the traditions and styles that mark their community, simultaneously, ranchers in the area largely have failed to act to protect their way of life. Outside of coffee time at the local Co-op mall, the ranchers in the Oldman region have yet to try to mount a spirited defence for the preservation of nearly a century of family-owned and -operated ranches in the Oldman River basin. While many ranchers speak of how they value the land for more than its monetary worth and wish ranching to be an option available to their children, they have been curiously silent in a political sense about the disappearance of the region's family ranches a little at a time. How historically have these ranchers moved from "winning the West" to letting it just slip away?

Individually ranchers have demonstrated innovation and ingenuity in keeping their operations afloat, but collective efforts to protect ranch land have not been as successful. Independently, many of them have responded to changing economic conditions by implementing business diversification strategies, such as niche marketing and guest ranching, or by having one or more members of the family employed off the ranch. As well, a few ranchers have opted to secure the future of their operations by means of trusts to preserve productive ranch land. The Southern Alberta Land Trust Society (SALTS) is one such organization.[43] SALTS land trust agreements are negotiated with individual producers and tailored to their own needs. The trusts prohibit subdivision of the land and other environmentally damaging activities, though they allow for oil and gas drilling. One advantage to the landowner is an income tax credit representing the difference in land value once development rights are removed. Over the past decade several groups of ranchers in the Oldman basin have discussed the possibility of a region-wide trust with conservation easements that would limit non-agricultural development. So far, however, nothing has materialized.

In part, the failure to act to protect ranch land from being cut up into acreage developments can be traced to a shared empathy and a deep understanding of the current financial realities many ranchers face. The rapid increase in local land prices has only worsened the situation. Most ranchers cannot afford to pay $700/acre and more for a parcel of land on which to graze cattle. To sell that same parcel of land for recreational or retirement property would bring in at least twice the going agriculture rate if not three times as much or more.[44] With operational costs steadily increasing, small family ranchers are simply getting by. With all their financial investment tied up in the land they work, even if they have children to pass it onto (and many don't have children interested in taking over), many ranchers must sell a portion of their land to acreage developers in order to secure enough money to retire and enjoy their "golden" years.

As well, in the last few years, frequently no one from the ranching community has been willing to represent their interests in the local municipal council. Scorn and ostracism have often beset the few who have publicly voiced criticism against development. In a community that values individuality and freedom, and continues to be intensely suspicious of, if not downright antagonistic towards, government, there is no place for public regulations that tell people how they should treat their land. For the ranchers in the upper Oldman region, government interference is how they lost the open West the first time and they'll be damned if they are going to allow more restraints to be put on their freedoms to do as they will on their land. As one rancher said in describing her commnity, it's a conservative and redneck community, "[v]ery anti-government, very independent, every man for himself, very free-enterprise, very capitalistic."[45]

HISTORICAL WOUNDS

Myths are not simply falsehoods, but rather popular beliefs and historical events tied together in a continuous dialogue. They tell how things came to be, how they are, and why they are. As Kittredge reminds us, the tales we tell ourselves have an enormous influence on how it is we understand the world and ourselves. Myths can mightily affect the course of events, suggesting possibilities but also leading people into difficult, even tragic situations.

Myths change, disappear, and are replaced by new emblematic narratives; yet they also have a tendency towards stasis. Robinson argues that for those who are the host population of myths, these narratives often become arrested beliefs—"not consciously held opinion but settled assumption, with a penumbra of related assumptions spreading away on every side."[46] Such myths persist and flourish in part because they become the accepted discourse of a culture, repeated and assumed, and rarely challenged. They also become their stigma. Similarly, this is the case with "myths of origins." When inserted into political, economic, and scientific discourse, myths of origins evoke reality; they speak to that "which simply is" and are therefore unalterable. Consequently, as much as they might reassure some of the equilibrium of the world, myths frequently represent "narrative dysfunction"[47] by distorting what is going on right now, and thus disabling people's capacities to respond effectively.

Like many myths, the story about the origins of settlement in the upper Oldman River region has a strong hold over the collective imaginations of many within the community. It links people together in a variety of ways, creating bonds between people and between individuals and the land where they reside. Living in this place is a deeply intentional act for most that make this corner of western Canada their home. Many of the residents sacrifice a better standard of living to wake up each morning in this land of expansive blue skies, golden prairies, and majestic mountains. Western tales such as this one also survive in part because they are seated within a real, living context. Agriculture remains a central economic mainstay in the region and an important identity marker not only for those who ranch or farm but also for residents of the region who are proud of their rural heritage. The tale of the founding settlers as simple, ordinary people who through courage, ingenuity, and self-reliance created a peaceful and productive life affirms a doctrine of individuality and freedom, instructing current residents on how they can live a life of authenticity. Yet could it be that these stories of the West also have survived because they avoid a more complex, ambivalent, and sometimes shameful picture of the proprietorship of a territory that requires stewards more than it does landlords, that requires co-operation more than it does self-reliance?

Returning to tales of the early history of the upper Oldman River region is a reminder that perhaps the ranchers have not yet learned the historical lessons that the "winning of the West" had to offer. As the history of the area reveals, even in the 1800s this escape was only temporary and for the most part illusory. In the stories of the First Nations, one is introduced to stories of displacement, genocide, and betrayal that accompanied the stories of the conquest of the frontier. In the accounts of explorers, trappers, and ecologically minded settlers, one can read about the extinction of species, the replacement of sustainable indigenous grasses with European hybrids, and the loss of topsoil. Further, in spite of the resistance of the many agriculturists to recognize the changes all about them, transformation is quickly befalling the community in the form of acreage owners. Be it through land-use planning, stricter bylaws, land trusts, or other means, discussion of possible solutions needs to happen to preserve agricultural land.

To be so individualistic that the thing you value most slips out of your grasp because of your antipathy to government and participation in political life suggests not only the imprint of historical wounds but also a contemporary disability. While the American and Canadian West are often envisioned as lands of hope, amidst our dreams and images of the West we must also recognize that the myth of the West as an infinity to which to escape was something it could never be. There were always restraints. Perhaps it is time to recognize these restraints and begin writing a new story about ranching in the upper Oldman River basin. As William Kittredge reminds us, "You cannot build a viable culture on the basis of half-truths, outright lies and expurgated stories. In the West we've been trying to do just that and it is not working. We need to tell ourselves a new story about the West."[48]

Notes

1   William Kittredge, "The Politics of Storytelling," *Northern Lights—A Selection of New Writing from the American West*, eds. Deborah Clow and Donald Snow (New York: Vintage Books, 1994), 42.

2   Marilynne Robinson, "Hearing Silence: Western Myth Reconsidered," *Northern Lights, A Selection of New Writing from the American West*, eds. Deborah Clow and Donald Snow (New York: Vintage Books, 1994), 50.

3   Robert Stacks, personal interview, June 22, 1997. Note: I have used fictional names for all those individuals I interviewed in order to protect their identities and privacy.

4   Paul Torrington, personal interview, Aug. 8, 1998.

5   Adam Lees Freebairn, *Pincher Creek Memories* (Pincher Creek, AB: Oldtimers Association, 1975); *Prairie Grass to Mountain Pass: History of the Mountain Pioneers of Pincher Creek and District.* (Pincher Creek, AB: Pincher Creek Historical Society, 1974).

6   Barry Watson, personal interview, March 5 1997.

7   Peggy Walsh, personal interview, February 21, 1997.

8   Sid Marty, *Leaning on the Wind—Under the Spell of the Great Chinook* (Toronto: HarperCollins, 1995), 36.

9   W.L. Morton, "A Century of Plain and Parkland," *The Prairie West-Historical Readings*, 2nd edition, eds. R. Douglas Francis and Howard Palmer (Edmonton: Pica Pica Press, 1992), 34.

10 Ruth Melindy and Clairise Nicholls, personal interview, September 15, 1996.

11 Potyondi, 125.

12 Ibid., 57.

13 Hugh A. Dempsey, *The Golden Age of the Canadian Cowboy* (Saskatoon/Calgary: Fifth House, 1995), 140

14 William Irvine, *The Farmers in Politics*, intro., Reginald Whitaker (Toronto: McClelland and Stewart, 1976), ix.

15 Potyondi, 104.

16 "Morden," *Prairie Grass to Mountain Pass*, 124–129.

17 The descriptor "crowded out" comes from a poem written in 1903 by H. Lake of Raymond, Alberta after reading a news item about seven old timers in the Pincher Creek district making preparations to leave and resettle with their cattle on open range in the Red Deer District. "Crowded out" is the term they used to describe their condition. Dempsey, 151.

18 Robinson, 57.

19 Andy Russell, *The Life of a River* (Toronto: Douglas Gibson, 1987), 12

20 Potyondi, i.

21 Patricia Nelson Limerick, *The Legacy of Conquest—the Unbroken Past of the American West* (New York/London: W.W. Norton & Company, 1987), 26.

22 Plains Hawk.

23 Ronald Rees, *New and Naked Land — Making the Prairies Home* (Saskatoon: Western Producer Books, 1988), 6.

24 Marty, 112.

25 Potyondi, 59.

26 Ibid., 77.

27 Albert Milton Morden, for example, won a medal and diploma for grain grown on fallow ground without irrigation at the Chicago World's Columbian Exposition in 1892–93. *Prairie Grass to Mountain Pass*, 128.

28 Potyondi, 120.

29 Ibid., 126.

30 *Survey of Pincher Creek* (Alberta Government and Publicity Bureau, Department of Tourism), 6.

31 Ibid.

32 Watson.

33 Ibid.

34 Gene Spencer, personal interview, October 8, 1997.

35 Ruth Melindy, personal interview, March 21, 1997.

36 Watson.

37 Alan Timms, personal interview, September 3, 1998.

38 *1986 Census of Canada*, Ottawa, ON Statistics Canada.

39 *1996 Census of Canada*, Ottawa, ON Statistics Canada.

40 Lana Sturby, personal interview, April 15, 1997.

41 Allan Pred, "Structuration and Place: On becoming of sense of place and structure of feeling," *Journal for the Theory of Social Behaviour*, 13, 1: 49

42 Melindy.

43 Wendy Dudley, "Land Trust Helps Protect Ranching Heritage," *Western Producer*, 8 February 2001.

44 Blair Stimly, personal interview, October 14, 1987.

45 Melindy.

46 Robinson, 63.

47 The term "narrative dysfunction" was first coined by poet C.K. Williams, but I happened upon it in Kittredge's "The Politics of Storytelling," 41.

48 Kittredge, as quoted in Gary Holthaus, "Homeland," *Northern Lights* 7,2 (Winter 1996): 16.

The Politics
of Development
on the Sunshine Coast

Bruce Milne

The Sunshine Coast is a series of small communities strung along an 80-kilometre ribbon of coastal highway. Langdale, Granthams Landing, Gibsons, Elphinstone, Roberts Creek, Wilson Creek, Davis Bay, Sechelt, Halfmoon Bay, Garden Bay, Madeira Park, Pender Harbour, Egmont—28,000 people, inclusive of those living in Sandy Hook, Tuwanek, and other non-incorporated communities. Six traffic lights, four governments, and an increasing number of four-way-stop intersections help to minimize direct collisions among competing interests. However, collisions do happen, of course, and when they do, they serve to illustrate the dynamic tensions that exist within this ribbon of communities.

The grand total of six traffic lights, for 28,000 permanent residents and more visitors, would mark the Sunshine Coast as rural for most observers. Those professional planners among us might more properly refer to it as ex-urban: as in non-urban, neither the city nor the suburbs. However, I will argue that urbanization, as a global process involving the spreading reach of urban money and urban lifestyles, fully informs cultural and economic life on "the Coast," with the result that this place is best seen today as a form of urban place. This essay will contend that tensions following from the co-existence of urban practices and rural values can help us understand the political dynamics found on the Sunshine Coast, as well as in similar communities in the Canadian West.

The development of urban forms, along with predictable resistance to urbanization, will be illustrated with reference to community debates about the development of new recreational facilities: specifically, the establishment or expansion of golf courses and the building of new indoor public recreation facilities (ice rinks and swimming pools). This is because citizens of the Coast have been divided by these issues in the last five years, and because increased demand for such facilities in this part of rural BC can be read as one marker of the spread of urban tastes and lifestyles. However, I will propose that local debates about these particular forms of development can be seen to draw on political values and priorities of a more general nature. To be specific, political positions in these Sunshine Coast debates aligned according to people's perspectives on the question of regional co-operation versus local autonomy; on support for nature conservation or for active development; and on people's wariness or enthusiasm towards the transition from a "traditional" resource economy to a "new" service economy based on tourism and recreation.

There does not appear to be any firm relationship between the urban/rural question and political positions taken in the debates identified above. Indeed, the discussion of political debates that follows will reveal the complexity that can emerge when various perspectives are aligned and complicated in specific local struggles. Cutting through the complexity, however, is the fact that urbanization marches on. This paper will illustrate the urbanization of rural life through recreation, specifically the spread of those urban recreational amenities considered necessary infrastructure for a local prosperity based on residential growth, tourism, and the attraction of "new economy" businesses.

Some of the political dynamics illustrated in this paper can also be found in the Banff–Canmore Corridor, along the eastern slopes of the Rockies, and in the Okanagan and other parts of the southern Interior (see Whitson, Urquhart, and Hanson, this volume). Many communities working to reshape their futures experience urbanization as both promise and threat, with consequences that can abound with ironies. The development of ecotourism, for example, may generate resistance to industrial forestry. However, it may also attract retail businesses selling outdoor clothing and kayaks priced beyond belief, as well as urbane clients for whom rural communities are just gateways to their "wilderness adventures." It can also lead to urban forms of residential development that raise local property prices and threaten community cohesion.

SITUATING THE SUNSHINE COAST

Located on the mainland of British Columbia, immediately northwest of metropolitan Vancouver, the Sunshine Coast has remained "rural" until recently because there is no direct road access from neighbouring urban areas. A 40-minute ferry ride to Langdale is necessary to reach the Coast from the Vancouver area in the south. At the north end of the Sechelt Peninsula, a longer ferry trip connects the Sunshine Coast to Powell River (pop. 24,000). Air access to Vancouver International Airport is approximately 20 minutes. The populated areas of the Sunshine Coast crowd the eastern shores of the Georgia Strait, with Vancouver Island to the west. The Coastal Mountain range rises immediately to the east, resulting in a ribbon of communities along the coast, with very little residential development more than two kilometres from the water. Geography shaped the Sunshine Coast as it developed, and continues to influence political and economic development today.

The relative proximity to Vancouver resulted in the historical development of the Sunshine Coast as part of the peripheral domain of Vancouver's "centre." The lack of direct access allowed resource extraction to proceed relatively undisturbed; but it also resulted in recreational development that was restricted to the affluent. Timber, sand, and gravel have been extracted since the 1880s to supply the construction demands of a growing metropolitan economy. However, by the first decade of the twentieth century, waterfront locations housed hotels and second homes for Vancouverites wealthy enough to enjoy recreational retreats. Over the years, several small residential communities developed around fishing, forestry, and leisure economies.

The residential population has developed significantly in the postwar era, particularly in recent decades. The vast majority of the current housing stock has been built since the 1960s. Residential growth accelerated in the 1980s, driven by retirees relocating from urban areas, and did not level out until the province-wide recession of 1998. Retirees have been attracted by the small-town atmosphere, the proximity to the Vancouver region and, compared to other locations on the southwest coast of BC, the low housing costs. This is especially true of Gibsons and Sechelt, where those over 65 represent 18 percent and 21 percent, respectively, of the population. In the mid to late 1990s this market levelled off, and anecdotal evidence from realtors indicates that during the late 1990s new residents were as likely to be younger families or couples, also attracted by a combination of quality of life and comparatively low housing costs.

Economic activity on the Sunshine Coast is relatively diverse. While it does not offer the range of opportunity found in larger urbanized regions, it has never been dependent on a single resource or industrial base. Tourism has been a part of the economy since the 1890s, and the more contemporary transition from reliance on resource extraction (fishing and forestry) began in the 1980s. Not surprisingly, considering the residential population growth, construction is the largest source of private-sector employment (15.1 percent), followed by retail trade (14.7 percent). Accommodation and food services employ just under 10 percent of the workforce, while business services employ 9.7 percent. The public sector—government, education, health, and social services—constitutes a combined 20.1 percent. The relative diversity of the economic structure, compared to other communities in rural BC, is evident when it is noted that logging and forestry provide only seven percent of the employment for the region. Another indicator of economic diversification is the large number of small businesses.

The population of the Sunshine Coast is largely distributed around two retail/service/political centres—the Town of Gibsons and the Municipality of Sechelt—separated by approximately fifteen kilometres of rural residential development. The population of Gibsons is officially just under 4000. However, there is a great deal of residential development in the surrounding region, so that the Gibsons market area includes close to 9000 residents. The Municipality of Sechelt has a population of approximately 8000 and the imme- diately adjoining jurisdiction, the Sechelt Indian Government District, has almost 1000 residents. Surrounding areas bring the population of the Sechelt market area closer to 12,000. The remaining 5,000 to 6,000 persons resident on the Sunshine Coast are distributed along 80 kilometres of coastal highway, with a concentration of some 2000 in the Madeira Park–Pender Harbour area, 25 kilometres north of Sechelt.

The three incorporated jurisdictions (Town of Gibsons, Sechelt Indian Government District, and Municipality of Sechelt) operate independently, and despite regular calls for co-operation and co-ordination, they remain autonomous in their decision-making capacity and in the pursuit of their defined interests. The Town of Gibsons has been somewhat curtailed by its limited tax base and restricted town boundaries. Much development here has occurred immediately adjacent to the town, under the auspices of the Sunshine Coast Regional District (SCRD). The SCRD Board lacks substantive powers relative to incorporated municipal areas and functions primarily as a provider of regional services such as water, transit, and recreational programming. It also provides planning services to the unincorporated areas and has established Official Community Plans for each area, even though final subdivision authority rests with the province. Nevertheless, the SCRD Board plays an important political role in the Sunshine Coast community and can be the site of fascinating political dynamics.

Electoral results over the past decade reveal that the politics of place on the Sunshine Coast are increasingly fluid rather than fixed. There are clear indications that party politics matter less to voters than local issues and the personal efficacy of candidates. The area is represented at the federal level by an Alliance MP (formerly Reform) who had served in Social Credit governments provincially and, many years earlier, had been a Conservative MP. I would consider him right of centre, with strong business leanings. Provincially the Sunshine Coast was represented until very recently by an NDP member who was first elected as a Liberal and, more recently, as the leader of the Progressive Democratic Alliance. I would call him a centrist with left-leaning sensibilities. Locally, environmental interests have a strong presence in the community, as do the interests of small business and the retail sector of the economy. Labour has a less visible role in politics on the Sunshine Coast, and the Sunshine Coast Labour Council is the smallest in the province. Local elections, however, are conducted without overt reference to political affiliations, and to date there have been no campaigns organized around slates of candidates.

There is, at the same time, a strong culture of local participation and involvement on the Sunshine Coast. Sechelt, for example, has seven active community associations, and there are strong community associations in other areas. A number of residents are also involved in national and international advocacy group activities, and as individuals, the residents could be considered relatively sophisticated in political terms. Nevertheless, I would argue that the Sunshine Coast remains economically and politically rather innocent. We have not experienced the intense capitalization of tourist destinations such as our neighbour Whistler. Neither have we been the object of intense residential commodification as has happened in the Lower Mainland or the Okanagan Valley. Politically, we remain naïve as to the interests of global corporations with a presence in our midst—in particular, Construction Aggregates Limited which operates the largest gravel mine in North America in sight of Sechelt's municipal offices, or forestry corporations such as Weyerhauser or Interfor.

There are many early indicators that suggest the Sunshine Coast is about to experience an intense and rapid transformation of place. Indeed, there are those in the community who promote this possibility as one of the area's primary attractions to outside investors. From this perspective, the Sunshine Coast currently lacks the capital to realize its full (commodified) potential, but this should be rectified as markets develop and this place is "discovered" by others.

However, this vision of the Coast's future is contested by other residents. In a poll conducted by the Municipality of Sechelt in 1997, a direct question on the issue of development was posed. Seventeen percent of respondents indicated they would prefer less development, 34 percent were content with current levels, and 49 percent wanted to see more development. Politically, these differences could be managed as a roughly even divide between those who desire the status quo or less in terms of development (51 percent) and those who would support additional levels of change (49 percent). Conversely, others might claim political support for development, on the basis of the 83 percent of respondents who indicate support for current or additional levels of development. Indeed, the political climate of Sechelt in the last few years has seen shifting coalitions of support for various forms and sites of development. These figures cannot be directly extrapolated to the Sunshine Coast at large. Certainly, those residents who choose to live in unincorporated and less developed areas may vary in their interests and commitments from those who reside in more urbanized areas. Nevertheless, Sechelt does comprise a significant portion of the larger population, and thus provides a statistically significant sample of the whole.

The following sections of this essay illustrate situations where the future development of the Sunshine Coast has been contested in public and political terms. These situations reveal, in their different ways, the dynamic political processes through which the "conditions of possibility" for the future of the Sunshine Coast are being established.

Golf courses have become fundamental features of the new residential, retirement, and tourism economies. Whether providing the draw (and the filter) for new residential compounds, expanding the opportunities for commodified leisure and thus profitability at resorts, or simply as sites for business networking, golf courses fulfil multiple functions in the new economy. The Sunshine Coast boasts three full-scale courses—two eighteen-hole and one nine-hole layout—and a par-three pitch-and-putt facility for good measure. There have, already, been marketing campaigns inviting visitors to the "Golf Coast."

Each of the full-scale courses required local government assistance to be established (the par-three course was developed by a private operator on private land). In each case, the course is situated on land granted or leased to local government from the province, with a sub-lease to the operators. The smallest course, an attractive nine-hole arrangement in Pender Harbour, is leased by the SCRD to a non-profit society. It operates with little fanfare and no political interference. In contrast, the Sunshine Coast Golf and Country Club, located in Roberts Creek (between Sechelt and Gibsons), is fully engaged in the public and political arena. It is a flashpoint of controversy with its neighbours, and has been the subject of hundreds of hours of SCRD staff attentions and Board deliberations over the past decade. It began innocently enough as a small nine-hole course located next to a sprawling natural park.

The Sunshine Coast Golf and Country Club (SCGCC) is a community-based non-profit society with a membership of approximately 700 persons, most of whom are resident on the Sunshine Coast. In 1988 the SCGCC approached the Regional District for assistance in expanding the course to include an additional nine holes of play. As the adjoining "undeveloped" parkland was already under Regional District control and had been designated for "public recreational purposes," it was seen as appropriate by SCGCC members to propose this land for a 30-hectare expansion of a community-based golf course. This view, however, was not shared by residents who were closest to the site.

The SCRD Board of the day resolved the immediate conflict by applying for the use of adjoining Crown land on behalf of the golf course interests. A 30-year Crown lease was granted in 1990 and in June 1991 a key 20-acre parcel of private land was purchased by the SCGCC in a deal brokered by the Regional District. In addition the SCRD Board agreed to release 2 corners of the park area (2.92 hectares) to be added to the base available for golf course layout. Preliminary approval for the course expansion was granted in September 1991 and a draft sub-lease on the Crown property was developed in June of 1992. However, before the golf course development could proceed, the land required rezoning, involving significant amendments to the Roberts Creek Official Settlement Plan. These amendments required a formal public hearing where the issues could be fully aired.

The debate centred on environmental impacts of a golf course on the surrounding lands: in particular, on the park and watercourses. The SCGCC did not consider such concerns to be warranted and, in fact, argued that a study of the environmental impact was unnecessary. The SCRD Board, when faced with balancing this political stand-off, agreed to support the golf course expansion subject to environmental concerns being addressed. The Board approved the rezonings, initiating the only changes made in recent decades to the Official Settlement Plan for Roberts Creek. The SCGCC agreed to pay for an environmental impact study, subject to developing an acceptable lease agreement and prior to proceeding with the course expansion.

Environmental studies in hand, construction and development were initiated and the opening of the Sunshine Coast's first 18-hole golf course occurred in July 1996. However, the lease agreement between the SCRD and the SCGCC had not been signed, and subsequent operation and maintenance of the new greens and fairways revealed problems that undid this uneasy truce between those wanting the environment of a championship golf course and those seeking to preserve the more natural ecosystem of the parkland. Thus, when a newly elected Regional Board took office in December 1996, they were faced with two outstanding issues on this file. The SCGCC was resisting signing a lease that would require "eco-friendly" greens maintenance; the neighbouring community, still upset over the loss of parkland, was opposing SCGCC proposals for light corridors and for reduced bio-diversity in previously agreed "buffer zones."

Each of these issues arose because on the Sunshine Coast, the low levels of winter light require high levels of artificial treatment of greens and fairways. However, the intensive use of herbicides and synthetic fertilizers to maintain playing conditions at "competitive" standards was considered a serious threat to the waterways and vegetation of the park. Buffer zones that had been established to provide transitional space between these incompatible uses were seen very differently by the parties involved. The golf club saw buffer zones as an extension of the golf course, to be kept free of shade trees or invasive weeds, and thus shielding the fairways and greens from the natural growth of a rainforest. Park supporters, conversely, who saw buffer zones as a way of protecting the park from the invasive horticulture of golf courses, believed that the buffer zones should be left in a more or less natural state. To make matters more complex, the buffer zone was supposed to be an "average" of 15 metres in width, but in fact varied from no more than a metre in some places to almost 10 metres in other places. The newly elected Board members were taken on a number of site tours—escorted through the park by the Friends of Cliff Gilker Park and through the golf course by the Executive and staff of the SCGCC.

Many presentations, community soundings, and painful deliberations culminated in an SCRD Board meeting held specifically for this issue. While Board meetings are always public, this one was convened in a local community hall to ensure room for all observers. Over 200 people attended and final presentations by the public were permitted. The SCGCC argued for the need for selective trimming within the park to increase winter light and for strict control over the buffer zones. The Friends of Cliff Gilker Park summed their arguments in the phrase: "not a twig, not a branch, not a tree." One side supported their arguments with claims regarding the economic and social benefits of the golf course, and the wide community membership in their club. The other side spoke of potentially contaminated water sources, of the assault on quality of life in the adjacent properties, and as advocates for all those beings who lived in the park but could not speak at public meetings.

The Board decision was dramatic. Members spoke to the issue pro and con, in terms that indicated a difficult intellectual and political balancing. With equal numbers of votes having indicated support for either side it came to the representative for Roberts Creek to make her final comments. A former law professor, suspected by the greens as not having deep enough roots in the community, Ms Morrison weighed the various arguments and laid her reasoning out before the public. On this issue she sided with the protectors of the park: allow the SCGCC negotiated and specified control in the buffer zones, but "not a twig, not a branch, not a tree" in the park itself.

As this is written in February 2001, the issues of the lease arrangements and the environmental practices on the golf course are not yet resolved. There is much added complexity in this case, and recently the SCGCC initiated civil proceedings against the Regional District. Out-of-court negotiations are proceeding, under direction of a new SCRD Board elected to office in 1999. A decade of community struggle between two visions of what people want for "recreation," and over what is required for the development of urban-style recreational amenities, clearly reveals that what are desirable (and even defining) characteristics of place are deeply contested on the Sunshine Coast.

At the same time as the community was divided over golf course expansion in the unincorporated area of Roberts Creek, a new golf course was proposed for development within the Municipality of Sechelt. This idea had originated with a previous mayor, who had arranged for a provincial Crown grant of land in an area expecting future residential development. The proposal was accompanied by the familiar arguments regarding economic and social benefits for the community and, in particular, arguments touting the benefits of the course as a catalyst for increased residential values. Quality of life would improve, property values would increase, and a rising tide of demand would stimulate new residential development with spin-off benefits echoing throughout the local economy.

From idea to execution, the Sechelt Golf and Country Club—an eighteen-hole championship course—took approximately six years. While no environmental studies were deemed necessary, public funds had supported a feasibility study and market analysis that became the basis of a private-sector business plan. To be sure, the council of the day had negotiated for a solid range of community benefits, including facilities for the local lawn bowling association and substantial lease fees based on gross revenues (inclusive of restaurant, lounge, and pro shop sales). However, the municipality also clear-cut the site (using timber revenues to pay for site servicing and creating a reserve fund for future ancillary developments in the area), negotiated favourable servicing agreements, and, to the chagrin of some adjacent property owners, allowed significant variance to the usual requirements for road development at time of subdivision. As noted above, no environmental impact study was required; furthermore, no environmental standards were referenced in the lease. When unexpected run-off during development damaged a salmon-spawning creek, there was limited public awareness of this, and no public response by local government. Four years later, when it was clear that projected revenue streams had been overestimated and the privately held company was delinquent in both lease payments and back taxes, a substantively different council (elected in 1996) supported a restructuring of the company. New terms included a "holiday" period for lease payments, a multi-year repayment of back taxes, and a 20-year schedule of lease payments that would no longer be based upon on gross revenues.

The Roberts Creek and Sechelt golf courses are no more than fifteen kilo-metres apart and they serve essentially the same resident population on the Sunshine Coast. Political values between two local governments serving the same population cannot be that disparate. In fact, one elected official (the author of this essay) has been involved in both negotiations since 1996. The narratives of these two courses illustrate the fluid and complicated nature of the balance between pro-development and conservationist forces. In each case, the balance between regional and more local interests, the relative values placed on conservation and simplicity versus the development of new amenities, and the particular attitudes of decision makers regarding the transition to a "new economy" helped determine the conditions under which urban forms develop.

What is important to note is that both developments proceeded. One devel-opment was initiated by local government on behalf of private business. The other was initiated by a community based non-profit society in a "rural" unin-corporated area; but it clearly spoke to aspirations held by some on the Sunshine Coast for new recreational (and business) options. It is thus clear that there are different arrangements which can provide for the capitalization neces-sary to realize urban forms of development. Moreover, as suggested at the outset of this section, golf courses can fulfil multiple functions in the new leisure and services economy. Welcome to the Golf Coast of British Columbia.

SWIMMING TOGETHER AND SKATING APART

Recreational infrastructure seems to bedevil the Sunshine Coast community. Not just golf courses, but more prosaic facilities such as swimming pools and skating rinks that are available in small centres throughout North America cause great public debate. In part, this is due to the fact that the Sunshine Coast is not centred but decentralized, with neither Gibsons nor Sechelt having sufficient tax base to build quality facilities alone. In such circumstances, common sense suggests that the disparate population come together to share resources and build facilities as needed and wanted. However, over the years common sense has been denied in the name of local autonomy, and a few inadequate facilities have been erected. There is a small public swimming pool in Gibsons, rebuilt in 1990 to accommodate four twenty-metre lanes. There is an even smaller pool in Pender Harbour, built as part of a new secondary school in 1982. This was not the result of a forward-thinking school board but rather a requirement for fire protection, paid for by local ratepayers rather than school taxes. There is an arena in Sechelt; but, built by volunteers in 1969, it has been deemed inadequate for at least a decade. It was not until 1999 that it was insulated to ensure holding ice at the start of the season in September.

Recreation facilities are a constant issue in community politics. However, for our purposes we can enter the continuing saga in April 1997, when Sechelt held a referendum to authorize negotiations on a public/private partnership that would build a twinned ice facility. The new rink would incorporate what could be salvaged from the current facility and would stay at the same location so that land costs would be minimal. The private sector proponents assured one and all that this would be a profitable venture, easy to finance.

Sechelt residents were asked to answer three questions on the referendum. With a 44-percent turnout, they said yes to building a twin ice facility. They supported the public/private venture (costs not to exceed $3.9 million) by almost two to one, but said no to any additional taxation to fund the facility. However, while Sechelt Council began negotiations based on the referendum results, other communities on the Sunshine Coast began a campaign against the proposed facility. While no other jurisdiction contributed to the costs of the Sechelt arena—in fact had expressly rejected such funding proposals over the years—many voices were raised against these proposals to finance a new facility.

For the most part these voices were centred in the Gibsons area. It was clear that the projected population of the Sunshine Coast couldn't support more than two sheets of ice for some years. Thus, some in Gibsons saw the proposal to build two sheets of ice at one facility in Sechelt as a willful dashing of their aspirations to have their own arena. The many financial benefits of a single twin ice facility were rejected, while the horrors of driving 35 minutes for ice time were carefully detailed in letters to local news editors. A south coast consortium—the Mount Elphinstone Recreation Complex Society (MERC), carefully named and managed to appear as more than a Town of Gibsons group—prepared a proposal for an arena on town land in Gibsons. This proposal was funded by the Regional District ($25,000) and the Town of Gibsons ($10,000).

The negotiations in Sechelt continued despite the reservations of their neighbours. It was the assessment of both the private-sector proponents (an Alberta-based company) and the Sechelt Council that other projects and proposals on the Coast were far from any implementation stage. For one, any other tax-funded proposal would need to pass a public referendum. No other jurisdictions were preparing for that consultative process. Meanwhile, at the Regional District Board table, directors elected in November 1996 on a platform of regional co-operation and a politics of mutual respect were also searching for a solution that would provide much-needed recreation facilities in the community. They agreed on a policy in early 1997 that entailed regional funding for decentralized community-based facilities. The Sechelt negotiations toward a public/private partnership posed some difficulties. Yet it was envisioned that, if successful, the Sechelt facility would be self-sustaining and any Gibsons-based ice arena would be managed as a local or neighbourhood amenity.

In December 1997, however, it became clear that financing for the Sechelt project would not be forthcoming without significant concessions on the part of the public partner. As the citizens had indicated by referendum that their support was conditional on no additional tax draw, and the private partners had earlier offered assurances that no such taxation would be necessary, Sechelt Council decided they could no longer pursue the partnership agreement. As disappointing as this was for community expectations, it did pave the way for the Regional Board to fast-track preparations for a coast-wide referendum on community-based facilities. The Regional Board took the issue to referendum in June 1998. Their proposal included an aquatic facility in Sechelt, an ice-based complex in Gibsons, and a smaller future facility (the nature of which remained to be determined) for Pender Harbour. The total capitalization of this plan was based on a $14-million borrowing over 20 years.

The complexity of community responses to capital-intensive recreational forms is instructive for anyone harbouring romantic notions of small-town cohesiveness or the homogeneity of "rural" life. Among supporters of the proposed recreational developments, people variously spoke of economic benefits from the construction of major facilities, of the multiplier effects of spending public funds, of increased retail opportunities associated with facility use, of increased tourism from hosting a variety of tournament or showcase events, and of enhanced residential values. This last supposed benefit was backed up with a multitude of anecdotal stories of people who had left the coast or had chosen not to locate in this place due to the lack of "competitive" facilities. In particular, it was argued that participants in the "new economy" were footloose, and therefore choosy, when it came to lifestyle issues. If the Sunshine Coast wanted to attract this new class of residents (whether workers, entrepreneurs, or retirees) a full range of urban amenities needed to be in place.

Supporters also spoke of quality-of-life enhancements, community pride, improved health benefits, and the advantages of public facilities providing (more or less) non-commodified leisure opportunities, compared to for-profit recreational options. Some also called attention to the beneficial results of a "coast-wide" process that would unite this ribbon of communities into a shared and mutually supportive project. In the view of supporters, the additional taxes necessary to fund such a multitude of benefits were seen as minimal. Those opposed to the facilities proposed in the referendum had a range of reasonable objections. The debt load would be a drain on our fragile economy, especially as it was public debt undisciplined by market forces. Any additional expenditures associated with using the facilities or associated retail purchases would simply be a reallocation of family income from current leisure choices with negative implications for existing business. If the private sector could not or would not provide the service, clearly the demand was less than touted by boosters, and government intervention was a recipe for waste.

Some opposed to the proposal also argued that after the tax increase had depleted the disposable income of families, many would not be able to avail themselves of the facilities. Rather than social benefits, then, there would be greater division between the haves and have-nots, and stress in some families to fund their children's participation in costly but popular sports. The annual costs of hockey equipment, travel, and fees were depicted as being especially expensive. Others wondered how there could be a need for capital-intensive recreation in a "rural" area where there were lakes to swim in (and to skate on occasionally), trails to hike, beaches to explore, and mountains to climb—all at no cost. Surely, those who suggested there was "nothing" for children and teens to do were limited in their imagination. The demand for capital-intensive, indoor recreation facilities, with their inevitable user levies (i.e., classic commodification), indicated an unhealthy urbanization in the community. Aside from creating traffic and congestion wherever the facilities would be built, the additional taxes necessary would make life on the Sunshine Coast unaffordable.

An additional dynamic that emerged clearly during the lead-up to the referendum was sub-regional autonomy or local vs. coast-wide perspectives. Local communities and neighbourhoods did not want to participate in, or contribute to, projects outside of their self-identified areas. This was especially true of Pender Harbour, the most northerly electoral area in the SCRD. However, similar dynamics emerged in other outlying areas and to a limited degree between the two urbanized areas. Residents of the Gibsons area already enjoyed a small aquatic facility and were reluctant to support a larger facility in Sechelt. Similarly, some residents in the Sechelt area expressed concern about supporting another arena "outside" of their area. These dynamics will not surprise those familiar with similar debates about building new recreation facilities in the Canmore–Banff corridor and the North Okanagan.

When the ballots were counted in June 1998, the citizens had supported the proposed recreation facilities 54 percent to 46 percent, with a voter turnout of 43 percent. Support was strongest in the unincorporated areas around Sechelt and in Sechelt itself. This is not surprising as those areas benefit the most when costs are shared by all areas of the Regional District. This allows them to share in the industrial tax base of the area's single pulp mill, located in the most southerly electoral district of West Howe Sound. However, in a dramatic rejection of the coast-wide approach, Pender Harbour electoral area voted 85 percent against the project.

However, the saga of recreation facilities is not over. Opponents of the proposal, upset with the results, launched a legal challenge of the process. The Regional Board considered a range of legal advice and decided it was not in the public's best interest to defend the referendum in court. Instead they initiated a new planning process utilizing a citizen-based steering committee. As this committee assessed the fallout from the referendum campaign and formulated new recommendations, local government elections intervened and a substantively new group of directors were elected to the SCRD Board.

The Board that took office in 1999 decided to move forward on recreation in a more cautious way. They are proposing to build two facilities: an ice-based community centre in Gibsons and an aquatic centre in Sechelt. The Board will respect Pender Harbour's clear rejection of any form of inclusion at this time. In addition, taxation for each facility will be drawn only from those areas considered adjacent to the proposed sites. That is, it will be a sub-regional or local approach to the provision of recreation facilities. The referenda necessary to acquire citizen approval of this new proposal will likely be completed by mid 2001. It is too early to predict what the results will be. Already one group has organized to protest the prospect that the region will not have a single centralized complex that would realize the economic benefits to be found via shared efficiencies of management and construction. Not to mention the enhanced residential values and retail opportunities that would be available in the immediately surrounding area!

For some residents on the Sunshine Coast, the inability of 28,000 people to co-ordinate their efforts to renew and improve recreation infrastructure is simply a failure of political leadership. However, this paper proposes that in democratic politics, proposals for development are open to legitimate contestation, and political processes must respect the authenticity of contradictory practices and interests. Thus, urbanization—if this means not only the spread of cities but the spread of urban money, urban tastes, and urban lifestyles and standards of living—occurs within parameters set by citizens whose interests and priorities are not completely predictable. The development of urban forms of recreation on the Sunshine Coast is therefore a product of decisions in which several different sets of values intersect in sometimes contradictory ways: regional vs. local identifications, values attached to preserving existing lifestyles on the Coast vs. enthusiasm for new amenities, and conflicting views on the need for a "new" economy.

POLITICAL HOMOLOGIES: SOME FINAL THOUGHTS

Similar complexities are also manifest if one looks carefully at other long-standing political debates on the Sunshine Coast. The question of restructuring municipal boundaries, for example, is an enduring issue. Some residents believe that the entire Regional District should be a single municipality governed by a mayor and council. Others suggest an expansion of the Town of Gibsons, while others propose incorporation of rural areas precisely so that they are *not* enveloped by neighbouring jurisdictions. Proposals to expand resource-extraction activities, whether forest resources or gravel aggregate, likewise provoke vigorous debates. Issues of contention on the Sunshine Coast are thus not limited to golf courses or recreation facilities.

Indeed, when we examine the political issues that have engaged Sunshine Coast citizens in recent years, opinion regularly divides according to people's views on regional co-operation versus local autonomy; on the need to develop vs. the need to conserve "nature"; and on the transition from a "traditional" to a "new" economy. Golf courses, swimming pools, ice arenas, municipal structures, and industrial expansion are all discussed and debated—and political coalitions forged and fractured—within a matrix established by these familiar arguments. Understanding the interplay of these ever-present themes, as political subjects shape their future, may thus help us to better understand the "conditions of possibility" within which the development of urban forms—as well as resistance to the continued urbanization of the Coast—will take place.

Underneath all these particular debates, moreover, there is a central tension which is seldom made explicit: between support for urban types of development, and resistance to development that is grounded in a valuing of the rural, and of what this place—the Sunshine Coast—has been in the not-too-distant past. Clearly, the growth rates noted earlier in this paper indicate the likelihood of continuing development. Indeed, it is in just this context that national and international retail chains have located on the Sunshine Coast in recent years. And although this is often the focus of criticism among businesses and residents with an established sense of place, the big chains can point to much evidence of support in the community. In addition, further large residential developments have already been approved, including a 700-plus residential project, centred on a new 18-hole golf course, and 2 separate properties rezoned and approved for hotels. All are in Sechelt and all now simply await favourable market conditions. All promise (or threaten) to bring new populations who could be expected to want more urban amenities.

Any observer visiting the Sunshine Coast will acknowledge that, to date, this place has not experienced the intense urbanization of other formerly rural communities like Canmore, the Okanagan, or Parksville and Qualicum. Observers could also note the proximity to Vancouver (and Seattle), the eager boosterism of local business associations, and the apparently untapped "recreational resources" of a beautiful environment (see Whitson, this volume), and see a future in which the imminent potential for further commodification and urbanization constitutes a landscape of attractive opportunities. However, this is also a future that for some current residents of the Coast is unthinkable.

This essay has implicitly argued that political coalitions are established through contingent engagements with others. Through political engagement, we develop shared or opposed perspectives on specific discursive agendas. Building political positions that prevail on any specific issue thus depends on the successful alignment of different interests and perspectives. In this sense, "public opinion" is a contingent and constantly reconstituted view of issues. It is this contingent alignment of shared aspirations that can authorize either the development of urban forms or the resistance to urbanization that sometimes prevails. What is striking, however, about this discussion of change on the Sunshine Coast is precisely the absence of explicit debates on urbanization. The underlying issue of urban forms displacing rural experience is itself displaced into other discussions: over process, over regional vs. local issues, over the pace of development, or over the transition to a "new" economy.

Further research would be required to discuss this with confidence. However, I would invite readers to consider two potential factors in the lack of explicit debate about urbanization in the events described here. First, there may be an implicit acceptance that urbanization will happen. Even those opposed may view continuing urbanization as inevitable, and prefer not to talk about it. Second, and perhaps ironically, there may be a complicit (though in my view mistaken) understanding among residents that they still share a rural, or at least non-urban, space. Such a view is consistent with marketing the Sunshine Coast as a holiday and retirement destination, while reassuring those that have chosen to live here that they have successfully distanced themselves from the perceived negatives of urban life.

I would argue that the latter is a naïve understanding of what constitutes rural experience, as Sunshine Coast residents are themselves complicit in the spread of urban tastes and standards in, for example, recreation and shopping. We cannot distance ourselves from our own daily practices and interests, and from our expression of these preferences in the context of local political debates. In as much as our lives are always lived *in loci*, our values and priorities are revealed most clearly in the politics of the real places we live in. And under current conditions (conditions established by the mobility of global capital and the reach of global communications media, as well as the contemporary mobility of people) the politics of place are inevitably about promoting—and resisting—urbanization, notwithstanding the explicit content of specific debates.

PART III

Defending
Real Rural Communities

Uneasy Neighbours

WHITE–ABORIGINAL RELATIONS AND AGRICULTURAL DECLINE

Murray Mandryk

PUNNICHY: TWO SOLITUDES

Surveying her neighbourhood in Punnichy, a small Saskatchewan farming town about 170 kilometres north of Regina, the woman counts 4 houses where the owners have purchased the adjacent lots. It's a common practice here, she says. Local white residents buy the properties and tear down the houses to ensure that neither private landlords nor the Saskatchewan Housing Corporation, a government agency, wind up renting them to Indian people coming into this community from the nearby Gordon First Nation.

"If you ask anybody about it, they'll just say that they want bigger lots," says the woman, who asks not to be identified because of the anger her comments would create in this town of 338 people.[1]

The kind of frank calculation she describes, however, is part of everyday life in some rural Saskatchewan communities where lot prices are low and white–aboriginal racial tensions can be high. As racist as it all might sound to an outsider, the rationalizations of Punnichy residents are expressed as much in the language of economics as they are in the language of prejudice. Having an Indian family renting next to you lowers property values, the woman says, in a matter-of-fact manner; it is really no different than when city residents oppose everything from commercial developments to halfway houses in their neighbourhoods.

"You know who lives in the house just by the yard," she continues. "Indians just don't know how to keep up their yard.... This is why people buy up the houses around them. It's the conditions that they live in." She is quick to admit that some of the white landlords who rent the dilapidated houses in town are every bit as responsible for the situation: since native people aren't really in the habit of complaining and have few housing options, bad landlords in town get away with failing to maintain their properties. Regardless of who is at fault, though, the net result is that having an Indian family move in next door to you means that the value of your home goes down considerably, she explains. That can be a big problem in a town where house prices are already devalued as a result of a sagging farm economy.

Doug Cuthand, Saskatchewan's most prominent and respected native journalist, agrees that racial tension in such rural communities "has a lot to do with economics." The 52-year-old Cuthand, who spent his first 11 years on the Sandy Lake reserve near Shellbrook in Northern Saskatchewan, can remember a time when both white and Indian people used horses and wagons to come to town, and when there might not have been quite so much tension: "There were a lot of marginal [white] farmers that weren't very rich either. We didn't have running water or anything. The thing is, though, nobody else was rich." While Cuthand doesn't deny that tensions existed 40 years ago, relative parity between poor white people and poor native people, at least near Shellbrook, eliminated one major source of it. "When we were growing up we were a pretty small population. In small towns we were definitely a minority. We were isolated on the reserves ... Of course, that has changed pretty rapidly."

Until very recently, native and non-native communities in rural Saskatchewan existed pretty much as two solitudes. In 1966 a mere nine percent of Saskatchewan natives lived off-reserve. Today, that figure is more than half. Population statistics from both Punnichy and the Gordon First Nation reflect how rural white people and Indian people have now become neighbours in the same communities. In 1974, the first year for which such statistics are available from the federal Department of Indian and Northern Affairs, 319 members of the 1,045 Gordon Reserve band lived anywhere off the reserve. By 1999, the band's population had grown to 2,537; only a minority—1,041—still lived on the reserve, where housing funds simply have not grown with the population.[2] Some of the population explosion can be attributed to the passage of Bill C-31 in 1986, leading to the reinstatement of many band members who had lost their status under the Indian Act through marriage or military service. Mostly, though, it can be attributed to the fact that First Nations' demographics are diametrically opposite to those for the rest of rural Saskatchewan (compare Coates, this volume, on rural BC). The province's native population is young and growing. By 2045, one-third of the population is expected to have native ancestry, compared with about ten percent today.[3]

Punnichy is typical of many small Saskatchewan farming communities. It's slowly aging and literally dying off. It recorded 338 residents in the 1996 census, a 7.4-percent decline from 1991. Moreover, the latest census data also indicate that, like most such small towns, Punnichy is old, poor, and white. In Punnichy, 22.2 percent of residents are 65 years or older. That is well above both the provincial and national averages. With so many seniors in town, the average income is only $17,431 annually—again far below the Saskatchewan average ($22,548) and the Canadian average ($25,196). Also, according to the 1996 census, 17 percent of Punnichy residents have less than a grade-nine education (compared with a provincial average of 16.2 percent and a Canadian average of 13.8 percent). And while Statistics Canada's numbers indicate that the majority of people in the community do not consider themselves to be part of a visible minority, the town's complexion is, in fact, changing rapidly. In the 1996 census, 70 of Punnichy's 338 residents claimed aboriginal descent.[4] Yet despite the prevalent perception of Western and small-town hospitality, the welcome mat hasn't exactly been out in Punnichy for its new residents. In a community whose residents abided by the tradition of never locking their front doors, complaints about break-and-enters, public drunkenness, and poverty have become commonplace. The doors are now being locked.

Punnichy's situation may be more extreme than some, but it is not unique. Indeed, there is good reason to think that the challenge of co-existence between rural white people and native people will soon be the most pressing problem in many parts of Saskatchewan. Given the starkly different demographic trajectories and the decline of the agricultural economy, rural resentment across the province is all too readily aimed at native people. The flashpoints can be housing, or taxation, or even the local school. At the same time, as this chapter will argue, promising possibilities for co-existence are emerging, rooted in mutual respect and shared interests, in places where native economic development initiatives are showing signs of success and helping to reinvigorate sagging local economies that have grown dependent on all sides on government transfers.

THE ROOTS OF CONFLICT

Close observers of race relations attribute the lack of understanding to years of living apart. "If people stepped back from it all, they'd see it isn't so much a racial problem," says Trevor Sutter, who covered native affairs for the *Regina Leader-Post* before becoming communication director for the Saskatchewan region of the Department of Indian and Northern Affairs. "It's a socio-economic problem ... I know of people in Punnichy who have never been to the reserve—who have never gotten to know their neighbors." There is little patience in small-town Saskatchewan, however, for exploring or understanding the root causes of such problems. Instead, the environment is ripe for people looking for examples of behaviour that confirm their stereotypes.

"They'll have their windows and doors wide open and the furnace blasting away," says the woman in Punnichy. "It's a heck of a waste of money."

Admittedly, such stereotypes aren't even always meant to be negative. Some of them are even expressed in admiration for what Punnichy residents view as values similar to their own—like the importance of the family. As one local businessperson, who also requested anonymity, puts it:

> If Joe comes to door, Joe gets let in and Joe gets to stay until there's nothing left in the house to eat. They just can't seem to make their money last.... I always said that in Punnichy, they are the best customers. If they have a dollar they spend it.

To a large extent, commerce defines local perceptions. One reason is that economic issues are particularly sensitive ones in Punnichy. Already struggling to compete with the big-box stores in Regina, the local business community has become increasingly, though not always happily, reliant on the less-mobile First Nations population. Frustration is evident. The local businessperson quoted above says that "about 60 percent of them don't like paying their bills." He describes some Gordon Reserve residents as being like "little children" in their business dealings, and unable to handle credit.

A related flashpoint throughout rural Saskatchewan during the past decade has been the exemption from provincial sales tax that status Indians have enjoyed on off-reserve purchases. For years the Saskatchewan government allowed such exemptions when a treaty card was produced. In exchange, the provincial Department of Finance could collect taxes on the sale of gasoline and cigarettes sold on reserves. It was an arrangement that actually worked in the province's favour, as it collected about $10 million more annually in gas and cigarette taxes than it lost on off-reserve purchases. Given that First Nation people were also exempted from paying tax on big-ticket items delivered directly to the reserve, it didn't make much sense for the government to bother with off-reserve taxation. For all that, the sales-tax exemption has also been wildly unpopular—especially in rural Saskatchewan. It has reinforced what for Doug Cuthand is the frustrating misconception that many Indians are rich and all driving new vehicles: "These guys [with money] are the minority. Even the chiefs ... I don't know of many of them that drive around in Grand Cherokees."

In the 1999 provincial election, the opposition Saskatchewan Party campaigned vigorously against the sales tax exemption. Rural New Democrat MLAs privately admitted that it was almost indefensible politically. The election results, in part, may have reflected this assessment. While Indian taxation wasn't the only unpopular government policy in rural Saskatchewan, it's noteworthy that New Democrats lost all but 2 of the province's 38 rural seats. Moreover, the NDP-Liberal coalition government formed after the election quickly dispensed with the policy in its 2000 budget and began charging status Indians the province's six-percent sales tax on off-reserve purchases. First Nations people reacted angrily, organizing protests and local boycotts in some communities. In rural communities, however, the change has been applauded. According to the woman in Punnichy: "It was like a thorn in your side. It ticked you off. Everything ticks you off, if you live next to it. They would brag about not having to pay taxes."

The Gordon First Nation, however, has had its own issues with the Punnichy business community. A few years ago, reserve residents boycotted at least one local merchant as a result of his decision to send his children to the high school in nearby Raymore, where there are fewer native students. He eventually sold his operation. "You can't get too political when you're in business," the local businessperson observes.

Even though economic grievances have created much of the hard feelings between the Indian and white communities in this area, there's likely no single issue more sensitive than that of the school. Local residents have complained that sending their children to school in Punnichy resulted in them getting an inferior education. The number of First Nations students who have learning disorders or suffer from Fetal Alcohol Syndrome has made it that much harder for teachers to give other students attention. The result, says the woman in Punnichy, is that "All the white kids are now being bused to Raymore. The whole high school is native."

The history of shared education goes back to the abandonment of the federal government's failed experiment in social engineering known as the residential schools. The source of the problem in the Punnichy area can be traced to one man: William Peniston Starr. He was the director of the Gordon Reserve residential school from 1968—shortly after it was taken over by the federal government from the Anglican Church—until 1984. During his tenure, the school was considered a model of success. The Gordon Dancers travelled across Canada and all over Europe in the 1970s; a boxing club that Starr organized was highly successful. But all pretenses of success were shattered in 1993 when Starr pleaded guilty to ten counts of sexual assault involving his former students. The incidents involved young boys between seven and fourteen years old. Court was told after Starr's 1993 guilty plea that he used a system of intimidation and reward to lure certain students into performing acts of fondling, masturbation, and oral sex. A student's refusal to participate would lead to the withdrawal of privileges like canteen duty, where they were given free soft drinks and food. Starr received a four-and-a-half-year sentence.[5]

The court ruling set off a series of lawsuits unprecedented in Canadian history. Four years after the conviction, more than 100 former Gordon Residential School residents had launched suits against Starr, claiming in court documents that they had suffered from nervous shock, anxiety, depression, emotional trauma, and personality changes. One of the victims told *The Leader-Post* in 1996 that at least six of the sexual-abuse victims had committed suicide. "In my heart and in my mind, I've killed Starr over and over for what he did to me," said the victim, who admitted attempting suicide twice himself.[6]

The magnitude of the Gordon Reserve scandal dwarfs any previous sexual abuse scandal, including Newfoundland's Mount Cashel orphanage, where 38 victims received compensation from the federal government. However, the

Gordon Residential School is not the only one in Saskatchewan about which such allegations have been made. Not long after the law suits began to flow from the Gordon scandal, more than twenty similar suits were initiated by former residents of St. Philip's School, on the Cote Reserve north of Kamsack, for alleged emotional, physical, and sexual abuse. Grant Severeight, who was an eleven-year-old resident of the school in 1961, explained in a 1997 interview he was whipped with a belt from a threshing machine after he tried to run away back to his grandparents on the reserve: "I was made to stand with my hands in the air and then whipped on my back and buttocks. It was severe. I had scabs for weeks."[7] By all accounts, Severeight's abuse at St. Philip's was not an isolated case. Other students suing for compensation testified how teachers—Oblate missionaries and lay teachers alike—would rub children's faces in soiled sheets to punish them for bed-wetting. Several of the St. Philip's lawsuits also allege sexual abuse.

While the percentage of First Nations people who attended residential schools is not high, the scars from them run deep and are still rather fresh. While the schools are almost as old as Canada itself, the last one in Saskatchewan operated until 1998. The concept goes back to 1879 when Nicholas Flood Davin, founder of the newspaper that is now *The Leader-Post*, prepared a report for Sir John A. Macdonald on an industrial school concept for Indian children. After examining American models, Davin recommended the creation of similar schools in Western Canada so that Indian children would be "kept constantly within the circle of civilized conditions…. The influence of the wigwam was stronger than that of the (day) school."[8]

There were fourteen such residential schools in Saskatchewan and as many as eighty in Canada—funded by the federal government and run by the Roman Catholic, Anglican, Methodist, and Presbyterian churches. Even without the particular terrors of sexual abuse, the assimilation policies practised by the religious administrators were, by all accounts, brutal. Mary Kehler of the Kawacotoose First Nation, in a 1996 interview, recounted her first Christmas at the residential school in 1945 when she was just seven. Her parents, who had travelled 25 kilometres by sleigh to see her for Christmas, were told that they wouldn't be able to go to the wash house to visit their children on Christmas Day unless they went to midnight mass. School officials supervised the visits, Kehler said, to ensure that no Cree or Saulteaux was spoken. Her mother spoke no English. "They were scared we would tell our parents how we are being treated," she said.[9]

Across Canada, more than 6000 lawsuits have been filed by former students stemming from the residential school experience. In 1998 the federal government issued an official apology to all Canadian aboriginal peoples for the "injustices committed against them"; Jane Stewart, then Indian and Northern Affairs Minister, pledged a $350-million community healing fund. The apology was a long time in coming. While the 1996 Royal Commission on Aboriginal Peoples offered detailed accounts of mismanagement and complaints of abuse at the residential schools, it appears the federal government had known for almost three decades that they were a failure. A 1967 report prepared by George Caldwell, a child-care specialist with the Canadian Welfare Council who examined nine residential schools, concluded that they were failing to prepare Indian students for life in a modern-day Canada. Caldwell wrote that children caught between the white culture of the residential school and the Indian culture were not "equipped to handle this struggle on their own."[10]

The lasting effects of the residential schools can now be seen in rural communities like Punnichy. One woman who worked in the Punnichy bar recalls overhearing a conversation between two Gordon Reserve residents, including a victim of Starr: "One of them just started crying. He was 40 years old, in a bar reliving what had been done to him, and crying. It was horrible. That's the damage that has been done."

While sympathy exists among Punnichy residents for the tragedy that some of their First Nation neighbours have endured, it too has its limits. When informed of the volume of suits in 1997, Starr told Trevor Sutter, who was then at *The Leader-Post*: "Good God. They are certainly not all legitimate."[11] That clearly is the view held by many in Punnichy, who say they've heard Gordon First Nations people brag about filing specious claims to get their share of federal compensation. Though there is a court process to validate each claim, some white Punnichy residents see the lawsuits as another example of Indians attempting to get something for nothing—one more thing that feeds the racial stereotypes and tensions in this town. Moreover, these settlements, ranging from $25,000 to $150,000 (significantly less than those for the Mount Cashel victims), generate complaints from Punnichy residents that this money does not help those who have been victimized. Dennis Hunter, chief of the Gordon First Nation, actually shares this concern. The settlements, he said in a 1997 interview, have "caused a nightmare out here. By handing out money to these kids without addressing their problems, it has caused more problems. They've been drinking, doing drugs, spending their money recklessly and they're only hiding the pain. They should have been given the help they needed before they were given the compensation."[12]

EMPLOYMENT AND ECONOMIC DEVELOPMENT

It may be no coincidence that some of the worst race relations in Saskatchewan exist in communities like Punnichy and Kamsack, communities where the most serious allegations of abuse from residential schools have emerged. But, according to Doug Cuthand, Punnichy and Kamsack also happen to be among the poorest economic areas for Saskatchewan Indians. There has been precious little economic development on the nearby reserves. While some of the problems that exist today can be attributed to prejudices, and to painful experiences like residential schools, Cuthand's view is that it is really the lack of employment and economic development opportunities that perpetuate them. Consider the complaints of the Punnichy woman cited at the outset of this paper, about the Gordon First Nation residents who have moved into her town. Asked why some in her community resent having Indians as neighbours, she claims: "Their work ethic is non-existent and they have every opportunity to get a job. You can't get them to work until at least lunchtime. As you're slogging it out from nine to five, they're sitting on their front steps ... You'd think they'd get bored." Cuthand has heard that refrain often: "I just shake my head over the way people are. There's an awful lot of parochial and narrow-minded people ... And it's not just white people." But the woman in Punnichy says those who would be quick to judge her community as racist tend to be people who have never experienced the reality of a decline in their school and their property values and an increase in petty crime. "You have to live with them to understand what it's like," she says. "Some would call it racist, but they don't live next to them."

There is no doubt that those living close to First Nations people are most likely to hold negative sentiments. A national survey conducted by the Angus Reid Group in July 2000 for the Department of Indian and Northern Affairs bears that out. The survey of 3000 people was designed with a disproportionately large Saskatchewan sample of 556 residents. It found that, in comparison with other Canadians, Saskatchewan people—and rural residents in particular—demonstrated much less tolerant views on several issues. For example, while 89 percent of the Saskatchewan respondents said they believed aboriginal people "are capable of earning their own way if given a chance," 70 percent of Saskatchewan people also agreed with the statement that "aboriginal people are too dependent on government." The Saskatchewan figure was significantly higher than the Canadian average. Agreement increased, moreover, among less educated, older, and rural Saskatchewan people. Asked whether "most of the problems of Aboriginal peoples are brought on by themselves," 39 percent of all Saskatchewan people agreed. Even more inclined to agree were those with no more than a high school education (48 percent), those 55 years and older (44 percent), those earning less than $30,000 a year (45 percent), and those living in rural areas (44 percent).

Treaty rights and aboriginal self-government were especially sensitive issues in the survey. Only one in five Saskatchewan residents agreed that working towards self-government should be a high priority. Three out of four strongly agreed that when land-claim agreements are signed, aboriginal peoples should have the exact same rights as any other Canadians—no more and no less. Four in ten Saskatchewan residents strongly agreed that it wouldn't be fair to displace people and businesses from their land just to make up for wrongs committed years ago. Just over half (55 percent) of Saskatchewan people thought that "Aboriginal peoples are taking advantage of the courts to get more out of the treaty agreements than was originally negotiated." By comparison, only 46 percent of all Canadians agreed with the same statement. But perhaps the most telling piece of information in the poll occurred when respondents were asked if they had "become more or less sympathetic towards aboriginal concerns over the past couple of years." Only 19 percent of all Canadians said that they were now less sympathetic. In Saskatchewan, however, the figure was 30 percent; in rural Saskatchewan, it was 37 percent.[13]

The poll results are no surprise to Sutter. "If you position any policy as a 'rights issue' or righting historic wrong," he says, people in rural Saskatchewan "can't see it…. They don't know their own history." Still, as troubled as race relations tend to be, when issues are framed in terms of economic development, they do seem to be more supportive of First Nations communities. "It's the only thing that resonates," Sutter says. As an example, he cites the controversy in the early 1990s over casinos. The White Bear First Nation near Carlyle in south-eastern Saskatchewan defied provincial gaming laws and set up the first Indian-run casino near the resort of Kenosee Lake, in Moose Mountain Provincial Park. Tensions escalated after a middle-of-the-night RCMP raid in which slot machines were seized. Interestingly, local residents sided with the White Bear Band and against the provincial NDP government in this dispute. "It [White Bear] basically had the support of Carlyle during the standoff," Sutter says, noting that the farming community was quick to recognize the economic benefit such a First Nations enterprise could bring to the area. "There was a common interest in this economic project."

Doug Cuthand, too, first noticed as a boy that the more First Nation and local white communities were linked economically, the better relations tended to be. With his father serving as an Anglican minister, Cuthand's youth was spent on the move, living in southern Alberta on the Blood Reserve and in northern Saskatchewan in LaRonge. His first real experience with racism was when he started school in southern Alberta. "I was about 14 and I was just shocked," he says. "The first day of school, they were just in your face." From southern Alberta, the Cuthand family moved to LaRonge, a community some 600 kilometres north of Regina that relies heavily on tourism, fishing, hunting, and the mining industry. The journalist says he was struck by the comparative absence of tension between whites and First Nations people there, even more than a generation ago. It had much to do with the fact that whites and natives in LaRonge tended to work side by side in the various industries of the local economy.

While working and creating economic wealth together doesn't necessarily obliterate racism, having First Nations people as active participants in the economy and workforce does seem to be a critical first step, Sutter agrees. "Where the standard of living is elevated, the community and the First Nation seem to have far better relations. Usually, the common bond is economic development. Money brings people together."

A prime example can be found in the northwest corner of the province where NorSask Forest Products, a state-of-the-art forestry operation exporting wood products around the world, is owned by the Meadow Lake Tribal Council. With annual revenues of $46-million and about 150 local employees, NorSask is just one of the many businesses that are giving the entire region economic hope. Besides NorSask, the tribal council's business interests include MLTC Logging and Reforestations Inc., MLTC Warehouse, Polar Oils Ltd., and MLTC Northern Trucking.[14]

In northeastern Saskatchewan, meanwhile, Kitsaki Development Corporation, owned by the Lac LaRonge Band, has revenues of almost $20-million and employs 530 people. Kitsaki has also branched into mining, catering, hotels, meat processing, wild rice, and environmental monitoring companies. Another northern Saskatchewan success story is a development company owned by the Peter Ballantyne First Nation; this company operates 17 businesses that had approximately $52-million in assets and more than $50-million in gross sales in 1999. Its extensive investment portfolio ranges from a minority share in companies such as Northern Resource Trucking (the majority of which is owned by Kitsaki) to full ownership of PB Tel Limited Partnership and Medi-Plus Pharmacy in Prince Albert. The latter was a twenty-year-old business purchased by Peter Ballantyne in 1995, when the previous owner fell into financial difficulty because of competition from large pharmaceutical chains. The band-run operation implemented a policy of old-fashioned, friendly service. The clean, well-organized appearance of the pharmacy plus the face-to-face contact contrasted with the less personal, warehouse-style approach of the bigger chain stores. Medi-Plus Pharmacy is now a successful business with a staff of 22 people that has seen its sales increase annually. It may also represent the changing face of race relations in Saskatchewan.

Another success story has emerged out of the Muskoday First Nation, a community of about 500 people located just southeast of Prince Albert. Muskoday's latest venture is market gardening. A quarter section of land on the reserve is now dedicated to the project, with 47 acres set aside for potatoes, 100 acres for hemp, and 3 acres for various vegetables. The most impressive number, however, is the 95-percent rate of seasonal employment on the reserve.

"For the last 20 years, since the highway went in … we sat and we watched economic opportunity go through one side of the reserve and out the other without capturing any of those dollars," Lyle Bear, chairman of the Muskoday Economic Development Authority, told *Seeds of Success* magazine, a publication produced by the Federation of Saskatchewan Indian Nations (FISN) to high-light business successes. "In order to do that, we had to develop, parcel, and market a product before we could expect that traffic to stop." Muskoday started in 1991 with a convenience store and gas bar on Highway 3 to take advantage of the high volume of northbound traffic. A restaurant followed in 1998. The Indian-run enterprises on Muskoday have become a big part of the business community on the northern edge of the grain belt in Saskatchewan. "We are fortunate here because of our uniqueness of geography, and we have good support from the surrounding neighbourhood, in Birch Hills and Prince Albert," Bear said.[15]

Circumstances do have to be right for such success stories. Geography is an important factor, and certainly northern bands with greater land bases and more riches from natural resources have a better financial foundation for success than the southern bands. But even in southern Saskatchewan, where local reserves and the largely rural white population are more inclined to come into conflict, there does seem to be a correlation between First Nations economic development and positive race relations. The Ochapawace First Nation near Broadview, 160 kilometres east of Regina, has ventured into several tourism-related businesses including a ski hill. Its success has allowed the band to expand even further into the hospitality industry, purchasing the Landmark Inn in Regina. Doug Cuthand's favourite example is shared tourism and resource development activity around Maple Creek in the southwest. "The people down there are redneck and proud of it," Cuthand said. "But they're not that hard to get along with."

Another development that is bridging the race gap in some places is First Nations' purchase of farmland under the Treaty Land Entitlement (TLE), the result of a 1992 agreement with federal and provincial governments to settle numerous claims going back to the establishment of reserves. The issue is not an easy one given the long-term economic and emotional investment that rural Saskatchewan farmers have in the soil. The agreement provided for the affected First Nations to acquire approximately 1.9 million acres of land for reserve creation. As of May 1999, 600,000 acres were being processed; about 270,000 acres were already set apart as reserve lands. Specific claim settlements—also in the implementation stage—will give First Nations another 110,800 acres for reserve creation. As of May 1999, about 38,000 acres were being processed for this purpose, with 32,700 acres already set aside for reserves.[16]

Surprisingly, there's been less resentment to First Nations buying up farm-land than one might expect. This may be because the 1992 TLE framework agreement will eventually pump $516-million into the Saskatchewan economy, with farmers being among the main beneficiaries. The TLE is widely cited as one of the major reasons why Saskatchewan land prices haven't fallen through the basement in tough economic times. The large number of aging farmers wanting to retire often have had no buyers willing to offer them fair market value for their land other than First Nations.

Perhaps the best example of this success in rural Saskatchewan is happening around the Carry-the-Kettle First Nation near the town of Indian Head east of Regina. Since 1992, the First Nation has spent $11-million under the terms of its TLE settlement to purchase 34,000 acres of local farmland—all of which has been leased back to local farmers. "The special thing about this situation is they have made it a policy to buy local and sell local," says Trevor Sutter, noting that the band's TLE officer has a reputation for taking less money rather than dealing with outside interests. He also cites the example of a 50-year-old farmer who couldn't make ends meet in his leaseback arrangements with Carry-the-Kettle.

The TLE officer reworked his lease to take into account low commodity prices. "It's offering an alternative to the rigid conditions imposed by the banks and the Farm Credit Corporation," explains Sutter, who adds that Carry-the-Kettle's fundamental approach is to keep farmers on the land and to keep the land in production. "It kind of reflects the nature of First Nations people who aren't transient. The common word in Indian Country is 'we're here to stay.'" The strength of local white–First Nations relations was demonstrated in February 2001, when some local band members protested the lack of accountability in payments made to off-reserve members. While the Saskatchewan branch of the Canadian Taxpayers Association condemned the situation as one more example of reserve mismanagement, Indian Head's weekly newspaper was considerably less critical, reminding local residents of the good things happening on the reserve.

The picture, of course, isn't completely rosy. One problem is that the lease-backs do nothing to develop a new generation of Indian farmers, who are further discouraged by the fact that the Indian Act still prohibits individuals from securing the large-scale capital investment needed to farm. The latter remains a sore point in rural Saskatchewan, where stories about business deals gone bad with local bands are plentiful. One farmer in the southeast says a band simply refused to pay him after his company delivered $10,000 worth of seed grain to a reserve. Because he couldn't take civil action, it took years to settle the dispute. Nonetheless, there has been progress in the past decade.

Native-run casinos have also played a major role in both First Nations' economic prosperity and in changing perceptions among their neighbours. The Saskatchewan Indian Gaming Authority (SIGA), owned by the FISN and 9 tribal councils, now has annual revenues of $77-million and employs approximately 2000 people at its 4 casinos in North Battleford, Yorkton, Prince Albert, and White Bear. The contribution of gaming to race relations, however, has been somewhat mixed. In the spring of 2000, a government special audit was ordered into SIGA's operations over allegations of inappropriate expense claims, especially by former president and chief executive officer Dutch Lerat. He was fired at the government's request after the initial allegations were made public. According to an internal Gaming Authority report, he used SIGA credit and debit cards to run up more than $500,000 in personal expenses in one year: groceries, videos, visits to Internet sites, sports car rentals, haircuts, vacations, limousines, hotel rooms, pet supplies, sunglasses, wrestling tickets, jewelry, fishing equipment, clothes, green fees, and golf equipment.[17] The whiff of financial mismanagement in First Nations ventures tends to linger with the rest of the Saskatchewan population, and reinforces negative stereotypes, especially in the rural areas.

"There's no question in my mind that it [the relationship between the two communities] has its ebbs and flows," says Northern Affairs Minister Keith Goulet, the province's first aboriginal cabinet minister. "I'm sensing that it has been on a downward spiral of late." But comparing the relationship now with ten, twenty, or thirty years ago, he says, there is little doubt of improvement. The minister attributes it to the increased participation by natives not only in the economy but in society in general. He points to the numbers. Just 10 years ago there were only 500 people working in the province's northern mines; now there are 1000. The social assistance dependency rate for First Nations people in Saskatchewan has dropped almost ten percent in the last three years alone. Perhaps most significantly, when Goulet went to university in 1965, he was one of only five native students on the University of Saskatchewan campus. This year, 2200 from the province's north alone were taking some form of post-secondary training. Seeing First Nation people going to the same schools, playing on the same golf courses, or even shopping in the same Wal-Marts, buying things for their families, does much to break down old stereotypes and substitute more positive images, he says.

People in parts of rural Saskatchewan are still less likely to encounter such positive images because of the endemic poverty and the residential-school legacy that corrode many lives on some reserves. The chasms in towns like Punnichy are deep, and negative stereotypes persist. But such problems are not indicative of every community. In others, traditional powwows are becoming events not only for the reserves, but also for the neighbouring towns and villages. At such events, where First Nations people celebrate and show pride in their aboriginal heritage, perhaps for the first time in the experience of their white neighbours, the non-native population often gains a greater understanding of native culture.

Doug Cuthand says that the advent of a provincial human rights commission has helped to institutionalize respect and give Indian people a body that will "take up their case and fight for them." But his hopes also rest on the possibility that native and non-native people are simply beginning to understand each other better because of increased contact. He points to the outpouring of sympathy his family received after the tragic death of one of his cousins—a local farmer who was well respected in the community by the other farmers with whom his cousin had done business: "The white farmers came to the reserve to pay their respects. They knew him and they respected him. It was quite touching. I was touched by that."

Relations between First Nations communities and their neighbors are in transition. In some parts of rural Saskatchewan—and, it must be said, rural Saskatchewan is no different in this respect from comparable communities across the rural West—relations are poor, and even sometimes worsening. Where poor reserves have existed outside small and often insular farm towns, with little real contact outside the most basic commercial interactions, long-held prejudices about Indians persist, and indeed are reinforced whenever poverty, alcohol abuse, or family dysfunction can be observed. In the context of agricultural decline and perceived threats to communities, local prejudices readily turn into resentment at what are perceived as "privileges": in Saskatchewan, tax advantages or hunting rights; in Alberta, oil royalties; in British Columbia, even the potential of "generous" land claims settlements (see Coates, this volume, on Northern BC, and Lawrence et al. on rural resentment in Australia). On the First Nations side, there is growing bitterness as the personal and communal devastation caused by the residential schools is more widely recognized and talked about. There is anger, too, at the reluctance of provincial governments in the West to make amends for this damage (Saskatchewan being a partial exception), and to settle land claims on a basis that would provide the foundations for better economic futures for First Nations.

At the same time, developments in other parts of rural Saskatchewan give reason for hope. Especially in the North, larger land bases and, in some cases, royalties and other income from natural resources have provided a foundation for steady and sometimes dramatic economic development. Outside the North, there are cases of wisely managed development that have improved standards of living on reserves and that stand as examples of what can be accomplished even in unpromising circumstances. Put together, these economic ventures have given both First Nations communities and their neighbours shared interests that forward-looking individuals on both sides can build on. Admittedly, the process remains a slow and arduous one. In some rural communities, it's still easier to buy the lot next to you rather than risk having an Indian as your neighbour. But as First Nations people continue to prosper, and as small towns increasingly rely on them to keep stores, schools, and government services open, there will be less reason for residents to object to their new neighbours.

Notes

1   Interviews conducted by the author with past and present residents of Punnichy in September 2000.

2   Statistics Canada population data provided by the Department of Indian and Northern Affairs.

3   This estimate is from a 1998 study on population projections conducted on behalf of the Federation of Saskatchewan Indian Nations.

4   Statistics Canada, 1996 Census.

5   *Regina Leader-Post*, 11 July 1995.

6   *Regina Leader-Post*, 22 December 1996.

7   *Regina Leader-Post*, 12 April 1997.

8   Ibid.

9   *Regina Leader-Post*, 23 December 1996.

10   *Regina Leader-Post*, 12 April 1997.

11   *Regina Leader-Post*, 24 January 1997.

12   *Regina Leader-Post*, 29 October 1997.

13   Angus Reid, "Public Views Regarding Aboriginal People," 2000.

14   Saskatchewan Department of Intergovernmental Affairs.

15   *Seeds of Success*, Fall 1999.

16   Interviews by the author in October 2000.

17   *Regina Leader-Post*, 18 October 2000.

Overcoming Cultural and Spiritual Obstacles to Rural Revitalization

Cameron Harder

Between 1985 and 1997, I served as pastor of a town and country congregation in rural Alberta. During that time I became acutely aware of the intense pain that farm bankruptcies cause—not only to the farmers involved but also to the community. Neighbours, fellow church, board, and club members, found their interests pitted against one another. Lenders foreclose on farmers; neighbours buy the farmer's land; relationships suffer apparently irreparable rifts. Shame, depression, and anger plague the lives of the insolvent farmers. I sensed that rural churches, because they include people who represent a variety of community roles and have a particular concern for the care of the community's "spirit," can have a critical role in the healing (and perhaps the making) of this pain. I did not have the tools, however, to help our congregation deal with the significant spiritual, theological, pastoral, and sociological issues involved. My research was an effort to gain some of those skills.

Over the past five years I completed formal interviews with twenty-nine farmers who were or had been in a process of bankruptcy or foreclosure and another thirty-five interviews with solvent farmers, lenders, input dealers, politicians, and others involved in the changes occurring in agriculture. Most were from the Prairie provinces.

All spoke of the diminishing size of their communities. One farmer said, "There used to be four families on our telephone line. We're the only ones left." Another said that her children, though they love farming, are reluctant to remain in a community in which there are virtually no others their age. A third noted that the regionalization of health and educational facilities was encouraging her neighbours to move into the nearest large centre where these services are located; now they farm from a distance. Her small community is being leached of its people and services. In the February 28, 2000 issue of *Maclean's* magazine, Jean Soggie gave voice to a common rural lament:

> [You have] to drive farther and farther for everything, whether it's to get the mail or buy parts for the combine or take your kid to the volleyball game or your uncle to emergency or yourself to that part-time job you are afraid to give up. It is having to drive farther and farther in older and older vehicles on the worst roads this side of Mexico. It is seeing my dad, who grew up with this country, from sod house to barbwire, telephones to paved roads to the Internet, disillusioned and saddened by the deterioration of the community he devoted his life to.

Beneath these obvious effects of rural depopulation is a less visible deterioration of the community's *spirit*. Some farmers, particularly those who have grown up on the farm and have ancestral links to it, report an intense bonding with the land. Michael said, "Farm families are connected to the land—like a living body."[1] For these farmers the pain of leaving the farm can be almost physical. As Brenda expressed it: "We have the roots of the land in us. Whether you are forced off the land, or choose to leave, it's like something that is planted deep inside you is just being ripped out."[2] Leaving the land, especially under coercion, leaves many farmers with feelings somewhat similar to those of war amputees—embarrassment at being seen in public places, grief, a profound sense of no longer being whole.

Among smaller and middle-sized farmers, even some of those who are solvent expressed a growing sense of disconnection from the land and their life purpose. Some said they feel a spiritual responsibility to be stewards of the land.

But their perception is that government and society favour large corporate farms which pay closer attention to their yearly shareholders' profit than to the complex needs of a piece of land over generations. Concern for long-term husbandry of the land's resources seems to have become identified with a sentimentalism that has no place in a hard-nosed business environment. Others said that they have the moral responsibility (and privilege) to supply bread to "feed a hungry world." Apparent over-supplies of wheat and other grain commodities have left them with the feeling that they are unnecessary anachronisms.

Including and overarching these concerns, two broad elements of community spirit appear to have been eroded: first, the community's sense of *hope*—its confidence that it has a meaningful future—and second, the community's *cohesion*—its willingness and ability to work together for a common future. It is on these two elements, particularly the latter, that this article will focus.

LOSS OF HOPE

The loss of hope is evidenced at personal, family, and community levels. Among those persons experiencing severe financial stress, depression is common.[3] Diane told how a deadening sense of hopelessness had settled into her life: "I've gone from being terrified to 'I don't care anymore.'" Nora spoke of the difficulty of simply getting up in the morning to face another day of anxiety and loss. "You're just drained emotionally, physically, and mentally," she said. The depression can be so paralyzing that the preparations necessary to fight for a good settlement or to prepare for an auction and a move simply cannot happen. Doreen says, "I felt like the lowest thing on earth. We had completely blocked the sale out of our minds. We didn't do anything to get ready for that sale." Wayne, a district agriculturist, admits that the most difficult part of his job is watching farmers give up hope. He says that they move from anger to blaming and finally a quiet despair.

Lynda Haverstock, a psychologist and farm counsellor for many years, as well as a former Saskatchewan Liberal leader, has observed that farm bankruptcy is a process of bereavement and that coping with it is a painful form of grief work. Connie agrees: "It's like a real death. It's every bit as stressful as a spouse dying." Ron goes further than that: "It's easier to cope with death than with what has transpired because this is an ongoing thing." In Saskatchewan the threatened or actual loss of a farm can take as long as six years, including negotiations with the banks, farm debt review, quit claims, court appeals, foreclosure or bankruptcy, a period of renting the land back from the lender, and final farm sale. As a result families are subject to prolonged and chronic stress. There is also a "futility factor" at work: the more hours a farmer puts in on the farm, the greater the stress he or she is likely to feel.[4] Diane said, "We worked harder and harder and harder, longer days and no help. We would do everything to try and make ends meet. But it was out of our reach." In other words, it was hopeless even to try.

For lifetime farmers the hopelessness partly reflects a fear that they are not suited for anything else, or that nothing else can be as rewarding. They may underestimate the value of their skills and abilities in another part of the economy. For farmers in their fifties or older, the despair may come with the evaporation of retirement funds. Andy lost his farm in the process of trying to set up his two sons in farming. He had co-signed their loans; when they lost their land, he also lost his, and therefore the equity for his retirement.

For families, the hopelessness is connected to the loss of a heritage to pass on. The farm often represents the collective effort and wisdom of several generations working a particular piece of land; the wisdom of managing it is part and parcel of the family's identity and its legacy for the future. To lose it is to lose one's past and future simultaneously. As Wayne lamented, "My kids won't have any opportunity to be on the land. We're the ones that broke the chain, passing the farm from generation to generation."

At the community level, hope fails as children find they have no future there and leave. Many of the bankruptcies have been among young farmers getting started in the business. Clark feels that the "whole system is saying to young people, 'No, you can't farm!'" Those children who cannot or choose not to farm have few options for employment in the area. As rural industries centralize, fewer and fewer off-farm jobs are available in smaller communities. John laments, "Here's one of our most precious resources—our young people—and they're gone, they're not coming back." The young people themselves feel it. In a video produced by teenage children of farmers in Manitoba, the youth express their discouragement this way:

> If we don't get something good to do here—if we can't make a decent living—if we've got no place to go and no one to turn to, then our only choice is to go to the city or keep running into the bush [that is, escape into drinking]. Either way a lot of us are never going to come back.[5]

The hopelessness is entrenched in rural communities by a sense that local people have lost control over their future. Critical decisions about the transportation, storage, and financing of their products are being made by large organizations far distant from those who feel their impact. The computerization of global markets has given powerful, detached, risk-oriented players freedom to impose rapid and devastating vacillations on market prices that can act in a domino fashion to destabilize economies around the world. In recent years farmers have found themselves incurring large debts simply to cover the losses of a single season's price collapse. At times (as with hog prices in the fall of 1998) it can be cheaper to trash one's product than to transport it to market.

LOSS OF COMMUNITY COHESION: CONFLICT, CANNIBALISM, SHAME

Of course it is difficult to know whether change is possible until a community has fully explored its options together. Here is perhaps the crux of the problem: interviewees reported a significant loss of community cohesion—that is, the ability to communicate and act together on matters essential to the community's well-being. A number of factors contribute to this loss.

Communities have been fractured by a proliferation of government programs, new technologies, farm lobby groups, and conflicting interests. Small farmers and acreage owners oppose developers of large confinement hog facilities. Organic farmers battle neighbours whose chemicals or genetically modified seeds drift onto their fields. The Western Canadian Wheat Growers battle for a freer market with National Farmers Union members who support the Canadian Wheat Board's marketing monopoly. Non-natives resent natives who have purchased farmland through the settlement of aboriginal treaties and then taken the land out of production.

Competition for shrinking profits has also diminished community cohesion. Older farmers complain that co-operative practices have been replaced by intense, even "cannibalistic" competition. Increasingly sophisticated mechanization has rendered the help of neighbours either unnecessary (one person can farm vast areas alone) or inadequate (when it breaks down it takes an expert to fix it). Shrinking profit margins, related to the rising cost of machinery, fertilizers, and other inputs, and to the relatively stable average price for some commodities over time, have pushed farmers to expand their holdings so that they can make an adequate living from increased volume. Al felt that some farmers were "waiting for their neighbours to go broke so they can gobble up their land." Some noted that when the farm economy is depressed it is often machinery bought at cheap farm-auction prices that allows neighbouring farmers to stay viable, while, at the same time, machinery dealers in the community lose out. To Bob, watching neighbours purchase his equipment was like watching "the vultures come in for the kill." Bill observed, "There's a lot of cannibalism."[6]

Farmers who saw their neighbours benefit from their foreclosure report feeling angry and betrayed. This sense that the trust one has invested in neighbours and lenders (essential in small-community relationships) has been violated is one of two critical socio-emotional experiences common in farm crisis that threaten community cohesion. Frequently foreclosures involve a lender and farmer from the same community, perhaps even members of the same church. The anger generated in the farmer is deeply personal and difficult to contain. It may express itself in threats or acts of violence towards lenders, family members, or self. Harold said that he had to stop attending church because the lender who oversaw his foreclosure was also a member of that congregation. He said, "I'm sure if I had kept coming I would have nailed somebody in the head and knocked them out. I was tight like a rattlesnake—ready to strike!" A farm-debt review mediator spoke of being greeted at the door of a farmhouse by a farmer holding a loaded shotgun. The farmer was not sure whether he was going to use it on himself or someone else. Lance spoke of visiting neighbours who had large armament caches, and Connie told of instances in which farmers she knew had shot at bankers. Rod tells of an older "teddy-bear sort of fellow" standing up at a farmers' meeting and saying that if he had a bomb right then he would go over to the bank manager's office to blow him up. Gary, a loans officer, admitted that the training of loans officers in his institution includes instruction in dealing with physical violence. He said secretaries are taught to listen for loud voices or noises from the officers' rooms and to knock on the door or ring the telephone to defuse the intensity of the situation. He watched one of his officers deal with four aggressive situations in one day and noted that it took a tremendous toll on the person. While it is difficult to assess the rate at which violent feelings express themselves in action,[7] these feelings reflect the way in which some farm people view the threat of removal from the land. They see themselves at war and their homestead under siege by their own community, with their family's survival at stake.

The other critical experience that threatens community cohesion is shame. I was struck in my interviews by how often interviewees said that they had been unable to talk to friends, family, even spouses, about their farm's financial difficulties. Nora described how her brother-in-law who farmed close by dealt with his bankruptcy:

He wouldn't come to us. We didn't know any of this until they had signed everything over to the bank.... It really hurts us that he went through this and felt that he couldn't come and talk to us. And then we say, like why hadn't we gone and talked to somebody when we were in that situation? [Nora and her husband had also gone through a bankruptcy.]

Dorothy said that to talk about her farm's finances would feel like stripping naked. Nor do others generally inquire. As Randy noted: "It's considered bad manners. You could ask somebody how they're feeling, but it was unthinkable that you would ask them how their financial situation is." Every interviewee agreed that a farm's financial woes are simply not a matter for conversation, even with one's closest friends.

To a certain extent, the silence that surrounds farm foreclosure is understandable. Farmers do not want to alarm local suppliers who may shut off the flow of necessary inputs. There may be an element of denial: "We'll be able to pull out of this. No point in upsetting others unnecessarily." Community members may be reticent to inquire because they do not know how they could help, or are not comfortable with the fears that a close encounter with another's insolvency raises in themselves. There may be an irrational fear that the problems are "contagious." They may feel that they will embarrass the other by offering care that the other may not be able to reciprocate (that is, "charity"). And, unlike other problems, there are no community-defined rituals for expressing care (such as bringing over a casserole when there has been a death in the family).

While these common-sense reasons account for the silence to some degree, they do not explain its duration and intensity. After all, as interviewees made it clear, rural folks normally depend on their neighbours for help in crisis. Neighbours are quick to help rebuild after a fire or take over the milking if one breaks a leg. Pat said that is what makes rural life so attractive to her: "Country people reach out to each other and give to each other that support when you're in trouble." In close-knit rural communities roles are overlapping and interdependent. Caring for the neighbours is part of ensuring that one's own needs will be met.

Crises related to a farm's general profitability, however, seem to be treated differently. Instead of rallying to help as for other tragedies, the community pulls back in an embarrassed, sometimes judgemental silence. Perry said bluntly, "If you are in farm crisis they'll avoid you like the plague.... People look at you from a distance; they ignore you; they don't ask how you're doing anymore." Or, as Marvin put it: "It's like you've got leprosy now."

Farm financial failure provokes silence and withdrawal because it is regarded as *shameful*. A "shame-full" person is perceived to be a poor risk in relationships, not a source of sound advice, not a good model of integrity or practical ability. Consequently he or she is considered unworthy of the community's respect, perhaps even dangerous to its well-being. The shamed are silenced and isolated to "protect" the community. A radio news reporter who covers agricultural stories told me that she once convinced some bankrupt farm families to tell the particulars of their story on air. Months later she learned that when their communities heard of their difficulties, these families were ostracized. They were snubbed in public settings and other people's children wouldn't play with their children.

This withdrawal of emotional support—even more than the absence of physical or financial help—is intensely painful. Mary Van Hook comments:

> Although some of the help from family, friends, and the church made an important difference in the financial situation of families, kind words and symbolic actions of concern were equally meaningful. Silence on the other hand was invariably interpreted as judgement or lack of interest. Receiving help generally strengthened relationships between the parties involved, and failing to help created further alienation. Numbers cannot describe the uplift created by supportive family and community members or the pain experienced when this help was not forthcoming.[8]

The withdrawal extends to the church as well. Randy says that the churches he has attended have had "some very fine people" in them. Yet, he says, "if you're having financial difficulties, stay the hell out of them, 'cause you're not going to get a second worth of sympathy or a pinch of help from them."

I have not yet found a good study that looks at the response of Canadian churches to farm bankruptcy. In the US, however, rural sociologists William and Judith Heffernan found in the mid 1980s that most farm families in difficulty perceived their congregations to be unresponsive, judgemental, or at best lukewarm towards them.[9] United Methodist leaders discovered that this was also true of their pastors. The pastors tended to lack insight into the farm crisis, denied there was a problem, withdrew from families in financial trouble—or expected that they would come to the pastor, and often didn't show up at the farm when it was being auctioned off.[10] Jerry, a rural pastor, told me that when a young farmer in his parish lost his land, "church folks lined up to get a piece of the action. One after another asked him or his wife, 'Are you planning to sell the elevator? What are you going to do with the combine? When's the back quarter going up for sale?'" Of the eighteen congregations represented in my interviews, I had reports of only four where the pastor provided significant support and two in which the congregation helped as well.

This shame around insolvency is not simply imposed by the community. It is also internalized by farm families. Those involved in bankruptcy, foreclosure, or debt review proceedings told me they felt "disgraced," "ashamed," that they had "let my family and myself down," and that they had "betrayed my folks and my neighbours." Similar responses are reported in several American studies and in anecdotal Canadian research.[11]

The feeling of being exposed and highly vulnerable is key to this shame. As Nora put it:

> Everybody knows, everybody finds out that *you* are the ones that are in trouble with the bank. And it's devastating. It goes like wildfire in a small town. Well the letters from the bank go to your local elevator agent. I mean it's all supposed to be confidential, but there are people in the community and coffee room who say [*whispered*], 'Hey did you hear…?' It's devastating. It's hard to walk in and hold your head up.

The sense of vulnerability leads to efforts to protect oneself from injury. Adam says: "You pull into yourself. You don't want to talk to people. You don't want to talk to your landlord. You don't want to see your banker."[12] If the community finds out about their financial situation, some farmers fear that all the creditors will want their debts repaid at once, or will take the farmer to court, or will damage the farmer's reputation so that no one will want to do business with him or her anymore.

The withdrawal also reflects a sense that one's *self* is no longer publicly presentable—that it is maimed, ugly, or shriveled. Harold told how he backed out of community leadership positions as his financial difficulties got worse: it was hard for him to hold his head up in the community. Others spoke of quitting favourite sports or avoiding neighbours in the town stores. Connie said that they stopped visiting in neighbours' homes because there was a sense of moral inequity: "they were not in trouble and you were."

In most cases they also reduced their involvement with the church. Marvin notes, "A lot of the ones that were in big trouble, there would be poor attendance from them." Ralph admits, "Our attendance has really dropped off in the church…. You look around at the church and the people that *aren't* there—and this is when I do go—I know the other ones are in the same kind of trouble."

Farmers in crisis may avoid church because the church can be a particularly painful part of their shaming. Religions tend to assign *worth* to human beings. They claim the right to speak for the Creator's attitude toward human creatures. So when one's religious community assigns a failing grade, it is not just behaviour that is being judged; it is as though one's *self* is being devalued—not simply by the community, but by God. Connie confessed to me: "I felt like I was cut adrift from God." Diane described a deadness that came into her faith life: "I don't say it's all God's fault or anything like that. I just don't know if I believe anymore. I don't care." This deep sense of a fundamental loss of worth—in their own eyes, in the community's eyes, in God's eyes—can be overwhelming. The desire to avoid any contact that activates those feelings takes over. As time goes on, it becomes more and more difficult to return to church. If approached by a pastor or congregation member, farm people in crisis often refuse to admit that anything is wrong.

Paradoxically, however, while farmers in difficulty want to hide, their sense of shame increases when they are *allowed* to hide, when no one seeks them out with respectful caring. The message they take is that the church must be on the side of their creditors, or else that their suffering is beneath notice. For many in my study, this was a shame almost worse than the bankruptcy itself.

UNDERSTANDING RURAL COMMUNITIES AS "HONOUR-BASED"

The devastating sense of grief and loss associated with farm bankruptcy or foreclosure,[13] and the resulting shame and isolation, can be accounted for if we respect the fundamental role that "farm pride" plays in rural Prairie communities. The term refers both to a broad set of values related to farm identity and to a narrower sense of one's personal place in the community. The former comprises a cluster of perceptions about what it means to be a farmer. These perceptions have roots deep in the settlement of the Prairies. Clifford Sifton, the political architect of Western Canada's agricultural landscape, is a good example. He promoted the Prairies to would-be pioneers as a fertile utopia where one could become a wealthy landowner in a few short years. Immigrants were lured to the Prairies by government posters claiming that simple hard work would be the road to success,[14] and by books with seductive titles such as *The Golden Land, The Land of Hope, The Wondrous West, Making Good in Canada, The Land of*

Opportunity and *The Last Best West*. The land was touted as a place where a "man" could make something of himself if he was willing to work hard. He could be "master of his own destiny." Sifton aggressively promoted the value of personal autonomy and control.[15]

Enamoured with such images farmers have come to understand themselves as independent, self-made, hard-working risk-takers, suppliers of the world's food, caretakers of the land. The failure to remain solvent and independent then becomes a repudiation of these foundational rural values. Lori, her own farm in trouble, admits: "The reason a lot of farmers don't ask for help is pride: 'We took out the debt—we'll pay it back.'"

The second element in farm pride has to do with one's personal sense of honour. Don, a rural pastor, says that his church members "feel it is better to go down on your knees alone than admit to your neighbours that you've failed." In this sense farm pride refers to the informal social status attributed to a farmer by the community.

This status was highly prized among those interviewed. It reflects the reality that in a small community one cannot escape the opinions of one's neighbours. Although transportation and communication improvements have given rural folks greater opportunity to choose with whom they will associate than in the past, the local community still provides the essential context for their lives. One's neighbours on the farm are likely neighbours in the pew, teammates at the curling rink, one's lender at the bank, and coffee colleagues at the local café. In a small community their "take" on you—your reputation—is your greatest asset. It opens doors to financial credit. It determines what positions you might be able to get on local boards and committees. It determines how much respect your children will get on the playground.

This is not unique to rural Canada. Anthropologist John Peristiany notes that honour is "the constant preoccupation of individuals in small scale, exclusive societies in which face-to-face, as opposed to anonymous, relations are of paramount importance and where the social personality of the actor is as significant as his office."[16]

As social "place," honour determines how one relates to others. Deference, attention, or obedience is given to those in a "higher" place while someone in a "lower" place may be helped, ignored, or instructed. Those with high honour have more substance in the community; their voices are given greater weight. Those with less are not as visible or audible. This is particularly true of those who lose honour in a substantive way—the shamed. As we have seen, they tend to withdraw from public view, to keep silent. And even when they speak, they are often not heard.

Honour may be *ascribed* on the basis of gender, race, inherited wealth, or family reputation, as in: "That Johnson kid comes from good stock." Honour may also be *achieved*. In rural Canada visibly successful farm management is an essential criterion. The names of the successful (especially those who give generously to the community) are engraved on the plaques in churches and public monuments. They are asked to serve on municipal councils. Their voices are respected at annual meetings.

Because honour provides access to critical community resources, protecting and enhancing it is essential to the well-being of oneself and one's family. This affects farmers both professionally and personally. Professionally, they may be loath to undertake innovative changes in their operation that are not respected in the community. For example, in Al Scholz's investigation of successful Saskatchewan rural enterprises, an organic farmer says that

> the issue of what the neighbours will think is a big factor in holding
> many farmers back from practising organic agriculture. It goes against
> conventional wisdom. To many farmers, weeds in the field translate
> into poor farming practices. They have been taught for decades that
> weeds are bad—a concept that has been carefully nurtured by
> industry—and they must be controlled at any cost. All too often, that
> cost is the farmer's net profit.[17]

One's personal reputation may come to constitute one's *self*. For many people in rural communities, concern for honour permeates their consciousness. It is reflected in the carriage of the body. It determines one's expectations for self and others. In such a context, William Miller says, "Honour is your very being. For in an honour-based culture there is no self-respect independent of the respect of others, no private sense of 'hey, I'm quite something' unless it is confirmed publicly."[18]

This is why the threat of bankruptcy or anything that might lead to public shame is so devastating. Farmers are trapped. As Michael put it, "The land and community are a part of us. You can't just put your hearts in a suitcase and move." If they leave the community they leave the source of their being. If they stay, the community may turn its face away from them—make them "invisible." Either way the self dissolves. People cease to exist.

This is not always well understood by those of us who are urbanites. As Michael Walzer points out, city dwellers tend to operate with the understanding that one's occupation is part of a personally controlled "career," a self-guided journey through a variety of jobs and activities.[19] They are able to move relatively easily from place to place because, in Emile Durkheim's words, theirs is a "portable self."[20] In cities, social relationships tend to be voluntary and the groups in which they occur are relatively unrelated to each other. The "self-contained" self is not constituted by such relationships, but enters into or withdraws from them as personal needs and interests dictate. Rural dwellers, however, live a life that is rooted in a particular place and regulated by their community. Their self is continually dependent on *social* sources for its maintenance.

The importance of honour to the growth of the social self, and the possibility of losing or gaining it through one's personal or professional behavior, intensifies the significance of social ranking in the community. There is a tendency to treat honour as if it were in short supply—that is, as if there was room at the top only for a few. With limited high-status positions available, this means that if one person is honoured, it may subtly reduce the social status of others.

The result can be competition for honour and envy that reduces the community's ability to work co-operatively for positive change. As one farmer from Newfoundland put it, in the federal government's 1998 survey of 7000 rural Canadians: "There is a rural mentality that if someone gets ahead, others get jealous and try to prevent them from doing so."[21] One family that was losing its land wrote in a letter to a farm columnist, "Some folks have been enjoying our predicament. I suppose that's because our downfall must seem to make their position or status higher or more superior."[22] Similarly, Bill commented,

> Some people in the farm community want to stand back and say, "He must have been a bad manager; he made his mistakes. The sooner he's out of the business, the quicker I'll be able to sell what I sell for more money and more profit." We have lost the ability in the farm community to work together for a common good and a common goal.[23]

Ironically, then, one of the dynamics that generates community cohesion (the growth of the self through honour) also limits it. This is particularly true for males. Honour is attributed to groups or families, but there is normally one person in the family group who represents and publicly defends the group's honour. The other members participate in the honour or the shame of that member. In rural communities that person tends to be the dominant male.

While the men are out competing for honour in the public arena, the women are supposed to look after the private arena where the family weaknesses are protected and cared for. In farm communities, however, the income picture is often so dismal that the majority of farm wives and almost half of farm husbands work off-farm to cover living expenses.[24] Several farmers told me they were ashamed that their wives had to go out to work. It can be a significant blow to a man's honour that his wife has to compete for wealth in a public occupation. It marks him in the community as a man who cannot provide for his family, cannot manage his home. He has exposed his family weaknesses to public view. It is shameful.

Men try to avoid shame by keeping up appearances on the farm. Honour is given according to the *apparent* prosperity of the farm, not the actual state of its books. So I met farmers whose operation is in the black because they buy old equipment and fix it up and because they do not always spray all the weeds in their fields. But they know others in the community look down on them. Other farmers are highly regarded because they have weed-free fields and modern equipment. Yet it is those expenses that eventually push them into bankruptcy. This creates the strange paradox that farmers who are in financial difficulty will sometimes put themselves in further debt to indicate to the community that they are doing fine. Lance, for example, said: "A lot of guys buy a new vehicle when they are getting into trouble. It's a sign to the community, and to yourself, that things are okay." Howard, a lender, observes:

> There is a lot of pressure to look like you know what you are doing … buying new equipment, driving a new half-ton, keeping the fields free of weeds…. It used to be that when I went into a farmyard, if everything is neat, tidy and in a row and shiny, then he is someone you want to do business with. Now it's the opposite. If I see all that stuff then I think that he is over-committed.

While women also try to keep up appearances, they are much more likely to ask for help. Sandra Petronio found that men in general show a greater desire than women do to conceal wounds.[25] If they cannot pretend that things are okay they try to focus blame on circumstances or on behaviour rather than on their character. In other words, men would rather assume *guilt* (action-focussed) if it helps avoid *shame* (being-focussed); it keeps their self-worth intact. Petronio found that women are slower to apologize. Instead they are more likely to invite sympathy and acceptance. They want others to share the shame or embarrassment. Men prefer to deal with it alone, apparently feeling that any public knowledge of their weakness, even if sympathetic, increases the shame.

Petronio's findings reflect the double-edged sword of our culture's patriarchal inheritance. It honours the men, but places them in competition with each other for that honour, isolating them from the support they need when honour standards are not met. Women, although they receive less honour, are also less involved in the competition for it. They cannot do much to increase their family's honour (though they are able to bring shame on the family). So they are less isolated from each other, more likely to ask for and receive help. Several times during the study I found myself in casual conversation with a farm couple at a social function. If I talked about my research it was often the women who, after a knowing glance at the husband, would lean across the table and confide that, though no one knew it, they were struggling financially. (I suppose that my position as a pastor, a non-threatening stranger and a researcher from outside the community, made me an unusually safe confidant.) One turned to her husband as he flushed with embarrassment, and said, "See Honey, I told you you're not the only one."

The women also expressed great frustration at their men's silence sometimes. Living and working in the interdependent environment of the home (and increasingly the town offices or businesses) they could not understand the men's apparent self-sufficiency. They felt that the men were too hard on themselves, unable to accept failure, and unable to accept help. "I have to force my help on him," one woman said.

From the men's point of view, of course, financial instability is an enormous threat. If they cannot stay in business, they may not be able to stay in the community. There are not many available jobs. It means the loss of their standard of living, the loss of their community, their land, their way of living, and, in a sense, their socially constructed self. The fear of it can be paralyzing. Many men find it hard to admit to themselves that they are in deep financial trouble, let alone admit it to others. This is especially true within the family. Farms tend to be handed down from fathers to sons. Managing the farm well shows respect for one's ancestors. It indicates that a man has been a faithful steward of what has been passed on to him. How can a farmer admit to his siblings or parents that he has disgraced the family by squandering their hard-won heritage and leaving nothing to pass on to his heirs? That is why he is likely to keep silent.

At the same time, women may be well placed to serve as a resource for male farmers when honour is lost, because they are less involved in the competition for it. Women, for example, are more apt to make use of processes for communal discussion of agricultural realities. From my observations, they seem to have a greater desire to involve the community in their distress when crisis comes and may be key to breaking the silence about bankruptcy in farm communities.

RECOVERING HOPE FOR RURAL COMMUNITIES

One can imagine the tensions that the dynamics of honour and shame create. On the one hand the community's respect is needed to provide substance to one's own sense of self. This creates a strong *centripetal* pull *into* the community. On the other hand, a variety of factors, many of which are outside of farmers' reliable control, are putting enormous stress on farm finances and creating the conditions for widespread bankruptcy and its accompanying shame. For those affected, the shame generates a *centrifugal* push *out* from the community, meaning less social engagement. The result of the tension is that increasing numbers of farmers find themselves pushed out of the centre of community life as a result of the shame of financial insolvency yet many of them struggle to hang on to their identities by staying in the community on its periphery. This poses both a problem and an opportunity for rural communities seeking to regenerate their economic vitality. The problem is that the very people most acquainted with the problems in the agricultural economy (those in financial distress) cannot easily share what they know without increasing their own shame, and so they remain silent. Nor are others likely to want to open their financial lives to their neighbours for fear of being found wanting in managerial ability and, as a result, losing honour. In the absence of honest conversation, it is difficult to initiate innovative, co-operative community enterprise. The *opportunity* is that many of these folks are still in, or in touch with, the community and could be a significant resource for considering its future if some way was found to reduce the shaming and to generate open conversation about economic alternatives.

In my experience there is real hope for renewal initiated through conversation at the local level. Unfortunately, globalization has left rural communities with a sense of impotence in regard to their own futures. It seems at times that any hope for agriculture must come from a high-level restructuring of the global economy. Certainly self-determination will not be handed to our rural communities by the global investors and multinational corporations who now exercise much of the control. However, every large structure has cracks in it. I am convinced that there are options for resistance and renewal that could make a substantial difference locally if rural people could find the grace and courage to work together.

In fact there are a number of rural communities across Canada experimenting with co-operative ventures that have promise for revitalizing their cultures and economies. The federally incorporated charity Women and Rural Development has helped establish 333 new businesses in rural Ontario, set up 21 rural women's business networks, and provides loans and training programs in farm diversification, economic literacy, communications, and marketing.[26] Farmers in Manitoba are swapping land to rotate crops, allowing farms to keep their land fertile without having to retool for a different crop each year. People in Bow Island, Alberta developed a farmer-owned edible-bean plant that processes beans grown in the area and injects $12-million annually into the local economy. Native groups in Powell River, BC have created the Wilderness Shellfish Cooperative, which includes a hatchery and processing plant.[27]

In his book *Don't Turn Out the Lights*, Al Scholz details a number of co-operative ventures in Saskatchewan that have revitalized local rural economies.[28] He describes the development of Western Grain Pelleting in Wilkie. Owned by 500 local residents, it produces a value-added product from previously valueless grain screenings and has spurred the development of an inland terminal and seed-cleaning facility in the area. In Lanigan, Pound-Maker Agventures is a community-controlled, 28,500-head cattle feedlot and ethanol plant that employs 50 people from the area and buys millions of bushels of wheat and barley from, and provides field manure for, local farmers each year. Lakeside Ventures, in the Dafoe area, presently a multi-million dollar machinery, seed, processing, and special crops company, began as a machinery co-operative among seven farmers. As Scholz notes, the benefits from community-owned, co-operative or semi-co-operative ventures have been enormous. True efficiencies increase. Workloads, and corresponding stresses, are shared. Members do not have to be able to do everything well but can focus on the work that fits their skills and interests. Lifestyle is enhanced: with others to cover, the time invested is more flexible. Participants are able to diversify and take on new ventures with lower risk. The employment and spin-off businesses generated provide educated children with a place to stay in the community. Population grows along with community services. The community develops cohesion as members from various walks of life are brought into close contact with each other.

Such ventures are not easy to initiate. As Scholz points out, they require committed leadership. And they depend on a willingness to trust and respect others. As communities shrink, that trust must be extended outside historic group identities. When asked why the Western Grain Pelleting venture worked so well in a community that had experienced decades of decline, one of the founders said:

> A key reason was the extra effort we made to redefine our community more regionally.... We had to swallow our pride, forget our 50-year history of petty competitiveness, and learn to work together with neighbouring communities.[29]

HEALING COMMUNITY DIVISIONS

As Jerome Martin points out in a study of successful rural communities, it is the development of the will, leadership, vision, information-gathering systems, and communication patterns necessary to work *co-operatively* that determines which communities manage to re-invent themselves.[30] Of course in a culture of honour and shame it is precisely the difficulty of nurturing that co-operation that is the stumbling block. The divisive competition for honour, and the shaming that isolates those whose experience of failure gives them key insights into the economy, must be challenged and deep conversation nurtured.

Rural churches can have a significant role in this regard in spite of (perhaps because of) their historic contributions to the problem.[31] This is true for several reasons. First of all, they offer a ready-made network for care that is still well respected and a ministry that is still desired in most rural communities. From her own experience of farm crisis, Pat says that what she wanted from the church was "just to know that you're there, that you care, that you'll lend an ear to listen—that you don't judge us—that we're a part of the church just like you. We need all of you. Don't run away."

Certainly there are obstacles which congregations that want to care must address. We have noted that financial problems tend to be well hidden. Awareness of a member's problems may come late—as auction notices are posted, as neighbours see machinery being sold and so on. Pastors, however, can watch for more subtle signs—especially the withdrawal of that person from church or community activities. Pastors are perhaps the only helping professionals that have permission to visit a home without invitation. They can explore possible problems, offer counselling and healing, and yet not raise eyebrows among the neighbours by the presence of their car in the farmyard.

Churches can also minimize another obstacle in rural culture: the need to maintain public honour requires reciprocity. To give assistance to neighbours when they cannot return it in some way shames them; it makes them dependent on "charity." Unrepayable help, however, *can* be given without shame to family members. Churches that emphasize the "family" character of their congregations and present their assistance as the sort of thing one does for family may circumvent the problem to some extent. Of course even if congregational members get past their fear of invading someone's privacy they may not feel equipped to deal with the strong emotions they may encounter. Clergy can help by introducing programs that train members in listening and care-giving skills.[32]

Most important in the church's gift of care is the simply "being there" that Pat mentioned, and when the problems are public, "standing with" people—at court, for example, when goods are seized or when auctions are held. Gail, a pastor, describes her own experience:

> Derek and I went out the day that they were coming to take their hogs
> away. We were just with them, and also watching to make sure things
> were done properly…. I guess in some ways they were little things, but
> they were signs of moral support to those people and I think it was a
> sign to people in the community that you can't just write these folks off.

By offering someone (whether the pastor or a lay person) to stand with the farmer at these times, the church does two things. First, while it does not remove the shame, it shares it. Second, when the church's representative indicates solidarity with a shamed one, it calls into question the practice of isolating one who has broken the "honour code."

A pastor who has listened to and stood with suffering parishioners has the opportunity to bring that hidden pain to community awareness in the way that he or she designs worship. Laments and prayers can give voice and legitimacy to the anguish felt by any in the community (not only farmers) who have been hurt by the farm crisis. Litanies can help to desacrilize our economic structures, presenting them as human constructs, not as fixed "orders of creation." Shame receives a great deal of its potency from the religious legitimization that social values are given. Theologian Walter Brueggemann writes that liberating liturgy adopts a "posture of refusal," indicating that God's people will not submit to these social contrivances as if they were divinely ordained.[33] Banners, stained glass, art, and sculpture, even children's worship projects, can become vehicles for the expression of symbols of suffering, protest, and hope that are drawn out of the lived experience of rural families.[34] These worship elements can hint at new ways of conceiving human life and alternative assumptions about what is most important that may energize a congregation toward change. At the very least they can let the sufferer know that what she or he is going through *matters* to the community.

Secondly, churches can be effective in de-shaming financial crisis because, to a great extent in rural Canada, they are still regarded as the guardians of morality. While interviewees indicated that all too often churches contributed significantly to the shaming by treating prosperity as a sign of God's favour (and bankruptcy as the loss of it), most religious traditions contain at least latent resources for challenging shame.

For example, my own tradition—Lutheran Christianity—insists at its heart that one's personal worth is *not* earned by one's own successes or failures. Nor is it determined by community judgement. Rather it is God's prerogative alone to bestow honour. And the witness of Jesus—whose attitude was scandalous to those who upheld the standards of honour in his own community—is that God does so *indiscriminately*, on the basis of Divine grace. A good illustration is the way Jesus deals with table fellowship. In ancient Palestine one's worth in the community could be assessed by who one ate with, and what position at the table one assumed: that is, "like eats with like" and "better folks take the higher places."[35] Jesus, however, refuses to choose meal companions on the basis of social standing. He eats frequently in the home of Pharisees (Luke 7:36–50; 11:37–44; 14:1–7), dines with friends and disciples (Luke 10:38–42; Mark 2:23ff.), with "sinners" and outsiders (Luke 5:29–32; 15:1–2; 19:5–17), even with mixed Galilean crowds that undoubtedly contained Gentiles, shepherds, peasants, perhaps even Roman soldiers, as well as curious members of Israel's elite (Mark 6:35–42). No one is excluded (or included) on the basis of their social performance.

Jesus also refuses to honour the socially respected with a special place at the head table (see Luke 20:42). Instead, he takes a towel and washes the feet of his guests—making the place of honour (closest to the host) that of the servant. What does this do to distinctions of honour and rank? In the traditional sense it eliminates them. If the host chooses the place of the servant, how can even the most distinguished guest claim special privilege at the table? The only way to gain honour in such a company is to forego it, Jesus says. So when his disciples begin to compete for the place of honour he upbraids them and reminds them that their value in the kingdom of God is a *gift* of God's grace (Luke 22:24ff). If we have any righteousness it consists in letting God be the determiner of our own and others' worth. That leaves no grounds on which to isolate and shame each other.

As the central figure of Christianity, Jesus hardly supports a "prosperity equals righteousness" ethic. He leaves a good job as a carpenter at 30 years of age, wanders around Palestine with friends, supported only by women's welfare, challenges existing mores, stirs up crowds thus alarming the Roman occupiers, claims to be God, and is eventually executed for treason and blasphemy. His crucifixion was a shameful death—one that the Romans used to humiliate condemned "provincials." It is hardly a success story, certainly not a mother's dream for her son. Yet the biblical witness is that God raises this "loser" from the dead, declaring him to be *the* Righteous One. In preaching and teaching, clergy can use powerful stories such as these to establish a new basis for relating to the sufferer—not as one who is worthless or God-forsaken because of his or her suffering, but as a full and valued member of the community.

Finally, churches can be catalysts for change in rural communities by generating shame-reducing and alternative-producing conversation. A few of the insolvent farmers I interviewed described how local churches (usually in some sort of ecumenical co-operation) established support groups for struggling farmers. The groups generally met somewhat secretly. They gave farmers a place where they could voice their pain and frustration, let go of the sense that they were alone in their failure, share survival strategies, and gain courage to speak in the larger community's discussions about its future.

A (very) few bold clergy have also introduced conversation in their churches about the economics of the farm crisis. They have used biblical passages (such as Isaiah 5:9, which reflects on those who would rather have land than neighbours, or Jesus's parable about the forgiveness of debt in Matthew 18:21–25) to elicit discussion about the worldview that informs our economic arrangements in agriculture. These conversations have been most fruitful when they moved very intentionally through several levels, beginning by inviting various people in the community—lenders, input dealers, farmers, health care workers, and so on— to share their stories. They described how the agricultural economy, and rural depopulation, had affected them. Then the conversation moved to a discussion of the current realities (requiring some careful fact-gathering by participants): how many have actually left the community? how much debt has been amassed and why? how have government policies and corporate decisions affected the present situation? and so on.

In this discussion it started to become clear that the facts are not equally valued by all. Some lament the growing size of farms, while others see it as a healthy evolution of agriculture. At this point the clergy had the opportunity to explore the deeper beliefs about human life—its worth, its purpose, its place in the world—that inform these values. Here the deep differences between members of the community came to light. While they sometimes turn out to be irreconcilable, it is really only here that it is possible to begin the struggle together that might lead to a common vision, and an active plan, for the community's future.

Notes

1   When I use a single name such as "Michael," I am using a pseudonym as requested by the interviewee. If I use a full name, it indicates that the interviewee agreed to have his/her real name given.

2   From an interview on the videotape *Borrowed Time* (Toronto: 49 North Productions, Inc., 1990).

3   Val Farmer, "Broken Heartland," *Psychology Today* 20 (4): 54–57, 60–62. This article cites studies by sociologists William and Judith Heffernan that found that 100 percent of those leaving farming in a northern Missouri county were depressed. Even several years later, 50 percent of those men and 72 percent of those women were still depressed. Farmer also notes that the distress is not only turned inward. He cites studies indicating increased levels of family violence in rural communities related to the farm crisis.

Molly J. Coye, "The Health Effects of Agricultural Production," in *New Directions for Agriculture and Agricultural Research: Neglected Dimensions an Emerging Alternatives*, ed. Kenneth A. Dahlberg (Totowa, NJ: Rowman and Allan, 1986), 181–2, notes that several studies have found that mental illness is significantly higher in rural than urban communities with approximately ten percent of the rural population defined as "those cases probably in need of psychiatric care." She argues that changes in agricultural structure engender changes in farm organization and in family work roles that have been found to be related to mental illness in other non-farm settings.

4   See Farmer, "Broken Heartland," 61, referring to a study by Norah Keating and Maryanne Doherty of the University of Alberta on the relationship between farm debt and the stress reactions of more than 700 grain farmers (men and women).

5   Almost Broadway Players, *Where the Rose Grows* (Sinclair, MB: Melita Rural Theatre Group, Malanka Productions, 1990), videotape.

6   *Borrowed Time.*

7   It is hard to know how much of this violence becomes self-directed. Although there is a good deal of anecdotal evidence, hard data on farm suicides is somewhat hard to come by. The ease with which suicide can be disguised as a farm accident—which then pays out insurance that can wipe out farm debts and give the children a good start—suggests a greater incidence of suicide than it is possible to assess with hard data.

8   Mary Van Hook, "Family Response to the Farm Crisis: A Study in Coping," *Social Work* 35 (Sept 1990), 429.

9   Referred to in Dennis Thompson, "A Flourishing of Faith and Service," *Christian Social Action*, June 1989. I was not able to locate the exact citation for this reference. Note that Thompson expresses the observation that churches in the United States became more sensitive to this issue by the end of the decade. My research would indicate that, in Canada at least, there is a long way to go.

10 Gladys L. Campbell, "Building Bridges of Understanding: National Program Division Responds to the Rural Crisis," *Christian Social Action* 1 (March 1988): 28–29.

11 See for example Mary Van Hook, "Family Response to the Farm Crisis"; Sara Wright and Paul Rosenblatt, "Isolation and Farm Loss: Why Neighbours May Not Be Supportive," *Family Relations* 36 (1987): 391–395; Marvin Anderson, "Going, Going, Gone: Selling the Family Farm," *Our Times* (March 1986): 26–31.

12 Interviewed by Farmer, "Broken Heartland," 61.

13 Note that I use these two terms somewhat interchangeably, although they refer to somewhat different realities. Bankruptcy is an action initiated by the farm; foreclosure is initiated by a lender.

14 The posters appear in David Goa, "Secularization among Ethnic Communities in Western Canada" in *Religion and Ethnicity*, ed. Harold Coward and Leslie Kawamura, (Waterloo: Wilfrid Laurier University Press, 1977), 13–17.

15 Described in Robert G. Moyles and Doug Owram, *Imperial Dreams and Colonial Realities: British Views of Canada, 1880–1914* (Toronto: University of Toronto Press, 1988): 117.

16 John G. Peristiany, ed., *Honour and Shame: The Values of Mediterranean Society* (Chicago: University of Chicago Press, 1966).

17 Al Scholz, *Don't Turn Out the Lights: Entrepreneurship in Rural Saskatchewan* (Saskatoon: University Extension Press, 2000), 90.

18 William Miller, *Humiliation: And Other Essays on Honour, Social Discomfort and Violence* (Ithaca: Cornell Press, 1993), 116. See also Gabriele Taylor's excellent discussion in *Pride, Shame and Guilt: Emotions of Self-Assessment* (Oxford: Oxford University Press, 1985), 55.

19 Michael Walzer, *Thick and Thin: Moral Argument at Home and Abroad* (Notre Dame: University of Notre Dame Press, 1994), 23–24.

20 Referred to by Christopher Lasch in *The True and Only Heaven: Progress and Its Critics* (New York: W.W. Norton, 1991), 44.

21 "'Rural Canadians Speak Out'—Summary of Rural Dialogue Input for the National Rural Workshop" (Government of Canada website), http://www.rural.gc.ca/discpaper_e.html, accessed 19 July 1999.

22 From a letter that appeared in Val Farmer's syndicated newspaper column on rural mental health issues, "Life After Farming Can Have a Soft Landing," http://www.valfarmer.com/getdoc.asp?Docid=133, accessed June 27, 2000.

23 *Borrowed Time.*

24 Forty-six percent of farm operators work off-farm according to the 1996 Census of Agriculture.

25 See Sandra Petronio, "Communication Strategies to Reduce Embarrassment: Differences Between Men and Women," *The Western Journal of Speech Communication* 48 (Winter 1984): 36.

26 See "WRED: Women and Rural Economic Development" at http://www.wred.org/, accessed July 26, 2000.

27 See "Canadian Rural Partnership Rural Dialogue Success Stories," at http://www.rural.gc.ca/success_e.html, accessed July 26, 2000.

28 Scholz, *Don't Turn Out the Lights.*

29 Margaret Skinner, quoted in ibid., 40.

30 Jerome Martin, ed., *Alternative Futures for Prairie Agricultural Communities* (Edmonton: University of Alberta Faculty of Extension, 1991).

31 To see some examples of how churches were involved in the revitalization of twelve mid-western American rural communities see the video "Healthy Communities: The Role of the Rural Church," available from The Center for Land and Theology, Dubuque, Iowa.

32 One that my own denomination has found very effective is called "Stephen Ministries." See http://www.stephenministries.org/, accessed July 27, 2000.

33 Walter Brueggemann, *Hope Within History* (Atlanta: John Knox Press, 1987), 12.

34 The Prairie grain elevator, fast disappearing, is one symbol that seems to make a powerful statement about the hopes, the suffering, and the identity of farmers. See Brock Silversides, *Prairie Sentinel: The Story of the Canadian Grain Elevator* (Calgary: Fifth House Publishers, 1997), 4; or Terry Johnson, "Twilight of a Prairie Icon," *Canadian Geographic* (September/October 1997): 28.

35 Excellent information on first-century customs regarding meals can be found in Jerome Neyrey, "Meals, Food and Table Fellowship," in *The Social Sciences and New Testament Interpretation*, ed. Richard Rohrbaugh (Peabody, MS: Hendrickson, 1996): 159–182; Scott Bartchy, "Table Fellowship," in *Dictionary of Jesus and the Gospels* 1992, 796–800; Kathleen Corley, *Private Women, Public Meals: Social Conflict in the Synoptic Tradition* (Peabody, MS: Hendrickson, 1989).

Work, Knowledge, and the Direction of Farm Life

Bob Stirling

A front-page article tells of a Saskatchewan farm couple who have just won $5-million in a lottery and intend to use the money to continue to farm. Their first purchase is an air seeder, an expensive piece of machinery that the farm is otherwise hard-pressed to afford. Family expenditures are also planned, but it is farm finances that are identified as the important drain on the winnings. Quipped the husband: "Before I go broke, I'll quit farming, that's for sure."[1] The story is a useful metaphor for the "farm crisis."

Winning a lottery is, of course, uncommon but the financial problems of farming are well known. Commodity prices are characteristically variable but also low. The price of wheat over the past decade, for example, has rivalled its low during the Great Depression. At the same time, input costs have risen. Not surprisingly, the financial margins in farming have become very narrow. Whereas during World War Two and the following decade net farm income was usually over 50 percent of gross farm income, by the 1990s it was often under 10 percent. Census data for 1995 show that typically over half of the income of farm families came from non-farm sources. Since the 1980s, a plethora of farm groups have formed to draw attention to farming's mounting financial problems. During recent winters, ones with increased and more extreme activity, their tactics included road blockades, a sit-in at the Saskatchewan Legislature, hunger strikes, the jostling and threatening of the Federal Minister of Agriculture, and countless treks to Ottawa to lobby politicians.

Framing the farm crisis as a financial crisis, however, is far too narrow an approach, one that underestimates the depth of the transformation that is underway. If commodity prices were to rise, or input costs fall, the crisis would scarcely be over. In fact, high farm incomes might well spur on even higher levels of farm consolidation. The Prairies have lost 156,000 farms since 1941, not especially because of farm bankruptcies, nor, until recently, because non-farm corporations have actively taken up farming. While low farm income surely encourages some farm families to buy out their neighbours, it does not account for the yearly pattern of farm consolidation. The dynamics of family farming go well beyond the immediate financial squeeze.

The farm crisis is, more precisely, a crisis in family farming. It is about who will produce food, and how, and who will control the product—in short, the productive relations including the nature of farm work. The crisis signifies a profound social upheaval or transformation that has been building for decades. Indeed we might well wonder why the shift away from populous small-scale family farming didn't happen much sooner.

What has made the family farming community sustainable to this point? Family farming is a type of farming in which families own all or most of their productive capital—land, buildings, machinery, and livestock—and do all or most of the productive work themselves. Typically they live in the communities where they farm, their farms are not large, and there are many of them. To say that the family-farming community is sustainable means that it can reproduce itself both physically and socially and, furthermore, influence new directions for itself. Obviously such a community must have a viable economic base. But, equally important, family farming must develop a supportive network of social relations, including neighbourly helping patterns and exchanges of advice. More generally, humans are social animals. For us, life, especially work and production, is inherently a collective activity. While farm work may seem isolated at times, it draws on a wealth of practices and knowledge built up over time and, of course, it depends upon class relations and a complex division of labour to give it value, meaning, and purpose.

Clearly the farm community must have an indigenous, vibrant culture and politics if it is to be sustainable. In this chapter I argue that this social component of family farming is also in crisis. Specifically, the control of farm work along with the knowledge about how to produce, factors which have been essential to viable Prairie farm communities in the past, are becoming secondary to a set of dependent "farm" skills that merely manage technologies owned and controlled by non-farm firms. This trend also has political implications for farm life and the possibility of its renewal. It encourages a social amnesia or collective forgetting about the importance of rural community and the means of resisting its demise. In short, it leads to a dependent farm politics. Against such a future, the conclusion to this chapter will "remember" some new directions.

WORK AS CONTESTED TERRAIN

Why should we privilege the area of work in an understanding of social transformation? What makes work any more important than, say, leisure or consumption?[2] For one thing, it is an important source of value. Humans couldn't exist without work and production. More than that, it is through work that humans develop society, their consciousness, and, indeed, themselves as social beings. The tools that humans have developed to facilitate their work illustrate a crucial human characteristic: the ability to engage in thoughtful, purposive action. The development and use of tools requires the union of conception and execution, of head and hands. The tool users, through their work, gain a deep knowledge of the processes involved and some control over what happens. As our knowledge expands, *we* also change. To recall a common example, as computer technology developed, our society changed and, in some measure, so did we as humans.[3]

There is nothing fixed in stone, however, about the nature of work. Even though it is crucial to the human condition, work can become something less than optimal for human growth. As capitalism evolved into its monopoly stage around the turn of the twentieth century, managers of large industrial firms found it necessary to try to control the work of their employees in ever more detailed ways. Following the ideology of Frederick Winslow Taylor and an increasingly popular Scientific Management school, they did this by appropriating workers' knowledge, codifying it, and setting out "scientific" principles which informed managers' decisions about improving productivity. The effect was to divide tasks into de-skilled, detail labour, replacing human with non-human control.

While Scientific Management became the mantra of owners and managers in the early 1900s, it was not universally or quickly adopted. Certainly the Great Depression limited the necessary investment in non-human technology. But equally important was resistance by workers. In fact, many struggles during the maturation of capitalism had to do with workers resisting the loss of their craft skills, control, and traditions. Not until large industrial plants became heavily "Taylorized" after World War Two did worker resistance become more regulated and bureaucratized through labour contracts and standards.[4] The point is that the nature of work, how it will be done, who controls it, and how the rewards of work will be distributed, at least in industrial settings, has been contested terrain between those who do the work and those who draw profit from others' labour. And if work is central to the human condition, as I argued above, then the stakes are high.

WORK AND PRAIRIE FARMING

There is a long literature that points out that the circumstances of farmers are not the same as the circumstances of workers under capitalist production. Indeed, Braverman thinks that farming work represents a counter example to the alienation and de-skilling of non-farm work.[5] It is true that Prairie farming has been pursued largely by families and that farm work obeys a family "logic" in a way that may not be as true for industrial workers. It is also true that workers are exploited at the point of production whereas the processes that draw surpluses out of farming also have to do with unequal exchange. Since farm families both supply the capital and do most of the farm work, to say that work for them is the same as work for the industrial working class is not immediately obvious.

Still, Braverman's depiction of farm work is a bit romanticized. Certainly large industrial capitalist farms such as industrial hog barns with their paid labour force operate like non-farm capitalists; their economic needs include the control of farm work. But even agribusiness corporations that are not directly involved in farming have an interest in controlling farm work as a way to advance the use of their inputs on farms, or to assure the supply and quality of farm outputs to their processing plants. And, like workers, Prairie farmers have resisted this tendency, more successfully before World War Two than currently. Elements of the history of Prairie farming illustrate this point.

The social setting

The creation of the Prairies as an agricultural staples-producing region and a home market for industrial goods was undertaken by the state as a "national policy" in the interests of central Canadian capital. Davis categorized it as a metropolis-hinterland relationship, one of unequal exchange between commercial and industrial capital as a dominant class and Prairie farmers as a subordinate class. It attempted to suck wealth to the metropolitan regions while leaving the Prairies and its farming regions underdeveloped. These economic and political structures set the broad features in space and time that came to be known as the Prairie frontier. They facilitated a new economic activity, family farming, created towns and cities, geographically located farm families, and recruited the population.[7]

Of course these were only structural tendencies; the domination of Prairie agriculture by outside interests was by no means complete. Farm people did resist. Certainly the level of every-day practice on the farm frontier was often one of serious hardship, stoic determination, and co-operation in the midst of competition. During the early part of the settlement period, many farms failed. But what is important to remember is that, ultimately, farms and communities did become established because of the formation of intricate helping patterns, systems of knowledge-sharing and reciprocity, and trust between farm families— all leading to the legendary growth of local "social capital."

The creation of local government can be seen as a natural extension of this practice. While there were various enabling policies in Manitoba and what became Saskatchewan and Alberta by the 1870s, the actual implementation of local government waited on local initiatives and determination. Indeed, the formation of co-operatives, regulation of grain handling and transportation, orderly marketing of some farm commodities, and the formation of political parties which captured the provincial states in Saskatchewan and Alberta and brought about many innovative programs, illustrate the importance of grass-roots initiative and resistance to threatening trends. Nor should we forget the farm women's and suffragette movements which took aim at formal, if not familial, patriarchy.[8]

If farmers, as the subordinate class, found a measure of success in their strategies to resist the domination of outside interests and create their own communities, and indeed they did, what are the main reasons? The initiative and vigour of people recruited to the frontier was one of them. Another was the relative isolation of the frontier from the "symbolic violence" of the metropolis, although education did convey the prescriptions of the dominant culture. Farmers' resistance also succeeded because of divisions that existed among the dominant class, particularly between the grain trade on the one hand, whose sharp practices threatened the whole project of the "national policy," and the central Canadian banks and industrial capital, on the other, which were loath to lose and wielded more clout. But ultimately it was because farmers had substantial control of farm work. Collectively they were the ones with the knowledge, skill, and initiative to turn inputs into farm commodities upon which Canadian capital and the country depended.

Farm work

The farming practised by Metis in the Red River and other Prairie settlements of the 1800s involved local knowledge and control of work. Of course the cultural practices were not immune to outside influences; European cultivars and tools were readily adapted for local purposes. As well, it was a different agriculture than the staples economy that was to follow, one largely based on subsistence production although it provisioned the fur trade and at times threatened to develop an export capability in grain to the United States. The defeat of the Metis did not entirely defeat their knowledge and skill in agriculture and transportation. Instead they were scattered more widely, which, at least in the case of the settlements along the North Saskatchewan, probably helped European agriculture take root as the early colonists learned and copied practices of their indigenous neighbours.

Although European Prairie agriculture was to supply an export staple and create a home market for manufactured goods, most commodity merchants and inputs manufacturers had little ability to control the details of farm production. Still, some did show interest. Flour millers such as the Ogilvies were keenly aware of the exceptional baking qualities of Prairie wheat and developed elaborate surveillance systems to source the best supplies each fall; they were major champions of policies that would enhance high-quality wheat production.[9] Similarly, machinery companies like International Harvester, anxious to capture market share, demonstrated their wares at local field days and held tractor schools. In these areas, however, the interests of capital arguably matched those of the new European farmers. Beyond that, no firm was so large or so dominant in its market that it could control farming practices.

Still, the control of farm work was contested terrain. For example, Jeffery Taylor has shown how educational institutions in early Manitoba advanced a dominant ideology with categories of meaning that defined "farmers"—men, women, and youth—and so attempted to create their identities and fashion their behaviour along lines that would be compatible with both the "national policy" and the interests of capital. Nonetheless, Cecilia Danysk finds in her study of the role of labour in early Prairie agriculture that work was firmly entrenched in the knowledge, skill, and control of farmers and farm wage labour.[10]

If we think of farm machinery and its main sources of motive power, the influence of farmers becomes obvious. Horse and oxen power required knowledge and skill at training, feeding, harnessing, and driving these animals, as well as a detailed understanding of animal health, breeding and bloodlines, and criteria for selection. These were farmer skills even after the universities began to develop knowledge about draft animals.[11] Farmers prided themselves in their horsemanship. They belonged to breed associations and held local competitions to hone and demonstrate their competence. Not every farmer was excellent in this department, of course, but even the slow learners were supported by a community network of shared knowledge and practice.

When tractors displaced horses, farmers developed the knowledge and skill to control them too. Their control was made somewhat easier by the fact that the major patent struggles over farm machinery had taken place a few decades earlier, meaning that many mechanical systems were now in the public domain. Internal-combustion engines were still well protected. While this seriously influenced the fortunes of some firms such as Massey, which had to license and ultimately buy tractor technology, it did not stop farmers from relatively rapid adoption and adaptation of tractor power.

Farmer initiatives to control machine technology took several forms. Collectively they pushed for machinery regulation with some success in the form of state and university testing facilities such as the Nebraska tractor tests, and much later, in Canada, the Prairie Agricultural Machinery Institute. They also formed co-operatives that began exclusively as buying groups but ended with the formation of Canadian Co-operative Implements Limited, which sold a range of other manufacturers' tractors under its own brand and had limited short-line manufacturing capacity.[12] CCIL's policy was to provide full documentation for its machines and to attempt to use off-the-shelf parts in its manufacturing.

Further, Prairie farmers along with their continental cousins invented machinery: among them, the Noble blade, disker, swather, air seeder, and a host of modifications to manufacturers' machines. In our research, the disker has been illustrative of the control that farmers had over machinery. In Southern Saskatchewan we found not one but many farmer inventors of the disker. Typically the inventors were males but in some cases the whole family was directly involved. Indeed the emergence of the disker appears to have been a collective community phenomenon in which the technology became part of the people's knowledge. When we asked one inventor if patents were involved he seemed perplexed at the question: "there was nothing to patent."

Finally, farmers co-operated at the community level in repairing machinery. One instance we uncovered involved a Case dealer who opened his shop during the winter months for farmers to work on their own machinery. When they needed help or lacked specific skills, the owner or his qualified mechanic would provide it. It appears that similar forms of sharing knowledge and skill were common among rural communities.

In other words, in the case of machine technology, farmers' strategies to control their work and to resist its control by outsiders drew on the people's knowledge. They could keep machines running longer and avoid capital costs, buy used, modify machines, and turn them to tasks that the manufacturer never intended or had overlooked. They developed welding and forging skills, aided by university courses. After World War One, North America fell in love with the automobile; mechanical knowledge and skill spread throughout the population. Even the experience of war had the effect of democratizing mechanical knowledge. So machinery developed as a relatively "open architecture," and would remain so until computerization and modular design became prime corporate strategies in the 1970s.

Farm production entails much more than machine technology, of course, but motive power was perhaps the central factor prior to World War Two. It was decisive in breaking prairie sod and, later, the heavy use of summerfallow in dryland farming. But it should also be said that farmers' control of machine technology was consistent with their control in other areas such as livestock, poultry and crop production, and building technology.

PRAIRIE FARMING IN THE POST-WAR PERIOD

The social setting

This period has been characterized as a period of "Fordist compromise" which entailed the legitimation and disciplining of labour, relatively high wages and high productivity, mass production and mass consumption, and the welfare state. As profits recovered during the war, new investments in technology became possible and work became increasingly Taylorized.[13]

Agriculture was part of this compromise. Generally in North America, the state attempted to maintain a cheap-food policy by encouraging farm production through increasing scale and productivity. This involved the wholesale displacement of farm labour and its replacement by non-farm inputs. In Canada, farmers struggled successfully to establish marketing boards and other "safety" nets but these probably only rationalized the process of transformation. A famous identifier of the pattern during this period was the 1969 report of the federal Task Force on Agriculture, which argued that we simply had too many farmers and that the smaller and inefficient ones ought to get out.[14] As a mechanism of symbolic violence against family farming, this coupling of smallness with inefficiency became another hallmark of the period. Structurally, the period was characterized by all of the familiar statistical trends. Farm numbers dropped, farm size grew, average production increased, the use of non-farm inputs—machinery, electricity, chemicals, fertilizers and loan capital—increased, while farm margins decreased.

The structure of agribusiness capital itself did not remain static. In the food business on the output side of farming, wealth and productive capacity became increasingly concentrated and the surviving firms became very large, typically with global reach. Segments of the food business, retail chains, slaughterers, millers, bakers and other processors, and commodity merchants struggled for control among themselves. The result was a high degree of integration from the farm gate to consumers through direct ownership, agreements, and contracts and marketing arrangements, particularly in livestock and poultry products, fruits, and vegetables. To gain advantage it now became necessary for large firms to increase their control of farm production, in terms of both quantity and quality.

A similar process took place on the input side of farming. World War Two brought better machinery but also better chemicals. After the war, firms had to find their civilian use; agriculture became one target. The use of weed and insect chemicals and of fertilizers mushroomed. In a sense, what was once farm production became industrial and non-farm production—another investment frontier for capital with over-capacity. This pattern, I argue below, threatens to become more complete with the advent of biotechnology and genetically engineered inputs.

Farmers confronted the strategies of capital and the state with a confusing array of strategies of their own. Perhaps most noticeable was the gradual transformation and eventual collapse of the agrarian populist hegemony that had provided at least a loose integration to family-farm resistance until the 1970s. It was no match for the new initiatives by agribusiness to penetrate farming. Indeed, the populist ideology itself had been built on a concept of "progress" which was easily turned by agribusiness and the state to the practices of early adoption of non-farm inputs, better efficiency, and higher production.[15] In this way, populist hegemony was eroded and replaced by a new hegemony dominated by agribusiness. Divisions between farmers, although always there, became more pronounced. Some actively sided with capital, seeing agribusiness as their natural ally, while others held to the older forms of resistance to outside control which were by now, perhaps, ill-suited to the challenge. In general, the collective solidarity and political organization of the previous generation of family farmers collapsed, though the collapse was neither immediate nor monolithic.

On an individual basis, farmers' strategies to control their life chances drew from time-worn practices. Their control of machinery through shared knowledge and innovation continued, though it would be increasingly interrupted by computerization and modularization. Family members supported the farm by finding off-farm work. But, in the end, as the well-known statistical trends have shown, the predominant strategy was to leave.

Farm work

While farmers, remarkably, have maintained some control over machinery work, the new forms of farming rely on new technologies, specifically chemicals and, more recently, biotechnology, that are largely beyond their control. The change began with the introduction of chemicals after World War Two. The universities and state research labs, which had been responsible for developing and protecting public knowledge in the earlier era, gradually shifted their focus from farmers to the companies. Patenting of products and of manufacturing and research processes became an essential strategy of the monopoly firms. Proprietary knowledge became embedded in the product. Use by farmers and the opportunity to modify products became strictly limited by patent law and contracts. This has become particularly true for genetically engineered products.[16]

Hence farmers' avenues for control of chemical and fertilizer technology have become seriously limited. Compared to machinery, purchasing used is either illegal or simply not a physical option. Facilities for reverse-engineering the products are not widely available. The technologies of chemicals and bio-engineering are not well understood by farmers, and experimentation and manufacturing are seldom attempted. There have indeed been attempts to gain some measure of control. Community networks have developed but only limited extensions of knowledge and control have resulted, for example, in developing legal strategies against manufacturers whose products have been defective, or in varying the way of mixing and applying a chemical so as to improve its performance or to make it suitable for slightly different applications. And one Saskatchewan-based group, Focus on Inputs, did reverse-engineer Monsanto's herbicide Roundup with the intention of manufacturing it when the patent expired. Farm support for the group folded, however, under threats from the company. It is doubtful that these areas of farm work will become farm "folk" knowledge, and under the control of farmers, any time soon.

Chemicals and bio-engineering are the new logic of farming. The language of company advertising and much of state extension work champions the "modern, progressive" farmer as knowledgeable, skilled, and in control when he or she merely follows the label, signs the contract, and applies the proprietary knowledge embedded in the non-farm inputs. In this discourse, the final mark of the skilled farmer is one who has, or appears to have, a positive net income and net worth, or is able to successfully negotiate an annual operating bank loan, or else is a deserving recipient of a state safety-net payment. This is the message in the state's current programs, which aim to raise farmers' management skills, encourage their use of commodity and futures markets, and, of course, drive up their use of non-farm inputs.

But in what sense is this a sign of farming skill? Certainly it takes knowledge and competence to manage a farm. Traditionally one had to know the physical, biological, and social characteristics of plants, animals, the soil and weather, machinery, buildings, and human labour in order to negotiate their combination into a successful growing system. And one had to have the skill to do the work. But increasingly this knowledge is embedded in non-farm inputs and marketing relationships. Farm management skill today requires one to determine whether or not the company supplying the input will make good on its advertising promises, and whether the market broker is reliable. Skill at the work of actually growing something becomes secondary in this new set of practices. But if control of the growing system is embedded in inputs and market relations, owned by non-farm companies, this new management skill is surely hollow, derivative of the strategies of capital, and dependent upon the needs of non-farm firms for a new investment frontier.

If farming becomes more thoroughly an adjunct of the corporate strategies of non-farm firms, then social capital, community helping patterns, collective knowledge, and ultimately political vitality will be lost to rural communities. Most obviously, farm numbers will continue to decline. Although farm wage labour may increase somewhat, even the current level of technology will mean that much less labour is needed. As farm scale increases and margins remain low, competition will increase. The integration of farmers with their corporate associates will grow. There are implications in this trend for farm politics. Farm managers and their families may stop voting and have a dangerously cynical attitude toward government, but their objective position will become increasingly that of *de facto* managers of capital's interests in agriculture. This is hardly the basis for fundamental resistance or for the building of an indigenous family-farm politics.

If this analysis is correct, then farm people should turn their attention to more steadfastly resisting the erosion of their control over farm work. Recall the case of the lottery-winning farm couple. It illustrated how non-viable family farming is as far as income is concerned. We might also note, however, that the couple's first purchase was an air seeder, a machine invented by a Saskatchewan farmer in the 1960s but quickly appropriated by agribusiness and turned into a centrepiece in the zero-tillage "revolution," a high-input type of farming where much of the technology is beyond local control. Or consider the cynical joke that has become popular in farming circles and is captured by the "Syd" cartoon in which, in the act of holding up a farmer, the thief says "Forget the wallet, give me all your herbicide and fertilizers!"[17] This kind of high-input agriculture is inherently beyond the control of family farmers. Can this trend be resisted?

For those who want to rebuild sustainable farm communities and rural life, some lessons from the past may be instructive and deserve to be remembered. For example, farm people would do well to emulate the desire and perhaps even some of the strategies of previous generations to control farm work. Today, that would surely involve developing and adopting farming systems that use fewer industrial inputs and that entail fewer constraints imposed by agribusiness interests. It would also mean sharing farm knowledge and skill not only at the level of local friendships and networks but also by forming broader organizations to advance, nurture, and protect farm control of farm work. The organic and low-input farming movements are obvious examples of such initiatives. At the same time, the challenge is greater to the extent that previous initiatives in farm machinery have been reversed. Co-op Implements is defunct and the watchdog functions of the Prairie Agricultural Machinery Institute have been reduced. These original strategies need to be revisited and extended to fertilizers and farm chemicals.

But our past also yields lessons in what not to emulate. Consider, for example, the blanket and even enthusiastic acceptance of "science" that was pervasive among farmers especially after World War Two. It is now clear that science comes in different flavours, with much of it turned exclusively to private rather than public interests, as Ralph Nader among many others points out.[18] Farm people need to join the struggle to return science to the public domain by insisting, for example, that university and government research always be public, by opposing patenting and trade agreements that make "knowledge" a form of private intellectual property, and by actively engaging in research themselves, contributing its results to a growing bank of "people's knowledge." Certainly there are examples of such initiatives: the Council of Canadians' campaign on genetically modified food; the networks of heritage farmers and gardeners that protect public varieties and species, and the companion efforts to protect public breeds; the endless examples of machinery invention and modification which can be found weekly in the farm press. Governments especially need to be pressured to fund and protect this public domain of knowledge.

Finally, farmers will have to return to a belief in the importance of small-scale agriculture and develop a "will" to defend it. Give or take a few thousand, Prairie farm numbers are now down to only some 15,000 in Manitoba and some 40,000 each in Saskatchewan and Alberta. Farm communities are not sustainable with such ridiculously low numbers of farms. We need more farmers, not fewer. Rural and urban people must recognize that the important issue is not only the quality of the food they eat but also the social relations under which it is produced. If we can campaign to stop our footwear and clothing from being made in sweatshops, surely we can campaign for non-alienating work and life in our farm communities.

Notes

1   Michelle Houlden, "Millionaires snap up machine of their dreams," *The Western Producer*, 18 May 2000.

2   These are questions that have gripped social thinkers for centuries. See, for example, Adam Smith, *The Wealth of Nations* (London: Dent & Sons, 1933); and Karl Marx, *Capital*, Vol. 1. (New York: International Publishers, 1967), Parts III and IV. A review is provided by Paul Thompson, *The Nature of Work An Introduction to Debates on the Labour Process* (London: MacMillan, 1983). Harry Braverman, *Labour and Monopoly Capital The Degradation of Work in the Twentieth Century* (New York: Monthly Review, 1974), ch. 1, provides an elaboration of the position used in this paper.

3   Canadian philosopher George Grant, in *Technology and Justice* (Toronto: Anansi, 1986), argues this point by way of criticizing the often-heard claim that "The computer does not impose on us the ways it should be used." Not only has the computer enhanced the homogenising processes in our society, for example, by treating us all the same so that we all "fit" in the same data banks, but even the verb "should" in the offending claim is part of a modern instrumentalist approach to life that has replaced the moral imperative "ought" of previous generations.

4   Bryan Palmer, *Working Class Experience: Rethinking the History of Canadian Labour, 1800–1991* (Toronto: McClelland & Stewart, 1992).

5   Braverman, op. cit., p. 109.

6   In the discussion that follows, where primary data are presented, they are based on a study of farm work supported by SSHRC grant #484-90-0027.

7   Vernon Fowke, *The National Policy and the Wheat Economy* (Toronto: University of Toronto Press, 1956); Arthur Davis, "Canadian Society and History as Hinterland Versus Metropolis," in R.J. Ossenberg, ed., *Canadian Society Pluralism, Change and Conflict* (Scarborough: Prentice-Hall, 1971), 3 - 32.

8   Jane Ursel, *Private Lives, Public Policy One Hundred Years of State Intervention in the Family* (Toronto: Between The Lines, 1990); Marjorie Cohen, *Women's Work, Markets and Economic Development in Nineteenth-Century Ontario* (Toronto: University of Toronto Press, 1988); and Sandra Rollings-Magnusson, "Canada's Most Wanted: Pioneer Women on the Western Prairies," *Canadian Review of Sociology and Anthropology* 37 (1997), 223–38. These writers among others have shown that while all forms of farm women's work were crucial to the sustainability of the family farm, the structure was patriarchal, e.g., in its homestead policies and in its family and inheritance laws, which no doubt encouraged farm family practices that tended to have a distinctly gendered division of labour, control of accumulation by the male head of household, and generally the subjugation of farm women. Nevertheless, farm women mounted spirited campaigns both against patriarchy and in support of family farming.

9   G.R. Stevens, *Ogilvie in Canada, Pioneer Millers, 1801–1951* (Montreal: Ogilvie Flour Mills Co., 1952).

10   Jeffery Taylor, *Fashioning Farmers Ideology, Agricultural Knowledge and the Manitoba Farm Movement, 1890–1925* (Regina: Canadian Plains Research Centre, University of Regina, 1994); Cecilia Danysk, *Hired Hands Labour and the Development of Prairie Agriculture, 1880–1930* (Toronto: McClelland & Stewart, 1995).

11   Grant MacEwan, *The Heavy Horses: Highlights of Their History* (Saskatoon: Western Producer Prairie Books, 1986).

12   Douglas Faller, "Degradation of Farm Work and Resistance to Deskilling in the Canadian Prairies: The Case of Farm Machinery," Unpublished master's thesis, University of Regina, 1998.

13   Various authors, e.g., Gary Teeple, *Globalization and the Decline of Social Reform* (Toronto: Garamond Press, 1995), would see two periods here instead of one, the first an era of Fordism, the second starting in the last quarter of the 20th century being an era of "globalization." At least in the case of farming, the jury is still out on this issue. Family farming on the prairies was always subject to global markets and firms, and the increasing penetration of farming by agribusiness in the late 1900s can be seen as merely an extension of earlier Fordist practices.

14   Task Force on Agriculture, *Canadian Agriculture in the Seventies* (Ottawa: Department of Agriculture, 1969).

15 David Laycock, *Populism and Democratic Thought in the Canadian Prairies 1910 to 1945* (Toronto: University of Toronto Press, 1990).

16 The case of Saskatchewan farmer Percy Schmieser is illustrative. When Monsanto's investigators found "Roundup Ready" canola growing on Schmeiser's farm, even though he had never bought the company's patented seed nor signed a use agreement, the company sued him. Media attention around the case revealed that even though patented varieties would readily out-cross, carrying their genes into fields where they were not wanted and perhaps even harmful, Monsanto had acted aggressively against farmers for allegedly violating its patents. (Ed White, "Monsanto, Schmeiser in gene battle," "Schmeiser seen as hero by many," "Monsanto suit about patent," *The Western Producer*, 8 June 2000.)

17 George Kynman, "Syd," cartoon, *Manitoba Co-operator*, 29 June 2000.

18 Barry Wilson, "Nader warns of corporate science," *Western Producer*, 21 February 2001.

A Good Place
to Grow Old?

RURAL COMMUNITIES AND
SUPPORT TO SENIORS

Norah Keating,
Janice Keefe,
and Bonnie Dobbs

In the past decade, Canadian governments have made dramatic changes in the organization and delivery of healthcare services. Many of these changes have been justified by the belief that the health needs of an aging population have outstripped the country's ability to pay. There has been a call for a reduction in public-sector responsibility and for a shift toward increased personal responsibility and involvement of family members in the health of seniors.[1] Some have argued that this approach to restructuring of healthcare amounts to "apocalyptic demography," the blaming of seniors for our healthcare woes.[2] Compared to other industrialized nations, though, Canada has a small proportion of older people. Significant increases in the number of Canadian seniors won't be apparent for another two decades, when most of the baby boomers will reach their sixties and seventies. Yet in Canada we have placed seniors front-and-centre in the healthcare debate.

We are just beginning to understand the impact of healthcare restructuring on the current generation of Canadian seniors. This is a formidable task since seniors differ tremendously in their abilities to withstand the move away from the publicly funded programs that have been part of the social fabric of Canada since the 1960s. People are more likely to be healthy if there is a good balance between their needs and the resources available to support them. Traditionally, rural communities are seen as being poor in terms of amenities and formal services, but rich in people willing to volunteer their help. Rural people are assumed to grow up and grow old surrounded by those friends and family who have supported them for a lifetime, and who will continue to support them through declining health. However, the notion that caring people can buffer rural seniors from poor health has been dealt a blow with the restructuring of healthcare in the 1990s. Rural residents, and seniors in particular, increasingly are isolated from formal services in both acute and continuing care, services that are necessary if informal caregiving is to be sustainable.

In this chapter we consider how rural seniors may fare in this new policy milieu. More than 20 percent of Canada's seniors live in rural parts of the country. Yet the policy lens rarely is focussed on their needs. Rural Canada has long been poorly served when it comes to healthcare resources, and may be particularly hard hit by healthcare restructuring that may lead to further reduction in these resources. On the other hand, rural seniors may be buffered from the negative impact of reduced public sector services because they have strong values about helping one another and because they have supportive networks of family and friends. The question then is whether, at the beginning of the twenty-first century, rural communities in Canada are a good place to grow old. We argue in this chapter that the answer could be yes if we make three policy responses to the needs of rural seniors. First, we need to think broadly about health and about how public policy in several government domains can support the health of rural seniors. Second, we need to support the family members and friends who provide informal care to frail seniors. Third, we need to customize policy solutions for the variety of rural settings that differ in access to services, availability of family and friends, and economic well-being. One policy solution does not fit all.

In order to understand whether rural communities support a healthy old age, we need to consider what health is. Health often is thought of as the absence of illness. From this perspective, the main focus of healthcare is on the treatment of acute illnesses, injuries, and chronic conditions. Physician and hospital services are central components of healthcare. A healthy older person is someone who is free of major illness or chronic condition. Thus, while a senior with osteoporosis could be treated to alleviate symptoms and prevent further deterioration, he would be considered by most to be in poor health since he has a chronic health condition. Since most seniors have one or more chronic health conditions, it is easy to understand how healthcare planners would see disaster looming.

In contrast to the idea that health is the absence of illness, there is a broader perspective on health that has been used in Canada since the mid 1980s. This view is that health is a resource that helps people adapt to or even change their surroundings in order to meet their needs.[3] Healthy people are able to interact effectively with their environment, changing their strategies to accommodate changes in their circumstances. Using this definition of health, how would we classify the health status of the senior with osteoporosis described above? In our work with rural seniors, we met a farmer in his early eighties who had osteoporosis and had had surgery to fuse some of the vertebrae in his back. While most people his age would long since have left the labour force, he had continued to farm with his son. His assistance helped his son to manage the farm, as well as giving the father a sense that he was still contributing. Because of the surgery, it looked like he would have to completely retire from farming. However, during his recovery he enlisted his son to help develop a mechanical lift to help him get into his tractor. With a cell phone to keep in touch with his wife, power steering in the tractor, and determination to carry on, he could continue to farm. This senior had managed his surroundings in order to remain operationally healthy.

The new health philosophy in action

Philosophically the main goal of healthcare restructuring in Canada is congruent with the broad definition of health described above. The goal is to move away from a medically focussed approach to health services toward one that is more social and that takes into account people's preferences and the environments in which they want to live. Flowing from this goal is the assumption that people should be cared for close to home, and that community-based care is more desirable than institutional care. As far as seniors are concerned, there is a widely shared belief that families are an integral part of the new approach to healthcare since family members know the person best. Families are seen as the mainstay of community-based care, with formal services available to augment family care if needed.[4]

Across the provinces and territories, the new philosophy has been implemented in various ways. Many jurisdictions have decreased funding to acute-care hospitals, increased emphasis on home care, formalized expectations of family involvement in care, and have regionalized program responsibility. All provinces are working within financial constraints that include reduced federal transfer payments. These changes appear consistent with bringing healthcare closer to home and more within the control of those who use healthcare services.

However, those who have tracked the shift of funds from institutional care to community care have noted that cost reduction has usually been a major goal, and that this has influenced how the shift has affected clients.[5] Reduced funding to hospitals has not been accompanied by funding that is sufficient to support increased levels of care in communities. In fact, much of the increased community care load comes from shorter average hospital stays, the result of which is often people going home with acute illnesses. Thus, services like home care now face greater demands, caring for acutely ill people who might otherwise have been in hospital. In turn, those requiring long-term care, such as frail seniors, now are lower on the list of home-care priorities.

One way that home care and other community-based services are being rationed is based on whether there are family members in the community. If there are, they are expected to be the first line of defence. Yet this so-called shift to families is ironic, given that families have already been providing the majority of care to their senior members with long-term health problems. This is especially the case, moreover, among rural families. Rural people share a set of values that stem from the early settlers who settled on the harsh frontier. These values include hard work and self-reliance, and expectations that family members will work together.[6] And indeed, estimates are that the informal network of family and friends provides 80 to 90 percent of long-term care in rural areas. Yet changes in the structure of funding to health and social services suggest that there is increasing pressure on informal caregivers to do even more.

Many provinces have included regionalization of the provision of healthcare services as part of healthcare restructuring. In Alberta, for example, there are now seventeen regions, each with responsibility for providing medically necessary hospital and medical services. Proponents of regionalization argue that this is a good structure since it allows for decision-making by people who know the communities they serve. Thus services should be more responsive to community needs. Detractors worry that regionalization will lead to increased disparity within provinces and across the country. Poorer regions may be able to provide few services outside of those mandated by the Canada Health Act. It is noteworthy here that while physician and hospital services are mandated, many community services such as home care are not.

RESTRUCTURING AND THE HEALTH OF RURAL SENIORS

Given these changes in the philosophy and implementation of health programs, we return to the question of whether rural communities are good settings for seniors to maintain their health as they age. There are different definitions of what is meant by rural, although statistical bureaus in many countries define rural based on geographic criteria of density and distance. In Canada, rural communities are considered to be those that have fewer than 10,000 people and are not within daily commuting distance from a city.[7] Both density and distance are important in determining how well rural seniors can maintain their health. Distance usually is defined as number of kilometres to a service centre that has essential services such as doctors, pharmacies, grocery stores, and banks. Distance is a good indicator of seniors' ability to gain access to needed services. It is an especially important indicator of rurality in Canada, where distance can be intensified by severe climatic conditions. Distance makes a difference, as well, to those whose network of family and friends is not in their home community. If seniors need care, informal caregivers who are not nearby often provide care at great personal and economic cost.[8]

The second criterion is density. Rural communities are sparsely distributed across the country and have small populations. Low population density is associated with less access to informal support networks. Low population density also means that it is inefficient to provide services such as home care, nursing homes, and hospitals because there are few potential recipients spread over a large geographic area.

In the remainder of this section, we consider three issues that will influence whether healthcare restructuring threatens the health of rural seniors, defined in this way. The first is how personal resources of rural seniors will influence their ability to get access to products and services they need to maintain their health. The second is whether erosion of formal health services will make rural residence untenable for some seniors. Finally we consider whether these barriers can be overcome though community support and strong informal support networks seen as part of the rural tradition.

Personal resources of rural seniors

What then are the unique features of rural seniors that might influence their ability to maintain their health? As a group, rural seniors differ considerably from urban seniors.[9] In many ways they appear to be disadvantaged. As a group they are older, have less education, and have lower incomes. More rural than urban seniors are in the oldest age group (over age 85). These are people who are most likely to have functional challenges such as poor eyesight, hearing, and muscle strength that may hamper their mobility. Age differences between the two groups are small. Eight percent of rural seniors are over eighty-five compared to seven percent of urban seniors. However, these differences may increase with current trends of people retiring to the countryside.

On average rural seniors have less education than their urban counterparts. About 30 percent of older rural residents have high school education or more compared to 50 percent of seniors living in cities. Similarly, higher proportions have limited incomes. About 65 percent have incomes of less than $15,000 per year compared to 50 percent of urban seniors. The combination of lower levels of education and income mean that rural seniors have less ability to purchase services they need or to negotiate with complex bureaucracies to get those services.

In contrast, rural seniors appear to have some distinct advantages. They are more likely to be married and to live in their own homes. As well, those who are unmarried or widowed are less likely to live alone. Being married is one of the best resources one can have in maintaining health and 67 percent of rural seniors are married (compared to 58 percent of urban seniors). One of the best buffers against the need to go into a nursing home is having a spouse who can provide support, transportation, and access to family, friends, and services. Living at home also has the great advantage of allowing for the continuation of long-time patterns of daily living in a familiar environment. Most rural seniors live in a house rather than in an apartment, condominium, or other shared housing such as lodges (86 percent compared to 58 percent of city dwellers), and relatively few live alone (25 percent compared to 33 percent of urban seniors). Almost 90 percent of rural seniors are Canadian-born and are no strangers to the challenges of distance and Canadian winters.

These statistics suggest that most rural seniors are well integrated into their surroundings. However, it is worth noting that those who are widowed may be disadvantaged. One of the ways in which widowed rural people adapt to their surroundings is by moving to a place that has easier access to services. Because of the inability to maintain a large family home and the limited availability of alternative housing such as apartments or condominiums, older widows in rural areas may choose to move into town. This pattern raises the question of whether rural areas can be sufficiently supportive to those of advanced age who have lost their spouses. Most people who move are women. Men comprise the majority (58 percent) of rural seniors due to the fact that young men come to rural areas to work in resource communities and older women are likely to leave if they are widowed.

Erosion of formal health services

In general, rural seniors lack access to the range of formal services found in cities. In fact, recent reports show that starting from this disadvantaged position, the restructuring of healthcare has resulted in further declines in formal services in rural areas. For example, New Zealand's restructuring of its long-term care system sharpened the gap between urban and rural, with rural communities suffering a broad depletion of services.[10] Closer to home, Ontario introduced a managed competition system as the centrepiece of its long-term care reform. Managed competition is intended to increase efficiency through a competitive process. However, the result was uneven levels of services across jurisdictions, and short contracts that precluded long-term planning. Recipients of services were uncertain of how to gain access to services or whether their current provider would continue to provide services. Unlike other provinces, Ontario has put substantial resources into long-term care facilities. The restructuring of publicly funded community services, combined with substantial re-investment in long-term care facilities, has made some rural elderly people vulnerable to institutionalization.[11]

Overall, rural areas are poorly served by health professionals. While 22 percent of Canadians live in rural towns with a population under 10,000 people, they are served by only 10 percent of physicians.[12] Rural areas often have inadequate levels of home care and mental health services as well.[13] In the past decade in Alberta, many rural hospitals have been closed, and rural communities have had increasing difficulty attracting physicians and other healthcare professionals. It seems that restructuring has not provided the solution to depletion of healthcare services in rural areas. Rural seniors may be better served by other kinds of services that support their independence. Most have access to some basic services in their communities such as grocery stores and pharmacies.

However, about twenty percent must go outside their neighbourhood for groceries or other services compared to only five percent of urban seniors.

Transportation is a key issue in understanding whether rural seniors are disadvantaged by lack of formal services in their communities. Access to services often hinges on seniors' ability to drive since they often must travel long distances to receive care. Not surprisingly, rural elders more frequently identify inadequate transportation as a barrier to healthcare services than do their urban counterparts.[14] Researchers in the United States have found that rural seniors living within reasonable driving distance of urban medical centres used healthcare services as frequently as their urban counterparts. However, in Canada many rural communities are located a considerable distance from major medical centres. In addition, the challenges of winter driving may make even nearby urban centres difficult to access. Seniors who are most likely to have stopped driving are older women who have chronic medical conditions, often individuals who are most in need of healthcare.[15] Since there is little public transportation in rural areas, those who no longer can drive must rely on others, typically family and friends, for transportation.

Community and social network support

Rural seniors may be able to compensate for lack of formal services by living in supportive communities and having strong networks of family and friends. Although rural communities are typified by values about helping each other, we are just beginning to learn about how these values translate into active support to seniors. The amount of informal support is influenced by two things: whether community members actively help each other, and whether seniors themselves have longstanding networks of family and friends nearby.

A small retirement community can be used to illustrate the difference between formal and informal sources of support, as well as the importance of the latter. This community is one to which many people move after they have left the labour force, often when they are in their early sixties. Thus when they arrive these young seniors have no existing support network in the area (an example of lack of a longstanding network of family and friends). Fortunately, community leaders believe that it is important to help the newcomers become integrated. Their strategy is to engage newcomers as volunteers and to socialize them to the community (an example of active community helping). A bonus of this arrangement is that it helps newcomers develop friendship networks that become important sources of support later in their lives.

Even today, people living in rural communities believe that it is important to help others and to be able to count on informal support if they need it. Rural seniors are more likely than city dwellers to expect that family and friends will be there for them, part of the cultural aspect of what is rural outlined above. These expectations are closely linked to idyllic images of a rural community lifestyle that includes expectations about high levels of support for others in the community. For the first time in Canada there is evidence to show that the image is true. One of the questions on the 1996 Canadian Census was whether the person had provided care to a senior in the past month. We looked at rural communities ranging from less than 2000 people up to 10,000 people and found that the smaller the community, the higher the percentage of people who said they had provided help to a senior. Figures for women were 20 to 24 percent and for men were 14 to 17 percent. As a comparison, 19 percent of women and 14 percent of men in cities of 100,000 had provided help to a senior. When it comes to community willingness to help older people, rural communities are advantaged, though perhaps the differences here are less than stereotypes might suggest.

Informal support networks

Rural communities are consistent in their commitment to providing assistance to seniors. However, they differ considerably in whether their older members are likely to have their own support networks of family and friends nearby.[16] This distinction is important since assistance from family and friends is a buffer against poor health and loss of independence. Thus it is the strength of the informal networks in rural communities that determines whether there exists a long-term care continuum adapted to meeting the unique needs of individual seniors.[17]

Many have argued that informal support is the keystone of continuing care to rural seniors and that formal support, at best, is a supplement to this care.[18] Yet local economies and related migration patterns can make a big difference in the likelihood that seniors will have family and friends nearby. For example, Alberta has a large number of resource-based rural communities. These communities differ in their mix of old and young. Mining and logging communities have high proportions of young people who are attracted there because of job opportunities. Most of these communities have few seniors. In contrast, farming communities have higher proportions of seniors who have farmed in the area and retired there. Farming communities typically experience out-migration of young people who need to go elsewhere for jobs. In contrast, remote communities often have relatively stable populations and seniors are embedded in longstanding networks of friends and kin.[19] Less is known about how economic migration of young people affects informal networks of rural seniors in these communities. However, the out-migration of young people may reduce the ability of seniors to age in place, because of a lack of readily available family caregivers. Such employment and migration patterns will inevitably affect whether seniors are embedded in longstanding networks of kin and friends who still live in the area and will provide informal care when needed.

Other kinds of rural communities, as noted above, will have high proportions of seniors not because young people leave but because older people move there at retirement. Older Canadians may relocate to rural areas because of overall attraction of living in a rural area, because of climate, or to reduce their cost of living. However, most older people who move toward these kinds of rural amenities are also moving away from family and friends.[20] The above discussion shows that in some kinds of rural communities, seniors are more likely than in others to have networks of family and friends who can provide social contact, who can check up on them, who are available to provide transportation if needed, and who can help seniors maintain their health and independence. Just as clear, moreover, is the fact that some communities need to develop strategies to help older residents remain in their communities.

The need for support and integration becomes especially important for seniors who have conditions requiring high levels of assistance. About 26 percent of rural seniors receive help for a chronic health problem. The majority receive all (44 percent) or some (25 percent) of their care from informal sources. Thus it appears that many seniors do receive help when they need it. However, this regular care can place heavy burdens on caregivers, increasing the vulnerability of those without strong networks. Rural caregivers consistently report more stress, more caring commitments, and less external assistance than urban caregivers.[21] Rural seniors who enter nursing homes are younger and in better health than their urban counterparts. Since there may be few community services available as a backup to informal support, seniors may be unable to stay at home if they can't manage by themselves. Despite their willingness to help, we may be expecting too much of informal rural support networks.

Some who do not have strong, resilient informal networks turn to formal sources for assistance. Rural seniors with higher incomes are, predictably, in a much better position than poorer seniors to compensate for a lack of informal assistance by purchasing paid help. Thirty-eight percent of those with income over $30,000 pay for professional assistance, compared to 25 percent of those with lower incomes.

It seems that seniors with nearby networks of family and friends, who live in small rural communities and whose informal network is large enough to provide care over long periods of time, might be in a good position to manage despite limited availability of formal services. Those who are affluent may be able to hire some of the services they need, although in small isolated communities, even those with financial resources may not be able to find people able to provide the services they need. Those without personal and people resources are, of course, at risk for negative health outcomes.

POLICY CHALLENGES

Rural communities have the foundation for a strong system of community care to their older members. Rural communities are supportive and caring, and seniors in some rural communities have good access to informal support. Yet rural seniors are disadvantaged in their access to formal healthcare services, to other services they need to live their daily lives, and in their personal resources. While it is difficult to determine the impact of healthcare restructuring on Canadian seniors, it is clear that further reductions in the availability of services will make rural seniors less able to access services necessary to maintain their health. The following are issues that need to be addressed if Canada is to support the health of rural seniors.

Use the broad definition of health as a basis for policy formation

The broad definition of health, which includes ability to interact with one's environment, requires that policy move beyond a focus on the provision of services covered under the Canada Health Act, by hospitals and physicians. If we are to help seniors maintain their health in this broad meaning, we need policies that are co-ordinated across what have historically been separate government domains. This is not an easy thing to do since we tend to have battles over turf or jurisdiction that inhibit departments from collaborating with one another.

One potential source of integration is provincial government portfolios with cross-department responsibility for seniors' issues. Many provinces, including Alberta, have ministers responsible for seniors. These ministers from the provinces, territories, and federal government meet periodically to discuss programs of benefit to Canadian seniors. However, only a few provinces, such as British Columbia, have a group of civil servants with expertise in aging, whose task is to work together to develop policies specific to the needs of seniors. The creation of such groups in all provinces and territories could enhance our ability to develop integrated programs for rural seniors. Restructuring makes this co-ordination particularly important since so much responsibility for program development and service delivery has been devolved to the regions.

Support informal caregivers

Rural seniors are poorly served by formal health and other services. One of the concerns about healthcare restructuring is the further erosion of such services. The result is increased pressure on family members and friends to do more. Yet families already are carrying most of the caregiving responsibility for seniors and are often doing so at great personal costs. We should not exploit their willingness to do what they can. Good health policy does not put caregivers at risk of burnout and, in turn, their loved ones at risk of institutionalization. Our recent analyses of public policies in Canada show that there are few programs to reduce the costs incurred by informal caregivers. Tax credits benefit very few. Most provinces have no public programs to provide caregiving leave to employed caregivers. Home-care services are spread so thinly that informal caregivers often get little respite.

There are ways in which informal caregivers can be supported. The main one is to make certain that there are formal programs in place to provide support to caregivers and care recipients. Caregivers provide care for longer if they get some support. Support can come from a number of sources. Adequate and accessible professional, diagnostic, treatment, and long-term care services are an essential component of health. We cannot afford further erosion of these services in rural Canada. Initiatives to encourage physicians to set up practice in rural areas should be applauded. As well, a current focus of the national health agenda in Canada is the development of a comprehensive home-care program that would serve the community care needs of people across the country. Such a program might do more for rural seniors and their caregivers than almost any other single policy initiative. If adequately resourced, home care can help people remain at home, reduce institutionalization, and provide a safety net for those without informal networks.

Customize solutions for the variety of rural settings

Support to rural seniors must take into account the fact that rural seniors have a diverse range of circumstances and live in variety of settings. Health is influenced by personal resources, informal networks, and formal services. People are healthy when there is a positive balance between their needs and available environmental supports. Thus, responsive models of community-based care to rural seniors must take into account all of the elements that influence health. For example, programs that allow for payment to informal caregivers might be especially helpful in economically depressed regions where personal resources such as education and income are low and where there are few formal services. Current social assistance policies do not allow people to stay on assistance while providing full-time care to a frail older relative. If we believe that such caregiving is a socially important job and family members wish to do that job, public policy should not inhibit them from doing so. Similarly, in areas such as retirement communities in which people are without existing informal networks, strong home-care programs can serve to keep people in the community. In remote communities, the negative impact of the closure of rural hospitals might be partially offset if buildings were refurbished as lodges or care facilities, so that those who need residential care can remain close to home. We believe that a good understanding of the ways in which rural communities differ in patterns of informal support and in use of formal services is essential to the development of models of care that will enhance the health of seniors in all types of rural settings.

A GOOD PLACE TO GROW OLD?

Are rural communities a good place for seniors? For those who have ample personal resources and strong, resilient informal networks, the answer may be yes. Rural values about supporting one another continue to flourish in rural communities. However, rural communities clearly are under threat. Resource communities have been hard hit by the vagaries of global markets and by the public-policy directions of the last two decades. The focus on individual and family, rather than public, responsibility seen in many governments across the country has led to the contraction of the public sector, to the detriment of those without the resources to negotiate their needs in the private sector. The shift from provincial governments to local communities to family and friends has been pursued, according to much official rhetoric, in the name of keeping people closer to home. Yet the cost-cutting agenda and the blaming of seniors for the demands they make on the healthcare system only serve to place additional stresses on family caregivers and on the cohesiveness of rural communities.

Notes

1   Alberta Health. Healthy Albertans living in a healthy Alberta. A three-year business plan. Edmonton: Author, 1994.

2   Gee, E. "Population and politics: Voodoo demography, population aging, and Canadian social policy." In E.M. Gee, & G.M. Gutman (eds.), *The overselling of population aging: Apocalyptic demography, intergenerational challenges, and social policy* (pp. 5–25). Don Mills, ON: Oxford University Press, 2000.

3   Epp, J. *Achieving health for all: A framework for health promotion.* Ottawa: National Health and Welfare, 1986.

4   Keating, N.C., J.E. Fast, I.A. Connidis, M. Penning, and J. Keefe. "Bridging policy and research in eldercare." *Canadian Journal on Aging* (supplement), 16 (1997), pp. 22–41.

5   Deber, R.B. and A.P. Williams. "Policy, payment, and participation: Long-term care reform in Ontario." *Canadian Journal on Aging,* 14(2) (1995): 294–318.

6   Keating, N.C. *Aging in rural Canada.* Toronto: Butterworths, 1991.

7   Beshiri, R., R.D. Bollman, and H. Clemenson. *Alternative definitions of rural.* (Working paper). Ottawa: Statistics Canada, May 2000.

8   Keating, N., Fast, J., Frederick, J., Cranswick, K., & Perrier, C. *Eldercare in Canada: Context, content and consequences.* Ottawa: Statistics Canada, 1999.

9   Comparisons between rural and urban seniors are from Statistics Canada. *1996 General Social Survey, cycle 11: Social and community support.* Public use microdata file documentation and users guide. Ottawa: Author, 1998.

10 Joseph, A.E. and A.I. Chalmers. "Restructuring long-term care and the geography of ageing: A view from rural New Zealand." *Social Science and Medicine,* 42(6) (1996): 887–896.

11 Cloutier-Fisher, D. and A.E. Joseph. "Long-term care restructuring in rural Ontario: Retrieving community service user and provider narratives." *Social Science and Medicine* 50(7–8) (2000): 1037–1045.

12 Society of Rural of rural communities. Physicians of Canada. 2000. Society of Rural Physicians of Canada introductory web page. http://www.srpc.ca.

13 Snustad, D.G., A.A. Thompson-Heisterman, J.B. Neese, and I.L. Abraham. "Mental health outreach to rural elderly: Service delivery to a forgotten risk group." *Clinical Gerontologist,* 14(1) (1993): 95–111.

14 Schoenberg, N.E. and R.T. Coward. "Residential differences in attitudes about barriers to using community-based services among older adults." *Journal of Rural Health* 14 (1998) 295–304.

15 Forrest, K.Y.Z., C.H. Bunker, T.J. Songer, J.H. Cohen, and, J.A. Cauley. "Driving patterns and medical conditions in older women." *Journal of the American Geriatrics Society* 45 (1997): 1214–1218.

16 Lee, G.R. and M.L. Cassidy. (1985). "Family and kin relations of the rural elderly." In R.T. Coward & G.R. Lee (eds.), *The elderly in rural society: Every fourth elder.* New York: Springer, 1985. Pp. 151–192.

17 Havens, B. and B. Kyle. "Formal long-term care: Case examples." C.N. Bull (ed.), *Aging in rural America.* Newbury Park, CA: Sage, 1993. Pp. 173–188.

18 Newhouse, J.K. "Rural and urban patterns: An exploration of how older adults use in-home care." New York: Garland, 1995.

19 Keating, N.C., J. Keefe, and A. Martin Matthews. "The social and caring context of seniors in rural Canada." Presentation to the annual International Conference on Rural Aging, Charleston, WV, June 2000.

20 Kivett, V.R., E. Dugan and S.C. Moxley. *Family supports and relationships of older urban and rural migrants in North Carolina.* Greensboro, NC: University of North Carolina at Greensboro, School of Human Environmental Sciences, Department of Human Development and Family Studies, 1994.

21 Keefe, J. *The nature of caregiving by community context: A profile of informal caregiving in Canada's rural and urban areas.* (Final report to Health Canada). Halifax: Mount Saint Vincent University, Department of Gerontology, 1999.

The Rancher and the Regulators

PUBLIC CHALLENGES TO SOUR-GAS INDUSTRY REGULATION IN ALBERTA, 1970–1994

Arn Keeling

> Trusting so-called authority is not enough.
> A sense of personal responsibility
> is what we desperately need.
> —*American author and biologist Rachel Carson, 1962*

As on so many rural properties in Alberta, the candy-striped flare stack of a sour-gas operation is clearly visible from the ranch house at Zahava Hanen's former cattle range in the Turner Valley. It marks the uncomfortable proximity of the traditional rural agricultural economy of Alberta and its dazzlingly profitable resource-extraction industries. Their uneasy co-existence through the middle of the twentieth century dissolved into confrontation in the 1970s, '80s, and '90s as the expanding oil and gas industry encroached on ranchlands and wilderness areas. The drama of the Wiebo Ludwig trial, the spectre of "eco-terrorism," and the murder of an oil industry executive are only the most recent and extreme examples of this long-simmering and acrimonious conflict.[1]

In the early 1980s, Hanen became one of many rural residents to challenge the expansion of sour-gas extraction and processing facilities near their homes. However, Hanen's was not, in any sense, the normal interaction a citizen might have with government and industry. Her battle with the provincial government Energy Conservation Resources Board (ERCB) and Imperial Oil Resources Ltd. spanned twenty years,[2] and she enlisted a galaxy of experts, well-known wilderness advocates, and public figures to assist in her fight. The historical significance of her case is that it marked the beginning of what became a groundswell of concern among Albertans over sour-gas processing, and prefigured the continuing struggles that we find today around the effects of natural-gas pollution. Hanen's case is also important because it highlighted the technocratic approach to both energy development and environmental conservation that characterized not only the industry at that time, but the Alberta government and its lead regulatory agency, the ERCB.

Examining the mandates and practices of the public agencies charged with regulating development is key to understanding conflicts between the industry and rural residents, because regulatory reviews have historically been one of the only public forums where Alberta citizens could voice concerns about the effects of resource-extraction operations. At first glance, the oil and gas industry appears extensively regulated; yet for decades the regulatory process failed to adequately respond to public concerns about the health and environmental impacts of development. While individuals may have sought redress through complaints to their MLAs or the Minister, crucial decisions about resource-extraction methods and their effects remained concentrated among a small body of technical specialists, political interests, and industry people.

Oil and gas revenues have played a major role in turning Alberta from a relatively poor province into a wealthy one, and related employment has provided important sources of income to many rural families. Indeed arguably, it is precisely the importance of oil in the Alberta economy that has made protest against industry activities very difficult. Nonetheless, as anxieties grew and individuals heard their own worries validated by the growth of global concerns about environment and health issues in the 1980s, public pressure would gradually force changes in the development review process, creating forums where, for a while at least, citizen concerns about the environmental effects of development were heard. This apparent victory would be reversed by new Alberta legislation in 1994 that undermined public input and prompted the current spate of conflicts.

The paper begins with a brief description of the pollution issues surrounding natural-gas processing and the regulatory framework in Alberta, which offered limited scope for public involvement up until the 1980s. Hanen's challenge to that regulatory order and the rising public pressure forced the government to accept the legitimacy of public input. Although the period considered in detail ends with the reorganization of the ERCB in 1994, the concluding section connects the events in which Zahava Hanen played a part, the changes that followed from her struggles, and the ongoing battles of rural residents today surrounding pollution and natural gas.

POLLUTION, NATURAL GAS, AND CONSERVATION IN ALBERTA

In the first half of the twentieth century, the oil and gas industry's birthplace— the Turner Valley, southwest of Calgary—withstood a pollution onslaught, as "sour" natural gas or the sulphur it contained was flared off into the surrounding atmosphere.[3] About half of Alberta's natural gas reserves are "sour," or laden with poisonous hydrogen sulphide and nitrous oxides, which must be removed to make the gas saleable. Though it was originally burned off as a waste product, conservation regulations in the 1950s forced industry to begin converting hydrogen sulphide to elemental sulphur—which itself became a lucrative commodity.[4] Sour-gas plants use a variety of catalytic conversion processes to remove hydrogen sulphide from the gas stream, recovering it as elemental sulphur. The remaining waste gases are incinerated to convert the remaining hydrogen sulphide to the distasteful, but less deadly, sulphur dioxide. The latter is the main compound implicated in acid rain and became the subject of major pollution battles before the ERCB.

Sulphur recovery rates from Alberta's gas plants remained low until the early 1970s. But as sulphur prices and public concern about the environment increased in the late 1960s, the ERCB issued higher sulphur-recovery guidelines to curtail emissions. The 1971 guidelines conformed to the "maximum desirable" federal emissions standards—a fact deployed repeatedly in the board and industry's defence. Stack-height requirements and stricter monitoring procedures were also instituted to ensure dispersion of sulphur dioxide plumes over larger areas.[5] Despite these changes, fewer than half of sour-gas plants recovered any sulphur at all, and public concern about the sour-gas industry grew as wells and plants materialized across the Alberta prairies and foothills. In particular, rural residents became concerned about the potential effects of sulphur dioxide on livestock health and soil fertility. They turned to a government regulatory regime that, by the early 1970s, seemed poised to respond to public concerns.

Before the 1970s, Alberta's rich oil and gas resources were administered by the Petroleum and Natural Gas Conservation Board (later the Oil and Gas Conservation Board [OGCB]), born in 1938 of efforts to stem the profligate waste of natural gas in the Turner Valley. Historian David Breen has chronicled its early development, showing how a world-class body of engineers, technical experts, and regulators exercised a broad public interest mandate in enforcing energy conservation, pricing, and export regulations.[6] The board's legislation, based on American models, was rooted firmly in the Progressive-era conservation ethos. Efficient and wise use of precious natural resources was the core of the conservation creed; legislation directed the Board to ensure the orderly and efficient development of the vast provincial oil and gas reserves.[7] During the explosive development following the 1947 Leduc oil strike, Board duties expanded to include the supervision of oil and gas exports (to ensure provincial needs came first), the resolution of industry disputes, and the conservation of sulphur from sour-gas processing.

The legislative death throes of the provincial Social Credit government yielded Alberta's modern conservation regulation framework. In 1970, the province created the Environment Conservation Authority (ECA) and, in 1971, it passed acts transforming the OGCB into the Energy Resources Conservation Board and creating Canada's first Department of Environment. For the first time, the regulatory purview encompassed pollution control and contained limited forms of public input into regulatory and environmental issues. The Environment Conservation Authority, in spite of its impressive name, constituted a government advisory body with little real power. Its original duties included holding public inquiries and issuing reports on environmental matters, and the Authority quickly became a prominent public-interest advocate.[8] However, the ECA's often pro-environment stance and its probing inquiries into energy developments quickly earned it enemies, and the government twice moved to curb the Authority's mandate during the 1970s.

Under the new provincial Department of Environment legislation, the minister was mandated to "do any acts he considers necessary to promote the improvement of the environment for the benefit of the people of Alberta and future generations."9 The department's jurisdiction included energy developments generally, and specifically the enforcement of environmental legislation and regulations. The department was ultimately responsible for approving energy projects and issuing development and emissions permits, but in doing so, it afforded minimal direct public input. Legislation also empowered the department to order and review Environmental Impact Assessments for major energy projects. Environmental impact assessment guidelines suggested mechanisms for public consultation by the development applicant, but included no provisions for formal public reviews or hearings. In any case, environmental assessments occurred infrequently: for the tens of thousands of energy projects proposed between 1971 and 1987, only eighty-two assessments were ordered.10

Perhaps the most significant legislative change in 1971 was the reorganization of the former OGCB. Though its structure and leadership remained, the new ERCB's duties now included the regulation of all energy developments, including coal, hydroelectric, and oil sands schemes. The board also assumed a significant new environmental mandate "to control pollution and ensure environment conservation in the exploration for, development and transportation of the energy resources of Alberta." The board regarded its new role as co-operating with industry and other government departments "to ensure that oil field producing practices do not lead to excessive pollution or the destruction or contamination of other natural resources."11

Considerable regulatory confusion ensued in the wake of these changes, as both the ERCB and the Department of Environment presided over environmental standards and enforcement. The "one-window" approval process advocated by the Alberta government meant all energy development approvals were routed through the ERCB, which in turn referred aspects of the applications for review to various government departments. The government bodies developed "roles" documents to delineate and co-ordinate their responsibilities, but the confusion, and public criticisms of the process, persisted into the 1980s.12

THE PUBLIC AND THE ERCB

In 1972, Environment Conservation Authority hearings provided the first-ever comprehensive airing of public concerns about sour-gas processing. The subsequent report reflected considerable public distrust of government and industry, and made dozens of recommendations to improve the regulations. It was particularly critical of government responses to public complaints:

There is evidence that employees in agencies and departments of government have in the past been less hospitable to the complaints of citizens than they should have been. In the circumstances surrounding the sulphur extraction industry where toxic and dangerous gases are being processed, a private citizen is given inadequate protection by the requirement that he prove beyond a doubt before a court of law that his complaint has its source in the gas plant.[13]

ECA chairman Dr. Walter Trost described public interactions with government and industry as "lonely," and suggested they faced a "psychological disadvantage" when opposing development.[14]

These hearings highlighted the fact that the public's ability to influence regulatory decisions was severely limited by a regulatory regime designed largely to promote the aims of resource conservation and development, rather than environmental or health protection. Indeed, the government appeared to view public involvement as a problem to be "managed" in the promotion of development goals. As this section shows, the increasingly loud demands of rural people and environmental advocates were frustrated by confusing and inadequate environmental protection bodies and the utilitarian mentality of the lead agency in resource administration, the ERCB.

Section 29 of the Energy Resources Conservation Act (1971) allowed the ERCB to hold hearings into proposed energy projects that "may directly or adversely affect the rights of a person." This power, unique among Canadian regulatory agencies, placed the board centre-stage in resource-use conflicts. As Vern Millard, ERCB chairman from 1976–1986, noted,

Under the new legislation ... (the board) had moved from an organization that was primarily devoted to dealing with technical oil and gas issues, and adjudicating between representatives of that industry ... to an organization that also had to consider developments where the interests of the public, or part of the public, could be substantially affected and were major factors in adjudicating the matter.[15]

The hearing process was a holdover from the board's industrial dispute-resolution mechanism, in which examiners consisting of board members and ERCB staff heard interventions regarding development applications. Thousands of applications and amendments were reviewed annually, but relatively few went to public hearings.[16]

The quasi-judicial process, which before the 1970s involved few people outside the industry, often concentrated on highly technical matters such as well spacing, plant design technology and well reserve capacity, issues falling squarely within the board's traditional conservation concerns. Cost-benefit analysis, a hallmark of utilitarian conservationist philosophy, dominated the board's considerations: "the ... overall objective of 'environment conservation' can largely be described as based on preservation of resources for use by man."[17] This undermined the inclusion of social and environmental impacts in decision-making because such issues were not considered strictly economically measurable. In fact, while the ERCB regarded pollution control as a "beneficial byproduct" of resource conservation, it required scientific proof of environmental damage before restricting development. Thus, the philosophy that justified natural gas and sulphur conservation joined forces with science to negate environmental concerns. Furthermore, interventions were confined to individuals or groups "directly and adversely affected" by a particular development. This, combined with the board's policy of "site-specific" consideration of individual applications, rather than hearing general concerns about oil and gas development, meant that cumulative impacts and broader environmental effects and issues remained effectively immune from challenge.

Nevertheless, faced with increasing public anxiety and frustration amid accelerating development, by the mid to late 1970s board tribunals began considering public appeals regarding the social and environmental impacts of the sour-gas industry. In the absence of other effective channels, these hearings became battlegrounds where (mostly rural) citizens sought redress for their complaints. Public participation jumped from about 10 percent of the hearings in 1970 to about 45 percent in 1977 and 1978, straining the board's traditional decision-making process.[18] The board was clearly uncomfortable in this role, as noted in its 1979 annual report:

> In general terms, the Board considers its jurisdiction encompasses
> matters of the environment and matters of the public interest, as well as
> the more clearly recognized matters of conservation and orderly
> development. It is, however, difficult to categorize in the absence of a
> specific case, just how far the Board is authorized to go in actually
> determining environmental and public interest matters. In the past, the
> Board has taken the position that it has the authority to consider such
> matters in a general sense, that is, whether such matters are so great
> that they should preclude a project from proceeding. If, however, the

Board decides the project should proceed, its jurisdiction does not extend to resolving those environmental or public interest concerns beyond conditioning the manner in which the project is developed.[19]

While the ERCB may have addressed non-technical concerns with reticence, by the end of the 1970s it had come to consider these interventions as legitimate and, indeed, sufficient expressions of public health and environmental concerns. Descriptions of public participation in Board literature intrinsically link public participation with environmental considerations. The acrimonious 1978 Cold Lake oil development hearings were an early participatory watershed: in their wake, the Board reviewed and altered its hearing process in an attempt to incorporate public concerns, and published pamphlets to help interveners participate in technical aspects of the Board's hearing process.[20] The ERCB also developed a local-intervener funding policy, whereby some local participants could recover their intervention costs. Environmental advocacy organizations were occasionally allowed to appear before the board to represent wilderness or recreational interests. However, citizens remained outside standard-setting processes such as the establishment of Alberta's new sulphur recovery guidelines in 1980, which were not open to public input.[21]

In this period of rapid oil and gas industry expansion, rural citizens discovered the somewhat arcane proceedings of the ERCB as their only outlet for concern and frustration. As observers lamented in 1980, "there is little other formal opportunity for public involvement in environmental regulation processes in Alberta."[22] The technically complex and legalistic ERCB hearings, others noted, put ordinary citizens at a disadvantage: "This, coupled with the concerns that they may have about the application may result in an intervener presenting a highly excited and emotional case involving matters outside the purview of the hearing and outside the Board's jurisdiction."[23] In the early 1980s, however, the rising tide of public environmental concern, as well as high-profile inquiries into the industry prompted by Zahava Hanen and other rural citizens, served to challenge regulatory assumptions and precipitated further reforms to the decision-making process.

THE RANCHER AND THE REGULATORS

As noted in the introduction, Zahava Hanen's fight was not a typical ERCB case. Although her dispute with Imperial Oil and the ERCB spanned nearly twenty years, I will highlight her involvement and impact as a local intervener and concerned citizen in ERCB hearing processes in 1981–2 and 1984. Hanen purchased the 2,867-acre Rumsey Ranch in the Turner Valley area near Millarville in the early 1970s, where she supervised a breeding-stock cattle operation. The land and grazing lease she owned surrounded almost entirely the Quirk Creek sour-gas plant, operated by Esso Resources Canada Ltd., a subsidiary of Imperial Oil Ltd., in turn owned by the American multinational oil company Exxon. In 1974, Esso applied to drill a well on her property, an action permitted under the provincial surface rights legislation. Hanen opposed the development on the grounds that the well construction and operation would have a detrimental effect on the value of her ranch. After she appealed to the Surface Rights Board and the ERCB, an amended application was approved. For the property incursion, Hanen won monetary compensation, which was subsequently increased by an Alberta appeal court.[24]

In April 1976, concern over gas-plant operations and well development brought area landowners to a special meeting chaired by the ECA's Walter Trost and attended by ERCB, Department of Environment, and plant personnel. The company's right of access remained the most prominent issue, Trost reported, as landowners felt legislation offered them inadequate protection from encroaching development. The meeting resulted in an agreement between the parties to "co-operate more fully in future to identify and solve their problems."[25] Subsequently, as Hanen herself discovered evidence of pollution on her ranch, she undertook an independent study to determine what effect plant discharges were having. In particular, polluted water from the plant continued to infiltrate the ranch land surrounding the plant. In 1981, Hanen called on then-environment minister J.S. Cookson to hold an inquiry into the operations of the gas plant, but was refused on the grounds that Esso seemed inclined to rectify pollution problems as they were reported.[26]

Later that year, Hanen received an opportunity to vent her frustration and concern, as the ERCB received a major Quirk Creek plant expansion application. The Esso application was made in conjunction with several proposals by Shell Canada Resources Ltd.[27] The plans proposed the construction of a pipeline from Shell's Moose Mountain and Whiskey Creek gas fields to the Quirk Creek plant for processing. In addition, Shell proposed a modernization of its Jumping Pound plant to include "deep cut" refining facilities, which would allow it to recover valuable natural gas liquids (used in the burgeoning petrochemical industry) from some Quirk Creek gas. The applications were attractive from a development standpoint because they extended the life of the relatively modern Quirk Creek plant, proposed no new plant, and furthered the "unitization" of processing, in which companies co-operated in developing, processing, and delivering natural gas and related products. Since the applications amended existing approvals, no environmental impact assessment was ordered, though the applications contained some environmental impact information.

For its time, Hanen's strategy in opposing the expansion was unique and effective. Rather than relying on emotional and scientifically unsubstantiated claims, she employed two competent lawyers, who drafted her interventions and represented her at the hearings. At Hanen's invitation, local farmers, environmentalists, and engineers submitted statements and testified before the board as the hearings stretched over months. Public advocate and ECA member Dr. Martha Kostuch appeared on Hanen's behalf, as did Andy Russell, a prominent Alberta environmentalist who resided at Rumsey Ranch and intervened representing the Canadian Wildlife Federation.[28] Hanen's intervention and her witnesses' testimony presented a comprehensive argument on environmental, technical, and economic grounds.

Citing a 1972 ECA report on gas processing [noted above], Hanen alleged that damage to crops, soil, livestock, and human health came from sulphur dioxide and other plant effluents. Three agricultural researchers also drew attention to the potential and documented long-term effects of sulphur dioxide deposition on soils. One scientist noted that the troubling incidence of selenium-deficiency disease in Alberta cattle may be related to gas-plant emissions, though scientific research had yet to prove a conclusive link. Another Alberta rancher testified to crop production damage on his farm that was bookended by two plants within three miles, saying company offers of compensation constituted recognition of significant adverse effects.

While the companies cited evidence that their plants conformed to ambient air standards, the interveners pointed to the poor enforcement by Alberta Environment, which rendered existing standards useless. In 1980 alone, Hanen's deposition noted, province-wide stack violations and ambient air standard violations numbered 1,135 and 1,104 respectively—none of which were prosecuted. One Hanen intervener, engineer E.L. Jones, pointed out that the simple existence of standards did not ensure adherence: "The 'co-operative' nature of the enforcement while fine for good relations does not give proper incentive to oil companies to follow the standards," he submitted.[29] Hanen's team also highlighted the fact that emissions monitoring focussed only on *known* major pollutants such as sulphur dioxide and nitrogen oxides, while ignoring the potential effects of trace heavy metals and carcinogens from stack emissions.

Finally, Hanen challenged the ERCB orthodoxy that pollution control was only viable where it was demonstrably economical. Using cost-benefit analysis, the ERCB standard of "best practical technology" was generally used to assess appropriate sulphur-recovery levels. For instance, tail-gas cleanup units processed waste gas before incineration, yielding 100 percent theoretical sulphur recovery, but were considered too costly for widespread use (although one was already in use at the Shell Waterton plant). Referring to the Board's legislative mandate, Hanen urged that the ERCB must consider zero emissions as a public interest goal, "even in the event (which is not the case) that the recovery of 100% sulphur or injection of gases resulting from the production of sour gas were not economical."[30]

The 1981–82 hearings were a partial success for Hanen. While the board rejected the development schemes, its decision was based not on the Hanen intervention; rather, the pipeline project was suspended for public safety reasons related to a proposed nearby recreational development, and the other applications were also nullified as a result. In fact, the Board decision on Moose Mountain and Whiskey Creek dismissed Andy Russell's concerns about wildlife as undocumented and E.L. Jones' suggested pipeline alternatives as unfeasible.[31]

However, the force of the Hanen intervention prompted the ERCB to launch an unprecedented separate study into her concerns, published in 1982. Board staff completed the study without further public input, despite calls for a public inquiry.[32] In the report, the Board itemized Hanen's concerns, including acid deposition, the presence of trace chemicals and other pollutants, lack of enforcement, use of technology, and the board's public-interest responsibility. Reticent to admit the presence of pollutants but noting the deficient scientific knowledge, the Board referred most of the pollution issues to further study. It refused, however, to impose more stringent guidelines in the interim. The Board bridled at the testimony on behalf of Hanen by federal acid-rain sub-committee member and former Speaker of the House of Commons John Fraser, who had outlined the federal strategies to combat acid rain. The 1981 acid rain sub-committee report, *Still Waters—The Chilling Reality of Acid Rain*, called for a cap on acid-forming emissions until the year 2000.[33] The ERCB found the cap unreasonable and even "discriminatory against Alberta" in light of the rapidly expanding industry. The adoption of Canada's strictest ambient air standards, as well as the delinquency of other provinces, was also used to justify the Board's rejection of the cap.

The report also refuted Hanen's challenge to cost-benefit analysis in favour of enhanced environmental protection. It rejected the mandated use of "best available technology" without regard to economics, saying that incremental sulphur recovery beyond the 96 to 99 percent already recovered would barely cover the cost of operating a tail-gas cleanup unit, much less the capital expenditure of installation. These expenses were "only justified where specific circumstances provide compelling reasons."[34] In addressing public access, the board reiterated its 1972 call on operators to improve their relations with local residents to improve the perception of the industry. Testimony regarding social and environmental impacts, the board maintained, remained relevant only in the context of particular applications. Such impacts were therefore "local" and, in the context of Quirk Creek, remained insufficiently proven.

In 1983, the Esso and Shell scheme was reconsidered after the latter revised its pipeline plans. The applications were revisited in a changed atmosphere, however. The *Still Waters* report had stirred national fears of dead lakes and deteriorating forests due to acid rain. Albertans' own anxiety about sour gas soared after the 1982 "blowout," or wellhead rupture at the Lodgepole well site near Drayton Valley, which killed two workers and spewed tonnes of toxic hydrogen sulphide into the atmosphere. The ERCB Lodgepole inquiry, which examined the public health and industrial safety aspects of the incident, included significant public input and dramatized the issue of public safety and resource extraction.[35]

An internal risk assessment conducted by Shell changed the Board's opinion of the pipeline application in late 1983, and that approval paved the way for the application to expand Quirk Creek processing capacity. However, Quirk Creek plant operations had not improved significantly in the intervening years, and Hanen opposed the development. Again, Hanen took the offensive at the second Quirk Creek hearings, hiring a research company to study the feasibility of enhanced sulphur recovery at the plant. Esso argued that it already agreed to a sulphur recovery level higher than that required of existing plants under the 1980 guidelines, and claimed still higher recovery would mean installing an expensive tail-gas cleanup unit. Such a move would be uneconomic, the company asserted, and based on scant evidence of deleterious environmental effect. The ERCB decision reflected lessons learned from earlier experiences with Hanen. The Quirk Creek expansion was approved, but with a markedly higher sulphur recovery rate of no less than 97.2 percent, which necessitated substantial plant upgrading including a tail-gas cleanup unit. In recognizing her need to gather technical and economic data to challenge the Esso application, the Board awarded Hanen substantial local-intervener costs.[36] Yet the Board remained careful not to consider claims of local environmental impacts, which it considered as yet unfounded.

The Hanen decisions were greeted by the interveners and the press as victories against unfettered industrial development. The *Calgary Herald* reported the hearings turned into "a complete inquiry into the sour gas industry."[37] Hanen's own reactions were mixed. While Hanen publicly greeted the decision as a positive step, she echoed the loneliness of opposing entrenched bureaucracy and industry noted by Trost a decade earlier. But she also felt that her intervention had transcended parochial concerns to publicize province-wide pollution issues.[38] By effectively placing the onus for pollution justification and control back on the protagonists of development, Hanen thwarted regulators' long-time strategy of ignoring problems and hiding behind standards.

OPENING THE DOOR: PUBLIC INVOLVEMENT AFTER HANEN

Sour-gas processing underwent increased scrutiny concurrent with and closely following the Hanen case. Individuals and groups appeared before the Board questioning development and citing growing evidence of pollution.[39] Public-participation processes at ERCB hearings were reviewed and often criticized for practices dating from the legislation's inception and identified a decade earlier. At the same time, the Board moved to defuse the increasingly confrontational atmosphere of its hearings, launching new public consultation policies—which Hanen also tested.

Albertans' interest in regulatory activities blossomed in the early 1980s. An ECA public-opinion survey in 1981 showed nearly 60 percent of Albertans believed environmental regulations were not strict enough. Still more thought regulators lacked the teeth to enforce standards. Rural inhabitants overwhelmingly fingered sulphur and other chemical emissions as the number-one environmental problem. The ECA also conducted a North American regulatory standards review in 1982 and launched a study (uncompleted) into the ERCB's role in environmental regulation.[40] But the ECA was undermined not only by the government, but through the apparent rivalry between itself, the ERCB, and the Department of Environment. After spending most of the 1980s developing an Alberta Conservation Strategy, the ECA was reorganized and effectively neutralized as a public-interest body by decade's end. As a prominent

ECA member noted, "The [renamed] Environment Council ended up with legislation which destroyed it and made it nothing more than a phony shell of its former self."[41]

In achieving effective participation, as in fighting pollution, the public itself pioneered. Community groups formed to examine development projects, including those in Cold Lake and Claresholm. Oil companies themselves played a role in these groups; Esso helped create and direct the Cold Lake group before citizen members took the reins.[42] Quirk Creek saw a similar development, as the stir caused by the 1981–82 hearings led to Esso's formation of the Quirk Creek Community Committee in 1983.[43] This committee's meetings and activities, however, reflected substantial company control, and Hanen rejected it as an effective way of pressuring the industry for tighter controls. By contrast, other community groups exhibited considerable independence, bringing concerns about local development before the ERCB and industry, and forcing legitimate public participation into development planning.[44] Another independent group helping rural residents was the Office of the Farmer's Advocate, established in 1973. The office fielded thousands of complaints annually, mostly regarding surface-rights issues.[45]

The ERCB responded with slow reforms to public input and pollution policies during the 1980s. At the start of the decade, the board and Alberta Environment signed an "accord" on Environmental Impact Assessments, which made ordering assessments the joint responsibility of the ERCB chairman and the Deputy Minister of Environment. Public and governmental review of the assessment was still contained to ERCB hearings, however, and critics still found the process frustrated public input at the formative stage. Assessment guidelines encouraged public participation, but in a fashion chosen and executed by the project proponent. Public involvement finally entered the standard-setting realm when the board and Alberta Environment began a review of sulphur-recovery guidelines in 1985. A task force solicited public input, though the public did not have a voice in the final decision.[46]

The ERCB approach to public health, social, and environmental issues softened in this period. In 1984, Board chairman Vern Millard noted the expanding list of issues tackled at Board hearings, including development alternatives, health issues and visual impacts, and denied the Board was "energy-development prone." That same year, he warned an industry gathering that companies needed to take public concerns seriously at Board hearings.[47] Reflecting its new role as a land-use co-ordinator between planners, industry, and landowners, the Board's annual reports began to include public-interest information alongside technical data. The board published a series of information bulletins called *Enerfax*, which outlined its role in development and the public role in board activities.[48] When Gerry DeSorcy replaced Millard as ERCB chairman in 1986, changes accelerated. The ERCB launched a sour-gas media campaign, and used more of its annual report to promote public participation. Public concerns "prompted a greater focus by the Board to search for alternatives to the public hearing process to solve some of the disputes," noted DeSorcy.[49] The focus shifted from the confrontational hearing process to "stakeholder" committees, in which the Board played the role of honest broker. For instance, several companies took the initiative in approaching communities before development, which then proceeded far more smoothly.

Typical of the Board's new "mediation" approach was its handling of the 1986 Gulf Canada application to pipe gas to Quirk Creek, which once again drew the ire of Zahava Hanen. Esso withdrew its initial application to process Gulf gas after Hanen submitted evidence of groundwater contamination at her ranch. Other Millarville community members also expressed concern. However, once Gulf and Esso amended their applications to appease public concerns, the Board granted its approval without a public hearing. The incident was lauded by the Board as an example of consensual decision-making.[50] To handle Hanen's ongoing concerns with Quirk Creek plant operations, the Board helped create the Quirk Creek Action Plan. The plan called for the company to undertake modifications to minimize operational problems and environmental effects, and urged improved communication with local residents. Hanen's pressure on the ERCB and Esso continued, albeit outside the public forums that she found inadequate, which resulted in significant modifications to plant operations and higher sulphur-recovery guidelines.

In 1989, the ERCB and Alberta Environment announced broad public-consultation guidelines for industry. Aimed at improving community relations between operators and the public, it called on both sides to undertake long-term consultation and co-operative efforts.[51] Board strategies to reduce confrontation appeared to work, reducing the number of hearings from 70 in 1982 to only 10 in 1992. Its central role in regulation was reconfirmed in the 1993 Alberta Environment Protection and Enhancement Act. This preserved the Board as the "one window" for development applications, while the renamed Alberta Environmental Protection branch continued to conduct environmental assessments and development reviews.[52] However, the effectiveness of much of this work would be diminished by subsequent changes.

As noted above, the Hanen case jump-started research efforts—demanded by the ECA in the early 1970s—into acid deposition and other long-term effects of gas-plant operations. But even though research increased in the 1980s, an adequate picture of long-term pollution effects remained elusive.[53] Meanwhile, public and scientific concern about the long-term effects of sulphur emissions remained, and still does.[54] In 1990, the board unveiled a ten-volume report on public safety and sour gas, and launched an advisory committee on the issue, which reported in 1994. Though a step forward in terms of public consultation, the 1994 report focussed on risk management and issues related to blowouts or other disasters. As the report itself noted, "public interest in the effects of long-term regular exposure to emissions from sour gas facilities appears to be higher than public interest in the topic of accidental releases."[55] Despite 30 years of public outcry, this concern has yet to be seriously addressed.

EPILOGUE: RENEWED CONFLICT

If, as has been suggested, the right of citizens to participate in decisions regarding development and the environment is an issue of democratic self-determination, then regulatory histories take on revolutionary overtones.[56] Participation processes in Alberta began in the early 1970s with the recognition that citizens have legitimate interests in the development of provincial resources. The creation of the Environment Conservation Authority and Department of Environment, and the overhaul of the ERCB, enshrined this interest in legislation and outlined a decent framework for public involvement at the local and policy-formulation levels. But clearly, this framework dissolved with the neutralization of the ECA. The resulting pressure on the ERCB to account for non-technical concerns about development strained its primarily technical expertise. Social and environmental concerns eluded the Board precisely because of their subjective, even emotional, nature. Citizens brought different experiences, assumptions, and values to development hearings than did the technocratic ERCB staff. The Board failed to comprehend that even its own cost-benefit analysis model of decision-making "involves a large measure of judgement and … must ultimately be characterized as political."[57]

Overall, the Alberta experience illustrates the difficulty of using traditional legal and policy systems to regulate the environment. The scientific uncertainty surrounding environmental impacts, the difficulty of measuring non-economic effects, and the social values of public health issues make conservation policy problematic for governments often more interested in promoting industrial development. Although significant changes began to take hold in the 1980s, public pressure, rather than policy-makers or regulators, was the driving force behind this change. Rural citizens such as Hanen showed considerable resourcefulness in overcoming technical and financial obstacles to have their concerns recognized. In challenging the decision-making priorities of regulators, citizens, particularly rural agriculturalists, exploded the compact between industry and government, and, by the late 1980s, once again seemed poised to take their place in overseeing development and protecting the environment. After continuing problems with pollution, Hanen herself eventually settled out of court with Esso in 1993, and relocated to another ranch.[58]

The Alberta government bias in favour of development was reasserted in the 1990s. Both environmental regulation and citizen participation would fall victim to the politics of deregulation and fiscal restraint under the Klein government. Under a 1994 streamlining plan, the ERCB and the (much smaller) Public Utilities Board merged and were renamed the Alberta Energy and Utilities Board. The new body maintained, on paper, most of the same functions as the former ERCB.[59] However, its capacity to fulfil these functions was seriously undermined by cutbacks and government policies that encouraged exploration and production activities (producing an explosion of small, independent companies), while simultaneously sanctioning a shift towards industry self-regulation. As a recent report by the Pembina Institute remarks, "during the period [1992–1998] that major changes were occurring in the oil and gas industry, the key provincial body responsible for regulating this industry [the AEUB] experienced substantial reductions in its financial and staffing resources."[60] In these circumstances, it is not surprising that environmental problems—and the familiar tensions around them—have re-appeared.

Indeed, recent controversies over development in Sundre, Pincher Creek, Rimbey, Lloydminster, and even Calgary provide a lamentable epilogue to the 23 years of ERCB history.[61] Farmers complain that their livestock are suffering, their throats are sore, and companies responsible for wells do not return their calls; yet they often find that their complaints are still not taken seriously. Instead, they are confronted with inadequate forums for public concerns about environmental and public health impacts, the denial of pollution by industry, and equivocation by regulatory bodies. Echoing Walter Trost's concerns of the early 1970s, the same Pembina Institute report cited above referred to the AEUB hearing processes as "harrowing." In these circumstances, the increasing anecdotal and scientific evidence of pollution, together with reduced opportunities for public input, have combined to undermine public confidence in regulators. This weakening of the regulatory regime has made more rural residents into activists, and the tradition of cantankerous rural advocacy represented by Hanen has direct echoes in present controversies, as farmers and communities continue to challenge a government-industry alliance that refuses to admit meaningful public participation into the development process. Unless this trend is again reversed, rural citizens may continue to resort to confrontational legalistic (or even extra-legal) strategies.

Farmers in Alberta are not fools; nor is the government. Each realizes that effective public forums on development provide opportunities for social, economic, and ecological resistance that the government and industry, with their neo-liberal development objectives, can ill afford to brook. Combined with the rapidly changing social and economic context faced by rural Albertans (and, indeed, Canadians), the regulatory changes of the 1990s constitute mortal threats to the self-determination and economic fortunes of agriculturalists. But even as the dervishes of development whirl deeper into the rural and wilderness spaces, the sources of effective resistance are being rediscovered on the familiar grounds of farms, ranches, and homesteads. The task remains to rebuild effective public-input mechanisms and restore democracy to development.

Notes

1   The individual cases of rural landowners in conflict with resource developers have become too numerous to mention. A useful overview of the sour-gas controversy in the 1990s is provided in Thomas Marr-Laing and Chris Severson-Baker, *Beyond Eco-terrorism: The Deeper Issues Affecting Alberta's Oilpatch* (Drayton Valley, AB: Pembina Institute for Appropriate Development, 1999). Some recent media coverage of Ludwig and the issue in general includes several articles by journalist Andrew Nikiforuk: "Pollution: Alberta's dirty secret no longer," *Globe and Mail* (16 July 1999); "It makes them sick," *Canadian Business* 72:2 (12 February 1999), 46–51; "Holy Terror," *Saturday Night* (February 1999), 51–58; and "Welcome to Alberta where seldom is heard a conservationist's word," *Outdoor Canada* 26:8 (Winter 1998), 22–27. On the conflict between resources and agriculture, see Roger Epp, "Alberta faces delicate balancing act between oil and public health issues," *Edmonton Journal* (3 March 1999), A13; Chris Varcoe, "Energy board task force tackles oilpatch disputes," *Edmonton Journal* (3 March 1999), F6; Andrea Maynard, "Second study links poor cattle health to sour gas leak," *Western Producer* (14 January 1999), 56; Alanna Mitchell, "Livestock may suffer, oil patch study finds," *Globe and Mail* (7 October 1998), A5A; Alanna Mitchell, "Cows, people sick; gas flares blamed," *Globe and Mail* (23 December 1996), A1, A6.

2   Carleton University History Collaborative, "Remembering Rumsey Ranch: A Case Study of the Pollution of a Cattle Ranch in the Alberta Foothills," unpublished study presented to the London Conference on Canadian Studies, November 1996. This paper formed the first phase of the Rumsey Ranch Project, co-ordinated by Prof. B.C. Bickerton at Carleton University. The paper you are reading emerged from a background study during a later phase. An earlier version was presented to the British Association for

Canadian Studies Conference, University of Wales, in March 1997. The author wishes to thank Carman Bickerton, Catherine Kiszkiel, and the Carleton History Collaborative. This paper has benefitted from suggestions by David Breen, David Whitson, and Roger Epp. Any errors and omissions are, of course, my own.

3   Natural gas was originally considered a waste byproduct of oil production, as gas was often found in solution with oil. On the early industry, see Fred Stenson, *Waste to Wealth: A History of Gas Processing in Canada* (Calgary: Gas Processors Association, 1985).

4   Sulphur conservation began in 1952 at Shell Canada's Jumping Pound sour gas plant west of Calgary and the Madison plant in the Turner Valley. Ibid., 191–2, 283–4. See also Bonar A. (Sandy) Gow, "Early Developments in the Canadian Gas Processing Industry: The Turner Valley Example," *Prairie Forum* 23:7 (1998), 247–65, for an overview of the development of gas processing technology.

5   ERCB, *Status of Environment Protection in the Alberta Energy Resource Industries* (Calgary: ERCB, 1972), 2.6.

6   David Breen, *Alberta's Petroleum Industry and the Conservation Board* (Edmonton: ERCB, 1993).

7   John Richards and Larry Pratt, *Prairie Capitalism: Power and Influence in the New West* (Toronto: McClelland and Stewart, 1979), 56 and Breen, 541. The intellectual roots of conservationism in North America are explored in Clayton R. Koppes, "Efficiency, Equity and Esthetics: Shifting themes in American conservation" in Donald Worster, ed. *The Ends of the Earth: Perspectives on modern environmental history* (New York: Cambridge University Press, 1988), 230–251; Samuel P. Hays, *Conservation and the Gospel of Efficiency: The Progressive Conservation Movement, 1890–1920* (Cambridge, Mass.: Harvard University Press, 1959); and Roderick Nash, *The American Environment: Readings in the History of Conservation* (Reading, Mass., Addison-Wesley, 1968).

8   P.S. Elder, "The Participatory Environment in Alberta" in P.S. Elder, ed., *Environmental Management and Public Participation* (Calgary: Canadian Environmental Law Research Foundation, 1975), 107–8. See also ECA, *Second Annual Report* (Edmonton: ECA, 1972). The ECA published two "First Annual Reports," one in 1971 and one in 1972, then numbered annual reports after that. Hereafter, the reports will be referred to as ECA, Annual Report and year.

9   Section 7 of Act, quoted in Donna Tingley, "Alberta Environmental Impact Assessment Process" in *Seminar on the Regulation of Environmental Impacts of Energy Projects* (Calgary: Environmental Law Centre, 1987), 3.

10 Elder, 123; Alberta, *Environmental Impact Assessment Guidelines* (Edmonton: Alberta Environment, 1985), 7; Tingley, 2.

11 ERCB, *Conservation in Alberta—1970* (Calgary: ERCB, 1971), 3. This annual report publication was renamed twice during this period—to *Alberta Energy* in 1983 and then *Energy Alberta* in 1985. Hereafter, the publication will be referred to as ERCB, Annual Report, and year. See also ERCB, Annual Report (1970), 5.

12 On the "roles documents," see ERCB, Annual Report (1971), 2. Critical appraisals included: Elder, 124–125; Constance D. Hunt and Alistair R. Lucas, *Environmental Regulation. Its Impact on Major Oil and Gas Projects: Oil sands and Arctic* (Calgary: Canadian Institute of Resources Law, 1980), 102–3; ECA, Annual Report (1971), 46–47.

13 ECA, Annual Report (1971), 34. R.F. Klemm, *Environmental Effects of the Operation of Sulphur Extraction Gas Plants* (Edmonton: ECA, 1972) provided a scientific prospectus for the hearings.

14 ECA, Annual Report (1972), 23–24.

15 Vern Millard, "The Public, the energy industry and the ERCB" in *Journal of Canadian Petroleum Technology* 23:5 (October 1984), 89.

16 Generally, hearings were held on fewer than 10 percent of applications, and fewer still contained public involvement. For instance, in 1984, when the ERCB handled about 12,700 applications for new energy facilities, only 68 public hearings were held. ERCB, Annual Report (1984), 32–33.

17 Hunt and Lucas, 146. The cost-benefit creed is captured in a 1971 review of regulatory legislation in the US, which noted that "in practice, damages have been tolerated if they were not immediately and obviously costly to economic groups—farmers, industrialists, sportsman and municipalities, for instance." Stephen L. McDonald, *Petroleum Conservation in the U.S.: An economic analysis* (Baltimore: Johns Hopkins University Press, 1971), 148.

18 ERCB, Annual Report (1985), 34.

19 ERCB, Annual Report (1979), 4.

20 The Cold Lake experiment in public participation is documented in Brian Plesuk, *The Only Game in Town: Public involvement in Cold Lake* (Edmonton: Alberta Environment, July 1981). See also ERCB, Annual Report (1979).

21 Task Force on Sulphur Recovery Guidelines, *Sulphur Recovery at Alberta Gas Plants: Phase I of a review of the guidelines* (Calgary: ERCB and Alberta Environment, September 1986), 2–3.

22 Hunt and Lucas, 110.

23 M.J. Bruni and K.F. Miller, "Practice and Procedure Before the Energy Resources Conservation Board," *Alberta Law Review* 20:1 (1982), 99.

24 Zahava Hanen Collection, Box 4, File F, Document 87, and 4.F.26. The Hanen papers, consisting of letters, reports, transcripts, maps, and miscellany regarding Hanen's pollution battles, were delivered to Carleton University in 1995 and became the subject of the Rumsey Ranch Project (see note 3). They have since been scanned and placed on a two-CD-ROM archive entitled *Remembering Rumsey Ranch* as a pilot project for research purposes. The CD-ROM has yet to be finalized for general release and the papers are in process for deposit at Carleton. The following account is largely a summary based on the documents: where documents are explicitly quoted, the collection shall be referred to as Hanen Collection, and box, file, and document number, corresponding to the inventory.

25 ECA, Annual Report (1976), 241. While her papers do not indicate if she personally attended the meeting, by at least 1978, Hanen was personally in contact with Trost (Hanen Collection, 4.F.52)

26 Hanen Collection, 8.B.16, 16.B.1

27 Aspects of the applications are dealt with in Hanen Collection, 7.B.1–6, 8.A.14, 8.C.4, 10.D.5.

28 ERCB, *Shell Proposed Moose and Whiskey Pipelines and Related Facilities*, Report 82–E (Calgary: ERCB, April 1982), appendix; Hanen Collection, 14.A.28

29 Hanen Collection, 11.B.7

30 Hanen Collection, 11.B.6

31 For these aspects of the decision, see ERCB, *Shell Proposed Moose and Whiskey Pipelines and Related Facilities*, 18, 25–26, 34, 43.

32 Shelley N. Phillips and Gale E. Pretash, "Acid-causing emission standards in Alberta: The standard-setting process, enforcement and forums," *Alberta Law Review* 23:1 (1985), 20–21.

33 Canada, Standing Committee on Fisheries and Forestry, Subcommittee on Acid Rain, *Still Waters—The Chilling Reality of Acid Rain* (Ottawa: Queen's Printer, 1981).

34 ERCB, *Sour Gas Processing in Alberta*, 5.4.1.

35 Peter McKenzie-Brown, Gordon Jaremko, and David Finch, *The Great Oil Age: The petroleum industry in Canada* (Calgary: Detselig Ent., 1993), 153. See also ERCB, Annual Report (1984).

36 ERCB, *Zahava Hanen and Rumsey Ranches' Request for Local Interveners' Costs RE: Esso Quirk Creek Gas Plant*, Report D84–18 (Calgary: ERCB, July 1984), 3.

37 See news clippings in Hanen Collection, 16.E.6, 16.E.7, 16.E.9 Also, "Quirk Creek (Esso sour gas) controversy continues," *Calgary Herald* (Jan. 17, 1984), F12; and "Full hearing (on sour gas development) needed," Editorial, *Calgary Herald* (Jan. 19, 1984), A4.

38 Hanen Collection, 8.C.4, 13.B.14

39 Relevant decisions include E81–9 *Panther Resources Processing Plant (near Camrose)*; D83–13 *Canadian Occidental Petroleum Ltd. Okotoks Gas Processing Plant (High River and Okotoks)*; D82–39 *Amoco Canada Petroleum Company Ltd. Approval of a Solution Gas Processing Plant St. Albert Area*; E83–20 *Examiners Report on Application by Consolidated Pipelines Co. 1983 (Gas Processing Plant Claresholm Field)*.

40 ECA, Annual Report (1981), 11–15; ECA, Annual Report (1983), 112.

41 Elder, 12. On government actions to rein in the ECA, see E.S. Hunter, ed., *The Roots of Public Empowerment: A History of the Public Advisory Committee to the Environment Conservation Authority* (Edmonton: ECA, 1993), 13; Phillips and Pretash, 19.

42 Plesuk, 33.

43 Hanen Collection, 4.D.1

44 ERCB, *Public Meeting to Consider Concerns Regarding an Uncontrolled Flow of Sour Gas and the Operation of a Sour Gas Plant in the Claresholm Area*, Report 84–B (Calgary: ERCB, 1984). This meeting was instigated by the East Claresholm Clean Air Association. Similar community groups arose to address concerns about sour gas in Caroline in 1986 and Northeast Calgary in 1991.

45 Office of the Farmer's Advocate, *Annual Report* (Edmonton: Office of the Farmer's Advocate, 1974–1995), *passim*. Research on the Office and some ERCB material provided by PearlAnn Reichwein to Carleton History Collaborative.

46 Task Force on Sulphur Recovery Guidelines, Appendix A.

47 Vern Millard, "The Technical and Other Aspects of Decisions of the Energy Resources Conservation Board" in *Decision-making: The role of environmental information*, proceedings of a seminar of the Canadian Society of Environmental Biologists, Alberta Chapter, May 17, 1984 (Edmonton: CSEB, 1984), 19, 20; Millard, "The Public, the energy industry and the ERCB," 91.

48 ERCB, *Enerfax: Information on the Development of Alberta's Energy Resources* (information pamphlet) (Calgary: ERCB, 1985).

49 ERCB, Annual Report (1986), 37; ERCB, Annual Report (1988), 7.

50 Hanen Collection, 2.E.33; ERCB, Annual Report (1986), 18.

51 ERCB and Alberta Environment, *Public Involvement in the Development of Energy Resources*, Information Letter IL 89–4 (Calgary and Edmonton: ERCB and AE, June 1989), Section 5.

52 ERCB, Annual Report (1992), 3; ERCB, Annual Report (1993), 26. In addition, the province created the Alberta Clean Air Strategic Alliance consultation body out of its 1991 Clean Air Strategy, the development of which contained public input.

53 Some of these reports included: Kimberly Sanderson, *Acid-forming Emissions: Transportation and Effects* (Edmonton: ECA, March 1984), 39; A.H. Legge, *The Present and Potential Effects of Acidic and Acidifying Air Pollutants on Alberta's Environment* (Calgary: Kananaskis Centre for Environmental Research and the Acid Deposition Research Project, 1988).

54 For a roundup of recent scientific studies, see Marr-Laing and Seversen-Baker, Section B; Alberta Environmental Centre, *Cattle and the Oil and Gas Industry in Alberta: A literature review with recommendations for environmental management* (Calgary: Alberta Cattle Commission, July 1996).

55 Advisory Committee to the ERCB, Reviewing Public Safety and Sour Gas, *Report and Recommendations to the ERCB on Public Safety and Sour Gas* (Calgary: ERCB, February 1994), 2.5

56 Elder, 106.

57 Hunt and Lucas, 144; Elder, 104.

58 Her legacy at Rumsey Ranch remains, however, as the company, the conservation board, and scientists set up a Groundwater Risk Assessment Team, later reformed as the Restoration Action Committee, in 1992 to tackle the problem of remedying the damage done to groundwater, soil and air quality at the ranch. Hanen Collection, 2.F.16, 2.F.20, 2.F.47, 2.F.110

59 ERCB, Annual Report (1994), 4–5.

60 Advisory Committee to the ERCB, Reviewing Public Safety and Sour Gas, ii; Marr-Laing and Severson-Baker, 3, 17. As an illustration of the declining public input into development, the Pembina report noted that in 1997, only 72 hearings were conducted on 19,551 development applications, and of those, only 11 featured citizen interventions.

61 See note 2, as well as David Staples, "In gas fight, score one for common sense," *Edmonton Journal* (2 January 2000), E10 [Rimbey]; "Outdated gas plants among worst polluters," *Canadian Press Newswire* (1 October 1999) [Rimbey]; Eva Ferguson, "Pollution killed cattle, judge rules," *Edmonton Journal* (9 July 1999), A5 [Olds]; Tony Seskus, "Gas plant's sulphur emissions anger Rimbey-area landowners," *Edmonton Journal* (13 June 1999); "Shell admits sulphur plant had problems initially," *Canadian Press Newswire* (19 June 1997) [Caroline]. Ian Urquhart, ed., *Assault on the Rockies: Environmental Controversies in Alberta* (Edmonton: Rowan, 1998) chronicles related development controversies on the Eastern Slopes of the mountains.

The Political De-skilling
of Rural Communities

Roger Epp

The global economy does not exist to help the
communities and localities of the globe. It exists to
siphon the wealth of those communities and places
into a few bank accounts. To this economy,
democracy and the values of the religious
traditions mean absolutely nothing.
—*Wendell Berry,* Sex, Economy, Freedom & Community

I know we all felt a little sad when the giant
backhoe toppled the last elevator—like we had all
lost something special. What will be the next thing
to go? Our school, or maybe just a portion of it?
As we head towards the next millennium we will all
have to cope with change—some for the better—
some for the worse. Is bigger better? I'm not sure.
—*Carol Huebner, Hay Lakes correspondent,*
The Camrose Canadian, *16 April 1997*

Schools and elevators matter in rural Alberta. They have mattered for a long time, much more than if they were merely facilities for the delivery of curriculum and grain. Schools and elevators have been central to traditions of local governance and co-operative enterprise. In different ways they have served as meeting places and as measures of a community's prospects. Their disappearance from the landscape in waves of efficiency-driven consolidation evokes deep fears of obsolescence in turn. For that reason, resistance to school closures, at least, is one of the few causes around which collective political action still happens in rural communities—difficult as it is to sustain where student numbers have declined and amalgamated boards stretch budgets over vast districts.

Rural Alberta is already filled with prophetic reminders of once-thriving settler communities. In the countryside outside of Camrose, not untypically, two very different kinds of monuments are particularly prominent. The first is small but proliferate. It is the plaque, affixed to a fence or planted just outside the fence-line facing the road, naming the one-room school that once stood on that spot. The second is a new, concrete-pillared, "world-class" grain terminal. It can be seen from a considerable distance towering against the horizon or lit up against the night sky; though it is not so Babel-like in proportion as to be visible throughout the 75-kilometre radius from which it will collect grain. A matter of boosterish promotion, its completion has prompted the rapid dismantling of the smaller elevators that drew farmers to the nearest village, to the conversation of the line-up, and, if time allowed, to the coffee shop.

The school plaques are not merely a sentimental evocation of Christmas programs and what must have been a limited, uneven education delivered by poorly prepared, poorly paid teachers. They also signify a vigorous agrarian-populist politics now buried beneath two generations of centralization, in which school districts were important sites of local governance and participatory practice—part of the institutional fabric of self-directed community affairs that made democratic politics an experiential reality. As a 1920 pamphlet of the United Farmers of Alberta urged its locals, the school should be made a "centre where the community can regularly meet and discuss all public questions" and thus "carry out the ideals of democratic government." Debates, organized courses, and readings would "develop the mentality, public spirit, and power of self-expression of every member." Agrarian self-defence against the vagaries of world markets and the indifference of a distant national government would be at the same time an "object lesson in true democracy."[1] Doubtless the schools and school boards could also be sites of intimidation and family rivalry. But that does not diminish the central place they occupied in locally anchored political strategies and the hope reasonably invested in them. Significantly, one of the most controversial, now forgotten, moves of the Social Credit government elected in 1935 was to consolidate 3750 local school districts into a mere 50 administrative units. This over the formal protest of 10,000 trustees—in itself a striking measure of participation—and of the many more ratepayers who crowded schoolhouses to pass resolutions and sign petitions. While the government's pretext was economic efficiency during fiscal hard times, the move also had a clear political subtext. It was consistent with a skillful usurpation of populist traditions in support of a more centralized, leader-dominated, managerial, and technocratic government that promised prosperity along with freedom from politicians. It was followed within four years by a similar consolidation of municipal government. Another round followed in the 1950s. The result in each case was to push further from reach the experience of local self-direction and the settings in which political skills could be exercised.

The world-class terminal, meanwhile, signifies a response to the dictates of competitiveness in a global economy. Its name—Legacy Junction—is intended to evoke sentimentality, but only that, for places left behind in the march of progress. The bravado of adaptation, free trade, efficiencies of scale, and niche markets masks a good deal of anxiety in places where rail lines have been abandoned and farmers now face the full shock of grain transport costs (while prices drop sharply); where Main Street retailers and equipment dealers cannot match city prices for mobile consumers; and where demographic indicators run sharply against provincial trends. Alberta may well have recorded strong population growth at every recent census interval and have the smallest proportion of seniors (less than 10 percent) of any province.[2] Across east-central Alberta, however, apart from transient pockets of oil and gas prosperity, population figures have been declining or, at best, stable—and aging in any case. In most communities between one-fifth and one-third of residents are older than 65. Alberta's population is among the most urban in Canada; only twenty percent is rural even by Statistics Canada's generous definition. A much smaller percentage is still engaged in farming as a means of livelihood, while agriculture—commonly redesignated as a business—is itself no longer the predominant economic activity in rural Alberta. Farm families in many areas exist in an uneasy, subordinate relationship with the energy sector, which is a source of lease income and off-farm wages, as well as disruption and environmental threat, and which (once pipelines are included) constitutes in some rural municipalities the largest, most influential source of tax revenue. Indeed, because of this, any slump in production in the province's conventional oil fields provokes local anxiety about the status of remaining reserves.

In this emerging political economy, communities with limited geological endowments are left to pursue riskier investment, say, in hazardous-waste treatment, tire incineration, or strawboard manufacture. The smallest village celebrates the arrival of Internet connections and anticipates the web page that will enable it to make its own hopeful pitch for jobs in cyberspace. As services are cut, as energy and forest resources are made available at a discount, the purpose of government at all levels is understood singularly in terms of soliciting investment. When in the name of "downsizing" the provincial government actually centralizes authority in key areas and takes control of much of the municipal tax base in order to create an attractive business climate for capital, which will concentrate in the cities, there is little resistance. The loss of the last vestiges of meaningful local authority and the prospect of further municipal amalgamation for the sake of efficiency prompt no protest.

Instead people are readily enlisted in a politics of anti-politics; for politics itself has become a dirty word. It denotes—and can only denote—well-pensioned, unlistening politicians, bloated bureaucracies, the domain of special interests, or merely time spent in disagreement where a show of unity would produce quicker, more impressive results. Government is routinely described as a business, and citizens as consumers or clients. For all that, rural Alberta's re-endorsement of the Klein government in the 1997 and 2001 elections was strikingly unenthusiastic. Mostly there is isolated complaint or silence—not so much consent as a despairing of alternatives. The suspicion that the so-called "Alberta Advantage" does not extend far beyond the major cities and the Highway 2 corridor linking them is confirmed by economic projections that show much of rural Alberta in the grip of a slow decline—one that is masked by provincial aggregate figures.[3] Third- and fourth-generation farmers in mid career entertain what, to them, had once been unthinkable: selling out. Active-treatment hospitals are closed or converted to long-term care facilities. At least a dozen schools in east-central Alberta alone have been closed in recent years. The development initiatives of community-minded people founder on the difficulties of speaking about, and for, a community interest in a world that increasingly presents only individual choices. Tellingly, the small-town credit unions established to keep capital in local circulation have succumbed to the mutual-fund frenzy in which individuals secure their retirement by diverting so-called ethical funds to investment pools managed from global financial capitals.

The crisis facing many communities in rural Alberta is real enough. At the same time, rural Alberta should not be written off as the "hopelessly conservative" region of common stereotypes. This claim is directed in part at the urban smugness that associates life beyond the acreage belts of Calgary and Edmonton with rednecks or even white supremacists.[4] It is also directed at the impoverished thinking of opposition political parties, which have had no other strategy for rural Alberta than a redistribution of seats to minimize its influence. But the most important audience for this claim is rural Alberta itself, depoliticized as it has been over two generations. Not only is it the historic site of robust, democratic-populist practices and communal traditions, some of which are still latent in local memory. More than that, the deep contemporary insecurities and the sense of abandonment it harbours have yet to find full political expression. Indeed, rural Alberta is an instructive vantage point from which to view the transformation of the state and political life under globalization.

The challenge, in turn, is a multi-layered one. Is it possible to reinterpret the threat to rural communities? Is it possible to rechannel, in constructive ways, the anger and suspicion now directed at various enemies: Ottawa, the "liberal elite," Hutterites, aboriginal peoples, even Ducks Unlimited, as it buys up farm land to preserve sloughs for American hunters? Is it possible to overcome an entrenched anti-political populism, which can neither resist nor think outside of the economic discipline of globalization, and to do so through the reinvigoration of local forums for speech and collective action? The balance of this chapter sets out what is best described as an exploratory position. It begins by reclaiming participatory politics as a property of rural life. It traces the loss of meaningful democratic experience through the perspectives of political economy and political culture. It concludes with an appeal to locality, place, and community— neither anachronisms nor bland pieties—as appropriate grounds from which to temper the discipline of globalization. The paper concurs in Christopher Lasch's judgement that "self-governing communities, not individuals, are the basic units of democratic society," and their decline, more than anything else, "calls the future of democracy into question."[5] In this light, the crisis of rural communities is not merely a matter of whether they share in the "Alberta Advantage"; it is above all part of a prolonged crisis of democratic politics.

The association of politics with the city is a well-worn conceit in our language. It is reinforced by the geography of the modern state, in which power is assumed to be located in, and to emanate from, a metropolitan capital. Jean-Jacques Rousseau's wry observation in *The Social Contract* (1762), that for every stately palace required by this centralization he saw "a whole rural district laid in ruins,"[6] is a rare, and germane, historical protest against what otherwise appears a natural feature of political life. Much of our inherited political vocabulary—the civic realm, the citizen—is related etymologically to the city. It bears all the venerable authority of classical republicanism. But meanings mediated over centuries are sometimes deceiving. While the ancient Greek *polis*, most notably, is conventionally translated as a "city-state," the word referred primarily to a way of life, an association, rather than to a certain density of population; and the novel democratic practices of its most famous example, Athens, emerged from a program of land reforms and debt emancipation that created an "Attica of smallholders."[7] Indeed, there is an intriguing recurrence at several points in Western history of strong democracy around small-scale agrarian communities: from the *landgemeinde* colonies of the late-medieval North European frontier[8] to the homesteading settlements on the northern plains of this continent. In the early part of the last century, American urban reformers such as Frederick Howe, Mary Parker Follett, and Jane Addams had to make the case that a vigorous democratic life could be lived equally in city neighbourhoods. The proposition was far from self-evident at the time.

The Great Plains agrarian revolt of the 1890s, writes historian Lawrence Goodwyn, was the "largest democratic mass movement in American history" and its most vivid "demonstration of what authentic political life can be." The movement embraced smallholders and landless alike. It was organized at a time when "throughout the Western grainary the increasing centralization of economic life fastened upon prairie farmers new modes of degradation." It built co-operatives, sent farmer-lecturers across the continent, made overtures to Southern blacks and urban workers, and, mostly in self-defence, fielded political candidates in state and national elections. Conversely, writes Goodwyn, the 1896 election in which the populist movement was partly defeated, partly co-opted, marked the "political consolidation of industrial culture"—complete with the introduction of corporate campaign financing and mass advertising—and, with it, the "decline of individual political self-respect on the part of millions of people."[9]

The agrarian populism that emerged a generation later in Alberta and Saskatchewan, planted partly out of the US experience, has been described similarly as having "contributed more to Canadian thought about the nature and practice of democracy than did any other regional or class discourse."[10] Much of that contribution was to highlight the central role of local institutions—co-operatives, municipal and school government, mutual telephone companies, voluntary organizations—in sustaining participatory practices and creating counterweights to the external forces against which farmers found common interests. The contrast with the Board of Trade boosterism that, at the same time, substituted for municipal politics in neighbouring towns is particularly striking. In 1926, the editor of *The UFA* proposed that Alberta farmers had "gained a quiet confidence in their own ability to carry on their own affairs in their own way ... learned much in their own schools of democracy, [and] obtained a deeper insight into the methods and possibilities of democratic political action."[11]

The marks of this learning are mostly encased in community histories, archives, and microfiche copies of period newspapers; but they are no less real, and no less contrary to political stereotype, for having been almost erased from memory. East-central Alberta is a case in point. The farming district of Gwynne–Bittern Lake was one of the first in the province to form its own chapter of the populist Society of Equity in the early years of the century. It helped send labourite William Irvine to the House of Commons in 1926 and 1930. Its active local UFA sponsored well-attended formal debates on a wide range of subjects, including, in 1932, the merits of the Soviet five-year plan in agriculture—evidence at least of a lively sense of openness to alternative ideas.[12] Further east, just off Highway 13, the now-dilapidated Avonroy Hall once hosted annual UFA picnics at which capitalist competition was routinely denounced and co-operation promoted. Chester Ronning returned here directly from Regina to report on the new Manifesto in 1933; the previous year, district farmers in a provincial by-election helped make him the first legislator anywhere elected under the farmer-labour coalition that became the Cooperative Commonwealth Federation.[13] Still further east is the town of Killam, whose co-operative association—begun as a bulk-buying society in a rural schoolhouse—was once the cornerstone of the provincial movement, along with Wetaskiwin and Edgerton, and whose members' willingness to defend it financially against bank foreclosure led to the creation of the first credit union in Alberta.[14] Similar stories of local initiative and practical political-economic critique can be unearthed throughout the region: "Prairie people worried today by globalization, resources and world markets, urbanization, and geographic inequalities of wealth and power, need to be reminded that they have faced these same problems repeatedly, and won victories."[15]

Nonetheless, apart from Thomas Jefferson's celebration of farmers as those "most virtuous and independent citizens," on whom the future of the young American republic depended,[16] the participatory citizenship that has been an important property of rural settler societies has attracted few patrons in the canon of political philosophy. The same is true generally of twentieth-century social and political thought. Trotsky spoke for modernization theorists across the ideological spectrum when he described capitalism as the victory of city over countryside, the future over the past. Such disdain is still commonplace on left and right. Raymond Williams wrote in his political-literary classic *The Country and the City* that two groups were responsible for the falsehood that a rural economy, rural life, and rural community had disappeared in Britain: on the one hand, the "sentimental ruralists"; and, on the other, "and more critically, the brisk metropolitan progressives ... whose contempt for rural society was matched only by their confidence in an urban industrial future."[17] A curious example of the latter is C.B. Macpherson, who spent much of his theoretical life championing participatory democracy over against the consumerist, party-dominated imitations familiar to North Americans. Yet his famous early study, *Democracy in Alberta*, is generally dismissive of the "inherent" conservatism of a dominant, homogeneous class of independent commodity producers—that is, farmers—who were trapped within a quasi-colonial economy, factors which combined to prevent Alberta's political maturation into a proper, two-party parliamentary system. Evidently Macpherson found nothing exemplary in agrarian political practice. Farmers were increasingly an economic anomaly, he wrote. They were mistakenly inclined to view society in their own image, when in fact "the day of that society is past."[18]

The alternate danger of romanticizing rural life must be acknowledged. There is no useful purpose in attempting to freeze a changing historical reality at some idealized point in the past, and from it either lamenting the present or imagining a more desirable future that glosses over contemporary problems. There is precious little sentimentality left in rural Alberta anyway. There are intimations of loss, however, and confusions about rural identity that present critical opportunities and perhaps political possibilities. As Williams puts it:

It is not so much the old village or the old backstreet that is significant. It is the perception and affirmation of a world in which one is not necessarily a stranger and an agent, but can be a member, a discoverer, in a shared source of life. Taken alone, of course, this is never enough... To make an adult, working world of that kind would involve sharp critical consciousness and a long active agency ... For we have really to look, in country and city alike, at the real social process of alienation, separation, externality, abstraction. And we have to do this not only critically, in the necessary history of rural and urban capitalism, but substantially, by affirming the experiences in which millions of lives are discovered and rediscovered, very often under pressure: experiences of directness, connection, mutuality, sharing, which alone can define, in the end, what the real deformation may be.[19]

THE COMPETITION STATE AND RURAL RESTRUCTURING

Globalization in popular usage evokes the experience of new human solidarities and the shrinking of distances. It is the World Wide Web, satellite photographs of planet earth, Mickey Mouse in China and Chicago Bulls t-shirts in Africa, multicultural societies, and lives lived between airports. These features are real enough. But they are, in a sense, secondary. Globalization is fundamentally a market-led phenomenon with enormous consequences for political life and human well-being. It denotes a complex set of processes, accelerated by technology and government fiscal crises, by which production, finance, trade, and consumption have been integrated—unevenly—on a world scale.[20] Products increasingly are international composites, with labour-intensive routine assembly done in low-wage countries. Capital is mobile; dollars, yen, and Deutschmarks criss-cross the globe electronically in the form of bond and equity investment, loan repayments, and currency speculation. Regional and global agreements lower trade barriers for goods and services. The same brand-name culture of Nike and McDonald's is ubiquitous for those who can afford it.

It is possible, of course, to overstate the novelty of globalization and therefore to neglect the ideological function of recent globalization talk in presenting a world without alternatives. In an important sense, while agricultural settlement in the Canadian prairies was a product of deliberate federal sponsorship, as an extension of the National Policy, the export orientation of farm production has always meant exposure to world markets. Moreover, rural economic restructuring is nothing new. The settlement system based on small homesteads and an extensive network of railroads and grain delivery points was under economic and technological pressure even before it was completed. Postwar mechanization allowed fewer farmers to produce more grain on larger farms. Improved roads made transportation possible over larger distances and facilitated the consolidation of schools, post offices, and trade centres. Good roads were a way out for people as well as products, even as services were brought in.[21]

At the same time, the distinctive marks of contemporary globalization can be seen in the round of rural restructuring dating back roughly to the debt and commodity-price crisis of the early 1980s. One is the deepening integration of family farms and farm communities into an international agri-industrial system of production, finance, trade, and consumption. The general patterns are the same across Western Canada and the US, Australia (see Lawrence et al, this volume), New Zealand, and Western Europe. Where the family farm persists as an economic anomaly—explained partly by the low return on investment and high risks of weather and disease, both of which discourage corporate investment outside of, say, intensive poultry and livestock operations—it is increasingly locked into global industrial and financial structures. This is true on the input as well as the output side. Capital-intensive farming means dependence on credit, expensive machinery, and the industrial products of applied biotechnological and chemical research. The newest features of the rural landscape are signboards for corporate seed, fertilizer, and herbicide products. Capital and input costs in Alberta, for example, have increased almost ten-fold over the past two decades, and as much as thirty-fold for weed and insect control (from $5 million to $150 million). Not surprisingly, the statistics also show increasing differentiation between large and small producers, and the squeezing out of the moderate-sized farms which traditionally constituted the strength of farm co-operative organizations.[22] On the marketing side, a recent trend in Europe and North America is towards direct contractual arrangements between individual farmers and food manufacturers that spell out production terms in detail. For large and specialized commodity producers, this relationship may resemble a business partnership, structured by shared ideology and interests. In other cases, Jefferson's independent farmer-citizen is "virtually relegated to the role of a semi-autonomous employee or piece-worker."[23]

The effect of restructuring on rural communities is equally striking. The concentration of land ownership and the related shift towards wage labour have a direct bearing on community viability. In east-central Alberta, it is not unheard of that an extended family—two generations comprising, say, three households—will own an entire township of land; and that the school in the nearest town will have only seven students in its kindergarten class. Such features are reminiscent of Australia's outback. Among the less tangible effects of restructuring are the shattering of any remaining ideological sense of a shared farm interest between large "agricultural professionals" and mid-sized family farmers; the withdrawal by individuals from community participation into farm-saving work (or private consumption); the loss of local leadership and the disappearance of co-operative practices.

A second mark of contemporary globalization arises from the kind of state transformation described in the introduction to this volume, whereby the purpose of government is increasingly understood in terms of creating a favourable investment climate, not protecting region or sectors, or playing "balancer" for the sake of broad social goals. That change is experienced by rural people as a kind of abandonment to market forces. Historical perspective is crucial in understanding this shift.

For roughly the first century after Confederation, the Canadian government took a direct interest in the development of Prairie agricultural settlement. It negotiated treaties involving real concessions with Cree, Blackfoot, and other First Nations people. It surveyed land, promoted immigration, sponsored railroad construction and subsidized grain transportation, established dominion experimental farms to assist farmers in unfamiliar settings, and built post offices in all the villages built up around grain delivery points. It did all this as if a governmental presence across a vast territory mattered—as if settlement mattered. Much of that has changed, and not simply because the Prairie farm vote has lost its national political clout. Globalization means an accelerated retreat from rural regions on the part of government, as is evident in such policy shifts as the phasing-out of the Crow benefit, the abandonment of "farm subsidies" under international trade rules, and the handover of agricultural research to the private sector along with legislative protection for "plant-breeders' rights"—all in the name of competitiveness.

The sense of abandonment by Ottawa is notoriously easy to generate in rural Alberta, but increasingly it is experienced equally, perhaps more acutely, in relation to the provincial government. The latter transformation can be outlined in three stages. The first begins with the election of a Progressive Conservative government under Peter Lougheed in 1971 and corresponds to the period of aggressive, interventionist "province-building" on behalf of indigenous capital that continued until the end of the oil boom in 1982.[24] The

Conservative banishment of Social Credit is commonly regarded as reflecting the ascendancy of the new Alberta—urban, professional, corporate. But electoral victory in 1971 required rural seats too. The Conservatives had appealed to rural and small-town voters on a promise to reverse depopulation and to raise their quality of life to a level equal to that in the cities. That meant improved roads, schools, hospitals; local access to government offices; and, not least, natural gas at reasonable rates. This platform reflected the principles and political instincts of Hugh Horner, who became deputy premier. But it was also vital to building political support for an export-oriented energy policy. The spectre of gas shipped to the US and eastern Canada, gas drilled from and transported in pipelines beneath farm land, when that same gas was available only to a limited number of farm households, represented no small political risk. Against the strong opposition of the private utility companies, which Horner knew farmers would distrust, the government in 1973 announced a massive program for delivering gas through local volunteer-run co-operatives, most of which were created only subsequently on the strength of considerable promotion and promises to subsidize much of the construction costs. In addition, the government created an agency—now under threat of privatization—to buy bulk gas from producers for sale to the co-ops.[25] The Lougheed government also subsidized the cost of gas, farm fuel, and fertilizers after the 1973 price rise. It established the position of Farmer's Advocate partly to deal with surface-rights disputes. It used its oil-royalty windfall, moreover, in several visible ways. It invested directly in irrigation works, grain cars, and, through a consortium, West Coast port facilities to gain economic leverage over against federal transport policy and federal regulatory or marketing agencies. It established, then expanded, the Agriculture Development Corporation (ADC) as the major source of farm loans and loan guarantees, especially for beginning farmers, many of whom nonetheless faced foreclosure in the early 1980s when credit that had been easily extended could not be repaid at shielded, but still higher, interest rates. Finally, the government embarked on a program of capital construction whose red-brick legacy can still be seen—if not always utilized—throughout the province: hospitals, schools, seniors' lodges, and provincial buildings.

The second stage is a transitional one extending roughly from 1982 to the Klein election in 1993. It can be characterized by deficit budgets, by more desperate and more expensive attempts at diversification in the collapse of the energy sector, and perhaps above all by cruder forms of patronage extended to particular rural communities. Foremost among them were Stettler, which returned Don Getty to the legislature in a by-election after the new premier had been defeated in an Edmonton riding, and Barrhead, the Horner fiefdom inherited by Ken Kowalski. Under new political pressure from the New Democrats, and later the Liberals, the Conservatives chose to shore up rural support. ADC farm loans and guarantees were expanded to an amount beyond $3-billion and every secondary road in the province was to be paved in a soon-forgotten 1989 election promise.[26] While opposition MLAs accused the government of having lost faith in rural Alberta, the premier gave assurances that its farmers were better protected than those in any other province. The Getty government also entered into long-term forest management agreements with Japanese pulp-and-paper companies, offering low royalties, massive loan guarantees, and infrastructure in return for investment in the sagging Northern economy.[27]

The third stage most fully resembles the reactive government role to global investors that is anticipated in the pulp-mill deals. In rural communities, this stage is reflected in the government's aggressive promotion of intensive pork production and processing—primarily for Asian markets—that evaporated before most of the controversial hog-barn proposals around the province had proceeded to construction. The parallels between the hog and pulp industries are instructive. In both cases, the government encouraged a form of export-oriented development that meant tolerating significant risks of environmental damage in out-of-the-way rural areas. In both cases, too, as in the energy industry of the 1990s, a regulatory vacuum has left communities deeply divided over the relative merits of economic opportunity and soil-and-water conservation. Fittingly, Alberta Agriculture's mandate is no longer about community development or farm extension; it is strictly a commercial one in relation to food and fibre processing.

This third stage, more generally, is about the foreign investment pitch known as "the Alberta Advantage," by which the government, as one columnist puts it, would "carve out a spot ... in the wildly competitive wilderness of the new world economy."[28] Its centrepiece is low taxation, a commitment that has dictated a singular cost-cutting approach to the deficit problem. Accordingly the province, having reduced spending on schools, has assumed control of education property taxes for the ostensible purpose of equalizing them across the province, but with the result that it can make further tax shifts in favour of corporations. The province has not only cut municipal grants; it has also eliminated a major revenue source for some communities—the machinery and equipment tax—on the grounds that it was a disincentive to new investment. It has imposed region-alization in education and health, and encouraged it among hard-pressed municipalities for the sake of similar efficiencies of scale. It has skilfully distanced itself from the difficult implications of deficit-cutting by leaving regional boards the task of allocating budgets, in effect, deciding which school or hospital facilities will remain open. It has made sure that it was seen to hit the cities first and hardest. Klein, it is often forgotten, secured the Conservative leadership in 1992 in a run-off with Nancy MacBeth, then the Health Minister, by committing himself to the defence of rural hospitals against the plans for regionalization and rationalization that were circulating in her department. But even in rural areas, the impact of cuts and the pitting of communities against one another could only be delayed.[29] Again, government's physical presence has receded. Rural communities repeatedly get the message that they are on their own, though with fewer resources and less political control over their futures.

CLIENTELISM AND ANTI-POLITICS

The acquiesence of rural Albertans that so puzzles outside observers is a direct reflection of an anti-political populism that is at least two generations old. It is reinforced by a complex, changing clientelist relationship with the provincial government. Some of its roots, paradoxically, can be found in early agrarian populist doctrines imported from the American Plains. This populism contained two contradictory impulses: on the one hand, towards local autonomy and direct democracy; on the other, towards technocratic, business-like government and non-partisanship. These contradictions frame much of the tension between UFA locals and the cabinet between 1921 and 1935—not simply over who set party policy, but equally over whether the ultimate aims of the farmers' movement were to be carried out at the local or provincial level. The Depression-era mystique built up around the unfathomable economic theories of Major Douglas, the 1935 election campaign that brought Social Credit to office, and the leadership of William Aberhart pushed populism's centralist, technocratic elements decidedly to the fore at the expense of its democratic elements. In the months prior to the election, Aberhart routinely addressed voters as consumers—promising to restore their purchasing power. He exhorted crowds to "put aside politics." As the election neared he forebade Social Credit candidates or study groups from debating with opponents. Social Credit supporters, meanwhile, brought numerous UFA rallies in country schoolhouses to a premature end by honking automobile horns or pounding on the walls.[30] The 1935 campaign left a deep split in rural communities. While the CCF absorbed some UFA members, many others simply withdrew from active politics.

Neither Aberhart's hold over Social Credit nor the homogeneity of the movement in the government's first term should be exaggerated. Backbench MLAs revolted; party supporters—urban and rural—collaborated formally and informally even with Communists.[31] But the premier did leave a distinct imprint on Alberta political culture, which Macpherson and David Laycock have described as plebiscitarian.[32] Aberhart did not make a speech in the legislature until 1939. His preferred medium of political communication—not debate—was radio. Moreover, he understood the role of "the people" as being simply one of demanding "results," and deferring to government experts who would implement the right policy. It was left to the leader to interpret and invoke the general will of the people, as the occasion required. Centralization of power in the hands of the provincial government was entirely consistent with this view. (Alberta's recent experience with policy roundtables and other manufactured representations of the general will has a longer history than the Klein government.) Laycock concludes: "The vacuity of public life contemplated for the average citizen in this vision indicates that Social Credit ideology also exceeded other Prairie populisms in projecting frustrations with current politics into an antipathy towards 'politics.'"[33] W.L. Morton's judgement is similar: "Social Credit was the end of politics in Alberta and the beginning of popular administration."[34]

The point is often made that populist parties in both Saskatchewan and Alberta moved in technocratic directions once elected. There are differences nonetheless. In Saskatchewan the CCF government was bound to some extent by grass-roots direction at party conventions; it attempted no equivalent consolidation of local government; and it relied politically on the support of a strong co-operative movement—above all the Wheat Pool—in which democratic practices were also sustained. The other factor that would set Alberta apart economically and culturally was oil. Already by the 1950s, half of government revenues were derived from oil. The province's population grew rapidly and the composition of its workforce changed, putting farmers in the minority.[35] The oil boom had three significant effects. It induced a dependence on the US-based oil companies that were in a position to develop the resource. It provided a focus for uniting "the people" against real or imagined federal encroachments on provincial powers. And it gave the government the fiscal means to spend generously compared to other provinces on such ideologically acceptable staples as health, education, highways, and welfare—primarily for the elderly—without having to resort to onerous levels of taxation.³⁶ Prosperity compensated for disillusionment with politics.

Throughout the Conservative years, oil and gas revenues have been the currency by which a "population of patrons and clients" was created—especially in rural Alberta.³⁷ The clientelist position essentially is one of passive support in exchange for government largesse. In Alberta this relationship reinforced the anti-political disposition already present. It resulted in vast improvements in rural infrastructure, while at the same time weakening political capacity at the local level. One of the most significant moves made by Lougheed's government to strengthen its position *vis-a-vis* municipalities was to terminate the practice of resource revenue-sharing and to slash the proportion of grant money that was given unconditionally from 61 to 13 percent.³⁸ In subsequent years lottery revenues have served as an additional means of patronage. While recent changes are intended to put the distribution of revenues at arm's length from the government, an aggressive lottery policy has had the effect of sucking money out of communities only to have MLAs return a fraction of it, on the basis of priorities determined in Edmonton, in cheque-presentation ceremonies staged for the local weekly newspaper. Generally rural Albertans "have learned that it is better to be a friend of the government than an enemy."³⁹

The most significant new mode of clientelism, however, is more individualized and potentially far-reaching. It corresponds with the Klein government's accelerated privatization push in many areas of service delivery. On the pretext of getting government out of business, privatization, in a sense, has deepened the connection between the two, creating a situation in which the operator of a private licence registry, for example, or a contracted social-services professional (perhaps a former government employee) now owes her livelihood directly to the government.⁴⁰ She is unlikely to risk a public complaint against government policy or identification with an opposition political party; she is even less likely to do so if she lives in a small community. The sources of political silence are multiple and reinforcing.

The problem with clientelism is that the passive client mentality is slow to change even when the patron has pulled the plug on the relationship. This is as true in rural Alberta as in rural Mexico. The legacy of two generations is a kind of political de-skilling that dovetails comfortably with a global market economy. At the height of Western separatist fervor in the early 1980s, John Richards wrote that the "average prairie citizen is probably less knowledgeable of political affairs, and less likely to participate actively, beyond the minimal act of voting, than his grandfather. He has converged to the North American norm."[41] He could have added grandmothers, in recognition of women's initiatives in what was a frontier society and their involvement at all levels in both UFA and, at least initially, Social Credit movements.[42] Agrarian populists, he wrote, understood that "the basis of a free society resides in forming a large number of people who can participate skillfully in democratic institutions ... But people only learn a skill if they practice it, and they will only practice democratic politics if democratic forums are locally available and they have jurisdiction over matters of substance."[43] The effects of political de-skilling are perhaps nowhere more evident than in rural Alberta's anti-political oscillation between passivity and resentment—the latter still sustaining the Canadian Alliance Party now that its Reform predecessor's more interesting Jeffersonian-populist strands have been set aside in the quest for corporate campaign financing. In an age shaped by bureaucratic and market forces, protest rather than argument is the predominant mode of politics when it is engaged at all; indignation is the predominant emotion.[44] Populism reduced to resentment is scarcely more demanding than passivity. It requires no face-to-face encounter, no expectation that an effective common purpose can be formed in democratic action.

A DEMOCRATIC POLITICS OF PLACE

The paradoxical challenge posed by economic globalization and by the corresponding transformation of the state is to recapture in rural Alberta a sense of locality as the immediate locus of political practice. This is not meant as a counsel of despair. Nor is it offered unaware of the skepticism it will invite on several grounds. First, such counsel runs counter to Enlightenment prejudice, economic rationality, much of modern political thought, and the North American culture of mobility—all of which understand the local as parochial and self-chosen in a way that the state (or the "world," or the market) is not. Second, it does not share in the tactical hubris that imagines that the global dragon can be slayed by some counter-hegemonic dragon of equivalent size— say, a transnational coalition of worthy interests, which, even if it could develop a closer scrutiny of economic transactions, could scarcely make political practice less remote. Third, it is easily confused with what has become a cliche ("think globally, act locally!"), which in conventional usage assumes an instrumental relation to place as the means to some larger end. Finally, it appears to treat the symptoms of the disorder rather than the disorder itself; that is, it projects a political "solution" to what is presented as an economic problem, and to that extent risks being dismissed as either irrelevant to practical people trying to keep small rural communities alive or, in other ways, naïve to theoretical people on the traditional urban left.

The contrary premise of this paper is a simple one. If there is to be a genuine alternative to the practice and discourse of globalization, it will lie in a political economy of place. For the most radical position that can be adopted against globalization's compression of time and space—its transience, its culture of consumption, its bottom-line ideology of efficiency—is one that strives to inhabit a particular place in a serious way. This position finds theoretical inspiration in diverse sources: from the cultural theorist Raymond Williams to the rural Kentucky essayist-conservationist Wendell Berry. It finds political opportunity—as well as danger—in the way that the processes of globalization and state transformation have undermined the authority of traditional political structures and leadership. It finds in local knowledge reassurance that there remain alive intimations of human agency, collective responsibility, and deep affection, beyond the reach of both scientific expertise and market metaphors—and beyond the view of general academic theories of the state or the world economy. Rural east-central Alberta is no exception. If anything it is comparatively rich in its potential for understanding the cultural contradictions of capitalism. Here, for example, as any discerning listener soon learns, land means much more than a commodity for exploitation or recreation. Land and the human marks made on it—even abandoned houses, halls, and churches—are repositories of intergenerational family identity and community memory. Land is where ancestors are buried. Land is the site of good work that feeds people, that engages parents meaningfully with their children. Land in combination with Prairie sky, light, and quiet represents an aesthetic sense of space that is not willingly abandoned even in hard times for the prospect of urban wage labour.

Montana writer Daniel Kemmis argues that meaningful citizenship can only develop out of a long-term stake in "real, identifiable places" shared by all those who "struggle to live well in such places." A public life demands that people collaborate across differences; that they acquire what he calls "practices of inhabitation," including democratic competencies; and that they create political spaces that overcome through "collaborative citizenship" the old suspicions between rural districts and neighbouring towns—acknowledging their mutual interdependence against the forces of bureaucratic indifference and corporate exploitation.[45] Such reclamations arguably are easiest to imagine in rural places for reasons, apart from size, that Berry gives: rural people "know how little real help is to be expected from somewhere else" and still possess the "remnants of local memory and local community."[46]

It is one thing, of course, to identify localities as the primary ground on which to rejuvenate democratic politics as well as community, and thereby to temper the grip of economic globalization. It is one thing, too, to promote community resilience, or just survival with neighbours, as a desirable goal. It is quite another thing to make any of this happen. Downsizing government according to the dictates of competitiveness or neo-conservative conviction cannot, of itself, reverse the process of political de-skilling. It merely reinforces an atomism in which people are "thrown back on themselves."[47] As Lasch writes: "It is either naive or cynical to lead the public to think that dismantling the welfare state is enough to ensure a revival of informal cooperation."[48] Or, for that matter, a vigorous democratic politics. In the current dispensation even the Prairie wheat pools have been transformed under global competitive pressures into corporate enterprises accountable to shareholders; grass-roots control by farmer-members has been surrendered. Markets do not create citizens, and they are no more inclined to repair local communities and their capacity for collective action. Instead they dissolve local attachments. What Lasch calls the "revolt of the elites" is premised partly on the growing ability of privileged, relatively transient participants in the global economy to detach themselves from the general prosperity of any particular place, from its standards of conduct, from any sense of obligation to it—indeed, "from the common life." This phenomenon is typically illustrated in the gated housing developments of major cities, but it is becoming no less a reality in rural Alberta. It runs parallel with the displacement of farming by both industrial agriculture and the energy industry, which have a more transient, short-term relationship to land.

There is, in short, no reason to be sanguine about the prospects of a democratic politics of place in rural Alberta. Meaningful local politics is a fragile thing in the best of circumstances. There is a great deal at stake here, nonetheless, in reviving alternative possibilities in the face of real insecurities and real desperation. For if resentment and bitterness towards government are the only socially sanctioned responses available, in the face of rural problems, one can foresee the potential to produce pockets of nativist extremism as these problems worsen.[49] But the scenario of armed, US-style militia survivalism is far too dramatic, even if, for a minority of people, gun control has been politicized along similar lines in the Canadian Prairies. The more plausible scenario is that people will simply continue to leave.

In the meantime, there are signs of an emerging rural realignment quite different from the party-political competition between card-carrying Progressive Conservatives and their electoral opponents. Berry frames this political realignment as follows:

> One of these parties holds that community has no value; the other holds that it does. One is the party of the global economy; the other I would call simply the party of local community. The global party is large, though not populous, immensely powerful and wealthy, self-aware, purposeful, and tightly organized. The community party is only now becoming aware of itself; it is widely scattered, highly diverse, small though potentially numerous, weak though latently powerful, and poor though by no means without resources.[50]

Part of the latter's weakness surely lies in the difficulty of speaking the language of community convincingly in the present political economy, against the domination of concepts such as "opportunity" and "competitiveness."

But a rebirth of politics in the form of parties of local community is not unthinkable even in rural Alberta. It has become a necessity in many places. As rural people come to understand that they are on their own, that the patron has pulled the plug, new *ad hoc* institutions and initiatives for community self-defence are proliferating mostly outside the domain of party politics. They have formed, for example, in response to the proposed closure of rural schools under the tyranny of provincial space-efficiency formulas that will dictate the demolition of existing buildings. They have formed among ranch people whose livelihoods are threatened by oil-company use and contamination of local water for deep-injection purposes. They have formed in the Rimbey area to bring an end to sulphur emissions from a natural-gas plant through skilful use of the remaining regulatory channels. They have formed in places like the County of Flagstaff in east-central Alberta (see introduction, this volume), and before that in the County of Forty Mile in the south, in response to the proposed construction of a massive hog-barn complex by Taiwan Sugar Corporation, on the invitation of the provincial government.[51] The challenge in every case is at least two-fold: to develop the required technical expertise, whether it concerns school policy, regulatory processes, or subsurface geology; and to learn, as a member of the Flagstaff group put it, "how to do politics," because "out here we've forgotten." Those political skills include articulating a position, listening, strategizing, researching, finding a consensus, depersonalizing conflict, and building external alliances.

There are limits, of course, to such community-defence initiatives. They cannot in themselves undo the global concentration of ownership in a handful of corporate food-chain clusters whose power rural people confront as a predatory cost-price squeeze on inputs and commodities. They are constrained by the loss of meaningful local authority, by the need to respond quickly to agendas set by distant investors and government policy-makers, by the personal rivalries and limited energies that mark real communities. Such initiatives can be unpolished in both their anger and their analysis. But by the experience they accumulate they push people—apolitical people—to ask real political questions: Why don't governments listen to us? Who has power in this society? Can we find reliable allies in other rural communities as well as in cities? More often than not, such initiatives are led by women, for reasons that may reflect the debilitating effects of a male-oriented rural culture of respect and shame (see Harder, this volume). By their existence they challenge the notion that globalizing processes are inevitable and that rural communities and family farms alike should be left to die the "natural death" to which economists have consigned them. Instead, from people like them, committed to staying where they are, the first flickers of a fresh political wind may yet blow out of rural Alberta.

Notes

An earlier version of this paper was first presented at the Parkland Institute's November 1997 conference and published as a Parkland research paper, "Whither Rural Alberta?" (1999). I am grateful to Sandra Read for her work as research assistant.

1   "How to Organize and Carry on a Local of the United Farmers of Alberta" (1920), quoted in David Laycock, *Populism and Democratic Thought in the Canadian Prairies, 1910–1945* (Toronto: University of Toronto Press, 1990), 92.

2   Statistics Canada, 1996 Census, *National Overview, Population and Dwelling Counts*; 1991 Census, *Profile of Census Divisions and Subdivisions in Alberta*.

3   "Rural Alberta in grip of a new recession," *Edmonton Journal*, 4 May 1999.

4   Rural communities like Provost and Eckville in particular have suffered unfairly from such stereotypes. While the former is associated with an Aryan Nations rally on a rural residence in 1990, more remarkable was the community's response at the time. It included denunciations from church pulpits, condemnation and ridicule in the editorials and letters pages of the local newspaper, and a protest by 70 percent of students in Grades 7 through 12 that later drew commendations from the Alberta Human Rights Commission. Arguably that kind of collective taking of responsibility could only have happened in a community of that size. See the *Provost News*, especially 12 September 1990, and 19 September 1990. In the case of Eckville, it was local people who testified publicly against their notorious former teacher, Jim Keegstra.

5   Christopher Lasch, *The Revolt of the Elites and the Betrayal of Democracy* (New York: W. W. Norton, 1995), 8.

6   Jean-Jacques Rousseau, *The Social Contract*, trans. Henry Tozer, Book III.13.

7   Simon Hornblower, "Creation and Development of Democratic Institutions in Ancient Athens," in John Dunn, ed., *Democracy: The Unfinished Journey* (Oxford: Oxford University Press, 1992), 4.

8   William TeBrake, *Medieval Frontier: Culture and Ecology in Rijnland* (College Station: Texas A & M University Press, 1985).

9   Lawrence Goodwyn, *The Populist Moment: A Short History of the Agrarian Revolt in America* (New York: Oxford University Press, 1978), passim, quotations at vii, xiii–xiv, 69, 296. See also John W. Bennett and Seena B. Kohl, *Settling the Canadian-American West, 1890–1915* (Lincoln: University of Nebraska Press, 1995), esp. ch. 14.

10   Laycock, *Populism and Democratic Thought*, 3.

11   Quoted in Laycock, *Populism and Democratic Thought*, 89. Cf. the account of what passed for small-town politics at the time given in Donald Weatherell and Irene Kmet, *Town Life: Main Street and the Evolution of Small-town Alberta, 1880–1947* (Edmonton: University of Alberta Press, 1995), ch. 2.

12   See, for example, an excellent community history, Louise Nordin and Nora C. Wylie, eds., *The Bitter 'n Sweet: The History of the Bittern Lake-Sifton District* (Bittern Lake Community Association, 1993), 209, 250–56; Anthony Mardiros, *William Irvine: The Life of a Prairie Radical* (Toronto: James Lorimer, 1979), 170–78.

13   See the accounts in *The Camrose Canadian*, 14 June 1933; 21 June 1933. The MLA, Chester Ronning, proposed in his first speech in the legislature that capitalism was "into its death throes," having "outlived its usefulness" (*The Camrose Canadian*, 15 February 1933).

14   Brett Fairbairn, "Visions of Alternative Futures: Three Cases from the Prairie Consumer Cooperative Movement," in Jerome Martin, ed., *Alternative Futures for Prairie Agricultural Communities* (Edmonton: University of Alberta Faculty of Extension, 1991), 105–10.

15   Ibid., 98.

16   See, e.g., "Notes on the State of Virginia" [1781–82], in *The Portable Thomas Jefferson*, ed. Merrill Peterson (New York: Penguin, 1975), queries XIX (p. 217) and XXII (227); and in the same collection, "Letter to James Madison."

17   Raymond Williams, *The Country and the City* (Oxford: Oxford University Press, 1973), 299–300.

18   C.B. Macpherson, *Democracy in Alberta: Social Credit and the Party System* (Toronto: University of Toronto Press, 1953), 226.

19   Williams, *The Country and the City*, 298. My former colleague, Kieran Bonner, makes a similar point in *A Great Place to Raise Kids: Interpretation, Science, and the Urban-Rural Debate* (Montreal and Kingston: McGill-Queen's University Press, 1997), ch. 10.

20   An accessible primer on the subject is Richard Stubbs and Geoffrey Underhill, eds., *Political Economy and the Changing Global Order*, 2d ed. (Don Mills: Oxford University Press, 2000), in particular Robert W. Cox, "Political Economy and World Order," 25–37. See also James Mittelman, ed., *Globalization: Critical Reflections* (Boulder: Lynne Rienner, 1997), including essays on rural communities in Mexico and southern Africa.

21   Jack Stabler, M.R. Olfert, and Murray Fulton, *The Changing Role of Rural Communities in an Urbanizing World* (Regina: Canadian Plains Research Center, 1992), 1–2.

22   Statistics Canada, *Agricultural Profile of Alberta*, for both 1991 and 1996 census years.

23 Patrick Cummins, "Restructuring Agriculture in Advanced Societies," in Terry Marsden, Philip Lowe, and Sarah Whitmore, eds., *Rural Restructuring: Global Processes and their Responses* (London: David Fulton, 1990), 55–56.

24 Larry Pratt, "The State and Province-building: Alberta's Development Strategy," in Leo Panitch, ed., *The Canadian State: Political Economy and Political Power* (Toronto: University of Toronto Press, 1977).

25 Fay Orr, *Harvesting the Flame: The History of Alberta's Rural Natural Gas Cooperatives* (Edmonton: Reidmore Books, 1989). One notable side benefit of the gas co-ops has been the partial integration into local affairs of Hutterite colonies, which in some cases are represented on boards of directors.

26 Peter J. Smith, "A Province Just Like Any Other?" in Keith Brownsey and Michael Howlett, eds., *The Provincial State: Politics in Canada's Provinces and Territories* (Mississauga: Copp Clark, 1992), 258–59. Smith also notes the reassertion of small-town business and farm elements in the party and in caucus during the Getty period.

27 Larry Pratt and Ian Urquhart, *The Last Great Forest* (Edmonton: NeWest Publishers, 1994).

28 Mark Lisac, *The Klein Revolution* (Edmonton: NeWest Publishers, 1995), 164. The patronage argument, with a special emphasis on the promotion of certain commodity groups to neutralize larger umbrella groups like the Wheat Pool and Unifarm, is also made by Barry Wilson, "Cultivating the Tory Electoral Base: Rural Politics in Ralph Klein's Alberta," in Trevor Harrison and Gordon Laxer, eds., *Trojan Horse* (Montreal: Black Rose Books, 1995).

29 See, for example, "Final bell ringing for rural schools," *Edmonton Journal*, 16 March 1997;

30 John Irving, *The Social Credit Movement in Alberta* (Toronto: University of Toronto Press, 1959), quotations at 105, 317.

31 Alvin Finkel, *The Social Credit Phenomenon in Alberta* (Toronto: University of Toronto Press, 1989), ch. 3.

32 Macpherson, *Democracy in Alberta*, ch. 6–8; Laycock, *Populism and Democratic Thought*, ch. 5.

33 Laycock, *Populism and Democratic Thought*, 293.

34 W.L. Morton, "A Century of Plain and Parkland," in Richard Allen, ed., *A Region of the Mind* (Regina: Canadian Plains Research Center, 1973), 178.

35 Ed Shaffer, "The Political Economy of Oil in Alberta," in Leadbeater, ed., *The Political Economy of Alberta*, 174–76; John Richards and Larry Pratt, *Prairie Capitalism: Power and Influence in the New West* (Toronto: McClelland and Stewart, 1979), ch. 3–4.

36 Finkel, *The Social Credit Phenomenon*, 122.

37 Lisac, *The Klein Revolution*, 118.

38 Jack Masson, *Alberta's Local Governments and Their Politics* (Edmonton: Pica Pica Press, 1985), 26–27.

39 Henia Martyniuk, "The rape of rural Alberta," *Edmonton Journal*, 21 May 1996. Also indicative of my clientelist interpretation are the cases where farm people with real complaints against the energy industry have, at considerable cost, exhausted all proper channels of appeal without redress, and then write a petitionary letter to the premier. Typically such letters make a fawning appeal for individual mercy in which the writer acknowledges having "voted Progressive Conservative all my life"—as if political affiliation should provide protection from the disruptions that befall others who live next door to oil and gas activity. (Copy in possession of the author.)

40 Lisac, *The Klein Revolution*, 127, 129.

41 John Richards, "Populism and the West," in Larry Pratt and Garth Stevenson, eds., *Western Separatism* (Edmonton: Hurtig, 1981), 79.

42 See, for example, Nanci Langford, "'All that Glitters': The Political Apprenticeship of Alberta Women, 1916–1930," in Catherine Cavanagh and Randi Warne, eds., *Standing on New Ground: Women in Alberta* (Edmonton: University of Alberta Press, 1993), 71–85: "The [United Farm Women of Alberta locals] not only encouraged women to develop knowledge and skills for participation in public affairs, they also gave their members opportunity to do so" (75–76). The farmers' movement in Alberta had supported women's suffrage. The UFA government, alone among provinces, supported the appeal of the "Person's Case" at all stages; Irene Parlby, one of the Alberta Five, was appointed to the first cabinet in 1921.

43 Richards, "Populism and the West," 76, 81.

44 Alasdair MacIntyre, *After Virtue* (Notre Dame: University of Notre Dame Press, 1984), 71.

45 Daniel Kemmis, *Community and the Politics of Place* (Norman: University of Oklahoma Press, 1990), 6–7, ch. 8, passim.

46 Berry, "The Work of Local Culture," in *What are People For?* (San Francisco: North Point Books, 1990), 168–69.

47 Charles Taylor, *The Malaise of Modernity* (Toronto: House of Anansi, 1991), 117.

48 Lasch, *The Revolt of the Elites*, 100–1.

49 See in this respect Catherine McNicol Stock's account of the Oklahoma City bombing in 1995 in the context of older traditions of producer radicalism, in *Rural Radicals: Righteous Rage in the American Grain* (Ithaca, NY: Cornell University Press, 1996).

50 Wendell Berry, *Another Turn of the Crank* (Washington: Counterpoint Books, 1995), 16–17.

51 Roger Epp, "Globalization hits home on the range," *Parkland Post*, Winter 2001, 13.